# DIGITAL HUMANITIES IN THE INDIA RIM

# Digital Humanities in the India Rim

Contemporary Scholarship in Australia and India

*Edited by Hart Cohen, Ujjwal Jana and Myra Gurney*

https://www.openbookpublishers.com

©2024 Hart Cohen, Ujjwal Jana and Myra Gurney (eds)

Copyright of individual chapters is maintained by the chapter's authors

ISBN Paperback: 978-1-80511-387-4
ISBN Hardback: 978-1-80511-388-1
ISBN Digital (PDF): 978-1-80511-297-6
ISBN Digital eBook (EPUB): 978-1-80511-389-8
ISBN HTML: 978-1-80511-390-4
DOI: https://doi.org/10.11647/OBP.0423

Cover concept by Thalan-Harry Cowlishaw, designed using original image provided by Freepic, https://www.freepik.com, CC BY-NC

Cover design by Jeevanjot Kaur Nagpal

# Contents

**PART 3**
**DIGITAL HUMANITIES AND TECHNOLOGY:**
**METHODS AND METHODOLOGY**

# List of Figures

Copyright to these graphs/tables belong to the authors that created them. Re-formatting for publication was by Desmond Devlin.

# Acknowledgments

I would like to express my sincere gratitude to everyone who has been part of the SPARC (Scheme for Promotion of Academic and Research Collaboration) Project on "Digital Humanities in the Indian Rim", an initiative of the Ministry of Education of the Government of India. First and foremost, I want to thank the Ministry of Education, Government of India for generous funding for the project; Pondicherry University, in particular the Department of English, for hosting the project and providing all of the necessary infrastructure for its successful execution. I deeply appreciate the support extended to me by IIT, Kharagpur. I would like to acknowledge the unwavering support and cooperation of my international collaborative partners: Professor Hart Cohen, Professor Rachel Hendry, Dr Michael Falk and Dr Helen Bones from Western Sydney University, Australia, and their active participation in and significant contributions to this project. Lastly, we are obliged to Open Book Publishers for kindly accepting our proposal and publishing this anthology on *Digital Humanities in the India Rim: Contemporary Scholarship in Australia and India.*

Dr Ujjwal Jana

I would like to acknowledge the following individuals from the School of Humanities and Communication Arts, Western Sydney University for their support:

Distinguished Professor Anthony Uhlmann (Acting Dean),
Ms Amanda McNamara, Executive Assistant to the Dean,
Staff and postgraduate candidates who contributed chapters to the book.

Thanks to Thalan-Harry Collishaw for his cover design concept, Bill Gurney for assistance with the cover design and Des Devlin for his work on the graphics and index.

Thanks also to Emily Rytmeister for her assistance in the early phase of this project. And many thanks to my colleague and co-editor, Dr Myra Gurney.

I would especially thank Professor Ujjwal Jana for his collegiality and strong support for this publication.

Dr Hart Cohen

# About the authors

**Ms Linda Aulbach** is a PhD fellow in Humanities and Communication Arts at Western Sydney University and holds an MA in Digital Humanities. She is committed to making contributions to the ethical development of Artificial Intelligence, exploring the impact of empathic AI applications on human relationships as well as discussing the concept of artificial empathy within a posthumanist perspective. Linda also holds a certificate in Human-Robot Interaction and continues to delve into the space of ethical AI and HRI, striving to foster a harmonious integration of cutting-edge technology with the fundamental aspects of human experience, definition and emotions.

**Associate Professor Tomasz Bednarz** has previously served as Director and Head of Visualisation at the Expanded Perception & Interaction Centre at UNSW Art & Design and UNSW Computer Science and Engineering. His past roles reflect his conviction of the need for a holistic approach to the wicked problems facing the collation, analytics and display of big data. His approach is expansive and encompasses the use of novel and emerging technologies. Over the last couple of years, he has been involved in a wide range of projects in immersive visualisation, human-computer interaction, computational imaging, image analysis and processing, visualisation, accelerated computing, simulation, modelling, computer graphics, computer games, computational fluid dynamics, machine learning, Artificial Intelligence, and multi-sensors assimilation.

**Dr Simon Burrows** is Professor of History and Digital Humanities at Western Sydney University. An historian of the enlightenment and the French revolutionary era, he is best known for his award-winning digital work on the French book trade. His many publications include *Digitizing Enlightenment*, which he co-edited with Glenn Roe.

**Dr Asha Chand** is a Senior Lecturer in Journalism and she is the Associate Dean International: South Asia in the School of Humanities and Communication Arts at Western Sydney University. She received the Nav Rattan (2023) and Hind Rattan (2019) awards in Delhi, India, and the Mahatma Gandhi Pravasi Samman award (2018) at the House of Commons in London for her teaching, research, and community work. In 2021 she won an Australian journalism teaching award from the Journalism Education Research Association of Australia (JERAA). In 2020, she became a Senior Fellow of the Higher Education Academy, UK and a fellow of Badugulang, Western Sydney University's Centre for Teaching and Learning Excellence. Dr Chand's research interests are in culture, society, migration, and marriage.

**Dr Hart Cohen** is Professor in Media Arts in the School of Humanities and Communication Arts and a member of the Institute for Culture and Society at Western Sydney University. He is currently the university's Discipline Leader for Communication and Media. Dr Cohen has published widely in the field of visual anthropology, communications, film and media studies and directed three Australian Research Council Projects related to the Strehlow Collection. Three films have been made in relation to these projects: *Mr. Strehlow's Films* (SBSi 2001), *Cantata Journey* (ABC TV 2006), and *Ntaria Heroes* (2016). Dr Cohen is co-author of the award-winning book, *Screen Media Arts: An Introduction to Concepts and Practices* (2009) and editor of the *Global Media Journal* (Australian Edition (2007–present) (https://www.hca.westernsydney.edu.au/gmjau/). His most recent book is *The Strehlow Archive: Explorations in Old and New Media* (2018).

**Dr Diane Colman** is a Lecturer in International Relations and Global Politics in the School of Humanities and Communication Arts at Western Sydney University. Her research focuses on the globalisation of ideas on social justice and their culturally sensitive, inclusive application to local challenges. Diane's interests have concentrated on the Asia-Pacific and include East Timor's struggle with Australia for sovereignty over its seabed and consequent control over the substantial oil and gas resources required for its development. This concern with development led to research on the developmental state, extending internationally influential ideas on the role of the state in socio-economic transformation by applying them to the challenges of culturally distinct Asia-Pacific countries with an emphasis on the sustainable, long-term interests of society in Korea and Papua New Guinea. Applying the conceptual framework of culturally sensitive collective action in a globalised world has led Diane to an interest in the intersection between popular culture and world politics, forging a new multidisciplinary approach to global power.

**Dr Ritam Dutta** works as an Assistant Professor at the School of Liberal Studies, University of Petroleum and Energy Studies. With almost 15 years of teaching experience in both India and the United States, he remains a dedicated educator. Dutta's scholarly pursuits revolve around the intersections of literature, culture, education, and learning in informal cultural spaces. He is particularly interested in understanding the complex relationships between cultural practices, cultural spaces, cultural texts, records, and informal learning and education. His areas of interest are South Asian and Indian Youth Cultures, Literary Studies, Translation Studies, Career Adaptability Studies, Environmental Humanities, Place-Based Education, and Digital Humanities. He has published several research papers in peer-reviewed national and international journals and have presented in international conferences. He was a Fulbright Visiting Lecturer in the India Studies Program, Indiana University, Bloomington, USA from 2008–2009 and was a guest faculty in Centre for Studies in Book Publication and Department of Comparative Indian Languages and Literature, University of Calcutta from 2015–2017 and 2019–2020. Dr Dutta is also a life-skill educator and a communication coach. He has been twice awarded the prestigious international Blackboard Catalyst award in the "Teaching & Learning" and "Student Success" categories respectively for his innovative pedagogical practices in 2021 and 2022.

**Dr Cameron Edmond** is a Lecturer in Game Development at Macquarie University, with a focus on Teaching Leadership. As a researcher, he is interested in the intersections between creative writing and coding, and how the two may inform each other in classroom settings. He is also passionate about inclusive teaching practices that empower students to forge their own interdisciplinary links. His research encompasses videogame narrative design, algorithmic and AI-powered literature, as well as data storytelling. He maintains a creative practice as a game developer and experimental poet under the name Uncanny Machines.

**Dr Michael Falk** is a computational literary scholar, and the author of *Romanticism and the Contingent Self*. In his work, he uses computational methods to study literature, and the tools of literary criticism to understand software. His work appears in *Frontiers in AI & Robotics*, the *Oxford Encyclopaedia of Literary Theory*, *Interdisciplinary Science Reviews* and elsewhere. He runs the Digital Studies program at the University of Melbourne.

**Dr Myra Gurney** is a Senior Lecturer in Professional Writing, Communication and Media in the School of Humanities and Communication Arts at Western Sydney University, Australia. Her PhD research into the Australian political response to climate change has been published in several books and journals including *Global Crisis: Media, War, Climate, and Politics* (2023). Dr Gurney has co-authored a foundational communication textbook, *Communicating as Professionals* (2024) and is a member of the editorial panel of the *Global Media Journal* (Australian Edition (2007–present) (https://www.hca.westernsydney.edu.au/gmjau/).

**Dr Aditya Ghosh** is an Assistant Professor, Faculty of Liberal Arts, ICFAI University, Tripura. His areas of interest are Indian writing in English, British Literature, Literary Theory, English Language Teaching, Dalit Literature and Digital Humanities. He was part of the Indian team of the MHRD, Ministry of Education, Government of India-sponsored SPARC (Scheme for the Promotion of Research Collaboration)-funded research project collaborating with Western Sydney University, Australia in 2019–2021.

**Ms Miyuki Hughes** moved to Australia in 2013 and graduated from WSU with a Bachelor's degree in Interpreting and Translation in 2022. She is an employee with NNA Australia, a Japanese business news media based in Sydney, and she maintains a strong interest in Japanese-Australian business ties.

**Dr Ujjwal Jana** is Professor in the Department of English, Faculty of Arts, University of Delhi, Delhi, India. Professor Jana's areas of academic and research interest include Digital Humanities, Translation Studies, Disability Studies and Literary Studies with interdisciplinary orientation. Professor Jana was a Fulbright Scholar in Indiana University, Bloomington, USA in 2007–2008. He was a visiting faculty member in the Departments of English, Leipzig University, Germany and University of Johannesburg, South Africa in 2014 and 2017 respectively. He received Hungarian State scholarship awards in the academic year 2021–2022 and 2022–2023 funded by the Tempus Foundation of the Government of Hungary to carry out collaborative research projects. He was the Indian Principal Investigator of the SPARC (Scheme for Promotion of Academic and Research Collaboration) sponsored International collaborative Project (2019–2023) on "Digital Humanities in the Indian Rim" in collaboration with Western Sydney University, Australia, funded by the Ministry of Education, Government of India. Professor Jana's Bengali translation of Amit Chaudhuri's Sahitya-Akademi-Award-winning English novel, *A New World* (2000) by the Sahitya Akademi, India's national academy of letters, was published in 2021. Presently he is the Indian Principal Investigator of another SPARC-sponsored International Project (2023–2025) on "Indian-European entanglements: exploring trans-cultural relationships through Digital Humanities", to collaborate with Ghent Centre for Digital Humanities. Ghent University, Belgium funded by the Ministry of Education, Government of India. He is currently carrying out a research project funded by the Indian Council of Historical Research, India on the 19th-century poet saint of Odisha, Bhima Bhoi, during 2024–2026. Professor Jana has edited an anthology on *Digital Culture in Humanities: Contemporary Trends* published by a Delhi-based publishing house in January 2023.

**Dr Peter Mauch** is a Senior Lecturer in Asian Studies at Western Sydney University. A modern Japanese historian, he has published *Sailor Diplomat: Nomura Kichisaburo and the Japanese American War* (2011). He contributed to the *Cambridge History of the Second World War* (2015), and *Planning for War at Sea: 400 Years of Great Power Competition* (forthcoming). He has written essays in such journals as *Diplomatic History, Diplomacy and Statecraft*, the *Pacific Historical Review*, and *War in History*. He is a newcomer to the field of Digital Humanities.

**Dr Willard McCarty, PhD**, FRAI, is Professor Emeritus, King's College

London, Fellow of the Royal Anthropological Institute (London), editor of *Interdisciplinary Science Reviews* (2008–) and the online seminar Humanist (1987–). He has spent decades contextualising Digital Humanities in the sciences of the human, for the last few years in the ongoing workshop Science in the Forest, Science in the Past (Cambridge, 2017–).

**Ms Rimi Nandy** is an Assistant Professor, Department of Languages, School of Arts and Humanities, Coordinator, Centre for Academic and Professional Support, Christ University, Lavasa, Pune, India. She has been teaching English Language and Literature at various institutions since 2011. Her research interests include Digital Humanities, narratology, media studies, postmodernism, posthumanism and Japanese Cultural Studies. She has published journal articles and book chapters in the field of Digital Humanities.

**Dr Gopa Nayak** has a D.Phil from the University of Oxford, United Kingdom and is currently serving as the Professor at Ram Charan School of Leadership, MIT World Peace University, Pune, Maharashtra. After completing her Masters in Sociology from Delhi School of Economics, and receiving Honours in Psychology from Ravenshaw College, she continued her studies in Hong Kong and the United Kingdom. Her academic interests are focused on English Language Teaching Translation Studies and Cultural Studies.

**Dr Meredith Rossner** is Deputy Director of the Research School of Social Sciences and Professor of Criminology at the Centre for Social Research & Methods at Australian National University. Her research focuses on emotions, rituals, the built environment, and technology in justice practices. Past and current projects include investigations into the emotional dynamics of restorative justice, therapeutic courts, the role of courtroom design on access to justice, and the use of video technology in courts. Meredith has published widely in the field of restorative justice, including *Just Emotions: Rituals of Restorative Justice* (2013). She is on the editorial board of the *International Journal of Restorative Justice*, a member of the Canberra Restorative Community and the Oceania Network of Restorative Practice for Sexual Harm.

**Dr P. Prayer Elmo Raj** is Assistant Professor of English, PG & Research Department of English, Pachaiyappa's College, Chennai-30. He is the author of *Postcolonial Theory and Literary Imagination* (2018), *Shakespeare and Critical Theory* (2019) and *Paper, Pen and Ink: Postcolonial/Textual Politics* (2019). His research interests include alternative epistemologies and critical/literary theory.

**Ms Navreet Kaur Rana** is a Research Fellow at the Jindal India Institute at O. P. Jindal Global University. Her research areas include cultural studies of India, anthropology of food and cultural analytics.

**Ms Lopamudra Saha** is a Research Scholar in the Department of English, Pondicherry University, India. Her broader area of research is Digital Humanities with particular focus on Electronic Literature produced in India.

**Dr David Tait** is Emeritus Professor of Justice Research at Western Sydney University and Honorary Professor in POLIS@ANU, Research School of the Social Sciences, Australian National University. He has led six experimental studies about court technologies and spaces, examining interactive visual evidence, remote witnesses, iPads for jurors, the prejudicial effect of the dock, distributed courtrooms (remote participants appearing in their 'correct' positions in the courtroom via video screens, with localised sound) and virtual courts. He is currently part of a project (in partnership with the Fraunhofer Institute and organised through the University of Montreal) developing an immersive virtual court platform for use in justice hearings and working out how this facility may impact on fairness, sense of presence and quality of communication.

**Dr Rebekah Ward** has recently completed her PhD. Her research focuses on the history of print culture, particularly the 20th century book trade. Rebekah's doctorate, which blends traditional archival research with Digital Humanities approaches, explores how Angus & Robertson used book reviews as a promotional tool. She has published in *Australian Literary Studies*, *Publishing History* and *History*, and presented widely across cognate fields of publishing studies, Digital Humanities and Australian history.

**Mr Julian Walker** is a Master's student at Western Sydney University. His research interests are centred around the Korean Provisional Government and the dynamics of Governments in Exile during the early 20th century. He seeks to use Digital Humanities techniques to analyse the responses of governments in exile to international dynamics during the 1920s.

# Preface

In 1987, two years before the first joint conference of the North American and European Digital Humanities organisations, I happened upon a sign of what such a collaboration as is proposed in this book might enable. Toronto semiotician Paul Bouissac, organiser of the International Semiotics Symposium that year, asked me to put together a short course on computing in the humanities to accompany the main event. Because of this I was allowed to attend other Symposium courses. In ignorance of semiotics but with a background in computing, I chose a course on Artificial Intelligence, about which I was curious. I knew nothing about the man who offered it—one Ragaswamy Narasimhan.[1] He turned out to be the doyen of Indian computer science and engineering, or more to the point, the man whom his colleagues in India often called Bhīṣma (भीष्म, 'the mighty one').[2] A handful of us met with him in a classroom at Victoria College, University of Toronto. The only equipment in the room was a chalkboard, chalk and eraser. We were to discuss, he told us, how a computing system that would learn as a human child learns, might be designed.

I have forgotten the details of the system that evolved that day. But two things I do remember. The first will come as no surprise to those who know Narasimhan's work: the brilliantly pragmatic, step-by-step, mathematically elegant reasoning from childhood behaviour to the questions that had to be asked to accomplish the (still) distant goal. The second is rather difficult to articulate but vividly memorable: a scent of the traditions of thought at play in Narasimhan's probing. Under the

---

1  Ramani (2008). https://www.tifr.res.in/~endowment/prof-r-narasimhan.htm. Bouissac told me that he invited celebrity scholars (like Jacques Derrida, who spoke at the Symposium that year) to raise the funds to bring the likes of Narasimhan to the event.

2  https://en.wikipedia.org/wiki/Bhishma

influence of Northrop Frye, another Bhīṣma, I was fresh from intense and protracted doctoral studies of the Biblical and Greco-Roman roots of John Milton's seventeenth-century epic, *Paradise Lost*. So, I was not unprepared to recognise in Narasimhan the phenomenon of two great cultures in which he had been educated, speaking as one.

Another way of putting my experience is to be found in philosopher Hans-Georg Gadamer's *Truth and Method*.[3] There he calls such an interchange as took place among us in that course a "genuine conversation" (*das eigentliche Gespräch*), which is not one that we lead, but one by which we are led. Few will ever be Narasimhan's equal, but bringing researchers in Digital Humanities from the India Rim together is a start at setting the scene for more such conversations. So many languages and traditions of thought to draw from!

What might they do? What has been done already offers groundwork towards a Digital Humanities worthy of the cultures thus assembled. Make no mistake, we are not there yet, despite the great technological centres, the promoters' rhetoric, swelling journal publications and books, the growing number of institutional centres, academic programs and appointments. One could be forgiven for concluding that 'DH' has arrived where it is proclaimed and is now only to be disseminated and replicated. Such a conclusion does not survive a closer, Narasimhan-critical look, however. On occasion Digital Humanities has sat at the top table, so to speak. Hence, we can conclude that an ambition worthy of the cultures of the India Rim is not in vain. But DH is an infant, and like all infants, preoccupied with itself.

Again, we learn from human childhood. The developmental psychoanalyst D.W. Winnicott, in his insightful *Playing and Reality* (1971), writes about the "transitional objects" to which a human infant becomes attached—a favourite blanket, say, or a teddy bear. The important thing, he argues, is not the object but how the infant uses it to begin connecting to the world, to begin the long process of acculturation by which she or he matures into a (potentially) useful member of and contributor to society. Like a child, incunabular Digital Humanities is far enough along to have latched onto some promising transitional objects and has indeed done some promising things with

---

3    Gadamer [1989] 2004, p. 385; Gadamer 1990, p. 387.

them. But there is so much more! What about suitability to the vocation of a scholar, communicating with and contributing to the vast and ancient intellectual world, translating its intellectual wealth into the terms of the present and much troubled world?

Hence, we arrive at the threshold of interdisciplinary research, to which the proto-discipline of Digital Humanities is unavoidably committed by the nature of its methodological orientation (McCarty, 2016). My guess is that well over 98% of the work going on in 'DH' has not yet arrived at that threshold but remains in service to the practitioner's 'discipline of origin'. Understandable that this should be so—one's starting point remains crucial. I like to quote Frye at moments like this: "It takes a good deal of maturity", he wrote in *On Education* (1988, p. 10), "to see that every field of knowledge is the centre of all knowledge, and that it doesn't matter so much what you learn when you learn it in a structure that can expand into other structures."

Such is the beginning to which Digital Humanities leads the scholar brave enough to go further. I say 'brave' because the expanding is neither easy (indeed, very challenging) nor does it tend to be professionally rewarding. Straying beyond disciplinary/departmental boundaries raises the hackles of colleagues on both sides of the borderlands. It is, after all, difficult to see unfamiliar work governed by unfamiliar parameters and conditions as research. And there are pitfalls. The American scholar Stanley Fish has famously thundered against both Digital Humanities and interdisciplinary research. About the latter he declares in his title that "Being interdisciplinary is so very hard to do" (1989), by which he means impossible. He is right about one thing: that pretension to a neutral, panoptic standing point is ultimately futile and pernicious in the attempt. As Foucault pointed out in *Discipline and Punish* (1975), "panoptic" denotes a vision of imprisonment and hegemonic domination. Against this is Frye's rendering of Alain de Lille's *centrum ubique, circumferentia nusquam*, "centre everywhere, circumference nowhere" (McCarty, 2006).

Bon voyage!

Willard McCarty
Professor of Humanities Computing (Emeritus)
King's College London

# Works Cited

Fish, S. (1989). Being interdisciplinary is so very hard to do. *Profession 89*, 15–22. https://www.jstor.org/stable/25595433

Foucault, M. (1995). *Discipline and Punish: The Birth of the Prison.* (2e). [Trans. Alan Sheridan]. Vintage Books.

Frye, N. (1988). *On Education.* Fitzhenry & Whiteside.

Gadamer, H-G. (1960; 1990). *Warheit und Methode Grundzüge einer philosophischen Hermeneutik. Gesammelte Werke, Band 1.* J.C.B. Mohr.

Gadamer, H-G. (2004). *Truth and Method.* (2nd rev ed). [Trans. Joel Weisheimer and Donald G. Marshall.]. Continuum.

McCarty, W. (2006). Tree, turf, centre, archipelago—or wild acre? Metaphors and stories for Humanities computing. *Literary and Linguistic Computing 21*(1+), 1–13. https://doi.org/10.1093/llc/fqi066

McCarty, W. (2016). Becoming interdisciplinary. In S. Schreibman, R. Siemens & J. Unsworth (Eds). *A New Companion to Digital Humanities.* (pp. 69–83). John Wiley & Sons.

Ramani, S. (2008). Rangaswamy Narasimhan: Doyen of Computer Science and Technology. *Resonance* (May). https://www.ias.ac.in/article/fulltext/reso/013/05/0407-0409 (10/8/24)

Winnicott, D.W. [1971] (1980). *Playing and Reality.* Tavistock Publications.

# 1. Introduction

## *Hart Cohen and Ujjwal Jana*

### Abstract

This chapter introduces the main rationale for developing a collaboration between India and Australia in the Digital Humanities (DH). We argue that the time is right to reflect the expansion of the footprint of the Digital Humanities to the sub-continent and to continue the collaborative ethos of DH in this ongoing exchange between India and Australia. We will provide an overview of the current state of the Digital Humanities in India and Australia and where the scholars from these research contexts fit in the global sphere of Digital Humanities studies.

\*\*\*

The countries of the Indian Rim (Australia, India and South Africa) are relatively new players in the Digital Humanities (DH) space and bring innovative research ideas and methodologies that could potentially influence how DH is conceptualised internationally. While this volume reflects Indian and Australian DH scholarship, and represents only two nations of the India Rim, our collaboration was conceived with the aspiration of including South Africa. We would therefore like to retain this title to reflect this original aim, and to suggest an ongoing interest in furthering this research to include South African scholarship in future work in the Digital Humanities.

This book represents a compilation of scholarship in the field of Digital Humanities by academics who teach and research in India

https://doi.org/10.11647/OBP.0423.01

and Australia. The field of Digital Humanities is still in an early stage of development, and while it appears to be dominated by Western countries to date,[1] this volume would set a departure from this tendency by reflecting a prior and ongoing collaboration between India and Australia. The groundwork for this volume was laid by a Ministry of Education, Government of India-sponsored SPARC (Scheme for the Promotion of Research Collaboration)-funded research project, "Digital Humanities in the India Rim". SPARC encouraged documentation of the best DH practices internationally and how these might be adapted to the Indian and Australian national contexts. This enhanced DH learning and teaching in our respective universities and upskilled DH researchers. The dissemination of the research outcomes from this project, including seminars and workshops over these last four years, are in part absorbed, adapted and reflected in the contents of this volume, which also includes a comprehensive bibliography.

The Australian contributions to the volume are, in the main, from academics in the Western Sydney University Digital Humanities Initiative[2] (with one exception). The proliferation of DH across Australian universities is a feature of its growth in recent years, though WSU is marked, firstly, by both having the inaugural Professorship in Digital Humanities in Australia, and secondly by hosting the Alliance of Digital Humanities Organizations (ADHO) annual conference in 2015. There are other substantial innovations within the Australian context (for example, Australian National Library initiatives such as the massive media database *Trove*, or the innovative initiative of an Indigenous music database, *Paradisec*), that are too numerous to account for in this introduction.

This book showcases a range of perspectives from India and Australia and by Digital Humanities communities of practice found there. In essence, as a collaborative field of research, the Digital Humanities and the various works of scholarship in this volume seek to understand shared challenges, points of similarity and difference, and a robust exploration of problems and practices. The shared and divergent

---

1   Notable non-western expansion of Digital Humanities scholarship is found in China as well as parts of the Global South such as Latin America.
2   See Chapter 2, Mapping Digital Humanities at Western Sydney University in this volume by Professor Simon Burrows.

colonial histories of India, Australia and South Africa have influenced their self-definition of Digital Humanities with emphasis on significant people and projects that have 'flavoured' the field in each region.

For example, drawing on Indian classical logic can lead to novel conceptualisations of the digital and of computation. Indigenous Australian traditions of representing and thinking about space can inform new ways of mapping, while traditional Southern African philosophies like Ubuntu can inform our practices of collaboration.[3]

Digital Humanities in India is in its formative stage and still has the potential to compete at the international level. By contrast, the North American and European DH landscapes are now well developed and are taken by many to define what the field comprises. Australia sits between these two extremes. There have been individual DH practitioners in Australia since the beginning of Humanities Computing (e.g., Burrows, 1987). As a field with a national body (the Australian Association for Digital Humanities, AADH), activities and infrastructure, however, it is still very new, and for this reason, still defining itself in the light of, and in some ways in opposition to, the international scene. Australia and India are, therefore, natural allies in learning from each other and disseminating innovative research ideas and methodologies of DH learning and teaching, and in understanding each other's shared challenges, cultivating innovative practices and contributing meaningfully to create new pathways and establishing dialogues in the field of Digital Humanities by moving beyond the more established Eurocentric traditions and practices. It is past time for India to consider forming a national body to represent Indian DH in the ADHO international committee.

The countries of the Indian Rim all have immense potential to make substantial contributions, and in many ways face similar challenges. There is an immediate need to look again at the approaches and methods of Digital Humanities by seeking inspiration in the newly developing research and learning practices of these regions.

---

3    Relation-oriented AI: Why Protocols Matter for Indigenous AI. Retrieved from https://dhdebates.gc.cuny.edu/read/debates-in-the-digital-humanities-2023/section/98dc1c8f-8583-4428-ac84-17ff072bdcad; Indigenous place names and meanings now on Google Street View, retrieved from https://www.abc.net.au/sydney/indigenous-google/8683718

# From post-colonialism to decolonisation

The topics covered in this book have been influenced to some extent by the context of the shared and divergent histories of British colonialism to which both nations, India and Australia, have been subjected and have also responded. In the late 20th century, post-colonialism dominated scholarly inquiries that sought to recalibrate how colonialism was embedded in the uneven relationships between those engaged in knowledge creation in the West and the Global South. Driven in the main by the paradigm of "Orientalism" (Said, 1979), post-colonialism sought to demystify the myths and mystifications of the West in regards the "Orient", or what we would now term the Global South. Post-colonialism emanated from non-Western scholars who like, Said, were educated in elite Western tertiary institutions with a focus on literary studies.

Decolonisation has moved the dial further in recent times by sharpening the post-colonial critique and extending its work to include not only demystification but a kind of co-creation, where the remaking of the idea of a person's ethnicity is a key feature of a decolonising process. For example, Aboriginality can be seen as a "thing in-the-making" where a person's subjectivity and identity is secured on its own terms as a feature of resistance to dominant ideologies. As Rigney (1999) notes:

> [t]o arrive at a rationale for liberation epistemologies and Indigenist methodology we must first understand the colonial history of Australia and its impact on the Indigenous Peoples and their struggles to be free from colonialism... (p. 110)

For the Digital Humanities, this decolonisation paradigm is felt most emphatically in the decolonisation of archives and "de-colonising methodologies" (Smith, 1999). Decolonising archives involves, for example, rethinking the idea of Aboriginality and as a "counter-archive" telling a counter-story about who benefits in the pursuit of knowledge. As Professor Patti Lather states, "[l]ooking through the eyes of the colonised, cautionary tales are told from an indigenous perspective, tales designed not just to voice the voiceless but to prevent the dying— of people, of culture, of ecosystems" (Lather in Smith, 1999).

# Overview of the book

The book is divided into three sections Part 1, Digital Humanities: Institutions, ethics, politics; Part 2, Digital Humanities and literature; and Part 3, Digital Humanities and technology: Methods and methodology. The three parts bring together chapters that have points of contact in approach and/or thematic content. The chapters in Part 1 offer general engagements underpinned by problem-exemplars to provide insights in relation to institutions where DH research has made an impact, examples of where ethics are examined in specific DH-related cases and where political concerns have been put into play by DH projects. Part 2 features chapters where DH is applied to literary concerns. It features predominantly (though not exclusively) Indian authors and in this sense suggests a strong focus for DH in current Indian DH scholarship. The chapters in Part 3 are focused on methods in which certain technological affordances, such as databases and other forms of data analytics, are prominent. Examples in this part show an articulation of technology within DH that spans a wide range of research interests. The chapters in each part show a distinctive focus and thematic interest but with an affiliation with the world of Digital Humanities research.

The following chapter breakdown offers a summary of the contents of the three parts and how the authors chose to isolate a problem-exemplar with their specific form of DH scholarship. In Part 1, Chapter 2, "Mapping Digital Humanities at Western Sydney University", Professor Simon Burrows describes and reflects upon the Digital Humanities experiment at Western Sydney University. It explores how the Digital Humanities Research Group (DHRG) has confronted the challenges of innovating a new research group to build capacity within their own unique institutional context. Western Sydney University is a particularly appropriate and mature subject for such a case study because it was home of the first Chair and earliest formally constituted research cluster in its field in Australia. The chapter charts the triumphs and disappointments of the university's Digital Humanities Research Group from formation to maturity, as it has struggled to establish a precarious financial independence whilst nurturing an emerging and diverse group of scholars and their digitally empowered projects.

In Chapter 3, "Netflix and the shaping of global politics", Diane Colman begins by outlining the meaning and importance of soft power in global politics and briefly detailing the consideration of popular culture in the International Relations (IR) discipline. She then provides a detailed description of the research design of her database project, taking account of positivist conventions in qualitative studies by utilising the hybrid methodologies in a Digital Humanities interdisciplinary approach. Colman's case study is Netflix, which, as a leading entertainment streaming service, has considerable capacity to influence its audiences' ideas about the world, projecting immense soft power worldwide. Examining the ideological basis of this power is important in understanding world politics. The creation of a comprehensive database that categorises all "Netflix Original" films according to a carefully selected set of ontologies provides the epistemological tools necessary to analyse how IR may be influenced by the "soft power" of streaming services.

Chapter 4, "Digital justice: Interactions and rituals in the virtual courtroom" is authored by David Tait and Meredith Rossner. Having completed several projects in relation to digital justice, the authors offer their analysis of how courts have increasingly made use of video technologies to allow witnesses and defendants to take part in cases remotely. The use of video technologies increased dramatically with COVID-19. Not only did individuals appear on screens in physical courtrooms, but courts themselves sometimes became entirely virtual in connection with their cases and those (appellants, witnesses, etc.) related to them. The chapter examines what happens to courtroom-based interactions and rituals when the physical courtroom disappears. For example, it compares the standard format of a video conference where participants are isolated into boxes in a "gallery" with an alternative approach where participants are brought together into a shared space.

In Chapter 5, "Artificial Intelligence ethics and empathy: How empathic AI applications impact humanity", Linda Aulbach argues that Artificial Intelligence (AI) has sparked huge debates about its impacts on individuals, cultures, societies and the world. Through AI, we can now support, manipulate, or even replace humans at a level we have not seen before. One of the core values of happy and thriving relationships between humans is empathy. The ability to understand another person's feelings builds the foundation of human connection. Within the past few years, the field of AI has taken on the challenge of becoming empathic towards humans to create more trust, acceptance and attachment towards its applications. There are now "carebots" with simple empathic chat features, which seem to be 'nice to have', but there is also a concerning development in the field of "erobotics"—the next (empathic) generation of sex robots, made for humans to fall in love with. The increased emphasis on feelings within AI leads us to focus on how good or bad empathy really is in an AI app or platform. On the one hand, there is a high risk of manipulation of humans on a deep psychological level, yet on the other, there is also reason to believe that empathy is necessary to truly reach an ethical 'gold' standard. This chapter examines empathic AI and its ethical issues with a focus on humanity and the posthuman. It will also touch on the question as to what happens if AI becomes more human than humans themselves ever contemplated.

In Part 2, Chapter 6, "Digital hermeneutics: Interpretation and the interpretational machines", P. Prayer Elmo Raj presents hermeneutics as a philosophical theory of interpretation and communication in the context of challenges to existing and emergent digital communication and information networks. Digital hermeneutics can be understood as the interaction between hermeneutics and digital technology. In a society where communication and information networks are digitally based, Raj asserts that one of the major challenges for hermeneutics is its social relevance and interpretation of knowledge. The pseudo-critical refutation of hermeneutics in the context of digital technology is common. To encounter the challenges offered by digital technology, Raj channels Heidegger's (1966) concept of a "productive logic" in deciphering the dynamics of digital technology and its relationship with human existence.

Chapter 7 features the work of Gopa Nayak and Navreet Kaur Rana, of O.P. Jindal Global University. Their chapter is titled "'Aboutness' and semantic knowledge: A corpus-driven analysis of *Yajnavalkya Smriti* on the status and rights of women". In this chapter, Nayak and Navreet utilise corpus linguistics, under the broad umbrella of Digital Humanities, with a focus on the computational analysis of text to derive semantic knowledge. They draw on Martin Phillips' concept of knowledge-free analysis and the proposition of 'Aboutness' (1985), to analyse a historical corpus developed from *Yajnavalkya Smriti*, the literary text originally written in Sanskrit and translated into English. The text is about the general code of conduct prevalent in ancient Indian society and is the basis of many modern Indian laws. The analysis focuses on semantic knowledge, free from any bias or prior information, and aims to help us understand the validity of laws, especially those pertaining to women's status and rights in modern India. The study consists of an (approximately) 36,000-word corpus, but it has the potential to become a prototype for large-scale studies using concordance, collocation, and semantic prosody.

In Chapter 8, "Building a book history database: A novice voice", Rebekah Ward tells the story of how she began a doctorate in book history and then, with minimal training, came to build a bespoke relational database to enable and complement her written thesis. This research was to be based on the Angus & Robertson Archive, held by the State Library of New South Wales (SLNSW), now containing over a million documents across hundreds of boxes. While finding a way to manage the sheer volume of records, Ward gravitated towards DH tools. In particular, she saw the value in linking two sub-series of archival materials (scrapbooks of reviews, and distribution ledgers). These collections were clearly related but remained distinct from each other in the physical archive. The solution to Ward's challenge was Heurist, an open-source data management application designed specifically for Humanities researchers. The platform can handle long, plain-text fields and interlinked heterogenous data; it is mutable; and it offers inbuilt searching, filtering, analysis and visualisation capacities.

Chapter 9 brings us to the work of Ritam Dutta with his humorous title, "Are we ready to 'screw around' together? Barriers to the institutionalisation of DH pedagogy in literature departments." This chapter focuses on the challenges of the learning environment in traditional teacher-centric classrooms and on teachers' beliefs about how students learn or should learn in the context of the limitations of Digital Humanities pedagogy in India. Dutta argues that DH is generally understood as an exploration of the "intersection between information technology and humanities," and has grown as an interdisciplinary field of research in Humanities over the last couple of decades. Nevertheless, studies on DH reflect on the difficulties with defining and locating the subject within discipline-specific boundaries. Because Digital Humanities research spans topics as diverse as archives and social media, it poses substantial questions about where it should sit in the curriculum in contemporary learning contexts. The question that Dutta asks is: can we conceptualise a role for DH pedagogy in India beyond skill-building to that of helping students to critically engage with socio-political concerns?

In Chapter 10, "Literary masterpiece as a literary bank: A digital representation of intertextual references in T.S. Eliot's *The Waste Land*",

Aditya Ghosh creates a repository where all the intertextual references of Eliot's poem *The Waste Land* could be stored. The chapter models a digital representation of all the intertextual references to which T.S. Eliot's *The Waste Land* alludes. It encompasses the references Eliot incorporated into his masterpiece from Classical and Biblical texts to those from contemporary literary texts, followed by an inventory of post-*The-Waste-Land* texts that borrowed from it in turn. There is an intellectual argument to be had about the changing paradigm of critical research work that is undertaken within the framework of digital technology. But with the prerequisite of an archival repository and the capability to quickly access multiple texts from various resources, this technology can facilitate the creation and dissemination of knowledge in the field of the Humanities.

In Chapter 11 "Hypertext as a 'palimpsestuous' construct: Analysing Shelley Jackson's *Patchwork Girl*", Lopamudra Saha analyses how the hypertext fiction, *Patchwork Girl* (1995), functions as a palimpsest in its postmodern multimodal rewriting of the myth of *Frankenstein; or, The Modern Prometheus* (1818). The traditional idea of the 'palimpsest' as a parchment is revised when it is newly introduced within a multimedia context. This enquiry also evokes the changing dynamics of readership emergent within this new media context, highlighting how hypertextual reworking promotes ideas of multivocality, fragmentariness, non-linearity and interactivity through the application of an intersemiotic paradigm.

Chapter 12 concludes Part 2 with "Narratives of the self: Comments and confessions on Facebook" by Rimi Nandy. Nandy argues that narratives are often structured around events, which are used to tell a story. The self is perpetually being constructed through these narratives of experience. Beginning with the anonymous messages sent using applications like Stulish, Sarahah and the earliest version of confession pages, Nandy identifies how commenting on the virtual self has undergone layers of transformation. The move from anonymity to identification indicates a change in the way identity is conceived. The chapter tries to situate the identity of a person in the context of the perceptions and responses of their online contacts or 'friends'. In contrast, the comments posted on Stulish are written by nameless, faceless authors in a striking similarity to confession pages. This research proposes to understand the reasons behind sharing such posts on Facebook, even if comments are negative in tone. The chapter references Anthony Giddens' concept of time-space 'distanciation' to show how, through their narratives, multiple tellers are building the complex networked identity of the end user.

Part 3: Digital Humanities and technology: methods and methodology is begun by Chapter 13, "Code against code: Creative coding as research methodology" by Cameron Edmond and Tomasz Bednarz. This chapter details the authors' process of iterations of exchange between themselves and a text. This 'hacking' of the text becomes a critical practice as an engagement with the coded artefact. The chapter presents creative coding as a research methodology and interrogates its benefits and challenges via the so-called "*Irritant*" case study. Machine writing such as Chat GPT has risen in popularity recently, with machine writing seen as a subset of the creative coding discipline. Emblematic of the contemporary turn in machine writing is Darby Larson's *Irritant*. Impenetrable by traditional reading standards, the text is governed by code. The reader of *Irritant* faces similar challenges to the Digital Humanities scholar attempting to analyse large textual corpora. As such, *Irritant* becomes a useful case study for experimenting with reading methodologies. The authors approach *Irritant* from a computational criticism perspective, informed by the same creative coding methods that spawned it. Their objective is to reverse-engineer *Irritant*: scraping its repetitions and variables using Python within a live coding environment. In this way, the authors position creative coding as a research methodology itself, especially suited for analysing machine-written texts. The analysis opens more questions around how the exploration of *Irritant* fails to unravel the novel's code, but instead reveals even greater thematic depth.

In Chapter 14, "Digital Humanities for a different purpose", Miyuki Hughes, Madeleine Leehy, Julian Walker and Peter Mauch explore the recent application of DH methods to an Australia-Japan Research and Industrial Collaboration (DAJRIC) database, and assess their potential utility to a project that sits outside of traditional scholarly work. The primary objective of the chapter is twofold: (i) to evaluate the effectiveness of this approach, and (ii) to consider the scalability of the pilot database to accommodate numerous yet-unfunded Japanese-Australian research projects. By developing a Heurist database, the project harnesses the intuitive design principles that make DH methods so effective and appealing for scholarly purposes to users unfamiliar with these research fields as represented by the Australia-Japan research and industrial database. Throughout this process, the project team has discovered the challenges of raw data, ontology development, and bilingual functionality that face a project of this scale, whilst also realising the potential of Digital Humanities' techniques to provide improved user interactivity and search functionality through identifying record types and their connections with each other, as well as data visualisation. These techniques, when applied alongside knowledge-organisation techniques, enable a scalable database that can organically grow thanks to hundreds of projects that will be entered in the future. As such, this project provides a valid example of how scholarly techniques within the Digital Humanities field can be applied successfully to projects that act as a gateway between academia and other sectors.

Asha Chand presents her work in Chapter 15, "Online dating: Transformations of marriage arrangements through digital media technologies in Australia's Indian community". Chand's research is focused on marriage and migration as twin global forces that have reshaped Australia's identity from a White nation to a multicultural melting pot. India has become Australia's largest contributor to immigration, with 673,352 permanent migrants, second only after England (Australian Bureau of Statistics, 2021 census). This study, a networked, mobile and global account, examines the use of new media technologies in finding potential partners for marriage, known to the Indian diaspora as a way of life. The research attempts to gauge an understanding of the sociological impacts of hyper-communication, especially the use of dating sites and social media such as Facebook, in forming intimate relationships online. The significance of the study emerges as it attempts to understand the issues of cultural negotiations specific to the Indian community, which is becoming visible through statistical data as well as through its social spaces in Australia. Bollywood, which has wowed Western societies, coupled with India's resurgence as a superpower, adds value and importance to this research.

Chapter 16 concludes Part 3 with "The digital mediation of film archives from the Strehlow Collection" by Hart Cohen. This chapter is concerned with the history of the Strehlow Research Centre (SRC), with a special emphasis on how the film collection has been handled at various points in the institution's history. As an archive and research centre, the SRC has evolved from an earlier series of controversies around cultural ownership to being a leading innovator in the digitisation of parts of its collection. The digitisation of the films of T. G. H. Strehlow has led the collecting institution sector, not only in technological innovation but also in outreach and engagement with its Aboriginal constituency. The example of the Strehlow Film Collection and its evolution as a database and focus for community engagement resonate with the issues that have recently emerged around archive/counter-archive projects and participatory archives, which have revived the role of archives in recovering spaces of cultural memory and cultural practice. The chapter will test the proposition that "… the archive as a site for creative intervention, enables new possibilities for preserving and representing individual memory within a larger historical consciousness" (Kashmere, 2021).

# Works Cited

Burrows, J. (1987). *Computation into Criticism: A Study of Jane Austen's Novels and an Experiment in Method*. Oxford University Press.

Dodd, M., & Kalrah, N. (2020). *Exploring Digital Humanities in India Pedagogies, Practices, and Institutional Possibilities*. Routledge.

Heidegger, M. (1996). *Being and Time*. SUNY Press.

Kashmere, B. (n.d.). Cache rules everything around me: Introduction to Issue #2: Counter-Archive. *Incite!* http://www.incite-online.net/intro2.html

Lather, P. (2006). Paradigm proliferation as a good thing to think with: Teaching research in education as a wild profusion. *International Journal of Qualitative Studies in Education 19*(1), 35–57. https://doi.org/10.1080/09518390500450144

Phillips, M. (1985). *Aspects of Text Structure: An Investigation of the Lexical Organisation of Text*. North Holland.

Risam, R. (2018). Decolonizing the digital humanities in theory and practice. In *The Routledge Companion to Media Studies and Digital Humanities*. (pp. 78–86). Routledge.

Rigney, L.I. (1999). Internationalization of an Indigenous anticolonial cultural critique of research methodologies: A guide to Indigenist research methodology and its principles. *Wicazo sa review 14*(2), 109–121. https://doi.org/10.2307/1409555

Roy D., & Dodd, M. (2024) Digital Humanities and their Discontents. In *Digital Humanities and Laboratories*. Routledge.

Shelley, M. (1818). *Frankenstein*. Lackington, Hughes, Harding, Mavor, & Jones.

Smith, T.L. (1999). *Decolonizing Methodologies: Research and Indigenous Peoples* (3e). Zed.

# PART 1
## DIGITAL HUMANITIES:
## INSTITUTIONS, ETHICS, POLITICS

# 2. Mapping Digital Humanities at Western Sydney University

*Simon Burrows*

## Abstract

This chapter discusses efforts to build research capacity in Digital Humanities at Western Sydney University. Western Sydney University is a particularly appropriate subject for such a study because it was the site of the first Chair and earliest formally constituted research cluster in its field in Australia. The chapter charts the challenges, triumphs and disappointments of the university's Digital Humanities Research Group from formation to maturity, as the group has sought to establish financial stability whilst nurturing an emerging and diverse group of digitally empowered projects. In particular, it focuses on how the group's leadership has leveraged conferencing, training and networking to build trajectory, reputation and velocity, and has strategically targeted seed-corn funding to support emerging Digital Humanities scholars. It also explores how my own award-winning and, by the standards of the field, positively venerable, project on the 'French Book Trade in Enlightenment Europe' has drawn on and developed the expertise and activities of colleagues, stakeholders and external collaborators, to bring training, research and funding opportunities to group members and students, and embed us in an ecosystem of 'like-minded projects'. In these ways, it is hoped that the Digital Humanities Research Group might be viewed as a living laboratory, and its experience serve

https://doi.org/10.11647/OBP.0423.02

as a guide to the perils and opportunities inherent in developing Digital Humanities.

## Keywords

Digital Humanities; Western Sydney University; academic capacity building; research groups; academic networks.

## Introduction

In recent years there has been growing interest and enthusiasm for Digital Humanities in the Indian Rim and other areas of the Global South. Whether we measure this interest in terms of practitioners, university course offerings, research centres dedicated to the field, regional associations, or affiliations to organisations like the Alliance of Digital Humanities Organisations (ADHO) or Centernet, it is clear that this is a growth area for the Humanities and Social Sciences, and one with significant potential for societal impact.

At first sight, the progress of Digital Humanities appears to face extra hurdles in the Global South, especially on account of infrastructure and resources. However, on closer analysis, whilst practitioners in these regions may experience these issues in particularly acute form, their colleagues in the Global North often face similar challenges. In this chapter, therefore, I wish to explore how Digital Humanists at one Australian university, Western Sydney University, have sought across the past decade to build research capacity and trajectory, particularly in the face of declining university funding. It is hoped that documenting our experience will be useful to others contemplating an investment in Digital Humanities—whether personal or institutional—both in and beyond the India Rim.

## The challenge of Digital Humanities

The prospectus for the ground-breaking global, online Building Digital Humanities symposium co-convened by Western Sydney University in November 2022, reflects thus on the novel challenges around work in the field:

Digital Humanities has presented a set of novel issues and dilemmas for both Humanities scholars and their collaborators, partners and facilitators in venues as diverse as the classroom, the library, industry, IT, government agencies and university research offices.

As Digital Humanities practices have increasingly challenged the lone scholar model of humanities research and embedded computational technologies at the heart of much cutting-edge scholarship, new challenges have arisen around infrastructures, collaborative models, approaches to scholarly attribution and accreditation, data-sharing, data-preservation, access to data, and appropriate training and career structures.

The choices policy makers, administrators and individual researchers take in response to these challenges have real world consequences, shaping, facilitating, or impeding individual careers, research agendas, or institutional or national initiatives.[1]

These observations are worthy of reflection, because the digital space is one of the most complex, rapidly changing, transformative and least understood challenges in the modern university. Digital Humanities, though only one part of this puzzle, is a particularly difficult one, due to the interdisciplinary and evolving nature of the field, and the large and ever-changing number of stakeholders, each with varied perspectives and interests. As a result, institutional engagements with Digital Humanities are perhaps best seen as ongoing and evolving real-time experiments.

Western Sydney University's experiment with Digital Humanities offers a particularly apposite and mature subject for such a case study, because the university created Australasia's first Chair in Digital Humanities and is home to the earliest formally constituted research cluster in the field. This means we can take a decade-long view of how the Digital Humanities Research Group (DHRG) has confronted general and particular challenges such as those outlined above, building capacity within our own unique institutional context even as it struggled to establish a precarious financial independence whilst nurturing an emerging and diverse group of scholars.

In particular, the chapter focuses on how the DHRG has leveraged

---

1    The 'official' conference website for Building Digital Humanities was decommissioned later in 2023. Recordings of the event have been archived at: https://www.westernsydney.edu.au/dhrg/digital_humanities/dh_downunder/past_events/dh_downunder_2022

conferencing, training and networking to build trajectory, reputation and velocity, and how it has strategically invested start-up funding to support emerging projects. It will also explore how my own long-term project on the 'French Book Trade in Enlightenment Europe' (FBTEE), which I brought with me to Western Sydney in 2013, has drawn on and developed the expertise and activities of colleagues, stakeholders and external collaborators, to bring training, research and funding opportunities to group members and students, and embed us in an ecosystem of 'like-minded projects'. In these ways, it is hoped that the DHRG might be viewed as a living laboratory, and its experience serve as a guide to the challenges and opportunities inherent in developing Digital Humanities.

Developing the Digital Humanities experiment at Western Sydney has been demanding, but, as many chapters in this book show, it has ultimately been worthwhile. As I write, colleagues working in the newly renamed Digital Humanities Research Initiative (DHRI) are leading on projects on themes as varied as 'Netflix and International Politics';[2] 'Cultures of Repair in Western Sydney';[3] and promoting research and industry partnerships between Japan and Australia.[4] All of these projects have been incubated within the DHRG, and none of the lead researchers involved had prior experience of Digital Humanities work. Further, all these projects have significant real-world applications. In this sense, the DHRG can be seen as a successful incubator of new, innovative, and often cutting-edge digital research across a wide frontier.

## International and local networks

Equally, the DHRG has developed a global profile, due to our engagements with, and birthing of, global networks in Digital Humanities. This approach dates back to the early days of the DHRG:

---

2    See Diane Colman's chapter on 'Netflix and the Shaping of Global Politics' in this volume.

3    On this project see: Abby Mellick Lopes and Alison Gill, 'Commoning Repair: Framing a Community Response to Transitioning Waste Economies', in Eleni Kalantidou, Guy Keulemens, Abby Mellick Lopes, Niklavs Rubenis and Alison Gill, eds, *Design/Repair*. Place, Practice & Community (Palgrave Macmillan, 2023).

4    To avoid confusion and for purposes of consistency, this chapter refers to the group throughout as the DHRG, except where the new name (DHRI) is significant to our story.

within months of his appointment as group leader, Professor Paul Arthur had secured us hosting rights to 'Digital Humanities 2015', the annual conference of the Alliance of Digital Humanities Organisations (ADHO).[5] This was a major coup for the university and Digital Humanities in Australia, and the first time ADHO had held its conference outside Europe and North America. The event had a mobilising impact within the university, conferring prestige on the group and arousing curiosity about Digital Humanities as a field.

In addition, Paul Arthur plugged us into other important international networks, most notably the Implementing New Knowledge Environments (INKE) partnership, directed by Professor Ray Siemens at the University of Victoria in British Columbia, Canada, a leader in the field of Digital Humanities globally.[6] Ray Siemens was for several years an adjunct at Western Sydney, and has subsequently served as visiting Global Innovation Chair in Digital Humanities at the University of Newcastle (NSW), one of our close regional collaborators.

Western Sydney has been a partner on several INKE-related initiatives. In 2017 and 2018, in partnership with the University of Sydney's Digital Humanities Research Group and with Ray Siemens as facilitator, we funded and convened the workshops from which the Canadian Australian Partnership for Open Scholarship (CAPOS) emerged. CAPOS duly won funding from the Canadian Social Science and Humanities Research Council.

The inaugural CAPOS meeting in 2019 was, as we shall see, a further turning point for Digital Humanities at Western Sydney.[7] The DHRG was also a named partner on a series of more ambitious INKE grant application, culminating in a successful application in 2019. This new funding covers the period 2020–2027. It commits Western Sydney to holding a major workshop each year in pursuit of the INKE agenda and establishes a funding stream to enable us to continue to send delegates to the annual INKE partnership gatherings in Canada. These exchanges have now been going on for almost ten years.

INKE proved a particularly rich choice of partner for international

---

5    Records of this conference are archived at http://dh2015.org/

6    The INKE partnership website is at https://inke.ca/

7    For details of CAPOS work, see https://inke.ca/canadian-australian-partnership-for-open-scholarship/

knowledge exchange for two reasons. Firstly, due to shared post-colonial contexts as former British dominions, it has empowered rich dialogues around indigenous knowledge and heritage issues. Secondly, it has allowed Western Sydney University to engage more closely with Victoria University's Digital Humanities Summer Institute (DHSI), the largest Digital Humanities training event in the Americas.[8]

Inspired by the DHSI model, in 2016, Associate Professor Rachel Hendery, who lectures in Digital Humanities, and Dr Jason Ensor, the DHRG's Research and Technical Development Manager, convened the inaugural Digital Humanities Downunder Summer School at Western Sydney. This event rapidly became the premier Digital Humanities training event in Australasia, drawing up to 100 delegates each year. The DHSI model leverages the collegiality of the national Digital Humanities community, who volunteer their time to train others in key approaches, techniques and platforms.

But DH Downunder's success has also depended on the efforts of Rachel Hendery, who has been instrumental in driving the event. This was not the original vision: Australia is a large country and so it was hoped that the event would circulate around the major cities. Circumstances dictated otherwise, however, and to date every event has been hosted in Sydney, except in 2019 when DH Downunder was hosted at the (relatively) nearby University of Newcastle.[9] Whilst this has helped to build local capacity and cement Western Sydney University's leadership in the field, long-term we hope the vision of a low-cost, circulating event will prevail.[10]

Besides CAPOS and DH Downunder, the DHRG has played a key role in establishing two further international networks. In 2016, with financial support from the Australian Research Council-funded 'Mapping Print, Charting Enlightenment' (MPCE) grant and my professorial 'establishment funds', the DHRG hosted the first Digitizing

---

8　The DHSI website is at https://dhsi.org/
9　The 2017 event was held at and co-hosted by the University of Sydney's DHRG, but the 2016, 2018, 2020 and 2021 events were hosted in person or, during the COVID-19 pandemic, online by Western Sydney alone.
10　As this book went to press, we were delighted to learn that DH Downunder 2024 will be hosted in Canberra at the Australian National University and the 2025 event will be held at the University of Melbourne.

Enlightenment symposium.[11] This was followed by a symposium at Radboud University (2017), and subsequent events at Oxford, Edinburgh and, following a break during the COVID-19 pandemic, Montpellier. Six years later, Western Sydney University hosted the aforementioned global, online Building Digital Humanities symposium, which we co-convened with the University of Pondicherry and corporate sponsors Gale. All of these initiatives provided opportunities for Western researchers and helped to build capacity. So, too, did the DHRG's participation from 2013 to 2018 in the annual 'Around the World Digital Symposium', an innovative 24-hour global event, organised by the University of Alberta, in which panels from over a dozen universities showcased their work in lightening presentations.[12]

In its early years, the DHRG was also connected to global networks through generous expenditure on visiting positions. In particular, we benefitted from extended annual visits by Professors Willard McCarty and Harold Short from Kings College, London. Recognised as being among the global founders and leading thinkers in the field, McCarty and Short advised on the initial business proposal for the DHRG and were instrumental in shaping our successful 'Digital Humanities 2015' bid. With such collaborations, the success of 'Digital Humanities 2015' and the launch of DH Downunder, Digital Humanities at Western Sydney University was making a mark internationally and within Australia, and generating excitement inside the university. By the time Paul Arthur left to take up a position at Edith Cowan University in September 2016, the group boasted over 60 members from across the university, including many of its leading researchers.

---

11  Most of the papers at the first Digitizing Enlightenment symposium were published in Burrows & Roe (2020). The 'Mapping Print, Charting Enlightenment' website is at https://int-heuristweb-prod.intersect.org.au/heurist/?db=MPCE_Mapping_Print_Charting_Enlightenment&website&

12  See https://aroundtheworld.ualberta.ca/category/archive/ for archived podcasts of all six 'Around the World' symposia. A publication to which a group of Western Sydney University academics contributed was led by University of Alberta 'Around the World' leaders. See H. Cohen, F. Sidoti, A. Gill, A. M. Lopes, M. Hatfield and J. Allen, 'Sustainability, Living Labs and Repair: Approaches to Climate Change Mitigation' in Chelsea Miya, Oliver Rossier and Geoffrey Rockwell, eds, *Right Research: Modelling Sustainable Research Practices in the Anthropocene* (Cambridge: Open Book Publishers, 2021), https://www.openbookpublishers.com/books/10.11647/obp.0213

# The composition of the DHRG

Many members of the group, however, were dipping their toes into unfamiliar waters. Their membership expressed a curiosity to know more, rather than a deep knowledge and engagement. Others saw Digital Humanities as a means of contextualising existing work. Most of these members brought energy and commitment, but the DHRG's ability to pursue key goals set by the university remained relatively limited—particularly when it came to growing research income from major competitive grants. The problem here was not success rates but underlying human capacity.[13]

At the heart of the DHRG were a small kernel of regular grant winners, several of whom were 'core' members for whom the DHRG was their institutional base. Prominent among them was linguist Rachel Hendery, in 2013 still an early career researcher. She soon won a series of major grants, culminating in her ambitious 'Waves of Words' project, which attempts to reconcile the linguistic, anthropological, and archaeological records relating to Australia's contacts with the wider world in the millennia preceding British colonisation. Also important was Professor David Tait whose work on the virtual courtroom in partnership with various jurisdictions internationally also involved multiple academic and corporate collaborations. Jason Ensor likewise played an important role. He was an investigator on my MPCE project as well as some of those run by Paul Arthur, and won Australian National Data Service funding for his own book-trade-related project, the 'Angus & Robertson Collection for Humanities and Education Research' (ARCHivER). Likewise, Dr Camellia Webb-Gannon participated in various projects relating to social media, including a study of 'Music, Mobile Phones and Community Justice in Melanesia'. Finally, Paul Arthur's involvements included the multi-partner DomeLab project and a collaboration with the Huygens Institute on Dutch-Australian cultural heritage and identities entitled 'Migrating People, Migrating Data'.[14]

Beyond these core members of group lay an outer kernel. Professor

---

13  The DHRG success rate in competitive grant applications submitted between 2013 and 2020 was around 50%. We had similar success rates when applying for other sources of funding.
14  For a list of DHRG projects see: https://logincms.westernsydney.edu.au/dhrg/digital_humanities/about_us

Hart Cohen worked with the group to publish, maintain and further develop his interactive site 'Journey to Horseshoe Bend'. In 2017 Hart joined the DHRG executive and became the group's deputy leader, overseeing development of an exciting MA programme. Likewise, two colleagues from Computing, Dr Tomas Trescak and Dr Anton Bogdanovych, devoted considerable efforts to Virtual Reality projects on 'Aboriginal Parramatta' and the impressive 'Uruk 3000 B.C.', which used insights from the genetic and behavioural sciences to 'breed' a population of avatars and model their behaviours. Tomas also contributed around a million lines of code as an investigator-developer to FBTEE, the project I brought with me from Leeds to Western Sydney, where initially I, too, was a member of this outer kernel. Supported originally by a British Arts and Humanities Research Council grant, FBTEE was already being recognised as a significant contribution to Digital Humanities by the time we transferred it to Western Sydney in 2013. One reviewer went so far as to assert that FBTEE did 'quite a lot' to bring the 'historical profession into the age of interactive digital technologies and GIS technology' (Caradonna, 2013). In 2015, FBTEE won further funding from the Australian Research Council, followed by the British Society for Eighteenth-Century Studies digital resource prize in 2017. This, as we shall see, was success we could leverage.

## Challenges for the DHRG

Expanding this small group of stalwart grant-winners became an important goal. By 2016, when I was appointed DHRG Leader, it was already clear that this would be a major challenge. There were structural reasons for this. The first stemmed from the nature of the Australian grant landscape, which places significant emphasis on track record. Because this takes time to accumulate, upskilling researchers' digital skills and building research trajectory was always going to be a five- to ten-year project. This timescale was problematic in a research culture where the main government-mandated research assessment, the Excellence in Research for Australia (ERA), took place every three years.

The second challenge stemmed from the internal structures of the university. Put simply, we lacked the resources to attract existing big-hitting established grant winners to submit their grants through the

DHRG. These researchers had existing relations with the university's research institutes and tended to submit their applications through them. These research institutes had been set up to concentrate research strength and underpin a rapid transformation of the university's research culture and international rankings.

By the time the DHRG was formed, the institutes were empowering Western Sydney's rapid rise up the Australian and global university research rankings. Their full-time members included many of the university's leading researchers, often on research-driven contracts. The research institutes also granted membership to 'school-based' members, regular teaching academics who, subject to performance, were accorded modest financial resources and, more importantly, significant administrational and academic support with grant applications.

The DHRG could not compete with these incentives, particularly because, as matters of principle, it operated an open membership and dispensed advice and support freely on grant ideation. It thus had a largely invisible input into several successful projects from which it did not derive direct benefit in university metrics. To be sure, this was not entirely one-way traffic. A number of institute members, particularly from the Institute for Culture and Society, have played leading roles in many DHRG initiatives. Nevertheless, these structural factors shaped our parameters of action.

## The search for self-sufficiency

In addition, by 2016 the university was signalling that the DHRG needed to stand on its own two feet financially. This was part of the group's initial design. From its inception, there was an explicit expectation that the DHRG would become, at the level of operating expenses, increasingly self-supporting over time. As a result, funding from the university's Research Infrastructure Funding (RIF) would be progressively withdrawn.

The group had several potential routes towards financial self-sufficiency. The most attractive from an economic point of view was through consultancy, since this might provide a relatively stable income stream. To incentivise consultancy activity, the university generously proposed that, in addition to any profits, the DHRG would keep the

16% matching funding offered by the Commonwealth government of Australia. A second route, theoretically, was through non-Commonwealth grant income. Like consultancy, this income carries matching funding, but such funding was not made available to the grant-winning unit. This was unfortunate for the DHRG, which has had significant successes in overseas grant capture. Other possibilities for raising funds included commercial partnerships, philanthropic donations or securing competitive internal grant funding. Finally, many of our conference and workshop activities could also be supported through sponsorships and registration income. The DHRG has tried most of these pathways, with varying degrees of success, and now finds itself in a sustainable position, but at the expense of having scaled back organisationally. The story of how we have achieved this, playing to our strengths and gradually focusing on core capacity, may provide pointers for other groups, especially those who are working with limited resources.

From the university's point of view, consultancy was for a while considered the priority route. A periodic review of the DHRG released in late 2016 called for the group to explore consultancy opportunities, and suggested we look at the Humanities Research Institute (HRI) at the University of Sheffield as a potential model. This model involved providing digital development support to other institutions. Unfortunately, our benchmarking exercise and further research suggested that the Sheffield HRI model was not suitable for the DHRG for three reasons. The first was financial. Outsourcing projects is more economically viable under Britain's Full Economic Cost (FEC) funding model, which provides host institutions with generous overheads, whereas universities have to match Australian Research Council (ARC) awards with significant cash and in-kind contributions. The second reason was capacity. The Sheffield HRI is a considerable operation which employs several academic technologists and has an impressive track record of digitising massive archives, making them accessible through text searching and metadata tools.[15] In contrast, the

---

15    The HRI's projects include the award-winning Old Bailey Online and successor projects, which are arguably, from a public engagement perspective, the biggest Digital Humanities projects undertaken anywhere. These projects can be consulted at https://www.oldbaileyonline.org/; https://www.londonlives.org/; https://www.digitalpanopticon.org/

DHRG lacked a specialism or track record and employed a single academic technologist, whose position as Research and Technical Development Manager also incorporated the roles of project management, group administrator, and active researcher. To operate as a viable consultancy, we would need to hire several more staff in an untested market. Finally, there was already a major competitor providing digital research services, Intersect Australia. Intersect is a not-for-profit organisation established by a consortium of universities in which Western Sydney University is a financial stakeholder.[16] Whilst not specifically focused on the Humanities, Intersect has worked on several Digital Humanities initiatives. Realising that it would struggle to compete in Intersect's space, the DHRG began to explore alternative consultancy possibilities with the University.

We were not without ideas. Jason Ensor had already pioneered an innovative and economical academic publishing model, and generously suggested we adopt it to develop a press with the university's imprimatur. The success of the university's Writing and Society Research Centre at sponsoring Giramondo Press suggested this might be viable.[17] We also explored commercialising Journal Finder, a tool developed by Jason and his partners in the Western Sydney University library to help researchers find appropriate, high-prestige publishing outlets. The former idea foundered on profit margins, the latter on Jason's pre-existing commitments to share Journal Finder as open source.

Our final and most successful proposal was to develop the DHRG's Experiential and Immersion Research Lab (EIRL), headed by Kate Richards. Kate had considerable experience of VR technologies and content creation before entering academia, and under her guidance the Lab attracted a couple of five-figure contracts. EIRL was also shortlisted, alone or in partnership, for three much bigger projects, including developing VR and XR content for the refurbished Hyde Park Barracks in Sydney and Villers-Bretonneaux war memorial site in France. Alas, none of these bids was successful. Eventually, it became clear that we would not be able to attract enough prestigious, specialised or cutting-edge, research-driven projects to maintain the income flow we required. Conversely, if we chose to focus on more mundane content-creation

---

16  For details on Intersect Australia and its services, see https://intersect.org.au/
17  See https://sydneyreviewofbooks.com/ and https://giramondopublishing.com/about/

assignments, it would not be viable to 'scale up' operations. The reason was simple. Creative salaries in Australia are substantially lower than university pay rates. It would thus be almost impossible to offer a competitive service.[18]

At this point, the DHRG was forced to face a brutal truth: we were not short of skilled scholars, but our strength lay in diversity, inter-disciplinarity, and a shared commitment to digital approaches. What we lacked was a critical mass of individuals with shared skills or expertise in specific methods or technologies. Without such shared competencies, we were likely to struggle to operate a successful consultancy operation. However, this same diversity opened avenues to interesting research collaborations, and these too might provide opportunities, particularly if we could upskill some new entrants to Digital Humanities. From 2016, this became a major focus for DHRG's new leadership.

## Building human capacity

A symptom and result of this shift was a revised strategy for building human capacity. This was reflected in the adoption of a more egalitarian leadership style through the formation of an executive committee (initially comprising Rachel Hendery, Jason Ensor, and me), regular member meetings, and a new budget formula. From 2016, one third of our resources were devoted to the personal development of core staff (that is, members formally assigned to the group, including research assistants), and another third to start-up grants. The final third went on general costs including commitments to overseas partnerships, such as INKE.

One positive side-effect of this new member-centred approach was a gradual increase in attendance at DHRG seminars. The DHRG has run seminar series throughout most of its existence, but as with other seminars at Western Sydney, it was a struggle to build regular attendance from a highly interdisciplinary group in a multi-campus university. At first, attendances were often barely a handful. However, from 2016, average attendances grew rapidly, to between ten and twenty at most

---

18    For creative salary data during this period (as of 4 June 2018), see https://www. payscale.com

seminars, abetted by the efforts of successive convenors: FBTEE post-doc Laure Philip, Michael Falk, and finally Hart Cohen. Further, Hart's 'The Artist and the Algorithm' seminar series successfully trialled a thematic approach, with the aim of publication. Other initiatives proved equally popular.

The start-up grant scheme proved a particular success and a key plank in the group's evolution, running annually from 2017 to 2020. The idea grew from Paul Arthur's decision after 'Digital Humanities 2015' to plough the small operating profit from the conference into a one-off competition in which members could apply for start-up money for their projects. This original call attracted several applications and not all could be funded. In 2017, the new executive committee decided to run a similar scheme every year, an idea members supported enthusiastically. The funding was limited: from around $8,000 per annum, we usually funded four or five projects. However, the DHRG also provided start-up-funding holders with in-kind support and advice. This allowed us to facilitate projects as required but without always granting the full sums requested. By this means the judging panel never rejected an application, though we did remodel some budgets. To make the grants as flexible as possible, our project eligibility requirements were deliberately loose: applicants had to be academic staff and members of the group, and projects had to fit broadly under the Digital Humanities umbrella. By this means, conference-type activities were eligible alongside projects requiring digital support or specialist equipment. We also asked for an (unenforceable) moral commitment to put any related grants through the DHRG, if not encumbered by previous collaborative obligations.

Projects funded by our start-up grants scheme included a 'Social Robotics' symposium, speaker expenses for conferences and, more often, funding for equipment, training, software or websites for emerging projects led by early career researchers. Several researchers accessed multiple grants as their projects evolved. This helped make the DHRG more cohesive and allowed the group leadership to become increasingly invested in their colleagues' work. The most significant start-up projects feature in this book.

Moreover, because we were always looking for cost-effective solutions, the DHRG increasingly advised applicants on open-source resources, above all the Heurist platform used by many of the projects discussed in this book.[19] Although Heurist presented at Western Sydney's first Digital Humanities event, the inaugural 'Around the World' symposium in May 2013, the DHRG's engagement with Heurist came much later, initially through two projects of much greater magnitude (Around the World, 2013). The first of these projects was my Australian-Research-Council-funded MPCE project, which built upon my work with FBTEE.[20] The second was the British AHRC-funded 'Libraries, Reading Communities and Cultural Formation' project, led by Mark Towsey of the University of Liverpool, on which the DHRG is a partner with special responsibility for digital development. Intersect Australia is also a partner on delivering this project. Neither of these projects began life as a Heurist project. Indeed, the original FBTEE database was published in June 2012. This was seven years before I met Heurist's developer, Ian Johnson, and promptly adopted Heurist.

## Leveraging success

Further, from 2012 to 2019, the DHRG helped to leverage FBTEE's reputation as a path-breaking project in Enlightenment studies and a model for other historical bibliometric projects. This included, as we have seen, the launch of the Digitizing Enlightenment symposium series, which grew out of conversations with Stanford University's celebrated 'Mapping the Republic of Letters' (MtRoL) project and MIT's 'Comédie française Registers Project'. Digitizing Enlightenment aimed to establish a collaborative network and conversation between digital projects treating the Enlightenment era.[21] As part of this initiative, Stanford's Dan Edelstein served as an external investigator on MPCE, and as a result Jason Ensor, Rachel Hendery and I all visited Stanford to work with the MtRoL team.

Equally, I became involved in a network of 'library historians' organised by Mark Towsey, and I attended their workshop on digital research in library history in Chicago in 2015 (Burrows, 2015). This led

---

19   For details of Heurist, see https://heuristnetwork.org/
20   The 'Mapping Print, Charting Enlightenment' online database interface is at https://int-heuristweb-prod.intersect.org.au/heurist/?db=MPCE_Mapping_Print_Charting_Enlightenment&website&
21   On MtRoL and CFRP see the project websites at http://republicofletters.stanford.edu/; https://www.comedie-francaise.fr/en/daily-registers#

to an invitation for Western Sydney University to take the lead on the digital development for Towsey's 'Libraries, Reading Communities, and Cultural Formation' project. This 1,000,000 GBP project involved 18 university and 'impact' partners across Europe, North America and Australia. It also helped build collaboration among DHRG researchers, as the project included innovative plans for incorporating weighted corpus linguistics tools, and this involved the collaboration of Rachel Hendery and another colleague, Robert Mailhammer.

FBTEE also developed collaborations with other leading book history projects, most notably two large European-Research-Council-funded initiatives. Alicia Montoya's 'MEDIATE' project, based at Radboud University in the Netherlands, looks at private library holdings across Europe in the long 18th century, whilst Damien Tricoire's 'Pamphlets and Patrons' project (PaPa), based at the University of Trier, examines networks of political patronage. FBTEE researchers advised on both projects in the pre-award stage and participated in knowledge and staff exchanges with both projects subsequently. In this way, FBTEE has embedded Western Sydney University researchers in an extensive network of like-minded projects. In the case of PaPa this collaboration extends to a unique database-sharing arrangement.

## Engagement with Heurist

The decision to migrate FBTEE resources to Heurist was thus a momentous one for both parties, particularly as, by then, the FBTEE team was developing a suite of successor resources under the auspices of the MPCE project. The end goal of MPCE had always been to create a single database containing all these resources, organised around a single event-based data model. However, by dint of a series of unfortunately timed staffing changes, drip-fed funding, and development issues, none of the daughter-resources quite mapped onto the original data model, whilst the original FBTEE data would require significant remodelling prior to integration into a combined resource.

By late 2019 it was also becoming clear that ARC funding and the university could not indefinitely support bespoke development for FBTEE resources. So, when Ian Johnson gave a presentation on the newly upgraded Heurist at the 2019 CAPOS conference, I seized the chance to test a system which promised flexibility and an almost unlimited capacity to restructure my database myself without needing any programming skills. Heurist proved to be as good as it sounded.

Within a day, following our first meeting, Ian Johnson and his developer, Artem Osmakov, built a demonstration database, uploaded the FBTEE data, and built an interactive website. In the months that followed, I designed a separate database for the MPCE data, along the lines of our original data model, and remodelled the FBTEE and MPCE data accordingly. Meanwhile, Ian and I identified areas where Heurist's existing functionality did not yet meet my requirements and worked with a succession of Professional Experience (PX) student computing teams at Western Sydney University to create the new tools I needed. To date, we have worked with over 20 students to develop new functionalities. These have then been rolled out to the wider Heurist community. Several of these students have been offered positions with Heurist, and one is currently employed with them.[22]

Essentially, Heurist is, as it boasts, a free, open-source 'research-driven data management system' that allows users 'to design, populate, explore and publish [...] richly structured database(s) [...] through a simple web interface, without the need for programmers or consultants'.[23] For Western Sydney University researchers, its key attractions have been flexibility, intuitive ease of use, and the in-built website creation tool and templates. Increasingly, as a user community, we have been able to support each other, too, assisting in database design. For efficiency reasons, wherever possible we have paid Heurist to design our websites. This is far cheaper than using a commercial website designer and saves researchers from significant time investment in learning a one-off task.

Heurist's flexibility and ease of use is perhaps best exemplified by the 'boot camp' Ian Johnson and I led for the post-docs on Mark Towsey's project in February 2020. The post-docs arrived with limited knowledge of how to construct a research database or the computational thinking involved, yet within two weeks they had designed their project

---

22  The work of the various PX team members is documented, along with the work of the rest of the project team, at https://int-heuristweb-prod. intersect.org.au/heurist/?db=MPCE_Mapping_Print_Charting_Enlightenment&website&id=117630&pageid=117628

23  https://heuristnetwork.org/

database.[24] This was all the more impressive because we needed to align their project with MPCE and a dump of newly-cleaned English Short Title Catalogue data brought to us under licence by Mikko Tolonen from the University of Helsinki's 'Computational History Group'.[25] In contrast, developing a bespoke tool would have taken months of a software engineer's time and cost tens of thousands of dollars.

In the months following the bootcamp, one by one the DHRG start-up-funding projects shifted to Heurist. At the same time, our corporate life was revivified following COVID-19 lockdowns by developments elsewhere, notably the 'Digital Humanities in the Indian Rim' project launched by Hart Cohen, Rachel Hendery, Michael Falk and Helen Bones in partnership with Professor Ujjwal Jana of the University of Pondicherry. This project and partnership remained funded throughout the pandemic and culminated in an online seminar series convened by Professors Hart Cohen and Ujjwal Jana involving Western Sydney University researchers and staff and students in Pondicherry, and Pondicherry partnered with us on hosting the Building Digital Humanities Symposium. Most of the chapters in this volume were first presented during the seminar series and showcase the development, diversity and richness of work taking place at this moment, particularly the Heurist projects.

The migration of Western Sydney DHRG projects to Heurist was timely, as it helped to compensate for the loss of internal development capacity. This progressive downsizing happened between 2017 and late 2019, following the resignation of Jason Ensor, who subsequently took up another position within the university. He was eventually replaced by Michael Falk on an *ad hoc* part-time basis. From mid 2018 to late 2019, Michael's position was supported by a combination of existing projects and a contribution from the School of Humanities. The role was

---

24  The online interface website for the project, constructed much later in the project with the assistance of Michael Falk, is at c18librariesonline.org

25  The ESTC can be consulted at: http://estc.bl.uk/F/?func=file&file_name=login-bl-estc. On the use by the Helsinki Computational History Group of cleaned ESTC data, see Mark J.Hill, Ville Vaara, Tanja Säily, Leo Lahti and Mikko Tolonen, 'Reconstructing intellectual networks: from the ESTC's bibliographic metadata to historical material', in *Digital Humanities in the Nordic Countries: Proceedings of the Digital Humanities in the Nordic Countries 4th Conference*, ed. by Costanza Navarretta, Manex Agirrezabal and Bente Maegaard (Aachen: CEUR-WS, 2019), pp. 201–19 at https://ceur-ws.org/Vol-2364/19_paper.pdf

discontinued altogether when Michael took up a lectureship in Britain at the end of 2019. However, by dint of fortune, he returned to Australia in 2021, where he took a position at Heurist that involved supporting several projects with which he was already familiar from his time at Western Sydney.

## Retrenchment and rebuilding

As COVID-19 began to impact university finances, Western Sydney University, like other Australian institutions, sought financial retrenchments. Research units were a particular target. The DHRG thus lost its central Research Infrastructure Funding a year earlier than previously expected. Outwardly, the most immediate impact of this was a change in the Group's name, since the term 'Research Group' was reserved for RIF-funded units: we now became a Research Initiative. Internally, the main impact was the loss of our remaining RIF funding and a 30% time allowance for the group leader. Both cuts could be weathered. The lion's share of the leader's time allowance had hitherto been spent preparing reports and attending meetings and key committees. These tasks were now no longer required, as the group ceased to be a university cost centre. This had collateral benefits, especially as the group leader could now return to the classroom. The funding cut also galvanised us to win a competitive internal grant offered by our school. The 'Building the Digital Humanities' grant secured funding for five discrete projects, all of which had benefited from the DHRG start-up funding scheme. To give it cohesion, the grant programme was tied together with a mentoring package and an end-of-grant symposium.[26] The project's results are visible in this book and in recordings from the Building Digital Humanities symposium.[27]

The projects funded by this grant are bearing fruit in multiple ways. The DHRG's new 'stars' are making significant contributions to their disciplines or fields of practice, as well as tangible differences to society in

---

26   The mentors on the project were Simon Burrows, Hart Cohen, Rachel Hendery, David Tait and Tanya Notley, a long-term member of the DHRG with research interests in social media and communications.

27   At time of writing, we are expecting to publish two volumes arising from the Building Digital Humanities symposium with Radboud University Press.

Western Sydney. They have also become adept at building the trajectory of a project. A case in point is Dr Diane Colman's aforementioned project on 'Netflix and Global Politics'.[28] This project has leveraged financial support from a variety of university sources including DHRG start-up funding, a grant for women researchers, and several summer student scholarships, a total package worth around $A 50,000. More significantly, perhaps, Diane Colman argues that Digital Humanities projects such as hers offer a means to marry traditional International Relations approaches with emerging research on soft power, which has hitherto been difficult to integrate into the empirical and realist frameworks favoured by International Relations specialists.

Over time, many DHRG projects have become more applied and socially transformative in their ambitions. In some ways, this had always been the case. For example, one of the DHRG's original core members, David Tait, was assigned to the group due to his innovative work with international partners on cyber-justice and the virtual courtroom. The importance of this work became clear during the COVID-19 pandemic, as many jurisdictions explored moving their courts online. More recently, engagement with Digital Humanities fed into Dr Alison Gill's project on repair cultures in Western Sydney and led Dr Peter Mauch and his partners at the Australia-Japan Foundation to envisage a database of fundable projects to promote Australian-Japanese research and business collaborations. Further, DHRG projects have become prolific users of the university's Summer Scholarships scheme. They have provided paid summer research internships to around a dozen students and provided a pipeline of future research students. For example, the summer research students I employed in 2020–21 and 2021–22 are now enrolled for PhD and Master of Research degrees respectively.

Diane Colman, Peter Mauch and Alison Gill's aforementioned projects were all among those supported by the Building Digital Humanities grant. The others were Dr Navin Doloswala's research on fire performance and the next iteration of Hart Cohen's mature project on 'Journey to Horseshoe Bend'. This project offers an interactive narration of the death-journey of celebrated Australian anthropologist and linguist Carl Strehlow across central Australia in 1922. All these

---

28   See Diane Colman's chapter on 'Netflix and the shaping of global politics' in this volume.

projects, with the exception of Horseshoe Bend, were showcased to a global audience in a 'special session' on the final day of the 'Building Digital Humanities' symposium on 23 November 2023, together with a further Heurist-supported project developed by Dr Katrina Sandbach.[29] Bringing together scholars with backgrounds in International Relations, History, Design, Communications and Anthropology, collectively these projects show the full diversity of the DHRG's work. As the finishing point of both the Building Digital Humanities grant project and the symposium, this seems an appropriate point to reflect on the past and future directions of the Western Sydney University DHRI.

The symposium itself marked another milestone for Digital Humanities at Western Sydney. The most ambitious event we had hosted since 'Digital Humanities 2015', and by registrations even larger, it marked a return to the outward-looking approach taken under Paul Arthur and revived by the India Rim project. This time, however, our networking is aimed outwards at promoting Digital Humanities to the wider global community. This approach aligns with the university's own priorities, which culminated in the award of the coveted number one world ranking for promoting UNESCO Human Development goals by the *Times Higher* in both 2022 and 2023.

Connections between Digital Humanities and development became increasingly clear as we planned the event, and for two main reasons. Firstly, many of the problems tackled by Digital Humanities, as well as the infrastructural challenges it faces, are in fact human development issues. This is particularly visible in the regions collectively known as the Global South, which includes most of the Indian Rim, but in different ways they affect universities and societies in the Global North also. The enthusiasm with which participants in the Global South embraced the opportunity to engage in, and frequently lead, our global conversation, was testimony to the need to discuss these challenges together. For example, 'minimal computing' has its attractions for researchers and citizens in rich societies, even as it is essential in the lands of the Global South. Secondly, it was obvious that a desire to engage in the sorts of conversations that took place at Building Digital Humanities was widespread. At Western Sydney, we originally wished to discuss

---

29   The special session can be watched at https://www.youtube.com/watch?v=sSy-Z-sYAGU

how to empower digital work in humanistic fields to inform our local discussions, but in fact similar challenges exist universally among practitioners. Thus, our symposium struck a chord internationally.

## Future prospects

As I write, the future shape of Digital Humanities at Western Sydney remains to be determined. Certainly, we will be developing international initiatives from the Building Digital Humanities agenda. One aspect of that will involve a traditional print and online publication from the symposium sessions, and at the time of writing we have just lined up a publisher. In keeping with the globally transformative aims of the symposium, commitments made to delegates, and our own group's commitments to Open Scholarship, we have negotiated for the book to be diamond open access—that is to say, free of charge without upfront fees for authors or a paywall for readers.[30]

Another aspect of this work will be developing networks, initiatives and global and local partnerships to support Digital Humanities in emerging spaces. These emerging spaces include the Global South, but they also exist within post-colonial societies such as Australia, most notably around the digital sharing and preservation of indigenous knowledges and wisdom. The historic abuse and continuing misuse of such material, even by sometimes well-meaning parties, means that this issue requires sensitive, informed and respectful dialogue. Whilst such issues are particularly pressing for post-colonial settler societies such as Australia, they are also important for the former colonial powers of Europe.

Finally, there will doubtless be further 'Building the Digital Humanities' events, particularly if we can find supporters as generous as Gale, Australia and New Zealand, who provided substantial cash and in-kind support for the inaugural event. This included the use of their license to the Cvent platform to organise the conference and the loan of a staff member, Damian Almeida, Training and Digital Communications Executive, who created the webpages and registration system and posted

---

30   Our expected publisher for these two volumes is Radboud University Press, contract pending.

session recordings. Blessed by this partnership, the event attracted over 140 (invited) speakers, 700 registered delegates, and several significant nominal sponsors, including ADHO.

The DHRI will continue to exist within the university as a funded entity. Its current INKE commitments—and a related income stream— remain active until 2027. Equally, collaborations around publishing, including this book, but also two volumes arising out of the Building Digital Humanities symposium, will keep group members active. Beyond these research activities, the DHRI is looking towards building possible teaching activities, and continues to attract research students.

Thus, if the group eventually ceases to exist, it will probably be because its original *raison d'être* has been overtaken by events. As digital methods become more mainstream in the humanistic disciplines, the services the group has hitherto provided may migrate elsewhere or become obsolete as knowledge is generalised. But to date there is no sign that the Digital Humanities are about to 'wither away'. Indeed, the case for including a robust training in—or at the very least encounter with—Digital Humanities in the undergraduate curriculum appears to grow stronger by the year.

What general lessons, then, can we take from the Western Sydney experiment? Especially in light of our setbacks around consultancy, it is important to understand your human capital, and how best to build upon it. At Western, once we identified the challenges we faced, we sought to build human capital by a combination of training events, start-up funding, strategic mentoring, high-visibility international partnerships and conference-style events and workshops. The university supercharged the group's initial development by strategic appointments, but developing existing talent has been a long-term process.

As our knowledge base and experience have grown, the DHRG leadership has become more creative, weathering cuts to central funding in ways that have had little impact on our capacity. At the same time, we have put ourselves at the heart of national and international networks and training events, culminating with our creative partnership with the University of Pondicherry and the Building Digital Humanities initiative.

Encouragingly for others, particularly in the Global South, the networks in which we are embedded are generally open, collaborative ones, and the digital platforms we have embraced have been open source with active user communities. They thus offer a model for groups in other institutional settings wishing to build capacity in similar ways. Finally, hosting repeated or one-off events has allowed us to build links with regular sponsors, including local partners like Intersect Australia and the Australian Research Data Commons, as well as international corporations, most notably Gale. By these means our workshops, symposia and summer school have become increasingly independent of our university financially.

Thus, whilst never generating the income that both we and the university would ideally have liked, we have realised and exceeded the university's founding vision for Digital Humanities research in other ways. Against a background of diminishing resources, we have learned to 'stand on our own two feet' financially, developed emerging talent, provided professional or research experiences to several cohorts of computing and summer scholarship students, and continued to play a significant leadership role in the development of the field at home and internationally. The experiment is far from over.

# Works Cited

Alliance of Digital Humanities Organizations. (2019). DH 2019 Conference. http://dh2015.org/

'Around the World'. https://aroundtheworld.ualberta.ca/category/archive/

British Library. (n.d.). English Short-Title Catalogue (ESTC). http://estc.bl.uk/ F/?func=file&file_name=login-bl-estc

Burrows, S. (2015). Locating the minister's looted books: From provenance and library histories to the digital reconstruction of print culture, *Library and Information History* 31, 1–17. https://doi.org/10.1179/175834891 4Z.00000000071

Burrows, S., & Roe, G. (Eds). (2020). *Digitizing Enlightenment: Digital Humanities and the Transformation of Eighteenth-Century Studies*. Liverpool University Press.

Canadian Australian Partnership for Open Scholarship (CAPOS). (n.d.). https://inke.ca/canadian-australian-partnership-for-open-scholarship/

Caradonna, J. (2013). Review of The French Book Trade in Enlightenment Europe Project. *French History* 27, 286–87.

Cohen, H., Sidoti, F., Gill, A., Mellick Lopes, A., Hatfield, M., & Allen, J. (2021). Sustainability, Living Labs and Repair: Approaches to Climate Change Mitigation. In C. Miya, O. Rossier, & G. Rockwell (Eds). *Right Research: Modelling Sustainable Research Practices in the Anthropocene*. Open Book Publishers. https://doi.org/10.11647/OBP.0213

Colman, D. (2024). Netflix and the shaping of global politics. In H. Cohen, U. Jana, & M. Gurney (Eds). *Digital Humanities in the Indian Rim*. Open Book Publishers.

Comédie Française Registers Project. (n.d.). https://www.comedie-francaise.fr/en/daily-registers#

C18th Libraries Online. (n.d.). Libraries, Reading Communities, and Cultural Formation in the C18 British Atlantic. c18librariesonline.org

Digital Humanities Summer Institute (DHSI). (n.d.). https://dhsi.org/

Giramondo Publishing. (2023). *About*. https://giramondopublishing.com/about/

Heurist. (n.d.). https://heuristnetwork.org/

Hill, M. J., Vaara, V., Säily, T., Lahti, L., & Tolonen, M. (2019). Reconstructing intellectual networks: From the ESTC's bibliographic metadata to historical material. *Digital Humanities in the Nordic Countries*, 201–219. https://ceur-ws.org/Vol-2364/19_paper.pdf

INKE. (n.d.). Implementing New Knowledge Environments (INKE) partnership. https://inke.ca/.

Intersect Australia. (n.d.). https://intersect.org.au/

London Lives. (2018). London Lives 1690–1800. https://www.londonlives.org/

Mellick Lopes, A., & Gill, A. (2023). Commoning Repair: Framing a community response to transitioning waste economies. In E. Kalantidou, G. Keulemens, A. Mellick Lopes, N. Rubenis, & A. Gill (Eds). *Design/Repair: Place, Practice & Community*. Palgrave Macmillan. https://doi.org/10.1007/978-3-031-46862-9_8

Mapping Print, Charting Enlightenment. (n.d.). https://int-heuristweb-prod.intersect.org.au/heurist/?db=MPCE_Mapping_Print_Charting_Enlightenment&website&

Mapping the Republic of Letters. (2013). http://republicofletters.stanford.edu/

Old Bailey Online. (2018). *The Proceedings of the Old Bailey 1674–1913*. https://www.oldbaileyonline.org/

Payscale. (2023). https://www.payscale.com

Short, H., Cohen, H., & Richards, K. (2013). Digital Humanities at University of Western Sydney (podcast). https://aroundtheworld.ualberta.ca/category/archive/atw2013-archive/

Tricoire, D. (2023). Pamphlets and Patrons: How courtiers shaped the public sphere in Ancien Regime France (PaPa). https://papa.uni-trier.de/

Western Sydney University. (2023). *Sydney Review of Books*. Writing and Society Research Group. https://sydneyreviewofbooks.com/

Western Sydney University. (2022). Special session at Building Digital Humanities (podcast). https://www.youtube.com/watch?v=sSy-Z-sYAGU

Western Sydney University. (2023). Digital Humanities Research Group. https://logincms.westernsydney.edu.au/dhrg/digital_humanities/about_us

Western Sydney University. (2022). Building Digital Humanities. https://www.westernsydney.edu.au/dhrg/digital_humanities/dh_downunder/past_events/dh_downunder_2022

# 3. Netflix and the shaping of global politics

## Diane Colman

## Abstract

This chapter begins by outlining the meaning and importance of soft power in global politics and briefly detailing the consideration of popular culture in the International Relations (IR) discipline. It then provides a detailed description of the research design of the database project, taking account of positivist conventions in qualitative studies by utilising the hybrid methodologies in the Digital Humanities interdisciplinary approach. International Relations as a discipline understands power on a global scale. Such understanding includes the concept of 'soft power' and the role of popular culture in projecting and universalising hegemonic state values. In the globalised world of today, the power of individuals often transcends state boundaries. This case study is about Netflix, which, as a global actor, is the leading entertainment streaming service. Netflix has considerable capacity to influence its audiences' ideas about the world, projecting immense soft power worldwide. Examining the ideological basis of this power is important in understanding world politics. The creation of a comprehensive database that categorises all Netflix Original films according to a carefully selected set of ontologies provides the epistemological tools necessary to suit the needs of IR studies.

https://doi.org/10.11647/OBP.0423.03

## Keywords

Netflix; international relations; database; soft power.

## Introduction

International Relations (IR) is a discipline that understands power on a global scale. Such understanding includes the concept of 'soft power' and the role of popular culture in projecting and universalising hegemonic state values. While a growing number of IR scholars are now using an ideational conceptualisation that draws on discursive theories from other disciplines, much of mainstream IR underestimates the power of popular culture to represent, reflect and constitute world politics. The reason for this is largely epistemological: as a social science, IR privileges positivist approaches and specifies the importance of data collection; the macro; the structural. Such approaches usually focus on the power of states as unitary actors.

But in the globalised world of today, the power of individuals often transcends state boundaries. As a global actor, the world's leading entertainment streaming service, Netflix, has considerable capacity to influence its audiences' ideas about the world, projecting immense soft power worldwide. Examining the ideological basis of this power is important in understanding world politics. The creation of a comprehensive database that categorises all Netflix Original films according to a carefully selected set of ontologies should provide the epistemological tools necessary to meet the tendency of IR to privilege positivist methodologies. This may well create legitimacy within the discipline and enable us to acknowledge and reassess the insights that the lens of popular culture brings to the study of IR, hopefully leading to a more complexly articulated and relevant theoretical basis for the understanding of what constitutes world politics. This chapter will begin by outlining the meaning and importance of soft power in global politics and briefly detailing the consideration of popular culture in the IR discipline. It will then provide a detailed description of the research design of the database project, taking account of positivist conventions in qualitative studies by utilising the hybrid methodologies in the Digital Humanities interdisciplinary approach.

# Soft power

The term 'soft power' was coined by political scientist Joseph Nye in his 1990 book, *Bound to Lead*. Since then, he has developed the term further whilst maintaining a central ideational definition. According to Nye, soft power is "the ability to get what you want through attraction rather than coercion or payments" (2004, p. x), "the ability to affect others and obtain preferred outcomes by attraction and persuasion" (2017, p. 2). Soft power, which Nye also calls "co-optive" or indirect power, rests on the attraction a set of ideas possesses, or on the capacity to set political agendas that shape the preferences of others (1990, pp. 31–35). Soft power is, therefore, related to intangible resources like culture, ideologies and institutions (Zahran & Ramos, 2010, p. 13). In fact, Nye's general conception of "power refers to more ephemeral human relationships that change shape under different circumstances" (2011, p. 3). This enlarges ideas about what exactly constitutes political power. Rather than power being understood in material terms, political power "becomes in part a competition for attractiveness, legitimacy, and credibility" (2004, p. 31). The ability to develop widespread understanding and acceptance of a country's values, motivations and interests becomes an important source of attraction and forms its soft power.

While he extended the idea to other states, most notably the USSR and China, in producing his extended scholarship on soft power, Nye specifically sought to explain how American global leadership was not in decline despite the challenge of other rising powers. The global reach of US influence could not be explained through military and economic power alone. He considered that many countries were attracted to, and approved of, US global leadership, providing less resistance to its pursuit of its goals as US power was understood as legitimate by other states. Nye specifically sought to influence foreign policymaking to ensure that America's global hegemonic position continued. Nye's idea of soft power is, therefore, an extension of Gramsci's concept of hegemony, which involves a combination of coercion and consent, as "domination" and as "intellectual and moral guidance" (1971, p. 215). Hegemony, as soft power, works through consent on a set of general principles that secures the supremacy of a group and, at the same time, provides some degree of satisfaction to the other remaining groups. Extending this

Gramscian notion to international relations, the cultural, economic, and social values of the hegemon are positioned as the civilisational values of the globalised society (Cox, 1983, p. 51).

This then leads to consideration of how such widespread consent to these hegemonic values is produced, secured, and reproduced over time. While Gramsci and Nye both focus on state power, they also both recognise that the soft, consensual part of this power comes from civil society rather than governments as "propaganda is not credible and thus does not attract" (Nye, 2017, p. 3). For Gramsci, the ruling class ruled most effectively when its control over society was least visible. This meant that his notion of the state included the underpinnings of the political structure in civil society. Gramsci thought of these in concrete historical terms: the church, the educational system, the press; all the institutions that helped to create in people certain modes of behaviour and expectations consistent with the hegemonic social order (Cox, 1983, p. 51). According to Nye, the generation of soft power is also affected by a host of non-state actors within and outside a country. Those actors affect both the general public and governing elites in other countries and create an enabling environment for government policies (2011, p. 69). Both concepts make reference to a set of general principles, ideas, values and institutions shared by, consented to, or regarded as legitimate by different groups, but that at the same time are resources of power, influence and control.

Nye highlights three sources of soft power:

> [...] culture (in places where it is attractive to others), political values (when the state lives up to them at home and abroad) and foreign policies (when they are seen as legitimate and having moral authority) (2004, p. 11).

Similarly, Gramsci considers the sphere of ideas and culture to be essential, manifesting a capacity to obtain consensus and create a social basis for it (Zahran & Ramos, 2010, p. 21). And so, it is to this third, cultural site of power that we will now turn.

# Popular culture and world politics

As indicated previously, the academic discipline of IR is particularly concerned with power in the global context. While this has traditionally focused on military and economic power, there is recognition that culture can also be considered as a resource of power, influence and control.

Taking culture seriously as a carrier of political values and norms is supremely important to global politics and has been seen as such since the 'cultural turn' in IR in the late 1980s. This coincided with an intellectual movement across the humanities and social sciences that challenged the orthodoxy of claims to objective, universal knowledge. Leading IR constructivists such as Nicholas Onuf (1989) and Alexander Wendt (1992) created a social theory of relations between states, that we live in a world of our own making and the world that we construct is one of varied identities and interests formed through social interaction and institutions. For Christian Reus-Smith (1989), cultural norms, principles and rules provide deep constitutive value to the development of institutional practices in the international system.

Exactly what is meant by culture is a contested term throughout the academy with many contradictions and complexities. Because of these incompatibilities, theorists who think about what culture is have tried to come up with less static and more open definitions of culture, which focus on how culture is related to meaning rather than trying to pin culture to a particular place at a particular time, or to particular objects. According to Stuart Hall, "culture ... is not so much a set of things—novels, paintings or TV programs and comics—as a process, a set of practices" (1997, p. 2). For Hall, "culture is concerned with the production and the exchange of meanings between members of a society or group" (1997, p. 2). Or as John Hartley defines it, culture is "(t)he social production and reproduction of sense, meaning and consciousness" (1994, p. 68). Culture has to do with how we make sense of the world and how we produce, reproduce and circulate sense. We circulate sense about the world in many ways, and one of the ways we do this is through stories. This is why another cultural theorist, Clifford Geertz, described culture as "an ensemble of stories we tell about ourselves" (1975, p. 448). The interrelated representations produced by these stories interact to constitute a frame of meaning which, through repetition, is transformed from being a culturally produced understanding into what is identified as 'common sense' as represented in the Gramscian tradition.

Formal cultural exchange has been an important aspect of statecraft for millennia, and the influence of high culture is well considered within both the academy and diplomatic circles. Most observers would agree that high culture produces significant soft power for a state. Yet there is often a clear distinction between high culture and popular culture.

> Many intellectuals and critics disdain popular culture because of its crude commercialism. They regard it as providing mass entertainment rather than information and thus having little political effect (Nye, 2004, pp. 44–46).

Far from being insignificant, however, Roland Barthes established that the banal, or "what goes without saying" (2009, p. xix) is eminently worthy of closer attention and analytical scrutiny. "It is that content, whether reflected favourably or unfavourably, that brings people to the box office. That content is more powerful than politics or economics. It drives politics and economics" (Wattenberg, quoted in Nye, 2004, p. 47). As Jutta Weldes and Christina Rowley say:

> Consumption is inextricably linked to the production and re-production of meanings—the maintenance of some, the transformation of others (whether through subversion, overt challenge or gradual change) (2015, p. 1).

For J. Furman Daniel and Paul Musgrave:

> [p]opular culture is more than a diversion from the serious stuff of international relations. It plays a greater role in shaping the world than mainstream international relations have recognised (2017, p. 513).

Popular culture can unite, either in a narrow way around a specific text, activity, location or person, or in a more general way, through a network of thoughts, feelings, and/or behaviours that interrelate to constitute it (Reinherd, 2019, p. 1). Wide-ranging or narrowly focused, popular culture is the commonality that weaves us together to help us find and make meaning, discover ourselves and each other, build community and solidarity, and make sense of the world and our place in it (2019, p. 2).

For soft power to be effective as a hegemonic tool, it must appeal to as large an audience as possible (Bruner, 2019, p. 12). It becomes obvious, then, that the most prevalent site for interacting with, and being heavily influenced by, cultural practices that produce, organise and circulate meaning through stories told about the world is what is most popular. Popular culture is for the public; it is for the masses. For everyday working people "who perhaps could not afford the 'finer' things of a society or culture but still find meaning and solidarity through so-called 'low culture'" (Reinherd, 2019, p. 1). There has been a growing awareness that popular culture can substantially affect and influence international relations by propagating and shaping world political ideas via mass media (Daniel & Musgrave, 2017, p. 512). Popular culture, according to Kyle Grayson, Matt Davies and Simon Philpott:

> ... has been identified as a critical site where power, ideology and identity are constituted, produced and/or materialized. There is a range of signifying and lived practices such as poetry, film, sculpture, music, television, leisure activities and fashion that constitute popular culture (2009, pp. 155–156).

But, when it comes to the power and influence of pop cultural forms, it is the 'movie' that reigns supreme. As Daniel and Musgrave say, "IR scholars should realize that more people have learned how the world works from Steven Spielberg than from Stephen Walt" (2017, p. 345).[1] Much of American soft power has been produced by Hollywood over almost a century of production. Nye quotes a former French foreign minister who observed that Americans are powerful because they can "inspire the dreams and desires of others, thanks to the mastery of global images through film and television" (Nye, 2004, p. 8). The promotion and export of the images, stories, sounds, and sights of popular movies help to create a common sense of world politics. Examination of these works shows how popular culture constructs national interests, creates ideas of belonging that delineate 'us' from 'them', and makes sense of world events. As award-winning filmmaker Ken Loach said at the 2019 BAFTAs:

> ... [f]ilms can do many things, they can entertain, terrify, they can make us laugh and tell us something about the real world we live in (Demianyk, 2017).

---

1      Stephen Walt is a professor of International Affairs at Harvard University, a distinguished and highly influential academic in the IR discipline.

According to Nye, the line between information and entertainment has never been as sharp as some academics imagine (2004, p. 47), and it is becoming increasingly blurred in the rapidly expanding global media landscape. The formation of entirely new types of media actors has empowered a broad range of civil society voices to the mediation of the world politics of today. Hegemony is in continuous need of "active agents, in this case, the producers of popular culture" (Dittmer, 2010, p. 62). One of the most powerful new non-traditional media producers is the hugely successful streaming platform, Netflix.

As we became more and more isolated from the world during the COVID-19 pandemic, many of us retreated into the worlds created in movies and television shows, streamed into our homes, on demand, 24 hours a day. While watching alone in our bedrooms is an individual experience, with so many of us watching the same movies, we are really engaging in a shared experience, a global experience. As the leading streaming platform, Netflix is a truly global media outlet. Its capacity to influence its audiences' ideas about the world through its streaming of popular cultural artifacts is clear. And so, it is important that the discipline of IR looks more closely at this powerful site of what it terms soft power.

## Netflix

> Stories move us.
> They make us feel more emotion,
> see new perspectives,
> and bring us closer to each other. (Netflix, 2023)

This is (at the time of writing) the pop-up on the Netflix 'about' page. It is easy to see the concept of culture as meaning-making here, as well as the consciously considered place Netflix reveals itself to hold. Founded in the USA in 1997 by Reed Hastings and Marc Randolph as a DVD mail rental service, Netflix launched the world's first DVD rental and sales website the following year, followed by its subscription service the year after, providing members with unlimited rentals for a flat monthly fee. In 2007, the Netflix streaming service was introduced, with membership surpassing 10 million by 2009. Netflix then began its push into international markets, expanding to Canada in 2010, Latin America and the Caribbean in 2011, the UK, Ireland and the Nordic countries in 2012 and many European countries in 2014. Membership extended to Australia, New Zealand, Japan, Italy, Spain and Cuba in 2015. It then simultaneously launched in an additional 130 countries in 2016. Netflix is now an undisputedly global media outlet with over 200 million subscribers in more than 190 countries around the world (Netflix, 2023). As a global actor, and the leading entertainment streaming service, Netflix clearly has considerable capacity to influence its audiences' ideas about the world, projecting immense soft power worldwide.

While media has always played an important role in shaping how we have viewed and approached global politics, the new digital media landscape of today has changed how new media platforms have depicted and mediated politics. Prior to the emergence of streaming platforms, global media corporations developed around and catered to either the state or business and advertisers. While the platforms developed by traditional broadcasters funnel users into larger media ecosystems (such as Fox and NBCUniversal), and others tie in with additional services or products (Disney, Amazon, Apple TV) and generate revenue from advertising, Netflix's financial success depends solely on the company's ability to attract and retain subscribers.[2] To ensure its existing users do not unsubscribe and join the competition, Netflix has devised, developed and refined the Netflix recommender system (NRS), which is a core feature of its business model and brand (Pajkovic, 2022, p. 216). This NRS is a sophisticated algorithm that Netflix utilises to recommend content to users and personalise nearly every aspect of a customer's experience on the platform. It is also imperative to its formulation of strategies to buy, develop, and distribute content to targeted audiences. In broad terms, the NRS is powered almost entirely by machine learning, using a combination of content-based filtering and collaborative filtering algorithms to recommend content. Content-based filtering relies solely on a user's past data, which are gathered according to their interactions with the platform (e.g., viewing history, watch time, scrolling behaviour, etc.). To produce recommendations and personalise a user's experience, these data are combined with other large and intricate data sets that contain information derived from the 15,000 film and television titles

---

2   Following its first subscriber losses in over 10 years, Netflix began offering lower cost subscriptions, 'Basics with Ads' from November 2022.

offered by Netflix worldwide, including items such as their genre, category, actors, director and release year (Wasko & Meehan, 2019, p. 10). All of this is vital to the success of Netflix, as its content is neither produced for the state nor for advertisers; it is sold directly to audiences, which means that the value is actually in the content itself (Khalil & Zayani, 2020, p. 8).

As competition for content increased with new players in the streaming sector coming on board, Netflix commenced its own original programming with the production of the television series *House of Cards*, *Orange is the New Black* and *Arrested Development* in 2013. Its first original feature film, *Beasts of No Nation*, was released in 2015. In 2019 Netflix's original film *Roma* won three Academy Awards. In 2020 Netflix Original Films as a collective were the most nominated studio at the Academy Awards. As Netflix positions itself as a creator of high-quality original content, with this as its competitive edge in an increasingly competitive streaming market, it has established new production hubs in London, Madrid, New York and Toronto and recently announced it will open a global post-production hub in Mumbai. According to Kasey Moore's (2022) analysis, by its 25th anniversary on 29 August 2022, half of the Netflix library consisted of Netflix Originals. These 'Originals' consist of in-house Netflix productions and programming produced by other studios with exclusive screening rights licensed by Netflix. As Netflix Chief Content Officer Ted Sarandos explains in an interview with Neil Landau:

> We use the word "original" to indicate the territory, where it originates. 'Netflix originals' is used in the US, because you can't see them anywhere else. For us, the word "exclusive" doesn't ring true to people. And "created by" doesn't either (Landau, 2016).

The customer is key here, and ensuring greater engagement with content is an essential element of the Netflix customer retention strategy. Data derived from the NRS is a crucial aspect of the acquisition process when determining which products to licence, but, more importantly, it also plays a significant role in the production decision-making process. Sarandos explained the process to Tim Wu at the Sundance Film Festival:

> "In practice, it's probably a seventy-thirty mix." But which is the seventy and which is the thirty? "Seventy is the data, and thirty is judgment," he

told me later. Then he paused, and said, "But the thirty needs to be on top, if that makes sense." (Wu, 2015).

Wu voices his concern at the capacity for the Netflix data-driven model to disrupt the traditional media establishment:

> Instead of feeding a collective identity with broadly appealing content, the streamers imagine a culture united by shared tastes rather than arbitrary time slots. Pursuing a strategy that runs counter to many of Hollywood's most deep-seated hierarchies and norms, Netflix seeks nothing less than to reprogram Americans themselves (Wu, 2013).

This seems overly dramatic—it is difficult to argue convincingly that Netflix has overhauled how power within the entertainment industry is organised—but it is very clear that it has managed to position itself alongside other powerful players through its clever use of data-driven strategies (Jenner, 2018, p. 4). Blake Hallinan and Ted Striphas refer to this as:

> [...] "algorithmic culture": the use of computational processes to sort, classify, and hierarchize people, places, objects, and ideas, and also the habits of thought, conduct, and expression that arise in relationship to those processes (Striphas, 2012).[3]

It is also in line with Shoshana Zuboff's 'surveillance capitalism' thesis, whereby human experience, in this case viewing popular culture, is translated into "behavioural data" and "fed into advanced manufacturing processes known as 'machine intelligence', and fabricated into *prediction products* that anticipate what you will do now, soon, and later" (2019, p. 372). Technologically targeted advertising "can easily have an impact on one's decision-making process in the activities they choose and in political decisions (Zuboff, 2019, p. 373); surely technologically driven cultural content can be equally influential.

This shows that it is important to consider "how algorithms shape our world" (Slavin, 2011), seeing how data-driven production processes might be forms of cultural decision-making (Hallinan & Striphas, 2016, p. 119). This opens up new considerations in the popular culture–world politics continuum in IR. If Netflix is to be seen as an agent of soft power,

---

3    See also Alexander Galloway (2006), *Gaming: Essays on Algorithmic Culture* (Minneapolis: University of Minnesota Press).

its establishment as a global media network means it is not just producing stories Americans tell about themselves; it is also representing, reflecting and producing stories about Americans to a wide international audience as well as influencing Americans' perceptions of 'the other' with its internationally diverse programming from countries around the world. I turn to the design of such a research program in the next section.

# Research design

As a purveyor of popular culture on a global scale, and particularly through its recommender system, Netflix mediates representations of the world. Such a source of influence on the ideas of a mass audience is central to international relations. We must, therefore, consider Netflix an agent of power and treat such a global source of influence seriously. If we can determine the ideological basis of the worldview represented through the popular culture resources mediated by Netflix, we can identify a vital piece of the story that Netflix is telling its audiences. The usual methodological approach of the cultural branch of IR would be to provide a close reading of Netflix films and tv shows, using the techniques of the literature, film and media studies fields, to produce a study that purports to demonstrate the politics of Netflix. Such studies would be used heavily in the teaching of international relations, providing rich subjects of meaningful insight into contemporary understandings of global politics. Unfortunately, though, such studies are not widely viewed as making a legitimate contribution to knowledge by IR practitioners based on their research design, even though they rely on evidence to generate knowledge claims. This is because IR defines 'legitimate scholarship' as 'proper social science', so that research imperatives related to the replicability and objectivity of these studies is called into question. "'Proper' IR knowledge is said to be generated through the objective examination of data" (Shepherd, 2019, p. 34) rather than the culturally subjective close-reading methodologies employed since the 'cultural turn'. As Steve Smith points out, this is because

> [...] ontologically, the (IR) literature tends to operate in the space defined by rationalism: epistemologically, it is empiricist and, methodologically, it is positivist. Together these define 'proper' social science and thereby serve as the gatekeepers for what counts as legitimate scholarship (2000, p. 383).

This means that "(S)cientific is a synonym for quality in IR" (King, Keohane, & Verba, 1994, p. 7).

So, despite the decades-long aesthetic turn in IR, it still privileges positivist approaches that specify the importance of data collection, the macro, the structural. For a study of the ideological basis of Netflix's soft power to be taken seriously, it needs to examine the world politics inherent in a large representational sample of Netflix content scientifically. Netflix Original content would be the most demonstrably representational object of the Netflix ideological base, particularly as such content is growing rapidly to constitute more than 50% of overall content. However, as a lone researcher, viewing a large number of episodes from Netflix Original series was completely outside the capacity of this study. I therefore, decided to concentrate on Netflix Original Films as the subject of research. The scholarship on popular culture and world politics usually cherry-picks overtly political films, films with a clear political message, specific genres, such as apocalyptic, dystopian films, or analyses specific films or sets of films in terms of significant world events to determine the zeitgeist. Yet, these films make up a small proportion of all the films produced and consumed by the mass public, a very small proportion of Netflix. To take seriously the causation of popular culture and how it influences the mass public to see the world in a certain way, we need to study the construction, production and reproduction of ideology on a macro scale. This is where the Digital Humanities comes in.

The creation of a comprehensive database that categorises all Netflix Original Films according to a carefully selected set of ontologies should provide the epistemological tools necessary to meet these quantitative requirements, bringing legitimacy to the study of popular culture and world politics in the IR discipline. The first step in the project consisted of identifying several proxies, including language, genre, etc., that point to a certain way of viewing the world. Data about writer, director, producer and stars is collected for all films. Ratings and maturity rating categories are included along with Netflix micro-genre descriptive categories (steamy, dark, suspenseful etc.). Reception is an important part of meaning-making, so various measures of this (Google rating, IMDb rating, etc.) are included. All of this data is collected from Netflix and various online sources before watching the film. While watching the film, data is then entered in relation to narrative elements of the film, including the protagonist, antagonist, hero, villain, setting and period. All of this data collection is reasonably straightforward and requires little understanding of world politics to provide a comprehensive data set of all Netflix Original Films. The more difficult aspect of the research was: how to determine the world politics inherent in this set of films?

While the world politics, the international relations of *House of Cards, Squid Game, Beasts of No Nation,* are easily discernible, how can this be objectively assessed in those films that make up the bulk of Netflix Original Films, which are less obviously political films? Leaving them out would mean discounting the considerable scholarship on the way the construction of unconscious ideologies work. The politics of these films are not flagged, they are not identified, the constitution and reconstitution of ideology are represented in such a way that audiences are not conscious that they are being ushered into a way of seeing the world through their interaction with seemingly non-political films. Leaving out those films not clearly identifiable as political would leave out the majority of films watched by the most viewers. If a study of the link between popular culture and world politics is to be taken seriously, it needs to look at the entire data set. So far, the database includes 697 films from 2015 to 2022, categorised according to 136 different genres. The only category indicating political content is Political Comedies, which includes just four films. These are the only films identified by Netflix with the term 'political'. But how to assess the world politics in films across this disparate set of genres? To determine this, I turned to the major ideological traditions of IR—realism and liberalism.

The major concerns of the International Relations discipline have been the causes of war and the conditions for peace. As most films are conflict-driven, the simple dichotomy of the key understandings of the two major competing ideologies provides a useful tool for categorising the worldview in films of any genre. Providing a simple choice between the anarchical, threatening worldview of realism and the rules-based, ordered worldview of liberalism ensures an applicable determination that is suitable for any film. Equally, by providing a simple assessment of how any conflict is resolved, either independently, as in the self-help mantra of realism, or cooperatively, as in the interdependent worldview of liberalism, as well as the compromise position if neither holds true, has a clear applicability to any film. Given the relational aspects of soft power to universalising values, these are considered while watching the film and categorised as well. Lastly, given the role of popular culture in reinforcing or contesting claims to common-sense understandings of power relations, how this is represented in the film is also assessed. This led to the development of a simple five-step ontology for data mining the international relations of all Netflix Original Films as follows:

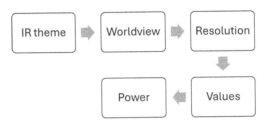

Fig. 3.1 Five-Step Ontology—International Relations of Netflix Original Films

At present, I have watched and categorised all films from 2015 to 2018, a total of 127 films. Of these, the most prevalent themes were freedom (20) and identity (19); 61 represented the world as anarchic while 66 presented an ordered worldview. Conflict in these films was resolved independently in 64 cases, cooperatively in 60 and via compromise in three cases. Prevailing power relations were reinforced in 66 and contested in 61 films. A more intensive data-mining analysis will provide a deeper picture of how these world politics are represented in various genres, what descriptions are given to the treatments of these various themes, the identity of the main protagonists, villains, heroes etc. After mining the data for noticeable trends and patterns in relationships between proxies, a detailed in-depth qualitative analysis via a deep reading of sets of films will add considerable depth to the investigation of the intertextuality between popular culture and world politics.

As Netflix increasingly internationalises its catalogue, this comprehensive database will provide considerable evidence for analysing and comparing the world politics represented in films across several countries and regions. For example, so far there are 51 films categorised as Indian Movies available for viewing in Australia. These are predominately Hindi-language films with 45 films in Hindi and just two each in Tamil and Marathi, one in Malayalam and one in English. They are mostly dramas (19) and comedies (14) with the remainder made up of an eclectic mix of romances (eight) crime movies (six), a couple of musicals and even an LGBTQ comedy. While I have only watched the six of these released from 2015 to 2018, they overwhelmingly represented an ordered vision of world politics. As an observation, they show very high production values and present India as a modern, economically aspirational country, guided by deeply traditional values—very much the impression presented to any Western visitor of the rich culture of this rising world power. It will be interesting to see if this trend remains constant with the dramatic increase in Indian content over the last few years.

As Netflix produces more and more content, we should begin to find out how data-driven production changes the Netflix worldview over time. This leads us to the subject of soft power—the audience of these films, the Netflix subscriber. As Netflix famously uses the recommender system, the algorithm that tells them what viewers want is an essential element in production decisions. So, this study, over time, extends to the role of the audience, the role of the mass public in the acquisition and production process. We should discover if Netflix's 'instrumentarian' methods are designed to cultivate "radical indifference [...] a form of observation without witness" as Zuboff's (2019, p. 379) thesis suggests, or if the subjects of power also have some agency, the causal concern missing from so much of the popular culture–world politics field. So, this project falls within Nick Srnicek's (2017, p. 28) concept of 'platform capitalism' whereby, over time, it "will distinguish data (information that something happened) from knowledge (information about why something happened)" by examining any changes in the Netflix worldview intertextually with what is happening in the world politics of today. The data-driven epistemology of Digital Humanities meets the disciplinary conventions for objectivity and replicability in the positivist tradition. In this way, the use of hybrid methods in the Digital Humanities should bring some legitimacy to the study of popular culture in the discipline of International Relations.

# Conclusion

This Digital Humanities project is in the preliminary phase, in which the work is concentrated on data collection. The data is complete for all Netflix Original Films from 2015 to 2018, a total of 130 films. The database is hosted on the Heurist academic data management system and this part of the project will be published on that network soon. It is very clear that, in more ways than one, this project on the global soft power of Netflix is an interesting addition to the field of Digital Humanities. While it is a comprehensive database, it also uses data-mining techniques to examine how data is used in the production of world politics itself. Such a digital method provides the tools to identify and navigate key ontological, epistemological and methodological challenges in determining the causal linkages between popular culture and world politics, showing that engaging with culture is not just a passive pastime, it is actually an act of *doing* politics on a global scale. Many scholars consider that film production and consumption have a powerful capacity to shape national identity (see Edensor, 2002; Dittmer, 2005; Philpott, 2010) and also have prominent roles in determining attitudes towards the foreign 'other', whether that be through the construction of the 'friendly other' or the 'enemy other'.

> In a relatively short period of time, Netflix built on existing business models from movie studios to pay TV, exploited the affordances of data-driven narrowcasting, and ultimately altered the way media is consumed (Khalil & Zayani, 2020, p. 8).

Netflix quickly recognised binge-watching as a way to promote itself and its original content, and it released new content on the same day in all its territories, establishing itself as a transnational broadcaster. Netflix is a driving force in changing how popular culture is organised and how viewing is structured for a global audience (Jenner, 2018, p. 4). There is no denying that Netflix is a commanding agent of soft power.

In global politics, the resources that produce soft power arise in large part from the values an organisation or country expresses in its culture; popular culture clearly constitutes an important source of the ideas that people use to judge the world and their place in it. As ideas shape actions, then this comprehensive database project can provide a pathway to show the linkages between popular culture and political actions in international relations. This will join:

Weber, Nexon and Neumann, and others in viewing novels, films, and the like as partly *constituting* world politics, because the experiences those artifacts induce can produce and reproduce ideas about world politics that even informed people believe (Daniel & Musgrave, 2017, p. 21).

While no claim is being made that films allow a reversal of power relations, they do allow audiences to formulate ideas and conduct speech acts within a discourse of power, potentially subverting power structures if a large enough proportion of the mass public is eventually hailed into a particular understanding of the processes that substantiate power on a global scale. According to Nye, "Those who deny the importance of soft power are like people who do not understand the power of seduction" (2004, p. 8.).

It becomes increasingly clear that developing novel methodologies and theoretical approaches for dealing with the changing dynamics of international power relations is imperative, especially as complex economic interdependence deepens and the power of non-state actors grows. By using hybrid Digital Humanities epistemologies in analysing the political trends in this audience-driven set of popular films, this research project will contribute to a better understanding of how power works through the production and normalisation of meaning and the processes of constructing the stories that are central to the study of power in global politics. By developing a fuller understanding of the constitutive production of hegemonic power on a global scale, this project should contribute to the evidence-based conventions of knowledge production in the International Relations discipline and extend our understanding of how hegemonic power is produced and maintained on a global scale.

# Works Cited

Barthes, R. (2009). *Mythologies*. Vintage Classics.

Bruner, S. (2019). I'm so bored with the canon: Removing the qualifier "popular" from our cultures. *The Popular Culture Studies Journal 7*(1), 6–16.

Cox, R. (1983). Gramsci, hegemony and International Relations: An essay in method, *Millennium 12*(2), 162–175. https://doi.org/10.1177/030582988301 20020701

Furman D.J. & Musgrave, P. (2017). Synthetic experiences: How popular culture matters for images of International Relations. *International Studies Quarterly* 61, 503–516. https://doi.org/10.1093/isq/sqx053

Demianyk, G. (2017, February 12). Ken Loach damns government over child refugees after 'I Daniel Blake' BAFTA Win. *Huffington Post UK*. https://www.huffingtonpost.co.uk/entry/ken-loach-bafta-child-refugees-i-daniel-blake_uk_58a0d95ae4b094a129ec2a20

Dittmer, J. (2005). Captain America's empire: Reflections on identity, popular culture and geopolitics. *Annals of the Association of American Geographers 95* (3), 626–643. https://www.doi.org/10.1111/j.1467-8306.2005.00478.x

Dittmer, J. (2010). *Popular Culture, Geopolitics and Identity*. Rowman and Littlefield.

Edensor, T. (2002). *National Identity, Popular Culture and Everyday Life*, Berg. https://doi.org/10.4324/9781003086178

Galloway, A. (2006). *Gaming: Essays on Algorithmic Culture*. University of Minnesota Press.

Geertz, C. (1973). *The Interpretation of Cultures: Selected Essays*. Basic Books.

Gramsci, A. (1971). *Selections from the Prison Notebooks*. Lawrence and Wishart.

Grayson, K., Davies, M., & Philpott, S. (2009). Pop goes IR? Researching the popular culture-world politics continuum. *Politics 29*(3), 155–163. https://doi.org/10.1111/j.1467-9256.2009.01351.x

Hall, S. (1997). *Representation: Cultural Representations and Signifying Practices*. Sage Publications & Open University.

Hallinan, B., & Striphas, T. (2016). Recommended for you: The Netflix Prize and the production of algorithmic culture. *New Media and Society 18*(1), 17–137. https://doi.org/10.1177/1461444814538646

Hartley, J. (1994). *The Politics of Pictures*. Psychology Press.

Jenner, M. (2018). *Netflix and the Re-invention of Television*. Palgrave MacMillan. https://doi.org/10.1007/978-3-319-94316-9

Khalil, J., & Zayani, M. (2020). De-territorialized digital capitalism and the predicament of the nation-state: Netflix in Arabia. *Media, Culture and Society*, 1–18. https://doi.org/10.1177/0163443720932505

King, G., Keohane, R., & Verba, S. (1994). *Designing Social Inquiry: Inference in Qualitative Research*. Princeton University Press.

Landau, N. (2016). *TV Outside the Box: Trailblazing in the Digital Television Revolution*. Focal Press. https://doi.org/10.4324/9781315694481

Moore, K. (2022). Netflix Original Now Make Up 50% of Overall US Library. *What's On Netflix*. whats-on-netflix.com

Netflix. (2023). 'About'. https://about.netflix.com/en

Nexon, D., & Neuman, I. (Eds). (2006). *Harry Potter and International Relations*. Rowman and Littlefield.

Nye, J. (1990). *Bound to Lead: The Changing Nature of American Power*. Basic Books.

Nye, J. (2004). *Soft Power: The Means to Success in World Politics*. Public Affairs. https://doi.org/10.2307/1148580

Nye, J. (2011). *The Future of Power*. Public Affairs.

Nye, J. (2017). Soft power: The origins and political progress of a concept. *Palgrave Communications 3*, 17008. https://doi.org/10.1057/palcomms.2017.8

Onuf, N. (1989). *World of Our Making: Rule and Rule in Social Theory and International Relations*. University of South Carolina Press. https://doi.org/10.4324/9780203096710

Pajkovic, N. (2022). Algorithms and taste-making: Exposing the Netflix recommender system's operational logics. *Convergence: The International Journal of Research into New Media Technologies*. https://doi.org/10.1177/13548565211014464

Philpott, S. (2010). Is anyone watching? War, cinema and bearing witness. *Cambridge Review of International Affairs 23*(2), 325–348. https://doi.org/10.1080/09557571003735378

Reinherd, C.L. (2019). Introduction: Why popular culture matters. *The Popular Culture Studies Journal 7*(1), 1–5.

Reus-Smith, C. (1999). *The Moral Purpose of the State*. Princeton University Press.

Shepherd, L. (2019). Authors and authenticity: Knowledge, representation and research in contemporary world politics. In C. Hamilton and L. Shepherd (Eds). *Understanding Popular Culture and World Politics in the Digital Age*. Routledge.

Slavin, K. (2011). How algorithms shape our world. *TEDGlobal*. http://www.ted.com/talks/kevin_slavin_how_algorithms_shape_our_world.html

Smith, S. (2000). The discipline of International Relations: Still an American social science? *British Journal of Politics and International Relations 2*(3), 374–402.

Srnicek, N. (2017). *Platform Capitalism*. Polity Press.

Striphas, T. (2012). What is an algorithm? *Culture Digitally*. http://culturedigitally.org/2012/02/what-is-an-algorithm/

Wasko, J., & Meehan, E. (Eds). (2019). *A Companion to Television*. (2e). Wiley-Blackwell.

Weber, C. (2005). *International Relations Theory: A Critical Introduction*. Psychology Press. https://doi.org/10.4324/9781003008644

Weldes, J. (2001). Globalisation is science fiction. *Millennium: Journal of International Studies 30*. https://doi.org/10.1177/03058298010300030201

Weldes, J. (2006). High politics and low data: Globalization discourses and popular culture. In D. Yanow & P. Schwartz-Shea (Eds). *Interpretation and Method: Empirical Research Methods and the Interpretive Turn.* (pp. 176–186). M.E. Sharpe.

Weldes, J. (Ed.). (2003). *To Seek Out New Worlds: Exploring Links between Science Fiction and World Politics.* Palgrave Macmillan.

Weldes, J., & Rowley, C. (Eds). (2015). So, how does popular culture relate to global politics? *E-International Relations.* https://www.e-ir.info/2015/04/29/so-how-does-popular-culture-relate-to-world-politics/

Wendt, A. (1992). *Social Theory of International Relations.* Cambridge University Press.

Wu, T. (2013). Netflix's war on mass culture. *The New Republic.* https://newrepublic.com/article/115687/netflixs-war-mass-culture

Wu, T. (2015, January 27). Netflix's secret special algorithm is a human. *The New Yorker.* https://www.newyorker.com/business/currency/hollywoods-big-data-big-deal

Zahran, G., & Ramos, L. (2010). From hegemony to soft power: Implications of a conceptual change. In I. Pamar & M. Cox (Eds). *Soft Power and US Foreign Policy: Theoretical, Historical and Contemporary Perspectives.* Taylor and Francis.

Zuboff, S. (2019). *The Age of Surveillance Capitalism: The Fight for a Human Future at the New Frontier of Power.* Profile Books.

# 4. Digital justice: Interactions and rituals in the virtual courtroom

## *David Tait and Meredith Rossner*

## Abstract

Courts have increasingly made use of video technologies to allow witnesses and defendants to take part in hearings. This use increased dramatically as a result of COVID-19. Not only did individuals appear on screens in physical courtrooms, but courts themselves sometimes went virtual. We examine what happens to interactions and rituals when the physical courtroom disappears. We compare the standard form of video conference based on isolating participants into boxes in a gallery, with an alternative approach, the metaverse court, which brings participants together into a shared space.

## Keywords

Metaverse; avatars; video conference; digital justice.

## Introduction

As a research paradigm, Digital Humanities has opened up the archive, most notably in literature, linguistics, archaeology, art history and history. Law is not far behind, with platforms to access Old Bailey cases from 1674 to 1913 (Digital Humanities Institute, 2023), or track offences such as blasphemy and Sabbath-breaking before the Court of Assistants of the Massachusetts Bay Colony from 1630 to 1692 (Massachusetts Court of Assistants, 2001). One significant Australian Digital Humanities database in the legal field lists convicts transported to the penal colony of Van Dieman's Land, including visual marks on their bodies produced by smallpox, tattoos or punishment beatings (Digital Panopticon, n.d.). Using digitised databases like this allows us to tell stories about the past that track patterns across long periods or multiple sites.

The digital revolution is not confined to unleashing floods of information. It has also transformed almost every type of communication, from texting to streaming of images. In this chapter, we focus on legal communication in one particular setting: justice hearings, and explore the possibilities starting to be opened up by immersive virtual hearings.

We are all so accustomed to video conferencing that, if we think of it all, we think of it as part of the fabric of everyday life. But as Garfinkel (1967) suggested, we can better understand a phenomenon if we stand back from it and treat something familiar or obvious as strange.

So, what are the aspects of video conferencing we might classify as strange?

- It brings people together into a shared conversation while isolating them in boxes in a gallery.

- It avoids the need for participants to meet in person, while bringing their faces uncomfortably close.

- Participants can see themselves looking back at them.

- All participants can see each other but nobody makes eye contact.

These paradoxes are not a necessary consequence of holding a meeting with dispersed participants. They result from the particular way video conferencing is organised—its origins were in a video call between two people to which additional participants could be added.

There is an alternative technology capable of being used for such communication, although rarely so employed: the computer game. Re-imagining a meeting as a game rather than a hi-tech phone call assumes the participants are together in a single shared space. A justice participant in this hearing game can see the entire courtroom from a first-person viewpoint as judge, litigant or witness. Others are seen in their assigned position, at the distance they would be in a regular court. When a lawyer questions a witness, the two interlocutors can turn to face each other (or they could turn away or look down), and when lawyers address the Bench, they can pivot to face the judge. Of course, a computer game used as a platform for a justice hearing can also be seen as strange:

- Users do not see images of the other participants; they see avatars representing them.

- If the avatars and the environment seem almost identical to real-world images (but not quite the same), this can produce what is referred to as an 'uncanny valley' effect.[1]

This chapter explores some of the rituals and interactions that are made possible by the two different technologies, the assemblages of actors, objects and actions that are brought together in the production of a justice hearing. It uses as the comparison case the physical courtroom and in-person hearing. These vary enormously, of course, between lengthy war crimes trials before an international tribunal and police courts that sentence motorists for speeding offences, so the descriptions are necessarily somewhat stylised.

At this stage of technological development, some of the prognosis about how the technology will work is somewhat speculative, although we do have some prior research, including randomised controlled trials, that offer some clues. No doubt some of our hypotheses will turn out not to be supported, but at least they might help to set the research agenda for the next phase of this research.

The issues to be covered are:

1. Producing subjects.

2. Producing deference and authority.

3. Moving rituals.

---

1     This term refers to digital images that are close approximations of the person being represented, which reportedly produce a dip in empathy compared to a less realistic image.

# Methods

This chapter is written as a reflective essay rather than a research report. As such, it draws on several studies carried out by the authors as well as a range of work by others. An important inspiration is the analysis of interaction rituals by Erving Goffman. The authors have undertaken numerous studies using this framework — of restorative justice, juvenile court and Indigenous court hearings, as well as federal and criminal courts. An underlying feature of this approach is the assumption that the identity of subjects is not just 'there' in the person themselves; rather it is negotiated, formed and developed in relation to others. The key unit of analysis is thus the encounter or the interaction between people in particular settings.

In outlining possible differences between a courtroom encounter using currently available video conferencing platforms and what we term the 'metaverse court', we are basing our reflections on a platform developed by the Fraunhofer Institute in Graz, Austria, and tested out by us in 2022 in the Harvard Visualization Research Lab in Cambridge, MA and the Cyberjustice Lab at the University of Montreal. This metaverse court prototype has several features that provide advances over other current avatar-based or immersive video conferencing approaches developed by Meta, Zoom or Microsoft—the avatars are highly realistic, the virtual environment is detailed and plausible as a courtroom, (apparent) eye contact is achieved with multiple participants, and, most importantly, all this is created without the need for intrusive 3D goggles. The downside is that bringing multiple participants together into this metaverse court requires powerful game computers with expensive graphics cards, good internet access, and the use of a cloud server. As a research platform, it allows researchers to test the strengths and weaknesses of the metaverse approach compared to alternatives. Many of the major IT companies are investing heavily in this area, which could transform some of our speculations into testable propositions.

Reference is made in this chapter to an earlier version of this platform (also developed by Fraunhofer), using multiple screens and multiple cameras. This platform was used in a randomised controlled trial in a comparison with a face-to-face condition. To achieve a hearing between four sites required 12 cameras, 12 screens and six simultaneous video calls, something that would be hard to sustain for real trials. Despite the extensive technical infrastructure required, the platform did not achieve what the metaverse court could—embedding participants in a shared environment.

## Producing subjects

One of the key arguments Goffman (2017) makes in his dramaturgical analysis of human interaction is that subjects (including the 'self') are produced as part of the process of interacting with others within a particular social setting. People learn how to behave in response to the constraints and possibilities offered by the environment. People entering a monastery learn how to become monks, while those entering a psychiatric institution learn how to become patients. As individuals embark on their 'moral careers', they learn how to act, move and interact with others and take on the role expected of them (Goffman, 1959).

What sorts of subjects do justice processes produce? In one of our previous studies, a comparison of two different children's court procedures, it was suggested that whereas a restorative justice procedure that focused on getting the young person to 'acknowledge' their shortcomings and 'agree to' some remedial actions proposed by adults might tend to produce an 'obedient child' as the ideal subject, whereas interrogation before a French '*juge des enfants*' which required agile thinking and the ability to formulate arguments might produce an 'argumentative citizen' as its ideal subject (Tait, 2018). The infamous Stanford Prison Experiment reportedly turned psychology graduate students either into sadistic guards or docile prisoners within a few days (Zimbardo et al., 1971). In both cases, the setting helps to shape the type of subject produced.

So, what sort of subjects do these two technologies—video conferencing and gaming—create? We know from two randomised controlled trials we have carried out that if a defendant is placed in a dock or box in a physical courtroom, they are almost twice as likely to be found guilty, compared to sitting alongside counsel, other things being equal (Rossner, 2017). The furniture in some way seems to shape the way the jury perceives the accused—perhaps the balustrade around the box informs the jury that the person needs to be constrained, or maybe the isolation from others suggests they are different (perhaps dangerous). Or perhaps sitting alone encourages disinhibited behaviour (though not in our experiment—the actor performed identically whether in a dock or beside the lawyer). There could also be different messages received by different jurors.

Whatever the mechanism, the effect is that jurors are more likely to consider someone they see in a dock as guilty. Appearing on a screen, on the other hand, whether alone or alongside counsel, according to our study at least, makes no difference to perceived guilt (Tait & Tay, 2017). This has two implications for the production of the subject in a virtual environment.

First, appearing on a screen can potentially have something of a levelling effect. For a video conference, everyone is in a box, and the boxes are usually of equal size. The impression given in a physical courtroom by elevating the judge and placing the accused in isolation is thus removed.

In a metaverse courtroom, the levelling effect could be even greater. The accused appears as an avatar, but if the avatars are drawn from a limited pool of standard images, any advantages or disadvantages potentially associated with body shape, beauty or age can be removed. Not all prejudice disappears: a name can provide cues about ethnic background, and if a person speaks, their accent can betray their origins.

There is a second implication of the apparent lack of impact of screen appearances for the metaverse courtroom—evidence could become relatively more important. In a video conference, viewers can guess (however incorrectly) whether a person is guilty, dangerous, or honest by how they look, although pixilation and voice distortion could be used to conceal the identities of protected witnesses (McKay, 2018). The image of an avatar on the other hand provides few, if any, cues about the person behind the avatar, and even a Metahuman avatar is unlikely to communicate all the subtle gestures (like shaking knees or sweating brow) that the image of the person on a video conference could provide. If the accused does not testify—and normally they do not—then the jury would have to rely on evidence, they hear without getting any assistance from glances to look inside the soul of the accused.

In the video conferencing environment, the boxes might hint at a form of equality, but judges still control the hearing. Indeed, in some ways, they may have even more control. In some in-person hearings, it can take some time for order to be restored when a person becomes verbally aggressive. If the person is on the screen they can be quickly muted, and the feed cut.

Participants in a video conference often have some control over their background, whether physical or virtual. A good lawyer will ensure that the background behind their client is consistent with the presumption of innocence. The availability of virtual backgrounds in all major video conferencing platforms means that even if defendants are in custody they can be seen in front of a bookshelf, a gurgling stream or a family room. The person can be positioned at a dignified distance from the camera—not too close to appear intimate and not too distant to appear remote. On the screen, the accused might be placed in the box alongside their lawyer, or in a central position, or even at the top. Meanwhile, a victim whose sporting career was terminated by an accident might have sporting trophies subtly positioned in the background to remind viewers of the impact the accident had on their life. A metaverse court however removes the opportunity for users to customise their environment—as with a physical courtroom, the courtroom design is given.

There are potential risks associated with seeing others only on screens. Empathy might be harder to develop (Bandes & Feigenson, 2021), and witnesses might be less likely to lie if they are confronted with the person whose life could be impacted by their testimony— alternatively they are less likely to be intimidated if they are separated from the accused by a screen, whether a physical barrier in a courtroom or a video monitor[2]—while judges might find it easier to pass harsh sentences if they do not see a real person in front of them. Indeed, on one occasion during the pandemic, a Singapore judge sentenced someone to death by Zoom (McLennan, 2021). Lawyers could feel that their theatrical talents are not put to such good use if the audience does not see them in person, although it could equally well be argued that most people's understanding of the law comes from a screen anyway (Guéry, 2015).

A critical part of the production of subjectivity is the way particular 'lines' are received by others and negotiated in the process of interaction

---

2    This is the one of the bases for the confrontation clause in the US Constitution.

(Goffman, 1955). In a video link, a witness or defendant will usually only see the person asking questions and miss out seeing the responses of other court participants. This could also be true in a video conference in which the image of the complainant is hidden from the defendant, or audience members are shown as black boxes (or, in a video streaming session, not shown at all). In the metaverse court, only the key participants will likely be shown, and of those who are, their appearance as avatars is likely to reduce the number of emotions that are expressed. So, it is likely that, with a reduced number of cues compared to a face-to-face hearing, a witness or defendant may be unable to adjust their performance in a way they would normally. The subjects that might be produced could therefore be less nuanced or flatter.[3] On the other hand, they might be less anxious, less intimidated, and therefore less likely to be traumatised by the experience.

As well as producing subjects, rituals such as justice processes may also produce or reproduce forms of organisation, such as hierarchy, authority or deference. It is to these that we now turn.

## Producing authority and deference

Courts are inherently hierarchical places. The spaces of courtrooms are segregated and organised by status. Judges, juries, lawyers, defendants, witnesses and the audience—everyone has their place, which they will soon discover if they sit in a place designated for someone else. Judges typically preside over the hearing from a Bench, which is elevated either by a small step as in most Scandinavian and Dutch courts, or, at the extreme, six steps as in the Irish court system. In many common law courts, lawyers establish their centrality to the process by sitting at a bar table which dominates the well of the court. In older French courts, prosecutors sit on a throne dressed in ermine in the front left corner of the room, a position once occupied by the king in the Paris 'parlement' (Garapon, 2001). When they stand to speak, they have the highest position in the room.

When the judge (and sometimes jury) enter a courtroom, the

---

3    This argument is somewhat speculative, but it does find some research support that compares live and video testimony, with child witnesses seen more positively and as more convincing if seen in the live setting. See Landström et al., (2007).

audience is expected to stand to show their acknowledgement of the authority invested in the judge. When participants or audience members leave the courtroom, in some jurisdictions at least, they are expected to face the Bench and bow. They are not, however, bowing to the judge as a person, but, at least in England and Wales where the tradition is perhaps most entrenched, they are bowing to the coat of arms behind the Bench, representing royal justice (England and Wales, n.d.).

The pattern of deference is further established by the style of language used in addressing legal professionals. Judges are referred to in some jurisdictions with the respectful honorific 'Your Honour'. In some English courts (including the High Court and the Court of Appeal) the judge may be referred to as 'Your Lordship' or 'My Lord'. Interestingly in Irish courts, where such titles were officially abolished in 1922, one can still hear senior judges being referred to as 'Your Lordship'. Lawyers in common law courts call their opponent 'My Friend' or if the opponent has taken silk (become a Senior Counsel or King's Counsel) they are referred to as 'My Learned Friend'.

Clothing may also serve to establish the place of different court participants in the hierarchy. Judges often wear robes, and in countries based on English tradition, wigs as well. Judges in Italy tend to wear a red sash with a white stripe as well. Lawyers often wear black robes, and, in England, King's Counsel have gowns made of silk and with a gold braid sewn onto the left shoulder. At the other end of the spectrum, a person in custody may in some US states (and elsewhere) be shackled in five places and chained to the floor. According to the 2005 Deck vs Missouri decision, such constraints were not to be visible to the jury, a position that a conservative Supreme Court has begun to roll back (US Supreme Court, 2022).

How can such markers of status be shown in a hearing where the participants appear on a screen? Using honorifics and wearing robes are relatively easy practices to bring across into the digital environment, but there are challenges with other rituals. A witness who stands up in a remote witness room to acknowledge the judge in a video conference may end up providing a view of their stomach to the other participants. Bowing has similar problems to standing, but a slight lowering of the head (or in some cultures, holding hands in a prayer position) could serve as an appropriate gesture of deference. However, new forms of ritual will likely emerge. There is no reason, for example, why participants need to sit for video hearings (also no reason why they should be prevented from doing so). One federal judge observed in Sydney presided over court from a standing desk in his chambers, while one of the lawyers in the case stood at a lectern.

A raised judicial Bench can be represented in a video conferencing screen by fixing the judge at the top centre of the gallery, something tax courts in the UK have done. There is an issue, however, with criminal defendants who appear by video link into a courtroom for a trial in which they say nothing (as they are entitled to do). Their face usually appears, larger than life, on a raised screen as a sort of exhibit. If the person scratches their nose or scowls, everyone can see. If one tried to design a degradation ritual to cause maximum invasion of a person's privacy, it would hard to improve on an approach that fixes a camera on a person's face for hours on end and projects the enlarged image high on the wall in a room full of strangers.[4] This is not inevitable—in many Dutch courts, the life-sized image of the remote participant is at the same level as the in-court participants and it is in front of the judge, not off to the side.

A metaverse court has more flexibility and can place the participants in their normal courtroom positions, including giving the judge an elevated Bench if desired, as well as locating them at appropriate distances from other participants to the right level of formality. Defendants can be placed alongside counsel, behind them or anywhere else that is considered appropriate to communicate the message that they are innocent until proven guilty. The courtroom layout can be adjusted for different parts of the process—just as in Indigenous courts where judges routinely move between a Bench and sitting around the Bar table.

It seems likely that judges may have to establish their authority in a different way than they would in a physical courtroom. In one of our studies, in which research participants took part in a hearing as 'witnesses' or 'litigants' in relation to a neighbourhood tree dispute and were randomly assigned to either a face-to-face or virtual multi-screen condition, those who saw the judicial officer in person regarded him as

---

4   The term was developed by Harold Garfinkel, with particular reference to court hearings. See: Garfinkel (1956).

more authoritative (Tait & Tay, 2019). One way of interpreting this is that there could well be an authority deficit in a virtual condition that needs to be addressed. This might mean additional preparation is required for lay participants, as well as reminders of the seriousness of the process and guidance as to the expected demeanour of participants. However, what is considered 'authority' might not translate into acceptance of the fairness of the process or the decision. It could rather be an indication of perceived social distance and lack of affinity ('the judge is not one of us'), which might produce a feeling of intimidation or anxiety. The social levelling produced by technology might produce more genuine engagement, rather than disruptive defendants feared by courts. More likely it will have different effects on different people, so a range of strategies is likely to be required.

## Moving rituals

Courtrooms are places of constant movement. When judges enter or leave the court, others stand. Streams of witnesses enter and leave the witness box, lawyers moving around to talk to each other, court officials scurry around, escorting witnesses, passing on documents or checking on recent court entrants, while audience members come and go.

Superficially it appears that in any sort of video-enabled hearing, the participants remain static—as faces in boxes (in a video conference) or avatars in position (in a metaverse court). In fact, these courts have their own forms of movement. When a person drops out of a video conference, including the judge, they typically appear in the gallery somewhere else, often in the bottom right corner. The active participants (e.g., lawyer and witness) might be 'spotlit' so they occupy two large boxes in the centre of the screen, while other court participants are relegated to the margins as thumbnails. The 'spotlighting' movement around the screen might be managed by the judge or a court official, or individual may 'pin' others in a similar way, for their own view only. Or a 'speaker' view (rather than 'gallery' view,) might be chosen so whoever is making the most noise at the time occupies the central position on the screen. This can mean that a person who coughs, laughs or shuffles paper becomes the central figure on the screen for a moment. This form of movement is therefore generally to and from the margins of the screen. If a defendant does not testify, they therefore remain at the margins, as a thumbnail, for the whole process, which is at least less intrusive than being placed on a large in-court screen for a hearing by video link.

Participants in a video conference who do not have a speaking role, such as judge's associates, court clerks, technology officers, journalists and members of the public are typically consigned to black boxes—frames with a name but no face. Alternatively, a streaming version of the software may be used, giving such groups viewing and hearing access, but not speaking rights or a box in the gallery.

Because participants in a video conference are framed in boxes it might be assumed that they remain somehow frozen in place and the viewer notices only those who are speaking at the time. However, the eye tends to detect movement ('visual attention capture'), so anyone who moves significantly is likely to draw attention. For example, during an observation in the Australian Federal Court during the COVID-19 pandemic (observed from the judge's chambers), two barristers were on the screen arguing their points in turn. When one barrister was making his argument to the judge, the other lawyer was preparing what he was about to say, so had switched his microphone to mute and was chatting to his solicitor, writing notes, and looking at documents. He was facing sideways to the camera. In a regular courtroom, this would have been entirely normal and unlikely to attract any attention. In the Zoom court, it was hard (for the observer anyway) to focus on what the speaker was saying because of the extensive movement in the box alongside. It did not seem to distract the judge, who could have changed the spotlighting arrangement if he wished, but it did illustrate the way small movements can be magnified in this technological environment compared to in a physical courtroom.

For a video conference hearing, it is possible to create 'pathways to court' that provide a trajectory through the process. Zoom and Teams provide waiting rooms and breakout rooms that can be used to manage entrances and provide opportunities for consultations, negotiations or sidebars (discussions between judges and lawyers). The Pexip software used in Irish courts takes this one step further with greater customisation of these side rooms for different categories of participants. The moving rituals therefore, within video conference hearings, are not within the gallery (apart from transitions from thumbnails to spotlit places), but between rooms at different stages of the process.

For the metaverse courtroom, participants could in principle move around the virtual space—lawyers, for example, could walk over to a position in front of the witness box to examine the witness or approach the Bench to confer with the judge, while witnesses could enter the courtroom and walk into the witness box. In the prototype version, participants remain in their correct position for the duration of the process. Movements are restricted to standing up or sitting down and moving the head and upper body (including of course the hands). These are tracked by the user's webcam.

The metaverse courtroom might appear as a less chaotic place than a real courtroom. Not only is less movement shown around the courtroom but support staff who work to help the judge, barrister or witnesses might not be visible at all—the fewer avatars that are shown, the less pressure on bandwidth. However, the concept of having multiple rooms, developed for video conference hearings, could be used. In addition to waiting and breakout rooms, a metaverse court could provide an evidence room—a 3D space that court participants, including of course jurors, can be invited to 'walk through'. For this purpose, court participants might use 3D headsets.

There is another form of movement that participants in a virtual hearing make. It is the transition between the local and remote environments. This is clearly the case when participants enter a virtual environment from the comfort of their home (or the discomfort of the prison video room). During the hearing itself, however, participants may seek relief from their screen by looking out of a window or staring at a wall. Lawyers meanwhile are likely to move their attention constantly between the virtual hearing space and their local desk space, giving them access to case files, legislation, and other documents being used in the process. This double presence—being present in both local and virtual spaces—means that moving rituals are an inherent part of online justice hearings. It provides material for backstage talk as participants discuss their local environments, particularly technical challenges such as internet reliability, forgetting to mute or unmute sound, and needing to log in again.

# Reflections

One of the possible impacts of both forms of virtual court that are examined here is a possible levelling effect, a narrowing of status differences. This seems to be the case if participants are all allocated equal-sized boxes in a Zoom gallery, but it could also apply to avatars drawn from a standard stock. The assemblage in this case would include constraints such as the Zoom boxes or the limited avatar wardrobe. But the assemblage would also include the rules about who gets to place participants in waiting rooms or breakout rooms, who decides whether to spotlight or use galleries at all, who allocates speaking turns or asks questions, and ultimately who gets to make decisions. So perhaps the appearance of increased egalitarianism is to some extent an illusion.

But it is an illusion that may have some benefits. An analogy with a physical courtroom might be that rather than the judge sitting far above the assembled multitude—six steps up as in Irish courts—they sit at about the same level, as in Danish, Swedish or Dutch courts. And rather than seeing the accused in a glass cage as in a French or English courtroom, they see them free and unconstrained, again as they would in a Danish, Swedish or Dutch court. In other words, the practices that are found in the jurisdictions that design their physical courtrooms according to human rights principles are closer to the practices made possible by the virtual court technologies being developed or used. The implication of this observation for future use of virtual courts is that jurisdictions that are the most conservative or restrictive in the design of their physical courts have the most to gain from virtual technologies.

Eliminating the human face as a source of information –which an avatar courtroom could do—sounds rather troubling, perhaps almost dehumanising. It could be justified perhaps for judges, who should arguably be seen to be neutral umpires who should try to leave their personal concerns at the door of the court, or for lawyers who have a responsibility as agents of the court. Standardised avatars for professionals might be considered just one step further than donning robes and sometimes wigs. But witnesses on the stand—is it not important to be able to detect a guilty conscience by the way the person fidgets, hesitates or avoids eye contact, in short, by their demeanour? And can't you generally tell if a person is guilty by whether they seem shifty, look uncomfortable when others talk about them or feign boredom when the nature of their alleged crime is outlined? The answer to these questions is 'No'; these cues are generally unreliable (Vrije et al., 2019). Relying just on oral evidence has been found to obtain more accurate decisions than having images of the witness as well (McKimmie et al., 2014). In a metaverse courtroom, having standardised avatars may thus avoid providing potentially misleading visual information about the person behind the avatar. The rituals in this interactive environment, however, may tell us what sort of legal world is being reproduced and what sorts of subjects are being created.

# Works Cited

Bandes, S. A., & Feigenson, N. (2021). Empathy and remote legal proceedings. *Southwest Law Review 51*, 20–39.

Digital Humanities Institute, University of Sheffield. (2023). *The Proceedings of the Old Bailey, 1674–1913*. https://www.oldbaileyonline.org/

Digital Panopticon, VDL Founders and Survivors Convicts 1802–1853. (n.d.). https://www.digitalpanopticon.org/VDL_Founders_and_Survivors_Convicts_1802-1853

England and Wales, Courts and Tribunals Judiciary. (n.d.). *Traditions of the Courts.* https://www.judiciary.uk/about-the-judiciary/history-of-the-judiciary-in-england-and-wales/court-traditions/

Heinsch, M., Sourdin, T., Brosnan, C., & Cootes, H. (2021). Death sentencing by Zoom: An actor-network theory analysis. *Alternative Law Journal 46*(1), 13–19.

Garapon, A. (2001). *Bien juger: essai sur le rituel judiciaire*. Odile Jacob.

Garfinkel, H. (1956). Conditions of successful degradation ceremonies. *American Journal of Sociology 61*(5), 420–424. https://doi.org/10.1086/221800

Garfinkel, H. (1967). *Studies in Ethnomethodology*. Harold Garfinkel. Prentice-Hall.

Goffman, E. (2017). *Interaction Ritual: Essays in Face-to-Face Behavior*. Routledge. https://doi.org/10.4324/9780203788387

Goffman, E. (1959). The moral career of the mental patient. *Psychiatry: Journal for the Study of Interpersonal Processes 22*, 123–142. https://doi.org/10.1080/00332747.1959.11023166

Goffman, E. (1955). On face-work: An analysis of ritual elements in social interaction. *Psychiatry 18*(3), 213–231. https://doi.org/10.1080/00332747.1955.11023008

Guéry, C. (2015). *Justices à l'écran*. Presses Universitaires de France.

Landström, S., Granhag, P.A. & Hartwig, M. (2007). Children's live and videotaped testimonies: How presentation mode affects observers' perception, assessment, and memory. *Legal and Criminological Psychology 12*, 333–348. https://doi.org/10.1348/135532506X133607

Massachusetts Court of Assistants. (2001). Records of the court of assistants of the colony of the Massachusetts Bay, 1630–1692. Internet archive. https://www.familysearch.org/library/books/records/item/372924-records-of-the-court-of-assistants-of-the-colony-of-the-massachusetts-bay-1630-1692-v-02

McKay, C. (2018). *The Pixelated Prisoner: Prison Video Links, Court 'Appearance' and the Justice Matrix*. Routledge. https://doi.org/10.4324/9781315111506

McKimmie, B.M., Masser, B.M., & Bongiorno, R. (2014). Looking shifty but telling the truth: The effect of witness demeanour on mock jurors' perceptions. *Psychiatry, Psychology and Law 21*(2), 297–310. https://doi.org/10.1080/13218719.2013.815600

McLennan, S. (2020, May 27). Singapore judge issues death sentence by Zoom. *Human Rights Watch*. https://www.hrw.org/news/2020/05/27/singapore-judge-issues-death-sentence-zoom

Rossner, M., Tait, D., McKimmie, B., & Sarre, R. (2017). The dock on trial: Courtroom design and the presumption of innocence. *Journal of Law and Society 44*(3), 317–344. https://doi.org/10.1111/jols.12033

Tait, D. (2018). Rituals and spaces in innovative courts. *Griffith Law Review 27*(2), 233–253. https://doi.org/10.1080/10383441.2018.1537074

Tait, D., & Tay, V. (2019). *Virtual Court Study: Report of a Pilot Test 2018*. Western Sydney University. https://courtofthefuture.org/publications/virtual-court-study/US Supreme Court, Deck v. Missouri. 544 U.S. 622 (2005).

US Supreme Court. Brown v. Davenport. US 596. 20–826 (2022).

Vrij, A., Hartwig, M., & Granhag, P.A. (2019). Reading lies: Nonverbal communication and deception. *Annual Review of Psychology 70*, 295–317. https://doi.org/10.1146/annurev-psych-010418-103135

Zimbardo, P.G., Haney, C., Banks, W.C., & Jaffe, D. (1971). *The Stanford Prison Experiment*. Zimbardo, Incorporated.

# 5. Artificial Intelligence, ethics and empathy: How empathic AI applications impact humanity

## Linda Aulbach

## Abstract

The development of Artificial Intelligence (AI) has sparked a huge debate about its impacts on individuals, cultures, societies and the world. Through AI, we now can either support, manipulate or even replace humans at a level we have not seen before.

One of the core values of happy and thriving relationships between humans is empathy, and understanding another person's feelings builds the foundation of human connection. Within the past few years, the field of AI has taken on the challenge of becoming empathic towards humans to create more trust, acceptance and attachment towards its applications. There are now 'carebots' with simple empathic chat features, which seem to be 'nice to have', but there is also a concerning development in the field of erobotics—the next (empathic) generation of sex robots, made for humans to fall in love with. The increase in emotional capacity within AI brings into focus how good or bad empathy really is. There is a high risk of manipulation of humans on a deep psychological level, yet there is also reason to believe that empathy is necessary to truly reach an ethical 'gold' standard. This chapter will examine empathic AI and its ethical issues with a focus on humanity. It will also touch on the question of what happens if AI becomes more human than humans.

https://doi.org/10.11647/OBP.0423.05

## Keywords

Artificial intelligence (AI); empathy; humanity; posthumanism; erobotics.

# Introduction

The development of Artificial Intelligence (AI) has sparked a huge debate about its potential impacts on individuals, cultures and societies more broadly. Through AI, we now can either support, manipulate or even replace humans at levels we have not seen before. AI has already infiltrated various aspects of our daily lives, significantly impacting how we live, work, and engage in the world. With the continuous development of more and better technologies, the effects will intensify and the ethical debates surrounding AI will become even more complex (Popkova & Sergi, 2020; Schwab, 2017).

To date, the evolution of AI has led to the development of increasingly intelligent systems that can analyse, predict, calculate, automate, and perform tasks faster, cheaper, and often more effectively than humans. Consequently, 'intelligence' is no longer solely attributed to the human species, challenging the conventional notion of what it means to be human. While 'hard skills' were previously highly valued in the labour market, there is now a shift towards promoting 'soft skills' such as interpersonal abilities like empathy, a shift which gives humans an advantage over their computational counterparts. Soft skills include the ability to experience and express emotions as well as creative and innovative thinking. However, AI technologies are already emerging that specifically target these human traits. Applications like DALL-E and Midjourney in the field of visual arts exemplify the potential for machine-driven creative outcomes (Miller, 2019). The field of emotional AI or empathic AI (AIE) is rapidly emerging, presenting both new possibilities and ethical dilemmas.

# Definition

AIE attempts to recognise and exhibit appropriate empathic responses based on human emotions. "Empathy accounts for the naturally occurring subjective experience of similarity between the feelings expressed by self and others without losing sight of whose feelings belong to whom" (Decety & Jackson, 2004, p. 71). Empathy works as an umbrella term for recognising, understanding and expressing emotions—three distinct areas in computer science that need to be developed to create a level of empathic AI (Spezialetti et al., 2020). At the centre of empathy are emotions, a term that has multiple theoretical models that differ significantly in regard to how they perceive and convey emotional signals, as well as how they interpret and evaluate emotional data (Yalçın & DiPaola, 2020). It seems that "there are as many theories of emotions as there are emotion theorists" (Beck, 2015). The concept of emotions lacks consensus in both philosophy and sciences (Stark & Hoey, 2021).

Terms like 'feelings', 'emotions', 'empathic' and 'affective' are often used interchangeably in public and even academic discussions (Stark & Hoey, 2021; Shouse, 2005).[1] According to Shouse, these terms differ in perspectives: feelings are personal and tied to individual experiences, emotions are social in nature, and affects are pre-personal (Shouse, 2005). In contrast, computer science understands human emotions from a physiological perspective, focusing on factors such as changes in heart rate, sweat, skin colour, or other bodily signals that can indicate specific emotions. Consequently, it may not be necessary to gather the same emotional data as in other models of human behaviour. The categorisation of emotions still heavily relies on the specific empathy model being utilised as the foundation (Stark & Hoey, 2021; Bråten, 2007). Regardless of the specific definition, it is clear that AI is taking on the challenge of understanding human emotions and expressing feelings in a way that makes humans think they are being met with empathy.

Apart from discussing emotions from either computational or psychological perspectives, there is also an ethical and philosophical debate about what it means for AI to *have* feelings (and not just *cause* feelings). Rust and Huang claim that "machines are more likely to experience emotions in a machine way, [...] it will be just as though machines can 'experience' emotions. In other words, machines will pass

---

1   In the context of this chapter, these terms are also used interchangeably, as this discussion focuses on AIE in general and does not go into the depth of the engineering background of these technologies.

the emotional Turing test."[2] (Rust & Huang, 2021, p. 161). Computational empathy may still impact humans significantly, whether or not machines *have* or just *simulate* emotions.

## Empathic robots

The exploration of human emotions in computer science was pioneered by Rosalind Picard with her book *Affective Computing* (1997). Picard argued that for computers to possess genuine intelligence and interact naturally with humans, they must be equipped with the ability to recognise, understand and even express emotions. As the groundwork for computational emotion recognition advanced, the field of social robotics also experienced significant growth.

Historically, the field of robotics has primarily focused on industrial and professional service applications such as those found in the automobile and mining industries. However, there has been a notable shift in recent times towards robots designed for human interaction. These personal service robots are gaining popularity, largely due to advancements in AIE (Bartneck et al., 2020). What was once a simple task-oriented robot, designed to improve personal productivity or reduce workloads, has now transformed into a social robot that places greater emphasis on personal interactions and experiences (Bartneck et al., 2020; Vincent et al., 2015).

In the 2004 IEEE International Workshop on Robot and Human Communication, Bartneck and Forlizzi defined social robots as autonomous or semi-autonomous robots that interact and communicate with humans by adhering to expected behavioural norms (Bartneck & Forlizzi, 2004). The authors developed a framework for classifying social robots based on factors such as:

- form: biomorphic (resembling lifelike objects, e.g., the bear-like nursing robot Robear), anthropomorphic (imitating humans, e.g., Sophia), or abstract, such as chatbots or online applications embedded with AIE (e.g., Replika);

- modality: communication channels (e.g., visual, haptic, auditory etc.);

---

2    A test used to check whether or not computational behaviour is distinguishable from that of a human.

- social norms: behaviour influenced by how others in a social group behave;
- autonomy: the capability to act without direct input from humans;
- interactivity: potential to exhibit causal behaviour (e.g., responding in reaction to certain actions of a human).

Park and Whang (2022) expanded Bartneck and Forlizzi's work, presenting a literature review on empathic AI and proposing a design concept for AIE robots. Their three-level evolution of AIE provides an overview of the current state of the technology and its future trajectory, with Type I AIE robots (domain-restricted, limited modality) already in use, ongoing research and development focusing on Type II (multi-modality but still domain-restricted), and theoretical explorations of Type III in academic literature (domain independent and intertwined multi-modality).

Currently, many 'low-level' (Type I) empathic social robot applications are in commercial and private use in various countries. One notable example is Softbank Robotics' semi-humanoid robot 'Pepper', which can recognise basic human emotions and is deployed in restaurants, banks, and retail stores worldwide to welcome and entertain visitors. Although its design is relatively simplistic, resembling a human in terms of its face, upper body, and arms, it is far less intimidating than the humanoid robots portrayed in the dystopian future depicted in the Netflix series, *Black Mirror*. Other robots, with varying degrees of human-like appearance, are utilised in elderly or disability care as well as child education and entertainment. The design and technology of all types of AIE robots are rapidly improving, and as a result, their impact on humans is likely to increase as well.

## Relationship between AIE and humans

The field of Human-Robot Interaction (HRI) draws from various disciplines such as robotics, psychology, social sciences and humanities (Bartneck et al., 2020; Billard & Grollmann, 2012). HRI Research aims to understand motivations, expectations, relationships and the impact of robot interactions to improve communication processes and enhance the human experience. The media equation theory suggests that humans respond to technologies in a similar manner to how they respond to other humans (Kolling et al., 2016). Building upon this idea, the computers as social actors theory (CASA) specifically focuses on human-to-machine (H2M) interaction, proposing that humans unconsciously treat machines as if they were social entities (Lee & Nass, 2010; Nass & Moon, 2000). Consequently, human-to-human (H2H) relationship insights are applied to human-to-machine communication, further driving the humanisation of robots (Lee & Nass, 2010; Kolling et al., 2016). The ultimate aim is to make machines more human-like, which leads to H2M communication becoming similar to H2H interactions, potentially having comparable psychological and social impacts (Bartneck et al., 2020; Nass & Moon, 2000).

Research has already demonstrated that people can form attachments to objects that are significantly less human-like, as they anthropomorphise (attribute human characteristics to) pets and objects (Hermann, 2022). Pet owners form deep emotional bonds with their animals, giving them names and talking to them in human language (Prato-Previde et al., 2022; Lindgren & Öhman, 2019). Owners of AI devices like virtual assistants Siri or Alexa, which resemble abstract social robots, also experience emotions throughout the lifecycle of these devices (e.g., purchase, use, disposal), and often experience emotional distress if anything happens to them (Hermann, 2022). In early 2023, the chatbot application Replika received a software update to remove the erotic roleplay function, resulting in a massive backlash for the company as it left its users heartbroken and devastated when their AIE companion suddenly ended their emotional relationship (Tong, 2023). The depth of psychological and emotional bonding varies depending on individuals' personality and mental health, however, it seems that everyone can (and will) become attached to an AIE robot to some degree, once it is being used (Wan & Chen, 2021; Yap & Grisham, 2019). Considering that AIE robots are becoming increasingly human-like and may soon act as equal social actors, any relationship with these applications could potentially impact humans similarly to how humans impact each other.

This topic, and the question of how technology (and the relationship between machines and humans) impact individuals and humanity is not new. Numerous media and communication studies have explored human relationships with technology, ranging from early internet use to recent developments in augmented and virtual reality (Rochadiat et al., in Ling et al., 2020; Bullock & Colvin, 2017). These studies explored, for instance, the impact of online interactions on offline relationships, examining changes in sexual activity or the increased number of complaints about a partner's online behaviour (Cooper et al., 2000; Underwood & Findlay, 2004). The diversity of research approaches and perspectives, and the significant impacts, demonstrate the opportunities and necessity of interdisciplinary exploration in the emerging field of AIE.

## The promises and challenges of AIE

While AIE is already a big part of ethical debates, it is useful to look into the reasons why empathic AI applications are being developed and— if done correctly— how it can positively impact humanity. AI that can show empathy promises to provide an enhanced user experience by dynamically adjusting to individual emotional states, thereby fostering personalised interactions that result in heightened customer satisfaction and engagement (Rust & Huang, 2021). Unlike human agents, empathic AI remains consistently attuned to emotions without fatigue, bias or fluctuations in mood, ensuring that every customer interaction is handled with the same level of care and attention. Customer service already benefits greatly from AIE, as seen in the adoption of various applications such as the aforementioned social robot 'Pepper', which is used as a receptionist in offices around the world. Not only will the service industry greatly benefit from AIE, empathy is also going to be a crucial element in AI applications for other fields, for example, education and health/elderly care (McStay, 2018). Learning experiences can be revolutionised by empathic AI applications by adapting educational content and approach to the emotional state and learning style of students, enabling a more personalised education and also offering promising solutions for children with additional needs (McStay, 2020). The inclusion of individuals with disabilities or special needs will be made much easier by incorporating AIE in assistive technology, offering emotional support and assisting with daily tasks in a way that promotes independence and increases quality of life. Empathic AI applications can be used as companions for humans dealing with various mental health issues or loneliness (Potimanios & Narayanan, 2020). AI, in general, is going to have a huge positive impact on the healthcare system, as it can greatly assist in analysing and monitoring health conditions (Topol, 2019). In addition to personal assistance, AIE can also be a support in professional settings where humans and robots collaborate. Enhancing machines with AIE fosters a more positive interaction, which may lead to more effective and efficient teamwork between humans and robots (Lyons et al., 2021; McStay, 2018).

However, all these opportunities can be seen as risky, if developed and applied in an unethical way. Customer service could become manipulative; education and healthcare could potentially have harmful effects on vulnerable people. While the threat of job loss due to AI is not new, emotional AI heightens the threat of replacing roles that rely heavily on empathy and human connection, making the displacement of workers in customer-facing or care industries even more profound. Additionally, the attachment to AIE applications may have a detrimental impact on individuals' mental health or even spark an existential crisis of humanity if humans come to prefer robotic sex over human reproduction. If not carefully designed and implemented, AIE could exacerbate racism and discrimination by perpetuating biases in data and algorithms, struggling to accurately recognise emotions across diverse populations (Johnson, 2006).

The ethical dimensions of emotional AI are closely entwined with broader concerns about privacy, fairness, transparency, and accountability in AI technology (Powers, 2012). Emotional data, being among the most intimate aspects of the human experience, magnify privacy concerns and underscore the necessity for robust data protection measures and informed consent protocols. Moreover, the potential for emotional manipulation and harm presents significant risks that warrant careful assessment.

As emotional AI technologies develop a greater resemblance to humans, the ease with which individuals may form relationships with AI robots increases. However, these emotional bonds carry the potential for negative impacts on mental health, akin to the devastating effects that can arise from human relationships. This complex landscape emphasises the importance of ongoing research to understand the impact of emotional AI and the development of appropriate regulatory frameworks to address ethical concerns (Park & Whang, 2022; Bartneck et al., 2020; Nass & Moon, 2000).

The approach to ethical empathetic AI also includes a philosophical discussion, as AIE may also challenge the way humanity defines itself. If intelligent agents take over not only physical tasks and abilities but are capable of reading and expressing emotions, the definition of what it means to be human is questioned. This is at the core of the posthumanism discourse, which critically discusses the concepts of human identity and existence (Braidotti, 2019; Nimmo et al., 2020; Ferrando, 2019). Delving deeper into the "crisis of the human" (Ferrando, 2019) and the ethical implications of AIE, one may find valuable insights by exploring the most sophisticated version of empathic AI applications: sex robots. These robots go far beyond the physical construction, as AIE now allows the addition of an emotional component to what is already an advanced compilation of human-like appearance and simulated human movements. The emotional capabilities render the name 'sex robots' obsolete—rather, a discipline called 'erobotics' has taken its place (Dube, 2021), shifting the focus onto 'eros' (love) and the many questions relating to humanity and its emotions. Imagine a user of an erobot developing feelings for it and treating it (or her/him?) as a companion or even officially as a partner. What psychological effects may arise? How are human-to-human relationships impacted? What does it mean for the value of sex, love and intimacy within society? What other effects does it have on humanity? These questions and examples are just the surface fragments of emergent debates in the field of erobotics (Sullins, 2021; Danaher & McArthur, 2017; Devlin, 2018) and exemplify the ethical discussion surrounding AIE, in which the Digital Humanities can also provide valuable insights into the socio-cultural impacts, ethical considerations, and humanistic perspectives on the development and deployment of AIE technology, particularly within the context of intimate human-robot interactions and the evolving dynamics of human-technology relationships in general.

The impact on both micro and macro aspects of society could be substantial. Ethicists have already voiced their concerns about erobots increasing the objectification of women, the potential use of child-bots in relation to paedophilia, and the possible problems and pressures on long-term relationships in relation to the potential of erobots always providing "what one desires" (González-González et. al, 2021; Zhou & Fischer, 2019). These concerns fuel the emerging need to program consent into a sex robot—another example of a complex multilayered discussion that involves questions about how much power we should retain or give to AI. However, the use of such applications may have therapeutic benefits or could lead to a decrease in human trafficking and exploitation (Belk, 2022; Sullins, 2012). Research in this area is ongoing and evidence can be found for both the promise and challenges of AIE. With fast-evolving technology, the ethical debate and the quick and ongoing development of guidelines and policies are necessary to ensure an ethical deployment of empathetic AI systems.

## Incorporating empathy

As noted, there is a lack of consensus about how to define emotions or empathy. Empathy has the potential to introduce a more individualistic approach to ethics (Nallur & Finlay, 2022). While the effects of AI are often discussed at a societal level ('ethics in the large'), a focus on the individual level ('ethics in the small') is seen as necessary, and AIE could enable this approach. With the capabilities of emotion recognition software, even large-scale applications can now take individual circumstances into account. This opportunity to incorporate empathy into AI applications empowers developers not only to avoid harm but also to assess the specific needs of each individual interacting with these systems. Multiple studies suggest that the inclusion of empathy in AI systems is a crucial factor for universal ethical AI (Srinivasan & Gonzales, 2021; Batista, 2021; Damiano, Dumouchel & Lehmann, 2015). Affective computing might serve as the "key to a human-friendly singularity" if AI reaches the level of singularity in the future (Hanson Robotics, 2022).[3] Thus, empathy seems to be necessary to reach an ethical 'gold' standard.

---

3    A state of AI where it supersedes humans (Kurzweil, 2005; Lunceford, 2018). The singularity is one of the possible scenarios of the future of AI, envisioning a point at which "super AI" or "Artificial General Intelligence" is reached (Goertzel, 2017, p. 1163). While alternative scenarios exist, the notion of the singularity serves as a focal point for contemplating the profound transformations that could occur once AI surpasses human capabilities. It is important to mention that there are a variety of interpretations regarding the future of AI, ranging from optimistic to pessimistic (Korotayev & LePoire, 2020; Thomas & Thomas, 2016). However, that is not explored in this chapter.

There is growing recognition of the value of empathy and improved mental health in society. This shift signifies a new perspective that considers emotions as complementary to rationality, influencing both prudential and ethical decision-making processes (Nallur & Finlay, 2022). In the traditional legal sphere, however, emotions have often been disregarded and invalidated in favour of the perceived rationality associated with the Rule of Law (Henderson, 1987). Henderson advocates for the integration of empathy into legal practice, asserting that a more comprehensive understanding of situations necessitates acknowledging their emotional dimension, which ultimately leads to more informed and improved decision-making processes. However, incorporating empathy into the realm of legal practice is complex and raises concerns about potential wrongdoing or exploitation due to cultural, individual or confirmation biases. This suggests that empathy, if taken into account when determining legal outcomes, could potentially yield harmful results.

As described earlier, there are various definitions of emotions and empathy, which make it incredibly hard, if not impossible, to create a 'gold' standard. Prinz (2011) discusses AI and emotions and presents a theory that addresses the "problem of parts" and the "problem of plenty". The former refers to the challenge of selecting the necessary components for detecting emotions in a specific context, while the latter pertains to how these components interact with each other. The fragmentation and interconnectedness of these components have given rise to multiple definitions of emotions. The absence of consensus regarding the precise nature of emotions and the true essence of empathy poses a significant obstacle in formulating universal guidelines, whether for the practice of law or the AI(E) industry.

As AI becomes increasingly capable of demonstrating empathy, the ethical considerations surrounding its use are struggling to keep up. McStay and Pavliscak offer emotion-specific ethics guidelines, calling upon practitioners to take action in their daily lives after considering certain ethics-related questions for their product or project, rather than providing a new standard similar to other ethical guidelines (McStay & Pavliscak, 2019). This proposal, still vague, nonetheless creates space for individuality and therefore manifests the core principles of an ethics of care. This normative ethical theory resolves around the individual, believing that generalised standards are "morally problematic, since [they] breed moral blindness or indifference" (Gilligan in Bailey & Cuomo, 2008). However, there is still no official guideline that incorporates empathy. This leads to the question of what happens if AI becomes more human than humans?

## Conclusion: AI(E) and humanity

Machines have already caused a significant transformation in what was once called the "physical economy", an era dominated by mechanical tasks during the Industrial Revolution of the 19th century. This transformation shifted the economy towards a more cognitive approach, often referred to as the "thinking economy" (Rust & Huang, 2021).

The emergence of intelligent technology led to ongoing debates about the very definition of 'intelligence', as there was a constant quest to identify characteristics exclusive to humans. With AI, even tasks such as solving complex calculations ceased to be classified as 'intelligent'. Rust and Huang claim that we have now moved into a "feeling economy" (Rust & Huang, 2021), which is yet again challenged by the emergence of AIE. The aim of developing intelligent technologies is to make them perfect, not allowing any mistakes, as this would be deemed unethical. This also means that, at some point, AIE may be 'better' or more empathetic towards someone compared to a human, as tiredness, lack of concentration or any other human factor might inhibit a human's ability to detect someone else's feelings. If empathy is currently the distinguishing factor between humans and machines, it may soon be time to find a new characteristic of being human. With that in mind, the question of whether AI will ever become 'more human' is impossible to answer, as the definition of such is constantly changing and may always be just one step away. Additionally, the pursuit of AI perfection might drive humans to explore their own progression into 'more-human humans', engineering and augmenting themselves towards perfection to bridge the gap between humans and flawless AI systems.[4]

---

4   This is linked to the transhumanist school of thought, which focuses on human enhancement through technology and tends to emphasise the potential benefits of such (Bostrom, 2014), as opposed to posthumanism, which focuses on the critical examination of the boundaries between humans and non-humans (Braidotti, 2019).

All of this is currently speculative; however, these hypothetical scenarios necessitate ethical discussions and regulations to navigate the potential implications effectively. Integrating humanistic perspectives into the design and development of AIE technologies is essential for ensuring that these systems align with human values, needs and experiences. Digital humanities scholars can contribute insights from the humanities and social sciences to inform the design, evaluation, and critique of affective AI systems, fostering more ethically and culturally sensitive approaches to technology development.

Ultimately, the notion of AI ever becoming 'more human' remains elusive, as the definition of humanity constantly evolves. It seems, however, that empathy is both the key for ethical AI as well as for humanity itself, where it becomes increasingly more important to focus on emotional abilities. Embracing this empathic humanity in the age of empathic AI applications involves leveraging such applications as catalysts for self-reflection, self-exploration and a redefinition of what it means to be human, so that we can ensure we stay 'more human' than any simulations of humans.

# Works Cited

Bartneck, C., Belpaeme, T., Eyssel, F., Kanda, T., Keijsers, M., & Šabanović, S. (2020). *Human-robot interaction: An introduction.* Cambridge University Press.

Bartneck, C. & Forlizzi, J. (2004). A design-centred framework for social human-robot interaction. *13th IEEE International Workshop on Robot and Human Interactive Communication* (IEEE Catalog No. 04TH8759), pp. 591–594. https://doi.org/10.1109/ROMAN.2004.1374827

Beck, J. (2015, February 4). Hard feelings: science's struggle to define emotions. *The Atlantic.* https://www.theatlantic.com/health/archive/2015/02/hard-feelings-sciences-struggle-to-define-emotions/385711/

Belk, R. (2022). Artificial emotions and love and sex doll service workers. *Journal of Service Research.* https://doi.org/10.1177/10946705211063692

Billard, A., & Grollman, D. (2012). Human-Robot Interaction. In N. Seel (Ed.). *Encyclopedia of the Sciences of Learning.* Springer. https://doi.org/10.1007/978-1-4419-1428-6_760

Bisconti, P. (2021). Will sexual robots modify human relationships? A psychological approach to reframe the symbolic argument. *Advanced Robotics* 35(9), 561–571. https://doi.org/10.1080/01691864.2021.1886167

Bostrom, N. (2014). *Superintelligence: Paths, dangers, strategies*. Oxford University Press, Incorporated. https://doi.org/10.1007/s11023-015-9377-7

Braidotti, R. (2019). *Posthuman Knowledge*. Polity Press.

Bråten, S. (2007). *On being moved: From mirror neurons to empathy*. John Benjamins Publishing Company. https://doi.org/10.1075/aicr.68

Bullock, A.N., & Colvin, A.D. (2017). Technology, human relationships and human interaction. *Social Work*. https://doi.org./10.1093/obo/9780195389678-0249

Cooper, A., McLoughlin, I.P., & Campbell, K.M. (2000). Sexuality in cyberspace: Update for the 21st century. *Cyberpsychology & Behavior 3*, 521–536. https://doi.org/10.1089/109493100420142

Danaher, J., & McArthur, N. (2017). *Robot Sex: Social and Ethical Implications*. MIT Press.

Decety, J., & Jackson, P.L. (2004). The functional architecture of human empathy. *Behavioral and Cognitive Neuroscience Reviews 3*(2), 71–100. https://doi.org/10.1177/1534582304267187

Devlin, K. (2018). *Turned On: Science, Sex and Robots*. Bloomsbury Sigma.

Ferrando, F. (2019). *Philosophical Posthumanism*. Bloomsbury Academic.

Kolling, T., Baisch, S., Schall, A., Selic, S., Rühl, S., Kim, Z., Rossberg, H., Klein, B., Pantel, J., Oswald, F. & Knopf, M. (2016). What is emotional about emotional robotics? In S.Y. Tettegah & Y.E. Garcia (Eds). *Emotions, Technology and Health*. Academic Press. (pp. 85–103). https://doi.org/10.1016/B978-0-12-801737-1.00005-6

González-González, C.S., Gil-Iranzo, R.M., & Paderewski-Rodríguez, P. (2020). Human-robot interaction and sexbots: A systematic literature review. *Sensors* (Basel) *21*(1). https://doi.org/10.3390/s21010216

Korotayev, A., & LePoire, D. (2020). *The 21st Century Singularity and Global Futures*. Springer. https://doi.org/10.1007/978-3-030-33730-8

Kurzweil, R. (2005). *The singularity is near: When humans transcend biology*. Penguin Books. https://doi.org/10.1057/9781137349088_26

Johnson, D.G. (2006). Computer systems : Moral entities but not moral agents. *Ethics and Information Technology 8*(4), 195–204. https://doi.org/10.1007/s10676-006-9111-5

Lee, J.-E., & Nass, C. (2010). Trust in computers: The computers-are-social-actors (CASA) paradigm and trustworthiness perception in human-computer communication. In D. Latusek & A. Gerbasi (Eds). *Trust and Technology in a Ubiquitous Modern Environment: Theoretical and Methodological Perspectives*. IGI Global. (pp. 1–15). https://doi.org/10.4018/978-1-61520-901-9.ch001

Lee, S.-K., Kavya, P., & Lasser, S.C. (2021). Social interactions and relationships with an intelligent virtual agent. *International Journal of Human-Computer Studies 150*. https://doi.org/10.1016/j.ijhcs.2021.102608

Lindgren, N., & Öhman, J. (2019). A posthuman approach to human-animal relationships: Advocating critical pluralism. *Environmental Education Research* 25(8), 1200–1215. https://doi.org/10.1080/13504622.2018.1450848

Lunceford, B. (2018). Love, Emotion and the singularity. *Information* (Basel) 9(9), 221. https://doi.org/10.3390/info9090221

Lyons, J.B., Sycara, K., Lewis, M., & Capiola, A. (2021). Human-autonomy teaming: Definitions, debates, and directions. *Frontiers in Psychology* 12, 589585–589585. https://doi.org/10.3389/fpsyg.2021.589585

McStay, A. (2018). *Emotional AI: The Rise of Empathic Media.* SAGE. http://digital.casalini.it/9781526451323

McStay, A. (2020). Emotional AI and EdTech: Serving the public good? *Journal of Educational Media : The Journal of the Educational Television Association* 45(3), 270–283. https://doi.org/10.1080/17439884.2020.1686016

Miller, A.I. (2019). *The Artist in the Machine: The World of AI-powered Creativity.* MIT Press. https://doi.org/10.7551/mitpress/11585.001.0001

Nass, C., & Moon, Y. (2000). Machines and mindlessness: Social responses to computers. *Journal of Social Issues* 56(1), 81–103. https://doi.org/10.1111/0022-4537.00153

Nimmo, R., Atkinson, P., Delamont, S., Cernat, A., Sakshaug, J.W., & Williams, R.A. (2020). *Posthumanism.* SAGE Publications Ltd.

Park, S., & Whang, M. (2022). Empathy in human-robot interaction: Designing for social robots. *International Journal of Environmental Research and Public Health* 19(3), 1889. https://doi.org/10.3390/ijerph19031889

Picard, R. (1997). *Affective Computing.* MIT Press.

Popkova, E., & Sergi, B.S. (2020). *Scientific and Technical Revolution: Yesterday, Today and Tomorrow.* Springer.

Potamianos, A., & Narayanan, S. (2020). Why emotion AI is the key to mental health treatment. *The Data Warehousing Institute.* https://tdwi.org/articles/2020/04/07/adv-all-why-emotion-ai-key-to-mental-health-treatment.aspx

Prato-Previde, E., Basso Ricci, E., & Colombo, E.S. (2022). The complexity of the human-animal bond: Empathy, attachment and anthropomorphism in human-animal relationships and animal hoarding. *Animals* (Basel) 12(20). https://doi.org/10.3390/ani12202835.

Prinz, J. (2011). Against empathy. *The Southern Journal of Philosophy* 49(1), 214–233. https://doi.org/10.1111/j.2041-6962.2011.00069.x

Rochadiat, A., Tong, S., & Corriero, E. (2020). Intimacy in the app age: Romantic relationships and mobile technology. In R. Ling, L. Fortunati, G. Goggin, S. Lim, & Y. Li. (2020). *The Oxford Handbook of Mobile Communication and Society.* Oxford Academic. https://doi.org/10.1093/oxfordhb/9780190864385.001.0001

Rust, R., & Huang, M.-H. (2021). *The feeling economy: How Artificial Intelligence is creating the era of empathy.* Springer. https://doi.org./10.1007/987-3-030-52977-2

Schwab, K. (2017). *The Fourth Industrial Revolution.* Portfolio Penguin.

Shouse, E. (2005). Feeling, emotion, affect. *M/C Journal* (6). https://doi.org/10.5204/mcj.2443

Spezialetti, M., Placidi, G., & Rossi, S. (2020). Emotion recognition for human-robot interaction: Recent advances and future perspectives. *Frontiers in Robotics and AI 7.* https://doi.org/10.3389/frobt.2020.532279

Stark, L., & Hoey, J. (2021). The ethics of emotion in artificial intelligence systems. *ACM Conference: Fairness, Accountability, and Transparency.* Association for Computing Machinery. https://doi.org/10.1145/3442188.3445939

Sullins, J.P. (2012). Robots, love, and sex: The ethics of building a love machine. *IEEE Transactions on Affective Computing 3*(4), 398–409. https://doi.org/10.1109/T-AFFC.2012.31

Thomas, J.C., & Thomas, J. (2016). *Turing's nightmares: Multiple scenarios of the Singularity.* CreateSpace Independent Publishing Platform.

Tong, A. (2023, March 26). AI company restores erotic role play after backlash from users 'married' to their bots. *Sydney Morning Herald.* https://www.smh.com.au/world/north-america/ai-company-restores-erotic-roleplay-after-backlash-from-users-married-to-their-bots-20230326-p5cvao.html

Topol, E.J. (2019). *Deep medicine: How Artificial Intelligence Can Make Healthcare Human Again.* Basic Books.

Underwood, H., & Findlay, B. (2004). Internet relationships and their impact on primary relationships. *Behaviour Change 21,* 127–140. https://doi.org/10.1375/bech.21.2.127.55422

Vincent, J., Taipale, S., Sapio, B., Lugano, G., & Fortunati, L. (2015). *Social Robots from a Human Perspective.* Springer International Publishing AG.

Wan, E., & Chen, R.P. (2021). Anthropomorphism and object attachment. *Current Opinion in Psychology 39,* 88–93. https://doi.org/10.1016/j.copsyc.2020.08.009

Yap, K., & Grisham, J.R. (2019). Unpacking the construct of emotional attachment to objects and its association with hoarding symptoms. *Journal of Behavioral Addictions 8*(2), 249–258. https://doi.org/10.1556/2006.8.2019.15

Yalçın, Ö.N., & DiPaola, S. (2020). Modelling empathy: Building a link between affective and cognitive processes. *Artificial Intelligence Review 53,* 2983–3006. https://doi.org/10.1007/s10462-019-09753-0

Zhou, Y., Fischer, M.H. (2019). Intimate relationships with humanoid robots: Exploring human sexuality in the twenty-first century. In Y. Zhou, & M. Fischer (Eds). *AI Love You.* Springer, Cham.

# PART 2
# DIGITAL HUMANITIES AND LITERATURE

# 6. Digital hermeneutics: Interpretation and the interpretational machines

*Prayer Elmo Raj*

## Abstract

Classical hermeneutics, firmly rooted in the interpretation of cultural artifacts, stands at the precipice of a transformative paradigm shift as interactive digital networks pervade our existence. This essay probes the fundamental transformation brought about by technology, positing it as a dynamic hermeneutic agent with a dualistic magnification-reduction structure. This challenges the conventional notion of technology as a mere replica of reality, demanding a critical re-evaluation of its interpretational potency and its profound impact on comprehension and consequence. Digital hermeneutics unfurls along two distinct trajectories: one focused on the analysis and interpretation of digital-native texts and databases, while the other delves into the intricate dynamics of intentionality in human-AI interactions. The proliferation of digital ontologies necessitates a refined interpretive logic capable of navigating the intricate terrain of humanities research. By engaging with foundational hermeneutic theorists, this essay underscores the materiality intrinsic to language and underscores the transformative potential embedded in signs, symbols, and narratives. It interrogates the implications of digital texts, dismantling established constructs of narrative identity and fostering avenues for dynamic and evolving expressions of meaning. By critically addressing the materiality

https://doi.org/10.11647/OBP.0423.06

of meaning sources and the transformative prowess inherent in digital texts, this comprehensive study lays a foundation for an enhanced hermeneutical framework adept at navigating the intricate web of contemporary communication and information networks.

## Keywords

Digital hermeneutics; interpretation; meaning; data; information.

## Introduction

Hermeneutics, as the philosophical theory of interpretation and communication, faces challenges occasioned by the existing and emergent digital communication and information networks. Rational interpretations are challenged by global and interactive digital (inter) networks. Classical hermeneutics neglects the intermediaries between the subject and the world. The emphasis on language ignores the materiality and technicity of the sources of meaning. Technologies are personally and collectively encapsulated into various configurations of signs and symbols that arbitrate comprehension and consequences. Nevertheless, language assumes a central position in the relationship between technology and interpretation. Hermeneutics, traditionally concerned with interpretation and understanding, extends its purview beyond the empirical domain of science to encompass the interpretative frameworks that underlie scientific inquiry. According to Ihde (1999), "hermeneutics needs to be understood, not only in relation to science, but in relation to the philosophies of science which, for philosophers, are often taken implicitly for science itself, or for how science is to be understood" (p. 346). In this sense, hermeneutics serves as a meta-discipline that elucidates the processes of interpretation inherent in scientific endeavours, illuminating the role of context, language, and preconceptions in shaping scientific knowledge.

Initially, hermeneutics (*kunstlehre*) is defined as the science of interpreting cultural productions. The fundamental aim of hermeneutics is to accomplish *verstehen* (Bulhof, 1980, p. 55), an understanding of human artifacts through interrogation to unveil causal factors. However, the 'dense web' of meanings is influenced by the author's intention and the reception of the readers. As a philosophical movement, interpretation and comprehension are considered to be an important faculty of human 'being-in-the-world'. Considering humans as interpretive beings, hermeneutics developed various approaches to interpretation and understanding.

Classically, technology has never been of any interest to hermeneutics. However, the inevitability of technology in the transmission of meaning and mediation between human beings and reality necessitated the extension of the understanding of hermeneutics. Technologically facilitated I-world relations offer new interpretations and entrée to the world. Ihde (1990) recognises technologies as having a hermeneutic nature by emphasising their "magnification-reduction structure". Technologies do not merely replicate the real world but selectively recognise the world around us in its hermeneutic function. In this sense, technology offers a delegatory function (Latour, 1994) in being an interpretational agency to humans.

The primary challenge facing the Digital Humanities does not stem solely from their integration with the material world—a transformation that varies only in degree. Rather, the critical issue lies in the absence of robust methodological and critical frameworks that should ideally facilitate both the generation of meaning and the development of functional digital products. The central epistemological challenge for the Digital Humanities lies in their inherent entanglement with technology to such an extent that it necessitates prioritising the functionality of solutions about interpretation (Smithies, 2017, p. 7).

Digital hermeneutics has laid two trajectories: one follows *kunstlehre* for the analysis, understanding and interpretation of digital native texts, texts corpora or databases. Another trajectory deals with the acknowledgement of the identicalities and contrasts between human and AI intentionality. Computers and software generate ontological and technological differences in interpretational methods in humanities. Ontology, here, includes the veracity and the texture of the object of interrogation. It establishes the object of linguistics, the context out of which the text derives its sense. The text is fashioned into a specific corpus so as to be interpreted.

Digital hermeneutics can be understood as the interaction between hermeneutics and digital technology. We live in a society where communication and information networks are digitally founded. One of the major challenges for hermeneutics in the digital network era is the creative social relevance and interpretation of knowledge. The pseudo-critical refutation of hermeneutics in the context of digital technology is of concern. To encounter the challenges offered by digital technology, we must evolve a "productive logic"[1] (Heidegger, 1996, p. 10) in deciphering the dynamics of digital technology and its relationship with human existence.

> Modern technology not only covers over or obscures the thinghood in things, it also covers over or obscures the Being of beings, and ultimately itself. Technology cannot be understood in terms of technology (Mitcham, 1994, p. 53).

In Heideggerian ontology, Technology[2] emerges as the principal antagonist to the essence of Being. Therefore, it exerts a profound influence on our perception and engagement with technological artefacts, analagous to Being's comprehension of the manifold manifestations of existence. Technology engenders comparable implications for our understanding of the diverse array of technological entities. Within the framework of ontological hermeneutics, which eschews inherent valorisation, there exists a reflexive acceptance of the Truth-event.

Departing from the classical notion of *techné*, Heidegger contends that Technology serves to veil reality, thereby advancing an understanding of reality as primal matter readily available for utilisation and manipulation. The conceptual apparatus of Being introduces a veil that obscures the interpretation of the plurality inherent in beings, analogous to an obfuscating effect on the comprehension of the multiplicity of technologies and technological processes. The nexus between 'being-in-the-world' and hermeneutics accentuates the pivotal role played by tools in mediating the relationships between human agents and their environment.

Typically, human actors direct their cognitive focus not toward

---

1   Heidegger's "productive logic" is an anticipation of the novelty of what is unveiled in the moment of discernment.
2   Heidegger examines the question concerning Technology (with capital 'T') in relation to Being and Thing. Technology, Being and Thing, in his argument, are interrelated. Technology's relation with Being and Thing is arbitrary, ambiguous and it observes each other.

the instruments employed but rather toward tasks in which they are engaged. Tools act as mediators that obscure the direct connection between humans and the world, instead moulding the perceptual landscape through which the world manifests itself:

> Things, in short, disclose the world. When somebody uses a tool or piece of equipment, a referential structure comes about in which the object produced, the material out of which it is made, the future user, the environment in which it has a place are related to each other (Verbeek, 2005, p. 79).

The significance of a tool typically emerges when it ceases to function as expected, drawing attention to its presence and necessitating a detailed examination of its structure. At this juncture, the materiality inherent to its functionality serves as a crucial intermediary in shaping the relationship between humans and the world. The transition of the tool from a state of seamless integration, known as 'ready-to-hand', to a state of conspicuous objectivity, underscores its pivotal role in mediating human-world interactions. Irrgang raises some pertinent questions:

> How is it that human behaviours and embodiment affect the associated social and cultural factors? How do we relate technologies in the lifeworld? What kind of relationship stand in direct correlation to technologies? How does the lifeworld shape technology and, conversely, how does technology shape the life world?" (qtd. in Tripathi, 2016, p. 148).

The emphasis noted here is the pertinence of the relationship between the human experience of life-world and the interceding tools. Ihde (1990; 2006) discusses how human-technology relations facilitate and transform our experiences. These relations also pave the way for the generation of structural aspects of technological mediation fashioning varied possibilities of experiences. Technological mediation regulates the relations between human activities and devices. We should be aware that:

> Technologies are not neutral instruments or intermediaries, but active mediators that help shape the relation between people and reality. This mediation has two directions: one pragmatic, concerning action, and the other hermeneutic, concerning interpretation (Verbeek, 2008, p. 94).

Language is a significant tool in the expression of "intelligibility of being-in-the world" (Heidegger, 1996, p. 151). The utilisation of language, whether in interpersonal discourse or introspective reflection, facilitates authentic comprehension and engagement with the world. This underscores an inherent, albeit passive, ontological interdependency between Being and language. However, this dialogue often overlooks the materiality inherent to language. While convenience remains associated with linguistic expression, the notion of value is contingent upon the interconnectedness within linguistic systems, as elucidated by Saussure. Emphasising the significance of reference, Heidegger diverges from prioritising tools in favour of examining signs as integral components of interpretation and signification. Consequently, the relationship between *Dasein* and language assumes a nuanced trajectory, wherein the focus shifts towards the realm of signs to attain consciousness. The articulation of inner conscience finds expression through what can be termed as the 'mode of silence', thereby indicating a shift towards introspective contemplation. This interplay between conscience and silence epitomises a journey of self-awareness that serves to orient one towards a deeper understanding of reality.

Ricoeur's (1991) hermeneutics is founded on written and stable forms of language like symbols, signs and narratives. Emphasising the ontological prominence of writing, he maintains that:

> The psychological and sociological priority of speech over writing is not in question. It may be asked, however, whether the late appearance of writing has not provoked a radical change in our relations to the very statements of our discourse (Ricoeur, 1991, p. 106).

In Ricoeur, we find the basis for the materiality of language and interpretational procedures. The semiotic and semantic interventions in the functioning of signs, symbols and narratives are external. However, concerning the transmission of meaning, Ricoeur is not concerned with either materiality or externalisation of language. The digital presence challenges Ricoeur's notion of narrative identity in terms of "mono-linearity and mono-ideality" (Romele, 2020, p. 7). Narratives that we hear or read have exploratory functions pushing language between explanation and instruction, through which our identities are configured. The texts we read are heterogeneous and they vary every time we read them. Digital texts are indefinite, it is a sequence and possibility of expression that anticipates the future. A story that took place in the past is expressed in the present and amplified towards the future like a video game. Moreover:

While stories are enclosed in an emplotment already decided by the author, computer games allow the player to move freely within a framework of few given rules. In some sense, computer games are the concrete realization of the speculations of postmodernity and the clumsy attempts of some literary avant-gardes (Romele, 2020, p. 7).

## Information and meaning

The relationship between information and meaning is implicit and indispensable. Floridi's (2005) understanding of semantic information is an affirmative relationship between data, meaning and truth (data + meaning + truth). The interconnection between data and information is an evolving domain. The fundamental principles of analysis can be appropriated in the context of application. The non-cognitive, affirmative and embedded domain includes objects such as databases, encyclopaedias and websites. The challenges facing the materiality of production and its interdependence with information from its locus and interpretation anticipate semiotic code and its corporeal implementation. The standard definition of information (SDI) includes data, data configuration and meaning. The data concerning SDI cannot be 'dataless' as it is deciphered with relational entities. Concerning relationalities, Floridi (2005) assumes data as "definable as constraining affordances, exploitable by a system as input of adequate queries that correctly semanticise them to produce information as output" (p. 357).

Translation introduces the work of reconfiguration into the syntactic and semantic framework. The primal intentions allow a process of interpreting the signs. The evocative and familiar data qualify as information even when they represent or transfer a truth. Sometimes, misinformation can be informative because it can be reduced to a notion of "non-primary" information. Non-primary information is presented through instances without data and differential objects. Further:

> A machine that always gives the same answer does not provide any information unless it stops responding, but the information it will give in this case (for example, the machine is broken) will be meta-information (Romele, 2020, p. 29).

Meaning and truth are embodied in information. The accentuation on uniformity and transmission of information communicates the preference over multiplicity. What lies underneath the theory of information is the relation of being and the relation within beings. Both these relations are distinct and individual, preserving the information to be communicated. The above-mentioned relations presume being/information as having an intrinsic value. When it comes to reality, information innately renders its ethical choices. While data processing is desired, the presence of information creates a paradoxical circumstance in hermeneutic relations. Further:

> Sometimes this understanding is merely in the background, as when a habitual user deals with the computer mouse, while at other times it is in the foreground when, for example, we have to confront new technological objects (Romele, 2020, p. 37).

Introna (1993) presents three different stances on information: a) information is the consequence of a process of transformation. Data is altered into information; b) significance of the receiver or user. The receiver should be familiar with the information he/she receives to make it meaningful; c) information aims to influence the choices of the receiver/receiving system. The condition on which data transform into information depends on how they become meaningful to the recipient. Hermeneutic relations set right the error that occurs in the process of communication. When a sender encodes his/her message to connect with the receiver, the sender anticipates the knowledge of the message in the receiver. The receiver is expected to interpret the message even when the signs or symbols are limited; an unrestricted series of meanings is expected. The relations between the symbols or signs and their meaning keep varying according to the context. Thus, a dialectic hermeneutic approach becomes fundamental within the information systems where the self-understanding of the sender and receiver contributes to the meaning-making process. This approach is based on the lived experience and how a message is appropriated in the lived experience. Given the context and perspective, interpretation within an information system is perpetual and never complete. Since data cannot be transmitted, interpretation becomes direct and contextual. Interpretation of a message also involves understanding the information. A sequence of knowledge system/s is involved in this process of understanding.[3]

---

3   See Claude E. Shannon and Warren Weaver, *The Mathematical Theory of Communication* (1949).

# Data and interpretation

The emerging digital constructs not only herald profound transformations at the individual level but also introduce unprecedented quantities of knowledge and information devoid of the regulatory mechanisms traditionally provided by philosophical underpinnings. Technology facilitates unrestricted access to vast reservoirs of human knowledge. The traditional figure of authority, epitomised by the professor who dictates what information to seek and prescribes structured arguments for and against, appears increasingly obsolete in the contemporary landscape. There is a burgeoning recognition of the necessity to incorporate the learning and application of computer code within educational frameworks, potentially engendering the emergence of a novel academic discipline centred on computation or data analysis. The intricacies inherent in code necessitate meticulous consideration at multiple levels. Beginning with the material engagement of users with code, encompassing both programmers and consumers, to the processes of reading and writing code, culminating in the execution and resultant experience of its functionality, it is imperative to foreground the comprehension of code as computational logic embedded within tangible technical devices (Berry, 2011, p. 63).

The advent of 'Big Data' has altered the interpretive processes and analysis of texts. This transition has underlined the significance of digitised textual corpora that are available for analysis. The presence and availability of digitised textual corpora have completely altered the manner of examining and interpreting the texts. These fundamental alterations are made in the way we use textual analytic methodologies to understand and gauge the meanings and character of textual corpora.

Digital hermeneutics involves text prospecting sensibilities. The available text-examining tools draw upon a specific theory of reading. The influence of Big Data is the extension of varied types of algorithmic and computational tools for interpreting texts. Technologies offer us the capability to deliberate a textual corpus in its hermeneutic intricacies and distinctions. The complexity of a textual corpus and how we excerpt different poetically significant elements or structurally entangled sequences provide interpretive intention to the corpus.

The focus is on various groupings of quantifiable textual features in a text to interpret. Big Data offers us an extraordinary sum of datasets and opportunities to engage, analyse and interpret textual corpora. The effort requires the extraction of critical information through deeper content analysis to pursue subtler nuances of textual corpora. The communicative purpose of a text, in digital hermeneutics, assumes multiple, contrasting and overlapping meanings. While traditional close reading presupposes the sole meaning of a text, we can analyse and understand the textual corpora based on its style and how it is embedded in wider literary contexts and interlinks. Consequently, the style becomes the substance of the text.

'Data' is a catchword in the contemporary digital world. Similar to:

> [...] industrial technologies of the past were accompanied by new social, cultural and political imaginaries, we can trace the ascent of 'data imaginaries' and 'data speak': visions and rhetoric concerning the role of data in society (Grey, 2018).

Data encompasses a variety of possibilities for the future and the relations that could appropriate practical tasks.[4] The data world:

> [...] draws on philosophical ideas about worlds, worlding, and world-making to look at how things are *sayable, knowable, intelligible* and *experiencable* through data (Grey, 2018).

The productive role of human thought is configured by the experience involving patterns, classifications and arrangements of space, time, causality and quantity. Hermeneutic thinkers like Heidegger and Gadamer challenged the Kantian emphasis on universal structures to highlight the importance of socially and historically positioned linguistic and cultural substructures in fashioning the worlds we exist. Language as a prospect of intelligibility offers conditions of possibility

---

4    "Companies see data as a lucrative new asset class and as a resource for streamlining their operations and for providing new offerings. Politicians see data as an instrument of reform by enabling transparency, accountability, participation and innovation. Journalists see data as a means to source stories and enrich their reportage. Activists see data as both an issue in itself and as a resource for intervention concerning everything from corporate and governmental surveillance to climate change and migration. Data is envisaged to make money, strengthen democracies, aid investigations and enable justice. At the same time, it has been subjected to numerous critiques. Data is also held to disrupt livelihoods, violate privacy, undermine democracies, deepen inequalities, distract from issues, and displace other forms of reasoning, sense-making and experience" (Grey, 2018).

for our experience considering the fundamental function. This position departed from the overemphasis on the information translation abilities of language.

The digital is deeply impacted by language because everything digital is deciphered into writing or is transcoded. The relevance of writing and its symbols are representative and performative. The translatability that exists between writing and the digital is decodable by human beings and transactable by machines. Information and communication systems have hybridised intellectual and material technologies.

The enunciation of expertise, communication of content and discussion about the transformation of matter are fundamental to writing and production systems. The physical patterns of information are made explicable through cybernetics. Expression and representation as techniques of manipulation are appropriated through informatics and algorithms. If the difference between signs and the technological is ontological, the material and technological understanding of the digital has hermeneutic underpinning.

Data worlding, as historically and culturally appropriated, is contingent on technologically influenced 'data a *priori*.' It not only defines but also offers various conditions of possibility of interpreting, understanding and engaging with different aspects of social life. The specific flair of interpretation and knowing various forms of experience are encircled within these conditions of possibility.

Consequently, data practices are to be understood as locating and innovatively contributing to meaning. Goodman (1978) reminds us that "worldmaking as we know it always starts from a world already on hand; the making is a remaking" (p. 6). The prospects of intelligibility offered by various modes of experiences and stances of reasoning are considered possible with the availability of data. Intelligibility also becomes possible with the presence of distinctive and emergent digital technologies. Therefore, the past and the present are involved in the making of possible meanings.

With the availability of digital data worlds:

> [...] we may examine how composites of conventions, norms, technologies, practices, methods, pieces of software, graphical user interfaces, data standards, data formats and aesthetic approaches are implicated in making things up and making things intelligible with data.

This might include looking at how horizons of intelligibility change from pre-digital to digital data worlds (Grey, 2018).

Various forms of experience, reasoning and sociality ascend with the advent of cultural objects related to digital data worlds. The world-making opportunities and capabilities of things such as digital platforms, apps, software, code libraries and digital tools make sense of data and assimilate data into varieties of social procedures and systems.

Computer scientists employ quantitative methodologies and computational models to generate scientific evidence and to 'explain' or 'simulate' phenomena, while historians predominantly use qualitative and hermeneutic approaches to comprehend the intricacies of past events. Despite both fields using digital infrastructures, data, and tools, significant disparities persist in their epistemological and methodological underpinnings and the researchers' self-conceptions within these disciplinary communities.

Variances in research design and methodology, such as quantitative versus qualitative methods, and in the analytical approaches, exemplified by machine-driven "distant reading" versus individualised "close reading" of textual corpora, as well as differing aspirations—ranging from the pursuit of general scientific laws to the creation of unique subjective interpretations in the humanities—result in the emergence of complex "boundary objects" within our intellectual exchange zone (Fickers, Tatarinov & Heijden, 2022, p. 5). Computation is conceptualised as a strategy aimed at organising reality using logical and quantitative techniques (Fazi, 2018, p. 1). The systematic approaches employed in computation are commonly perceived as straightforward formulae designed to encapsulate the intricate dynamics and multifaceted nature of the world. From this vantage point, computation is construed as a process that simply acquires and portrays reality by employing binary calculations of probabilities. Following the interactive paradigm within computing, the deductive algorithmic processes must be supplemented by the unpredictable nature of environmental input to introduce the inherent unpredictability of the real-world context into the computational framework.

Furthermore, investigations into ubiquitous, pervasive, embedded, and physical computing underscore the imperative of imbuing computational processes with characteristics akin to empirical scenarios (Fazi, 2018, p. 3). In this vein, both the technical and cultural discourse surrounding situated computing endeavours to emphasise the mediated accessibility of computational devices within the context of tangible reality. This accessibility primarily manifests through the physical interaction between users and machines, thus necessitating a material or embodied engagement.

Interaction, therefore, evolves into a practice intertwined with the spatial orientation of computing devices within the physical environment and our interactional dynamics with them. The computational realm extends beyond the digital domain, encompassing a broader spectrum of operations, yet both are grounded in discrete processes involving counting, measurement, and quantification. This foundational discrete nature predates the formal instantiation of computation within finite-state machines such as computers. Nonetheless, this instantiation underscores the inherent alignment of principles: both the computational and the digital rely on the discretisation of reality.

The digital, functioning as a method of information processing, employs digits—such as the binary digits of zeros and ones—to represent and manage data. Similarly, within the computational sphere, discreteness is expressed through various quantifying mechanisms, including models, procedures, representations, symbols, numbers, measures, and formalisations. Whether engaged in digital or non-digital computation, the act involves organising reality into abstracted relations among these quantifiable entities. Both the entities themselves and the relations between them can be subject to logical manipulation, resulting in an output corresponding to a given input.

Consequently, computing transcends mere numerical computation; a computing machine serves as a 'meta-medium,' capable of representing numerous other media while augmenting them with novel properties. These achievements hinge upon the fundamental discretising nature of computation. A computer possesses the capability to execute any task that can be articulated in finite, well-defined terms through a sequential series of executable instructions (Fazi, 2018, p. 48).

# Hermeneutic relations

Ihde's philosophy of technology, predicated upon the framework of the Husserlian model of intentionality, underscores an emphasis on cultivating a phenomenology of human-technology relations. In this perspective, the experiential interface between humanity and technology assumes a paramount significance. The nature of what is experienced becomes inextricably intertwined with the modalities through which it is experienced. Ihde maintains that "there have been technological revolutions in imaging technologies which created the ways for material things to 'speak' and more, thus leading to a 'material hermeneutic' which will change all previous histories and interpretations." (2020, p. 35–36). Ihde postulates that the nexus between humans and technology, like other interpersonal relations, unfolds within the expansive domains of consciousness and intentionality, thereby accentuating the intricate interplay of subjective awareness and purposive engagement. Within this framework is the recognition that the human-technology dyad is not merely a uni-dimensional interaction but rather a multifaceted fabric of experiential encounters. Such encounters are intricately woven into a technologically saturated culture.

Ihde's proposition accords primacy to the lived experience of technology, contending that it is through the prism of experiential recognition that the profound implications of technological mediation upon human existence can be apprehended (2022, p. 112). While Ihde's stance offers valuable insights into the subjective dimensions of human-technology relations, it arguably elides certain structural and systemic dynamics that underpin the contemporary technological landscape. By foregrounding individual experience, Ihde risks eliding broader socio-political forces that shape and constrain the contours of technological engagement, thereby potentially occluding critical inquiry into issues of power, inequality, and technological determinism. While the emphasis on intentionality foregrounds the active agency of human subjects in shaping their technological milieu, it may inadvertently obscure the myriad ways in which technology itself exerts a formative influence on human consciousness and behaviour.

Ihde, in his presentation of "hermeneutic relations," recognises the symbiotic interplay between human agency and technological mediation.

The experience of technology assumes an ontological dimension similar to that of an "other self-like" entity. Central to this schema is the notion of engaging in a "special interpretive action within the technological context," (1990, p. 40) where human actions and observations are imbued with interpretive significance, engendering a dialectical process of meaning-making through reading. For instance:

> The engineer in the case "reads" his dials and if one creeps up, indicating that Quad X is overheating, he merely has to turn a dial and watch to see if the heat begins to turn to normal. If it does, all right, if not, he may have to call a building manager to find out what has broken. Here the engineer is engaged in experiences *of* a machine (Ihde, 1990. p. 41).

The engineer engages in a form of interpretive engagement with the instrumental panel of the machine, wherein the dials and indicators serve as mediators through which the engineer grasps the machine's state and functionality. This interpretive act, characterised by a reflexive interplay between observation and action, epitomises the essence of hermeneutic relations. The technological artefact assumes a quasi-autonomous agency, necessitating a reciprocal engagement on the part of the human subject.

Of particular importance is Ihde's elucidation of the contingent nature of hermeneutic relations, wherein the efficacy of interpretive action is contingent upon the allegiance of the technological artifact as a mediator of meaning. The engineer's ability to discern the operational status of the machine hinges upon the fidelity of the instrumental panel as a faithful representation of the machine's underlying state. Therefore, the hermeneutic relation is predicated upon a delicate equilibrium between the interpretive prowess of the human subject and the fidelity of the technological artifact as a mediator of meaning.

Reading technology as a means of accessing knowledge about the 'world' transcends the conventional purview of existential inquiry to explicate the interpretive relations that underpin the interface between humans and technology within the fabric of our lived reality. Ihde urges us to see the scientific objects "which are techno constructed to be 'seen-read' though the specific style of interpretation which is a scientific hermeneutic" (Ihde, 1997, p. 123). At the heart of Ihde's exposition lies the recognition that technological artifacts serve as mediators through which human subjects access and interpret the underlying realities of their environment. Ihde highlights how technological objects, despite their material instantiation, transcend their immediate physicality to signify something beyond themselves.

> You read the thermometer, and in the immediacy of your reading you *hermeneutically* know that it is cold [...] but you should not fail to note that perceptually what you have seen is the dial and the numbers, the thermometer "text". And that text has hermeneutically delivered its "world" reference, the cold (2006, p. 42).

When one reads a thermometer, for instance, the perceptual encounter with its dial and numerical display serves as a hermeneutic engagement through which the ambient temperature, or the 'world' reference, is understood.

Thus, the act of reading technology becomes synonymous with deciphering the textual cues embedded within its material form and thereby facilitating a deeper understanding of the surrounding reality. Ihde explains the concept of "technological otherness," wherein the technological artifact assumes a quasi-autonomous agency that stands in contrast to the frailty of human existence. This acknowledgment of the ontological disparity between human subjects and technological objects underscores the asymmetrical power dynamics inherent within human-technology relations. Technological otherness, therefore, not only amplifies the potency of technological artifacts as mediators of knowledge but also underscores the inherent vulnerability of human subjects vis-à-vis the formidable capabilities of technology. The invocation of technological otherness raises pertinent questions regarding the ethical implications of ceding agency to technological artifacts and the concomitant erosion of human autonomy.

The discourse on digital hermeneutics unveils an examination of the interpretive processes within the technological milieu, foregrounding the intricate interplay between reading, writing, and the material instantiation of language. Reading involves technologies and writing has a 'product'. Writing is recognised as a technologically encapsulated form of language (Ihde, 1990, p. 81) where the act of inscription mediates the perception and transmission of meaning. This technologically mediated aspect of writing engenders a transformative dynamic, whereby our understanding of language and meaning undergoes a perceptible shift.

The representational isomorphism between text and the corporeal space of perception sheds light on the nuanced interrelationship between technology, perception, and cognition. The correlation between text and vision constitutes a "representational isomorphism with the natural features of the landscape" (Ihde, 1990, p. 81) that underscores the profound influence of technological mediation on our perceptual experiences. This differentiation between representational and perceptual isomorphism introduces a crucial distinction that warrants closer scrutiny. The difference is visceral, where technology influences the textual artefact. Technologies as artefacts become virtually any material entity that can be engaged in praxis.

This aligns with the assimilation of the artifact into a human-directed or referential praxis vis-à-vis the external world. This is exemplified by the elementary act of retrieving a stone and propelling it. However, in the majority of cases, humans tend to enact some form of rudimentary technical adaptation to the artifact before its utilisation (Ihde, 1998, p. 46). When the representational isomorphism vanishes from a text, there are no demonstrative references other than a technologically encapsulated form of language. The perceptual object concurrently corresponds to the demonstrative references. The technologically embodied sensitivities are different in the printed text based on the referential clarity. Ihde observes: "Textual transparency is hermeneutic transparency, not perceptual transparency" (1990, p. 82).

The assertion that textual transparency equates to hermeneutic transparency rather than perceptual transparency emphasises the differential processes at play in the interpretation of technologically mediated artifacts. While the representational isomorphism between text and vision may facilitate a certain level of interpretive clarity, it remains imperative to interrogate the extent to which this clarity is contingent upon technological mediation. Textual transparency is achieved through hermeneutic procedures rather than perceptual immediacy, which prompts critical reflection on the epistemological implications of technological mediation in shaping our understanding of language and meaning.

Ihde's observation regarding the developmental trajectory of writing and its divergence from oral speech underscores the intricate historical and socio-cultural dynamics that corroborate the evolution of language and communication. The advent of digital technologies has precipitated a paradigm shift in the dissemination and reception of textual artifacts, necessitating a re-evaluation of traditional conceptions of writing and interpretation.

Writing can be assessed, deciphered and interpreted in terms of its linguistic transparency. Therefore, writing becomes an "embodied hermeneutic technics" (Ihde, 1990, p. 84). The role of writing as a technologically mediated form of communication is where the transparency of linguistic expression shapes the perceptual landscape of the textual domain. The notion that writing fashions the world of the text through its capacity for linguistic transparency illuminates the intricate interrelationship between language, meaning, and the experiential structures engendered by technological mediation.

Ihde navigates the complex terrain of human-technology relations within the framework of hermeneutics, elucidating how the mobility from embodiment associations to hermeneutic relations is contingent upon the interplay between human subjects and technological artifacts. The enigmatic nature of this connection, particularly exemplified in his illustration of the control panel as an intermediary between the observer and the referent object, underscores the fluidity and complexity of technological mediation within the perceptual realm (Ihde, 1990, p. 84).

The formulation of the *I*-(technology-world) (Ihde, 1990, p. 86) relation emphasises the continuity and interdependence between human subjects, technology, and the world they inhabit. The ever-altering human-technology relations pose challenges to hermeneutic relations. The position of technicity in hermeneutic relations depends on the intermediary between the instrument and the referent. Perceptually, the user's visual position depends on technology. Therefore, "To read an instrument is an analogue to reading a text. But if the text does not correctly refer, its reference object or its world cannot be present" (Ihde, 1990, p. 87).

The interpretive act of reading instruments parallels the reading of texts, and underscores the significance of technological artifacts as mediators of meaning and understanding. However, there exists the potential limitations and ambiguities inherent within technological mediation, particularly in instances where the referential clarity of the text or instrument is compromised. Without placing the human-technology relations on the hind side of the hermeneutic relations,

Ihde deliberates on the various positions from which the perceptual and the human-technology interact. When technology functions, the technology-world relation maintains its hermeneutic transparency. However, the I-(technology-world) relation is a continuity signifying the relation as a hermeneutic meeting of perceptual relations with technology variations. Interpretive technologies allow the extension of hermeneutic and linguistic possibilities through machines, while reading maintains the perceptual position in relation to the technology. The transformation collectively guides us toward the differences between text and interpretation/meaning:

> The transformation made possible by the hermeneutic relation is a transformation that occurs precisely through *differences* between the text and what is referred to. What is needed is a particular set of textually clear perceptions that 'reduce' to that which is immediately readable (Ihde, 1990, p. 88).

Interpretive technologies as facilitators of linguistic and hermeneutic possibilities through machines punctuate the transformative potential of technological mediation in expanding the horizons of human understanding. The argument that hermeneutic transformation occurs through the differences between the text and its referent invites scrutiny regarding the epistemological foundations of interpretation, and the extent to which technological mediation shapes our understanding of reality.

Hermeneutic relations involving technologies explore the intricate dynamics between perception, interpretation, and technological mediation. The vertical modifications within hermeneutic relations accentuate the transformative potential inherent in the act of reading the world as a readable text. The plasticity within hermeneutic relations is contingent upon the linguistic constructs employed, highlighting the malleability of meaning within interpretive frameworks. The conceptualisation of digital protocols as facilitating the translation and retranslation of perceptual phenomena into analogues of writing represents a significant advancement in understanding the role of technology in mediating human experience. These translation processes as transformations from perceptual gestalt to transmittable codes underscore the transformative power of technological mediation in shaping the perceptual landscape (Ihde, 1990, p. 93).

The mobility from embodied relations to hermeneutic relations transpires from the human-technology continuum. These relations are convoluted as the differences are emphasised through embodied and perceptual inconsistencies. The relation between perception and interpretation is tangled. Perception is interpretational because the process of perception and perceptual relations can be supposed as reading, which involves decoding and interpreting. Nevertheless, specialised technics are involved in the process of reading, making it a specific act. The perceptual position alters in embodiment relations and hermeneutic relations encompassing various interpretive actions.

Hermeneutic transparency is imperceptibly altered through perceptual transparency. Reading with a specific point of reference is not essential to generate a perceptual object. Therefore, the praxis surrounding the perceptual relations accomplishes immediate interpretive examination. Hermeneutic transparency does not incline towards the interpretive affirmations that evolve out of a text. It maintains the extemporaneity through corporeal mobility. In embodiment relations and hermeneutic relations, technology does not attempt to accomplish objectiveness. It remains without any alteration. Nonetheless: "When the technology in embodiment position breaks down or when the instrumentation in hermeneutic position fails, what remains is an obtruding and thus negatively derived object" (Ihde, 1990, p. 94).

While Ihde adeptly navigates the complexities of the human-technology continuum, the assertion that embodied and hermeneutic relations encompass various interpretive actions raises questions regarding the ontological status of these relations. The tangled relationship between perception and interpretation underscores the epistemological challenges inherent in discerning the boundaries between these modes of engagement. Moreover, Ihde's delineation of hermeneutic transparency and its imperceptible alteration through perceptual transparency invites scrutiny regarding the ontological status of technological mediation within interpretive frameworks. That technology remains without alteration in embodiment and hermeneutic relations raises questions regarding the extent to which technological artifacts influence and shape human perception and interpretation. The negative implications of technological breakdowns in embodiment and hermeneutic positions prompt reflection on the fragility of human-technology relations and the potential disruptions to perceptual and interpretive frameworks.

The embodiment relations and hermeneutic relations are differentiated by the existential association between humans and the world. Interpretive strategies and signification processes also are distinguished in these relations. Technology could influence the existential aspects of interpretation because the practical context remains in a state of transition. When technologically inclined praxis is controlled, the referential focus is constrained.

In the progress of technologies, enhancement of instrumentality and materiality advances. The existential sense of embodiment relations is not constrained by isomorphism because hermeneutic variations establish themselves.[5] Within embodiment relations and hermeneutic relations, technology intervenes to facilitate the perceptual and existential association with the world. The technology's materiality, therefore, would vanish. An affirmative materiality emerging from instrumental technologies encompasses the hermeneutic relations. "The bodily-perceptual focus *upon* the instrumental text is a condition of its own peculiar hermeneutic transparency" (Ihde, 1990, p. 97).

Ihde's nuanced differentiation between embodiment relations and hermeneutic relations within the context of human-technology interactions underscores the multifaceted nature of interpretive strategies and signification processes. His elucidation of how technology influences the existential aspects of interpretation amidst a landscape of perpetual transition is both insightful and pertinent. However, critical scrutiny reveals certain conceptual ambiguities and tensions within Ihde's framework.

While Ihde highlights the transformative potential of technology in shaping the existential associations between humans and the world, his characterisation of technological intervention as facilitating perceptual and existential engagement warrants closer examination.

---

5   Citing the relation between music and technology, Ihde writes: "computer-produced music clearly occurs much more fully within the range of hermeneutic relations, in some cases with the emergence of random-sound generation very close to the sense of otherness, which will characterize the next set of relations where the technology emerges as other" (1990, p. 96).

That the materiality of technology vanishes within embodiment and hermeneutic relations raises questions regarding the extent to which technological artifacts influence and shape human perception and existential understanding.

Ihde's depiction of an affirmative materiality emerging from instrumental technologies within hermeneutic relations presents a somewhat deterministic view of technological mediation. The proposition that the bodily-perceptual focus upon instrumental text constitutes its peculiar hermeneutic transparency overlooks the complex interplay between technological artifacts and human agency in shaping interpretive frameworks.

The proposition that hermeneutic variations establish themselves within embodiment and hermeneutic relations implies a deterministic view of technological mediation, wherein the influence of technology on interpretive strategies is portrayed as a foregone conclusion. However, a critical examination reveals that human agency, and socio-cultural factors also play a significant role in shaping the interpretive landscape.

Digital technologies are hermeneutic technologies encompassing hermeneutic relations as they can curtail the distance between the world and its representations (interpretations). Digital technologies can bridge the gap between the text and its interpretive process. The materiality of digital technologies explores the information to communicate it to the hermeneutic self. The connection between the materiality of digital technologies and information is a social actuality anticipating digital traceability. Reality is digitalised through symbols and signs making sense and meaning to the hermeneutic self. Digital traceability is independent of sense and meaning. They are defined autonomously from each other without any specific signification. The nature of the interpretation of signs, in digital traceability, is mechanical and material. It is a challenging venture:

> A difficult exercise for us human beings, who are above all semiotic animals that approach what surrounds us by its significance, as a message that we must interpret since the world is not merely reduced to what is shown here and now (Bachimont qtd. in Romele, 2020, p. 23).

Digital technologies accentuate "a process of symbolic distanciation from the world and it is only on this basis that they appropriate the entire world and become effective into it" (Romele, 2020, p. 21). It is within the subtleties of distanciation and appropriation of digital traceability, Romele locates digital hermeneutics. The

> [...] digital is structurally based on a performative distanciation from the world that the digital cannot realize its aspiration of being the world, but rather continues to need the world as its interlocutor and as its "otherness" (Romele, 2020, p. 21).

Hermeneutic relations between division and appropriation locate a space in digital traceability. Ricoeur inclines towards "fusion of horizons" to balance the appropriation of approaches involving interpretation (Romele, 2020, p. 20). The interaction between the object and the text, and the intention of the author and the reader are connected through various approaches to appropriating texts.

With the development and ubiquitous presence of 'technoscience', the interpretive activity has gained further momentum. Digital hermeneutics inclines heavily on materiality offering new possibilities of how we read and interpret the text. The relationship between human beings and the computer is a system that offers mind to the machine. It is a connection between digital information and human perception. The materialist nature of phenomenology and technology assumes that the juxtaposition of human corporeality with artificial instantiation serves to catalyse the evolution of hermeneutical discourse. Artificial intelligence serves as the nexus through which human cognition and computational prowess converge via a corporeal conduit.

The automaton, bereft of corporeal form, lacks the perceptual and kinesthetic faculties inherent to organic embodiment. Notwithstanding, a demarcation persists between electronic and corporeal vessels, yet the automaton proffers an expanded hermeneutic paradigm, thus enhancing its function within the interpretative praxis. The ensuing perceptual phenomenon engenders a process characterised by its amalgamation of scientific rigor with hermeneutic inquiry. The instrument extends itself as a human embodiment by becoming 'virtually transparent' in the interpretive activity. Thinking happens differently for a computer or thinking never happens. It is only through an illusion that human resemblance is assumed in a computer.

# Works Cited

Berry, D.M. (2011). *The Philosophy of Software: Code and Mediation in the Digital Age*. Palgrave Macmillan.

Buholf, I.N. (1980). *Wilhelm Dilthey: A Hermeneutic Approach to the Study of History and Culture*. Martinus Nijhoff Publishers

Fazi, B.M. (2018). *Computation: Abstraction, Experience and Indeterminacy in Computational Aesthetics*. Rowan and Littlefield.

Fickers, A. et al., (2022). Digital history and hermeneutics: Between theory and practice: An Introduction. In A. Fickers and J. Tatarinov (Eds). *Digital History and Hermeneutics: Between Theory and Practices*. De Gruyter. https://doi.org/10.1515/9783110723991

Floridi, L. (2005). Is semantic information meaningful data? *Philosophy and Phenomenological Research 70* (2), 351–370. https://doi.org/10.1111/j.1933-1592.2005.tb00531.x

Goodman, N. (1978). *Ways of Worldmaking*. Hackett Publishing.

Gray, J. (2018). Three aspects of data worlds. *Krisis: Journal for Contemporary Philosophy 1*, 3–17. https://archive.krisis.eu/three-aspects-of-data-worlds/

Heidegger, M. (1996). *Being and Time*. SUNY Press.

Ihde, D. (1990). *Technology and the Lifeworld: From Garden to Earth*. Indiana University Press.

Ihde, D. (1997). Thingly hermeneutics/technoconstructions. *Man and World 30*(3), 369–381. https://doi.org/10.1023/A:1004267804953

Ihde, D. (1998). *Expanding Hermeneutics: Visualism in Science*, Northwestern University Press.

Ihde, D. (1999). Expanding Hermeneutics. In M. Feher, O. Kiss, L. Ropolyi (Eds). *Hermeneutics and Science*, Springer Netherlands.

Ihde, D. (2006). Postphenomenology and the lifeworld. In M. Geib (Ed.). *Phenomenology and Ecology*. (pp. 39–51). Simon Silverman Phenomenology Center.

Ihde, D. (2020). Language and hermeneutics. *Technology and Language 1*(1), 34–36. https://doi.org/10.48417/technolang.2020.01.07

Ihde, D. (2022). *Material Hermeneutics: Reversing the Linguistic Turn*. Routledge. https://doi.org/10.4324/9781003153122

Introna, L.D. (1993). Information: A hermeneutic perspective. *Proceedings First European Conference of Information Systems*. Henley on Thames (UK).

Latour, B. (1994). Technical mediations. *Common Knowledge 3*(2), 29–64.

Mitcham, C. (1994). *Thinking through Technology: The Path between Engineering and Philosophy*. The University of Chicago Press.

Ricoeur, P. (1991) *From Text to Action: Essays in Hermeneutics II*. Northwestern University Press.

Shannon, C.E., & Weaver, W. (1949). *The Mathematical Theory of Communication*. University of Illinois Press. https://www.doi.org/10.1002/j.1538-7305.1948.tb01338.x

Smithies, J. (2017). *The Digital Humanities and the Digital Modern*. Palgrave Macmillan.

Tripathi, A.K. (2016). The significance of digital hermeneutics for the philosophy of technology. In M. Kelly & J. Beilby (Eds). *Information Cultures in the Digital Age*. (pp. 143–57). Springer Fachmedien Wiesbaden.

Verbeek, P.P. (2005). *What Things Do: Philosophical Reflections on Technology, Agency, and Design*. Penn State University Press.

Verbeek, P.P. (2008). Morality in design: Design ethics and the morality of technological artefacts. In P.E. Vermas et.al., (Eds). *Philosophy and Design: From Engineering to Architecture*. (pp. 91–103). Springer.

# 7. 'Aboutness' and semantic knowledge: A corpus-driven analysis of *Yajnavalkya Smriti* on the status and rights of women

## Gopa Nayak and Navreet Kaur Rana

## Abstract

This essay establishes the use of computational methods to study the semantics of a historical corpus compiled from the ancient Indian text of *Yajnavalkya Smriti*. Although the use of corpora has been extended to the study of computational semantics, in addition to grammar usage and patterns of language, they have mostly been limited to word-sense disambiguation, structural disambiguation or analysing a semantic space in terms of calculating semantic distances and determining relations between words within a corpus. This study adopts the use of computational semantics on 'aboutness' and 'knowledge-free analysis' within a limited aspect of 'aboutness' based on the methodology of Philips (1985).

The text-only corpus of this study comprises 36,000 words of verses of the *Yajnavalkya Smriti* text translated by Vidyarnava (1918; 2010) from the original Sanskrit to English. In this study, 'aboutness' and 'knowledge-free analysis' aim to find the semantics of collocations and bring out bias-free information on the inheritance rights and the status of women in ancient India as described in the text. The application of the ubiquitous yet rarely applied concept of 'aboutness' is used to derive semantics in an unprecedented manner from an ancient historical text.

This research on 'aboutness', which has seldom been used in computational semantics (Yablo, 2014), opens up avenues for further research on corpus analysis for extracting semantic knowledge from ancient texts to minimise knowledge bias.

## Keywords

Corpus linguistics; *Yajnavalkya Smriti*; 'Aboutness'; semantic knowledge.

## Introduction: Digital Humanities and corpus linguistics

Corpus linguistics involves the study of digitised text with the help of computational tools and digital methodologies involving concordances and software tools within the broader field of Digital Humanities (DH, hereafter) (Bjork, 2012; Hockey, 2000; Kirschenbaum, 2016; Schreibman, 2012; Svensson, 2016). Corpus linguistics had existed much earlier than the inception of DH, but DH emerged as a superset that accommodated lesser-studied or relatively later-developed disciplines. While corpus linguistics is often considered the basis of quantitative research, DH has the potential to uncover both qualitative and quantitative features of a corpus. Building a corpus and analysing it computationally is fundamentally a DH project. As Hockey (2000) explains, DH involves applications of tools and techniques of computing to research on subjects that are loosely defined as "the humanities", or in British English "the arts". Digital Humanities are thus computer-supported humanities (Simanowski, 2016).

A corpus is essentially a collection of natural language consisting of texts, and/or transcriptions of speech or signs, constructed with a specific purpose. A corpus may contain a text in one language, as in a monolingual corpus, or in multiple languages, called multilingual corpora. A diachronic corpus, on the other hand, is a corpus containing texts from different periods and is used to study the progress or change in language.

The corpus under investigation in this study is a text-only corpus which is a classic scripture named *Yajnavalkya Smriti*, originally written in Sanskrit by the sage Yajnavalkya, now translated into English. It contains a substantial amount of Sanskrit vocabulary. It is a historical corpus and is considered closed as it cannot evolve. It is estimated to have been written around the third to the fifth century CE. The corpus designed for this study has been collected from the scanned scripture available in digitised form at a web portal that supports archived documents. The digital format is an English translation of the 1010 verses, including a commentary along with a detailed glossary. However, the corpus used here for analysis consists of verses only from the edited version of the text translated into English by Rai Bahadur Srisa Chandra Vidyarnava with commentary and notes (1918; 2010).[1] Although this corpus is compiled from an ancient text and may therefore be considered a historical corpus, the focus is on the semantic knowledge of the corpus rather than semantic change (McGillivray, Hengchen, Lähteenoja, Palma, & Vatri, 2019). On the other hand, this research draws on the digitised version of the translated text in English. The digital version opened up the use of computational tools in analysing this ancient text (Allan, & Robinson, 2011; deGruyter. Lamoureux, & Camus, 2024; Martin, Norén, Mähler, Marklund, & Martin, 2024).

## 'Knowledge-free analysis' and 'Aboutness'

This study draws on the concepts of 'knowledge-free analysis' and 'aboutness' as discussed at length by Martin Phillips in his book titled *Aspects of Text Structure: An Investigation of the Lexical Organisation of Text* (1985). The book elaborates on knowledge-free analysis of non-linear lexical structures, also called macrostructures, through language patterning using graphs. However, for our study, we restrict ourselves to a limited aspect of 'aboutness' in order to find the semantics of certain collocations from our corpus. Phillips states that the reader has a psychological sensation that a book is 'about' something and he argues that this 'aboutness' is not adequately accounted for in any kind of linguistics analysis (Phillips, 1985, p. vii). In his study, Phillips tried to capture 'aboutness' by dropping all non-functional words and thus understand the 'aboutness' in the literal meaning of words in the text. These texts included five science books and novels by Virginia Woolf,

---

1    https://archive.org/details/yajnavalkyasmrit00yj/page/n9/mode/2up

Graham Greene, and Christopher Evan. The literal meaning of a word is contextual and is always associated with the neighbourhood of the node word. Quoting Phillips, "the crucial point concerning aboutness is that it is a type of meaning arising from the global structuring of text" (Phillips, 1985, p. 30). Following his research hypothesis:

> [...] knowledge-free analysis of the terms in a text [...] will reveal evidence of systematic and large-scale patterning which can be interpreted as contributing to the semantic structure of text and hence as constituting a major device through which the notion of content arises (Phillips, 1985, p. 26).

'Aboutness' as a concept was expanded by Yablo (2014) as "the relation that meaningful items bear to whatever it is that they are on or of or that they address or concern" (Yablo, 2014, p. 1). Bruza, Song and Wong (2000) sought to define 'aboutness' in terms of a model of Information Retrieval (IR), arguing for a linguistic analysis of a text in line with Hutchins (1977) and explaining aboutness under a semantic network. Although the concept of 'aboutness' was studied by Yablo (2014) and Bruza, Song and Wong (2000), it was Phillips' model of aboutness in terms of deciphering the meaning of the text that has been widely adopted in corpus-based research on the Fukushima War (Kalashnikova, 2023), the COVID-19 lockdown (Herat, 2022) and social tagging (Kehoe & Gee, 2011) among others. A "knowledge-free analysis of text [...] contributing to the semantic structure of text" (Phillips, 198, p. 26) is also the premise on which the methodology of this study is based.

Since the concept of 'aboutness' is used in this study to derive meaning, the concepts of semantic prosody and semantic preference deserve attention. The relationship between semantic prosody and computational methods was revealed by Louw (1993) and subsequently, in a later study, semantic prosody was defined as "a form of meaning which is established through the proximity of a consistent series of collocates" (Louw, 2000, p. 57). Hunston (2002, p. 142) explains that "semantic prosody can be observed only by looking at a large number of instances of a word or phrase because it relies on the typical use of a word or phrase". Sinclair is of the opinion that semantic prosody refers to the usage of a word that "gives an impression of an attitudinal or pragmatic meaning" (Sinclair, 1999). Kalashnikova (2023) along the lines of Sinclair (1998) and Stubbs (2009), confirms that semantic prosody reveals conscious views or intended actions. Thus, semantic prosody could describe the pragmatic or semantic sense that arises when a keyword and its specific collocates are in the vicinity of each other. For instance: "bad weather" and "bad company" derive a negative connotation whenever they occur together. The word "bad" itself has a negative sense to it, but when it is used in the phrase "Not bad at all", it indicates positivity. Such is the impact of the company words keep! Most of the time, semantic preference and semantic prosody have been used to describe the same phenomenon, but at other times the two are considered different but closely related. Therefore, the need for precise definitions of the two terms arises. Partington (2004) has described the difference between the two in his claim that semantic preference and semantic prosody have different operating scopes. While 'semantic preference' relates the node item to another item from a particular semantic set, 'semantic prosody' can affect wider stretches of text. 'Semantic preference' can be viewed as a feature of collocates, while 'semantic prosody' is a feature of the node word. Partington (2004, p. 151) also adds that these two terms interact. While semantic prosody "dictates the general environment which constrains the preferential choices of the node item", semantic preference "contributes powerfully to building semantic prosody".

The relevance of semantic preference and semantic prosody to this discussion is that we have limited our computational study to obtaining collocates only, and no other concepts, because we want to derive the most pristine semantic sense out of the text in order to justify a 'knowledge-free analysis'. Applying other concepts like semantic prosody and semantic preferences would have given us information about the possible usage of a particular word or characteristic features of collocates, both of which are not the intent behind this computational exercise. Also, collocates, in this case, are the first level of analysis and by applying semantic preference and semantic prosody we run the risk of introducing a bias or reducing the degree of 'knowledge-free' analysis.

The following section includes the source of corpus, the process of making the corpus, and the methodology to comprehend and draw conclusions on the status and rights of women from the text.

# Design of the corpus

*Yajnavalkya Smriti* along with the *Manu Smriti* are widely acknowledged as the texts that describe the codes of conduct, moral duties and statecraft in the Indian subcontinent in ancient times (Bhat, 2006; Bhattacharji, 1991; Tomy, 2019; Tharakan & Tharakan, 1975). While *Manu Smriti* has been widely read and researched, *Yajnavalkya Smriti* remains less so. *Yajnavalkya Smriti* is less popular as a reference in the legal history of India compared to *Manu Smriti*, a comprehensive document on the fundamental religious and philosophical conventions observed by the people of India. *Manu Smriti*, or the 'Code of Manu', which has made a lasting impact in India, has been studied even in modern India for the ordinances and decrees it contains relating to the law. It lists the obligations of the kings and rules of their administration of justice based on Dharma. *Yajnavalkya Smriti* is next to the *Manu Smriti* in authority and recognition. The codes mentioned in *Yajnavalkya Smriti* are largely based on *Manu Smriti* but are more liberal on certain matters than *Manu Smriti*, particularly on women's right to property, inheritance and criminal penalty (Thukar, & Thakur, 1930). Justice M. Rama Jois (2004) in his book, *Legal and Constitutional History of India*, argues that *Yajnavalkya Smriti* deals exhaustively with subjects like the creation of valid documents, the law of mortgages, hypothecation, partnership and joint ventures and emphasises that *Yajnavalkya Smriti* is scientific and more methodical than *Manu Smriti*.

Robert Lingat, a French-born academic and legal scholar whose area of practice was classical Hindu Law, in his book *The Classical Law of India* (translated by J. Duncan M Derrett) (Lingat, 1973), also states that the text in *Yajnavalkya Smriti* is closer to legal philosophy and transitions away from being Dharma speculations found in earlier Dharma-related texts such as the Vedas, Upanishads and Puranas and focusses more on the practices and not on the moral or religious aspects of these practices. Not only as the less studied scripture, but as a liberal document *Yajnavalkya Smriti* remains worth exploring to understand the historical rights and privileges of women mentioned in this ancient text, especially when this document is referred to even in 21st-century India for reference in the legal field (Darshini, 2001; Deodhar, 2010; Tharakan & Tharakan, 1975).

While the rationale for using the text of *Yajnavalkya Smriti* lies in the relevance of the text to the interpretation of the legal system in India even today, the justification for using the translation (1918) can be explained only because this remains the only translation of the ancient text available in English. The digitised version of the translation (2010) available on the University of Toronto website also adds to the reliability and validity of the text. This translated text has been the source of reference for recent publications in different fields of study by scholars (Acevedo, 2013; Ambedkar, 2020; Kiss, 2019; Nongbri, 2018).

The entire text of this ancient scripture consists of three chapters, namely *Achara Adhyaya* (meaning 'proper conduct' and consisting of 368 verses), *Vyavahara Adhyaya* (meaning 'legal procedures' and consisting of 307 verses) and *Prayashchitta Adhyaya* (meaning 'penance' and consisting of 335 verses). There are 1010 verses in all the three chapters. The available text is comprehensive and comprises the verses, detailed commentary on these verses called *The Mitakshara*, and an exhaustive glossary authored by Balambhatta. For this study, the verses without commentary or glossary were chosen. We chose only the verses as part of our corpus because the commentary and glossary, if included in the corpus, would have affected the statistical analysis and in turn would have influenced the semantic findings. To keep the semantic discoveries unbiased, the text had to be scrutinised with a neutral perspective. Thus, although the entire text was 1894 pages, it was reduced to 127 pages, which is approximately 6.7% of the original text in this study.

## Methodology

The methodology adopted for this study focuses on the notion of the context and 'aboutness' and will be implemented to examine the corpus of *Yajnavalkya Smriti* to be discussed in the following section. The methodology applied here is independent of any natural language understanding or knowledge representation system and thus supports knowledge-free analysis. The text can be interpreted as per the readers' understanding but interpretations vary and can be prejudiced.

The study aims to bring forward an analysis based solely on the findings from the Antconc (3.5.8) concordancer tool instead of intuition or experience. Paul Doyle (2005), in a conference proceeding, interpreted the term 'knowledge-free analysis' adopted by Phillips (1985) as an analysis that did not depend on semantic notions originating with the introspection of the researcher. Rather it dealt empirically with the "syntagmatic patterning of the textual substance" itself (Phillips, 1985, p. 26). Assuming that the meaning of a content word, which he has referred to as a node, can be established by the company it keeps, Phillips analysed the collocations of the node word inside a span of four words on either side, dropped all non-function words and attempted to group all such nodes on the basis of these collocations, and displays this distributional network by a statistical technique known as cluster analysis.[2]

Extrapolating from this method and attempting to derive wider notions about the situation of women in ancient India as per the text, the heuristics that are applied in this study examine the collocation of the words through the target words, "women", "man", "wife" and "husband", with the help of a corpus analyser tool, AntConc (version 3.5.8). To continue with the knowledge-free analysis, it is necessary to find out the collocates of the target words. The neighbourhood of the target words will help to extract a semantic sense out of collocates.

The significance of the concept of collocation has long been recognised in theoretical linguistics. It was first brought to light by Firth in 1957 (Bartsch, & Evert, 2014). The study of collocation has evolved in the form of semantic approach, lexical approach (Halliday, 1966; Sinclair, 1966), and the integrated approach (Mitchell, 1971). The study of collocation forms an integral part of corpus-driven approaches and has been widely adopted (Farghal & Obeidat, 1995; Ahrens & Jiang, 2020). In this study, a corpus-based approach is adopted to uncover the status and rights of women in ancient India through a semantic analysis. To derive an absolute semantic sense, word clusters of the normalised collocates are considered. The subsequent section discusses the relevant collocates and their clusters. Once the collocations are determined, and non-functional collocates are dropped, the remaining collocates will be analysed semantically. For clarity, the relevant verses are also quoted alongside the collocates.

In relation to the FAIR principles, i.e., Findable, Accessible, Interoperable, and Reusable (Wilkinson, Dumontier, Aalbersberg,

---

2    Cluster analysis aims to detect and graphically to reveal structures or patterns in the distribution of data items, variables, or texts.

Appleton, Axton, Baak, & Mons, 2016) as they apply to the development of software, the focus of this research was on the use of software rather than its development. However, this research created a corpus with a clear research intent (Barker, Chue Hong, Katz, Lamprecht, Martinez-Ortiz, Psomopoulos, & Honeyman, 2022). The AntConc software used in this research is a freeware corpus analysis toolkit for concordancing and text analysis developed by Laurence Anthony, a professor at Waseda University in Japan. Anthony (2009) explains that this is a standalone, multiplatform software tool developed by him in collaboration with linguists to extract data from digital texts. This is the first step in interpreting the text. The unique feature of this toolkit is that it works effectively with files made in Microsoft Word and accepts character sets and token definitions making it easier to use, especially for analysing a historical text. Anthony (2013) reiterates the effectiveness of AntConc as a tool for corpus linguists to analyse texts, and demonstrates its popularity. Bjork (2012) claims that the use of AntConc for extracting data from a corpus is effective. Thus, the AntConc software follows the FAIR principles since it is accessible as free software and has been used by researchers other than the team that developed it.

The CARE principles, including Collective benefit, Authority to control, Responsibility, and Ethics (Carroll, Herczog, Hudson, Russell, & Stall, 2021) were also taken into consideration in this research on an ancient text. While collective benefit was embedded in this research, which aims to uncover knowledge-free semantics of an ancient text, the 'authority to control' feature does not apply. Responsibility and ethics were guiding principles. Personal biases that could influence the outcome of the research were controlled by using this software.

## Keyword selection criteria

Drawing inference from the research on keyword analysis (Baker, 2009; Kehoe & Gee, 2011; Scott, 1997), this study conducted the keyword selection and included eight relevant keywords: "woman" / "women", "husband" / "husbands", "wife" / "wives", "man" / "men" (the name of a woman or man as common nouns are not present in the text owing to its nature as a treatise on law). The concordance and collocates are analysed in their respective clusters.

The total collocations of the regular expression[3] '**wom.n**' (this regular expression will search for both woman and women) are 82 in number (refer to Figure 7.1). After normalisation, dropping non-functional words, and considering only relevant collocates, we came across the following:

- Collocates of woman/women: *stridhana*, property, debt, paid by, childless women, never independent, menstruating.

- Collocates of man/men: intercourse, fined.

- Collocates of husband: respected by, devoted, wife alone.

- Collocates of husbands: No relevant collocates of 'husbands' were found in the context of a wife. The collocates spoke about the general conduct of all wives towards their husbands. However, this was not the case with the keyword "wives".

- Collocates of wives: eldest, others.

- Collocates of wife: loving, same class, unchaste, deprived, devoted to wife alone.

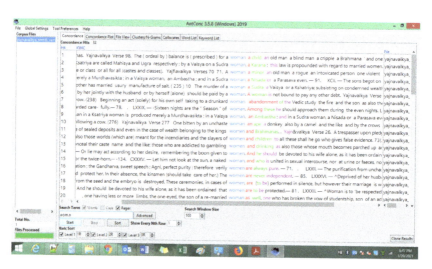

Fig. 7.1 Concordance of regular expression 'wom.n'.

---

3    A regular expression is a sequence of characters that define a search pattern. The dot (.) is a special character used to match, at most, one character.

# Analysis of findings

This section describes each collocate along with the cluster.

## Collocates of woman/women

*Stridhana* is one collocate of the regular expression 'wom.n' referring to the ownership rights of women for any tangible property. *Stridhana* is a compound word formed of two words: *stree*, meaning woman, and *dhana*, meaning money/wealth. In this case, money equates to the tangible property or assets that a woman owns. In the corpus, *stridhana* is suitably defined along with the ownership rights in the verse 143 of the second chapter, the *Vyavhara Adhyaya*. The English translation of the verse defines *stridhana* as whatever is presented to the woman by her parents or siblings during her wedding. In the subsequent verses (verse 144(2) of *Vyavhara Adhyaya*), it is said that if the women passes away without issue, her kinsmen can take the property (the *stridhana* is demonstrated by "it" and the woman as "she"). Verse 145 of *Vyavhara Adhyaya* further goes on to explain the inheritance rules if a woman is childless (childless being one of the collocates of woman). The relevant cluster for the collocate is "The property of a childless woman". The verse explains that if the woman is childless, the property goes to her husband. This is also indicative of the ownership rights of the women.

> Verse 143.
> What was given (to a woman) by the father the mother the husband
> or a brother or was received by her at the nuptial fire as also
> that which was presented to her on her husband's marriage to another wife
> or any other is denominated (stridhana) a woman's property."

> Verse 144.
> If she pass away without issue her kinsmen should take it.

> Verse 145.
> The property of a childless woman married according to any of the
> four forms such as the Brahma and the others goes to her husband; it
> will go to her daughters if she leave progeny; and in other forms of
> marriage it goes to her parents.

The next collocate of woman is "debt", which has been used multiple times and brings to light the fact that a woman could borrow money, and under what circumstances she is liable to pay it back. The cluster, "A debt agreed to by her" of verse 49 of *Vyavahara Adhyaya* is sufficient to demonstrate that a woman could borrow money as men could, although it is not very clear from this cluster whether women could borrow money for their own needs or only to meet the requirements of their family. Other clusters extracted from the same verse throw more light on this fact: the cluster "which was contracted by her jointly with the husband" and "or by herself (alone)". The cluster "which (debt) was contracted by her jointly with the husband" clearly states that the husband and wife could take a debt together. It also indicates that "woman" and "man" can jointly take up financial responsibility. The other cluster "or by herself (alone)" implies the independence and equality women enjoyed in the ancient era, as they could take independent decisions regarding financial responsibilities. The cluster "paid by a woman" also establishes this fact.

Although the collocates above point towards the financial liberty and responsibility women enjoyed, there is corpus evidence that proves that women were considered to be dependent and impure during menstruation. Verse 85 of *Achara Adhyaya* indicates that women are always dependent on their kinsmen—father, husband and sons. The cluster collocate is "never independent". Similarly, a menstruating woman is considered impure according to verse 168, *Achara Adhyaya*, which suggests avoiding food touched by menstruating women.

> Verse 49.
> A debt agreed to by her or which was contracted by
> her jointly with the husband or by herself (alone) should be
> paid by a woman. A woman is not bound to pay any
> other debt.
>
> Verse 85
> When a maiden, her father; when
> married, her husband; and when old, her sons, should
> protect her. In their absence, the kinsmen (should take
> care of her.) The women are never independent. —
>
> Verse 168.
> What has been touched by a menstruating woman, or what has been
> publicly offered, food
> given by one who is not the owner, or what has been

smelt by a cow, or the leavings of birds, or what has been wilfully touched with feet (these foods) let him avoid.

## Collocates of man/men

There are 67 concordances of man and men (Refer to Figure 7.2) searched using the regular expression '<space>m.n<space>', but with relevance to women or with respect to men's duties towards women, the collocate "intercourse" is relevant. It speaks about "unnatural" intercourse as a punishable offence and deems that the man practising it should be appropriately fined.

"Intercourse", "improper part" and "fined" come under the same cluster. The original verse recommended a fine of 24 panas to be imposed on a man who had intercourse with a woman in an "improper" way (verse 293).

Verse 293.
If a man have intercourse with a woman in an improper part
 or make water or void excretion he shall be fined twenty-four panas
 so also he who has connexion with a female devotee.

Fig. 7.2 Concordance of regular expression 'm.n'.

## *Collocates of wife*

"Wife loving" is a collocate that draws our attention towards the conduct of a husband towards his wife. The cluster worth considering is "He should be wife loving" or "It is [...] expected of a husband to be wife loving" (*Achara Adhyaya*, verse 121).

"Same class" is a collocate of wife and the entire cluster is "wife of same class". This is evidence enough that marriages across castes (the term class is used for the four varnas, Brahmin, Khatriyas, Vaishyas and Shudras, in the text) was a norm at that time (*Achara Adhyaya*, verse 62).

"Unchaste wife" as a collocate refers to the conduct of a wife. The translated verse (*Achara Adhayaya*, verse 70) states that an unchaste wife should be deprived of all authority and should be unadorned. "Deprived of authority" is a collocate of wife. The way that the ancient text has described the duties of both men and women is also evidence of their equal status in ancient India.

Similarly, the collocates of wives, "eldest" and "others", clearly indicate polygamy. The cluster is "religious duties are to be performed by the eldest and not by the others".

> Verse 121.
> He should be wife-loving, pure, maintaining the dependent, and be engaged in the Sraddha, and
> the ceremonies, and with the Mantra "Namah" he should perform the five sacrifices.

> Verse 62.
> In marrying a girl of the same class the
> hand should be taken, the Ksatriya girl should take
> hold of an arrow, the Vaisya should hold a goad, in the marriage with one of higher class.

> Verse 70.
> The unchaste wife should he deprived of
> authority, should he unadorned, allowed food barely
> sufficient to sustain her body, rebuked, and let sleep on
> low bed, and thus allowed to dwell.

> Verse 88.
> When there exists a wife of the
> same class (savarna), religious works are not to be performed by a wife
> of another class. When there are
> wives of the same class, then religious duties are to be
> performed by the eldest and not by the others.

## Collocates of husband

Another cluster which included "husband" as a keyword in the context of "woman" is "to be respected by her husband" (*Achara Adhyaya*, verse 82). "Respected by" and "her husband" form the collocates of husband and are self-explanatory. Similarly, "devoted to" and "wife alone" form the cluster of the same sentence and are collocates of "husband", and they are indicative of the fact that a husband is also expected to be devoted to his wife (*Achara Adhyaya*, verse 81).

> Verse 81.
> Or lie may act according to her desire,
> remembering the boon given to women. And he should
> be devoted to his wife alone, as it has been ordained
> that women are to be protected.

> Verse 82.
> Woman is to be respected by her husband, brother, father, kindred,
> (Jnati), mother-in-law, father-in-law, husband's younger brother, and
> the bandhus, with ornaments, clothes and food.

# Discussion

Two important concepts have been discussed in this chapter. The first is 'knowledge-free analysis' and the notion of 'aboutness', and the second is the revelations about the status and rights of women as described in the *Yajnavalkya Smriti*. The study was based on the rationale that 'aboutness' can be adopted as a methodology to extract semantic knowledge from a given text. This is based on established research and thus can inferentially be applied to discover an unbiased, neutral viewpoint about any given text. While it is inevitable that there will not be a final interpretation of any text, approaching the same text with the concept of 'aboutness' has the potential to discover unknown or lesser-known meanings of texts. The less well-known the text is, the lower is the degree of 'aboutness', thus reducing the chances of any bias that can creep in when deriving semantic sense from the text.

The semantic knowledge derived from this study through the knowledge-free analysis of the corpus, developed from the translated text in English of the original Sanskrit, revealed details concerning the rights and status of women in ancient India. Although women appeared to be dependent on their kinsmen, such as fathers and husbands, they had ownership rights or *stridhana*. These rights were gained through the gifts a woman received from her parents and siblings, yet these rights were passed on to her husband if she died without a daughter. Otherwise, the property of a mother is passed on to the daughter. These ownership rights of women, prevalent in ancient India, were not granted to women until recently in 21st-century India. The daughter's equal right to inherit their parent's property was passed only as recently as 2005.

Women, according to this text, could not only pass on these ownership rights but they enjoyed financial liberty and were expected to carry the burden of economic liability and could borrow money. In addition, a detailed description of the duties and responsibilities of both men and women in social institutions such as family and marriage are provided in the text. These descriptions reflect the status accorded to women in ancient India.

In the context of marriage, love and loyalty formed the bond between men and women. Unlike the practices prevalent in modern India, where caste remains an important criterion for arranged marriages, the text shows that ancient Indians married across castes. Explicit instruction on the practice of conjugal relationships and punishment for men indulging in "improper" sexual intercourse reflect the respect accorded to women. Women also partook of religious activities and sacrifices alongside their husbands and were given respect.

There is some evidence to suggest that feminine reproductive processes such as menstruation were not viewed without prejudice, and there are instances when they were considered impure.

## Conclusions

The conflicting discoveries from this analysis suggest that assessing a text computationally nullifies the probability of introspection, thus making this a knowledge-free analysis. The conflict reflected in the computational analysis adopted in this study could have been compromised by human intervention or bias. However, computational analysis with a knowledge-free approach has led to an objective exposition of the text.

This study shows that computational methods, when applied to semantic outcomes, produce unbiased results. This contradicts the common view that computational methods should only be employed in certain research areas, which excludes semantics because of their complexity (Jenset & McGillivray, 2017). However, the results of this research reaffirm McGillivray's (2020) view that the combination of computational modelling of semantic analysis with linguistic intuition can drive a methodological shift in research on historical texts. This can open new avenues for interdisciplinary research in corpus linguistics. This study could act as a trigger for research on other ancient texts that are digitalised, leading them to be analysed in a new light using the lens of corpus linguistics. It is past time to study ancient texts to find a new perspective or to reaffirm the established one with knowledge-free analysis. The corpus compiled for this research can pave the way for new research examining it from many different angles including social, economic and political critiques involving caste-based systems, laws, penance, conjugal laws and inheritance to name a few.

The findings of this research do not in any way attempt to make other approaches to the critical analysis of ancient literature redundant. On the other hand, it provides an effective alternative to critically analyse texts, particularly those that are large in volume. Moreover, this research shows that the focus of the research when computational coding is used can make the analysis objective and less time-consuming. As ancient literature becomes digitised, linguistic research can exploit computational tools to unearth evidence effectively, with benefits in terms of the time spent and the volume of material covered.

# Works Cited

Acevedo, D.D. (2013). Developments in Hindu law from the colonial to the present. *Religion Compass 7*(7), 252–262. https://doi.org/10.1111/rec3.12052

Ahrens, K., & Jiang, M. (2020). Source domain verification using corpus-based tools. *Metaphor and Symbol 35*(1), 43–55. https://doi.org/10.1080/10926488.2020.1712783

Allan, K., & Robinson, J.A. (Eds). (2011). *Current Methods in Historical Semantics* (Vol. 73). Walter de Gruyter. https://doi.org/10.1515/9783110252903

Ambedkar, B.R. (2020). *Beef, Brahmins, and Broken Men: An Annotated Critical Selection from the Untouchables*. Columbia University Press. https://doi.org/10.7312/ambe19584-008

Anthony, L. (2009). Issues in the design and development of software tools for corpus studies: The case for collaboration. In P. Baker (Ed.). *Contemporary Corpus Linguistics*. (pp. 87–104). Continuum Press.

Anthony, L. (2012). AntConc (Version 3.3.5) [Computer Software]. Waseda University. http://www.antlab.sci.waseda.ac.jp/

Anthony, L. (2013). A critical look at software tools in corpus linguistics. *Linguistic Research 30*(2), 141–161.

Barker, M., Chue Hong, N.P., Katz, D.S., Lamprecht, A.L., Martinez-Ortiz, C., Psomopoulos, F., and Honeyman, T. (2022). Introducing the FAIR principles for research software. *Scientific Data 9*(1), 622. https://doi.org/10.1038/s41597-022-01710-x

Bartsch, S., & Evert, S. (2014). Towards a Firthian notion of collocation. *Vernetzungsstrategien Zugriffsstrukturen und automatisch ermittelte Angaben in Internetwörterbüchern 2*(1), 48–61.

Bhat, P.I. (2006). Protection against unjust enrichment and undeserved misery as the essence property right jurisprudence in "Mitakshara". *Journal of the Indian Law Institute 48*(2), 155–174.

Bhattacharji, S. (1991). Economic rights of ancient Indian Women. *Economic and Political Weekly 26*(9/10), 507–512.

Bjork, O. (2012). Digital Humanities and the first-year writing course. In B.D. Hirsch (Ed.). *Digital Humanities Pedagogy: Practices, Principles and Politics*. Open Book Publishers.

Bruza, P.D., Song, D.W., & Wong, K.F. (2000). Aboutness from a common-sense perspective. *Journal of the American Society for Information Science 51*(12), 1090–1105.

Carroll, S.R., Herczog, E., Hudson, M., Russell, K., & Stall, S. (2021). Operationalizing the CARE and FAIR principles for Indigenous data futures. *Scientific Data 8*(1), 108. https://doi.org/10.1038/s41597-021-00892-0

Darshini, P. (2001). Women and patrilineal inheritance during the Gupta Period. In *Proceedings of the Indian History Congress*. (Vol. 62, pp. 7–77). Indian History Congress.

Deodhar, L. (2010). Concept of the right of Stridhana in the Smirtis. *Bulletin of the Deccan College Research Institute 70*, 349–357.

Doyle, P. (2005). Replication and corpus linguistics: lexical networks in texts. http:/www. corpus. bham. ac. uk/PCLC/COL-ING_2005_paper. Pdf

Farghal, M., & Obiedat, H. (1995). Collocations: A neglected variable in EFL. *Review of Applied Linguistics 33*(4), 315. https://doi.org/10.1515/iral.1995.33.4.315

Firth, J.R. (1957). Modes of meaning. *Papers in Linguistics 1934–51*, 190–215. https://doi.org/10.1111/j.1473-4192.2007.00164.x

Halliday, M.A. (1966). Some notes on 'deep' grammar. *Journal of Linguistics 2*(1), 57–67. https://www.doi.org/10.1017/S0022226700001328

Herat, M. (2022). Nothing short of devastation: Disabled writers' responses to the COVID-19 lockdown during the first year of the pandemic. *Medical Research Archives 10*(6). https://doi.org/10.18103/mra.v10i6.2797

Jenset, G.B., & McGillivray, B. (2017). *Quantitative Historical Linguistics: A Corpus Framework* (Vol. 26). Oxford University Press.

Jois, R. (2004). *Legal and Constitutional History of India: Ancient, Judicial and Constitutional System*. Universal Law Publishing.

Kalashnikova, O. (2023). Exploring the Fukushima Effect: A Corpus-Based Discourse Analysis of the Algorithmic Public Sphere in Post-3/11 Japan (Doctoral dissertation, Friedrich-Alexander-Universität Erlangen-Nürnberg (FAU)).

Kehoe, A., & Gee, M. (2011). Social tagging: A new perspective on textual 'aboutness'. *Studies in Variation, Contacts and Change in English 6*(5). https://varieng.helsinki.fi/series/volumes/06/kehoe_gee/

Kirschenbaum, M.G. (2016). What is digital humanities and what's it doing in English departments? In *Defining Digital Humanities*. (pp. 211–220). Routledge.

Kiss, C. (2019). The Bhasmāṅkura in Śaiva texts. *Tantric communities in context 83*.

Lamoureux, C., & Camus, E. (2024). Moving Forward in Administrative History: Encoding the Département de La Seine and Paris Yearbooks (1883–1970). *Journal of Open Humanities Data 10*(1). https://doi.org/10.5334/johd.186

Lingat, R., & Derrett, J.D.M. (1973). *The Classical Law of India* (Vol. 2). [trans from the French with additions by J. Duncan M. Derrett]. University of California Press.

Louw, W.E. (1993). Irony in the text or insincerity in the writer? The diagnostic potential of semantic prosodies. In *Text and Technology*. (p. 157). John Benjamins.

Louw, W.E. (2000). Contextual Prosodic Theory: Bringing semantic prosodies to life. In C. Heffer and H. Sauntson (Eds). *Words in Context: In Honour of John Sinclair*. (pp. 48–94). ELR.

Martin, B.G., Norén, F.M., Mähler, R., Marklund, A., & Martin, O. (2024). The Curated UNESCO Courier 1.0: Annotated Corpora for Digital Research in the Global Humanities. *Journal of Open Humanities Data 10*. https://doi.org/10.5334/johd.181

McGillivray, B., Hengchen, S., Lähteenoja, V., Palma, M., & Vatri, A. (2019). A computational approach to lexical polysemy in Ancient Greek. *Digital Scholarship in the Humanities 34*(4), 893–907. https://doi.org/10.1093/llc/fqz036

McGillivray, B. (2020). Computational methods for semantic analysis of historical texts. In *Routledge International Handbook of Research Methods in Digital Humanities*. (pp. 261–274). Routledge. https://doi.org/10.4324/9780429777028

Nongbri, I.H. (2018). Women in Brahmanical Literature: Some aspects. *XVI 1*, 79–97.

Partington, A. (2004). Utterly content in each other's company: Semantic prosody and semantic preference. *International Journal of Corpus Linguistics* 9(1), 131–156. https://doi.org/10.1075/ijcl.9.1.07par

Phillips, M. (1985). *Aspects of Text Structure: An Investigation of the Lexical Organisation of Text*. North Holland.

Schreibman, S. (2012). Digital Humanities: Centres and peripheries. *Historical Social Research/Historische Sozialforschung*, 46–58.

Simanowski, R. (2016). *Digital Humanities and Digital Media: Conversations on Politics, Culture, Aesthetics and Literacy*. Open Humanities Press. https://www.doi.org/10.26530/OAPEN_612791

Sinclair, J. (1966). Beginning the study of lexis. In C.E. Bazell, J.C. Catford, M.A.K. Halliday, & R.H. Robins (Eds). *In Memory of J. R. Firth*. (pp. 410–30). Longman.

Sinclair, J. (1999). A way with common words. In H. Hasselgard & S. Oksefjell (Eds). *Out of Corpora: Studies in Honour of Stig Johansson*. Rodopi B.V. Amsterdam.

Svensson, P. (2016). Humanities computing as digital humanities. In *Defining Digital Humanities*. (pp. 159–186). Routledge.

Stubbs, M. (2009). Memorial article: John Sinclair (1933–2007): The search for units of meaning: Sinclair on empirical semantics. *Applied Linguistics 30*(1), 115–137.

Thukar, A., & Thakur, A. (1930). Proof of possession under the Smritis. *Annals of the Bhandarkar Oriental Research Institute 11*(4), 301–335.

Tharakan, S.M., & Tharakan, M. (1975). Status of women in India: A historical perspective. *Social Scientist*, 115–123. https://doi.org/10.2307/3516124

Tomy, A.C. (2019). Property Rights of Women under Hindu Law: From Vedas to Hindu Succession (Amendment) Act 2005. *Supremo Amicus 10*, 24.

Wilkinson, M.D., Dumontier, M., Aalbersberg, I.J., Appleton, G., Axton, M., Baak, A., ... & Mons, B. (2016). The FAIR Guiding Principles for scientific data management and stewardship. *Scientific Data 3*(1), 1–9. https://doi.org/10.1038/sdata.2016.18

Yajnavalkya, V.B., & Vidyarnava, R.B.S.C. (1918). *Yajnavalkya Smriti: With the Commentary of Vijnanesvara Called the Mitaksara: and Notes from the Gloss of Balambhatta*. AMS Press.

Yājñavalkya, V., & Chandra, S. (2010). Yajnavalkya Smriti: With the commentary of Vijnanesvara, called the Mitaksara and notes from the gloss of Balambhatta. http://www.archive.org/details/yajnavalkyasnnrit.

Yablo, S. (2014). *Aboutness* (Vol. 3). Princeton University Press.

# 8. Building a book history database: A novice voice

*Rebekah Ward*

## Abstract

This chapter recounts my lived experience as a novice Digital Humanist. It is deliberately anecdotal, rather than theoretical, in style and form. The chapter tells the story of how I commenced a doctorate in the field of book history, then, with minimal technical training, came to build a large relational database that both enabled and complemented my written dissertation as well as providing value for future users.

My research is centred on Angus & Robertson, the largest 20th-century Australian bookseller and publishing house. I was particularly interested in Angus & Robertson's use of book reviews as a promotional tool. The company archive contains millions of miscellaneous documents and, even when limited to certain subsets, there were thousands of undigitised pages to interrogate.

In response to that scale, I turned to the Digital Humanities, using the Heurist platform to design a bespoke database schema then populate the requisite fields with metadata from the physical documents, and subsequently enriching the records with secondary research. The resultant Angus & Robertson Book Reviews Database, which has been published online, remains a living database that at the time of writing contains 152,000 records, each with several fields, amounting to over a million data points.

https://doi.org/10.11647/OBP.0423.08

In this chapter, I explain design decisions as well as obstacles that I encountered whilst building the database without prior technical skills. I also share how the database has allowed me to tell previously untold stories about Angus & Robertson, book reviewing, and the 20th-century Australian print industry. The chapter concludes with a discussion of the ongoing potential of this specific database and how platforms like Heurist extend important opportunities to novice Digital Humanists.

## Keywords

Database; Angus & Robertson; Heurist; Digital Humanities.

## Prologue

I started my book-historical PhD at Western Sydney University (WSU) in 2020, intending to investigate the promotional strategies of Angus & Robertson, the largest 20th-century Australian publishing house.[1] I was particularly interested in how the publishers were routinely distributing hundreds of copies of their books to the newspaper and periodical press (review copies) at home and abroad to solicit book reviews. This process was intended to saturate the market with information about the books while bypassing the need for paid advertising.

My research was based on the Angus & Robertson Archive, held by the State Library of New South Wales (SLNSW). That Archive, now containing over a million documents across hundreds of boxes, is one of the largest collections of publishing files in the world. According to its curators, it is "one of the most significant literary collections in Australia" (Edmonds & Peck, 2016), rendering it a cornucopia for scholars. However, the Angus & Robertson Archive also presents several obstacles to research. It is difficult to identify relevant materials because many records currently remain undigitised and the indexes are incomplete. When identification is possible, the scale of materials proves unwieldy. I limited my research to a discrete sub-series of reviewing

---

1    For more information about Angus & Robertson, refer to A. W. Barker, *Dear Robertson: Letters to an Australian Publisher* (Sydney: Angus & Robertson, 1982).

records, but even that required me to sift through 134 undigitised scrapbooks containing tens of thousands of book reviews, as well as a set of complex business ledgers which tracked Angus & Robertson's distribution of review copies.[2]

Despite that scale, I was reluctant to narrow the scope of my project (which was to include all genres of books published in 1895–1949) or only interrogate case studies at the risk of reaching unrepresentative conclusions. Book historian Simon Eliot speaks of the need:

> [...] to see the forest, not a host of additional trees [...] any number of individual studies would not be sufficient, because you could never be certain that you had assembled a reliable sample (2002, p. 284).

A similar argument is made by literary scholar Franco Moretti, who—with a debt to Pierre Bourdieu's theory of the literary field (1996)—argues that literature cannot be:

> ... understood by stitching together separate bits of knowledge about individual cases, because it isn't a sum of individual cases: it's a collective system, that should be grasped as such (2005, p. 4).

To "see the forest" and grasp the "collective system", while also finding a way to manage the sheer volume of records, I knew that I wanted to use Digital Humanities (DH) tools. This choice was partly inspired by exposure to innovative work being done by Western Sydney University's Digital Humanities Research Group,[3] and my prior use of quantitative methodologies as part of my Masters' thesis (Ward, 2018). In particular, I saw the value in linking the two sub-series of archival materials that I was working with (the scrapbooks of reviews, and the distribution ledgers of review copies). These collections were clearly related but remained distinct from each other in the physical archive, with no way to easily move between them.

---

2    The distribution ledgers are contained within 'Angus & Robertson Ltd Business Records, 1885–1973' (SLNSW, Angus & Robertson Archive, Collection 3, Series 1, Sub-Series 1 at ML MSS 3269 Boxes 23–24); and the scrapbooks of reviews are held at 'Angus & Robertson Book Reviews in Bound Volumes, 1894–1970' (SLNSW, Angus & Robertson Archive, Collection 3, Series 4, Sub-Series 1 at ML MSS 3269 Boxes 478–531).

3    This collective has, since 2021, been known as the 'Digital Humanities Research Initiative'. For more information, see Simon Burrows' chapter on "Mapping Digital Humanities at Western Sydney University."

My intention to use DH tools was complicated by a significant obstacle: my relative lack of technical skills. This is not an uncommon experience for doctoral candidates commencing projects that involve the Digital Humanities. The current scholarly landscape demands that all researchers have at least some familiarity with DH, even if not defined as such, and also means that people from all disciplines find themselves conducting DH research. History is particularly impacted, with Adam Crymble (2021, p. 1) asserting "no discipline has invested more energy and thought into making its sources and evidence publicly available, or in engaging publics through digital mediums, or transforming their pedagogic practices with the help of technology", albeit with some residual "divides between the traditional and digital scholar". As a result, many people working in the DH—directly and indirectly—do not possess technical skills upon commencement of their project. Even the Department of Digital Humanities at King's College (London) does not impose technical requirements upon students entering the PhD in Digital Humanities (established in 2005 as the first dedicated DH PhD), a program that explicitly aims to produce "digitally adept scholars". Rather, students in that PhD come with varying levels of computing expertise and are free to conduct "research of any kind that involves critical work with digital tools and methods" (McCarty, 2012, pp. 36–37). Such shifts in the makeup of DH work have been enabled by the increasing availability of low-threshold digital tools as well as the rise of team projects that bring together discipline-specific researchers and computing experts. This, in turn, makes for richer scholarship and novel findings as more people can participate in the field.

Unfortunately, newcomers to DH often struggle to find ways to upskill, even when they are interested in doing so. There are still few dedicated opportunities for those who do not study computing to flexibly learn such skills, although there are increasing moves to incorporate digital skills into undergraduate programs, self-paced online learning options, and some dedicated, short-term DH certificates (see, for example, Spiro, 2012). In *Technology and the Historian* (2021), Adam Crymble describes the 'Invisible College' whereby researchers "pick up technological skills through informal channels [...] developed to fill voids left within the traditional structures of universities, which were slow to adapt to the growing demand for new skills". These informal channels, including social media, workshops and online discussion groups, rely on a self-learning model, often complicated by a lack of institutional funding and technical support.

In my case, I came to the PhD with few technological skills beyond familiarity with basic computing functions and more detailed experience with the Microsoft suite. I had no experience with programming, coding, digital textual analysis, GIS mapping or data mining. My undergraduate degree, also completed at Western Sydney University, had not included DH content or tools, nor had I completed any formal DH training as part of my Master of Research program. Even once enrolled in the PhD, there were few internal opportunities to rectify this gap. Western Sydney University does not run structured DH training for postgraduates outside of the coursework for the Master of Digital Humanities degree. The university does offer digital support for researchers via Intersect, including online training in programming (R and Python), surveys (Qualtrics and REDCap) and data analysis and visualisation (namely using Excel). I completed a few of these courses but found they were often geared to scientific disciplines and were mostly intended for intermediate users. Further, many of these workshops were based around skills training rather than broader methodological training which, as Mahony and Pierazzo (2012) reflect, is a more transient approach. I, therefore, struggled to see how I would be able to usefully adapt the skills presented in these workshops to my project. Other than trying to arrange and fund my involvement in external workshops, I had limited opportunities to learn advanced technical skills, particularly within the time and space afforded by a three-year full-time PhD in Australia. In the early stages of my doctorate, then, one of the overriding questions was how I could effectively and efficiently utilise DH tools in my project whilst also working towards a timely completion.

## Project design

There were several possible solutions to this technological dilemma, each of which would determine the project direction. The solution that I chose to adopt was Heurist (HeuristNetwork.org), an open-source, not-for-profit data management application. While there are alternatives, most notably Omeka, Heurist was the most appropriate choice for my project for several reasons. The platform was designed specifically for Humanities researchers so it can handle long, plain-text fields and interlinked heterogenous data. The platform is also mutable and offers in-built searching, filtering, analysis and visualisation capacities. Furthermore—perhaps most significantly in my case—Heurist is low-threshold: the creation and maintenance of a database does not require any prior expertise in coding, nor does it take an onerous amount of time to produce. There was no charge for creating and hosting the database, the Heurist team is always responsive to requests for bug fixing, and the flexible budgeting structure meant that the costs for additional services (creating the associated website, including building new capacities specifically for my project) were viable within my limited candidature funds. Finally, the platform was already being used by other research teams at Western Sydney University, allowing me to draw on their expertise and experience with the platform.

The suitability of Heurist to my work was soon evident. Within just a few hours I was able to create the core structure with some consultation from my doctoral supervisor, Professor Simon Burrows, whose own book history database is now hosted by the same platform.[4] Heurist offers a range of templates so it is possible to use preconfigured record types, vocabularies and fields (then tailor them as necessary) but it is equally possible to create entirely new versions for specific projects. The original sketch of a schema—drawn up in March 2020—is illustrated in Figure 8.1. At that time, I envisaged the database would contain five record types (highlighted in purple), each containing multiple fields, with relatively straightforward connections between them as indicated by the directional arrows. Many fields were plain text (such as author occupation, editor name and book title), but some were temporal (such as the date of review and book publication) or geospatial (latitude/longitude). Others called on standardised Heurist vocabularies (such as yes/no for the presence of illustrations, and male/female/other for gender) or bespoke terms lists created for this project (such as types of newspapers and length of reviews).

---

4    The *Angus & Robertson Book Reviews Database* can be accessed at https://heuristref.net/Rebekah_ARBookReviews

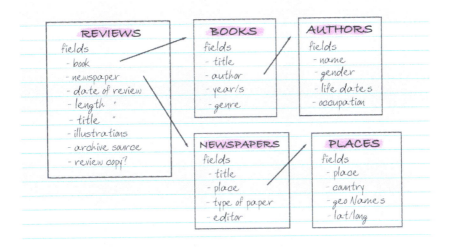

Fig. 8.1 Initial database schema (as of March 2020).

This schema has, unsurprisingly, undergone several changes since March 2020. Such changes are inevitable over the lifecycle of a DH project, since it is impossible to know at the outset precisely where a project will end up. This is especially true when dealing with primary sources, where greater engagement with the materials continually alters research plans, even more so when the associated database is being designed by a novice. Rather than having to wait until the end of data collection to start the construction of the database, though, Heurist allows for incremental creation. In my case, the database structure expanded significantly over time and now contains ten record types with more connections between the various nodes. The current version of the database schema is illustrated in Figure 8.2. I was also able to change the fields contained within record types, edit terms lists and create new relationships between records, all without coding changes or impacting existing data.

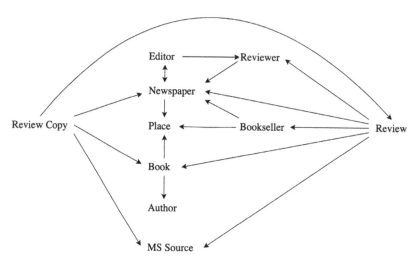

Fig. 8.2 Revised database schema (as of April 2023).

All changes to the database structure were designed in response to the complexity of the physical records. For example, as I processed more reviews it became apparent that Angus & Robertson were frequently sending review copies to the press via booksellers. Many reviews named specific local retailers as the source of their copy or encouraged people to buy the book from a designated local store. I first added a plain text field for booksellers within the review record type. However, it soon became apparent that booksellers were not minor characters in this story: they were significant agents in Angus & Robertson's promotional strategy. Consequently, I created a separate bookseller record type and then linked those records to the reviews as needed.

Having created the requisite structures, I started to manually populate the database using information drawn from the Angus & Robertson Archive. Some data were directly added via the Heurist interface. Other cleaned, delimited data were uploaded as CSV files. This process required high-level decision-making at every stage. Names, dates, newspaper mastheads and book titles had to be carefully standardised across the database to avoid misattribution or distortion. This was not just a case of accurately typing the information that appeared on the physical documents, though it was also vital to minimise this type of human error. In most cases, dates and mastheads had been handwritten onto the clippings by staff at Angus & Robertson or the various newspaper offices, resulting in significant inconsistencies and some errors over time. To take a straightforward example, in regional New South Wales, competing Bathurst newspapers were recorded in archival materials as the *Bathurst National Advocate* and *Western Times* and, elsewhere, as the *Advocate* and *Bathurst Times*. Sometimes, such differences reflected actual name changes in the mastheads but often it was just a case of varying usage. Ensuring that such duplicate records were merged in the database was important to avoid skewed statistics. Yet, this proved difficult to achieve completely when dealing with more than 58,000 reviews of 1,950 books in 2,660 unique newspapers or periodicals, so it became an ongoing process in my project.

Another issue that I faced during the input stage was related to the temporal data. Some reviews had incomplete or illegible dates, or no dates at all. Approximate dates could be assigned based on known information, including by examining the dates of reviews located on the same page of the physical archive, as the scrapbooks had been prepared in rough chronological order. To acknowledge this in the database, I created separate fields for confirmed and fuzzy dates within the reviews record type, as well as an overarching decades field. At this stage, though, my novice status interrupted the development of the project. I failed to correctly standardise the format of the dates as YYYY-MM-DD before uploading the data, instead using DD-MM-YYYY. This resulted in significant errors. Thankfully, the aforementioned mutability allowed by Heurist meant I could redo this stage relatively quickly without impacting other data. Working through this case did serve to remind me that, wherever possible, it is best to troubleshoot such issues before uploading the data.

Once the initial input stage was complete, I was able to enrich the database records in a variety of ways. Firstly, inferences were drawn from the physical records. For example, I added a field for the length of the review. Given time constraints, it was not possible to precisely count the words or even lines for the 58,000 reviews in the database. In lieu of that fine-grained data, I classified all reviews into one of five length categories (capsule, short, medium, long, feature). Clear boundaries for each category were established at the outset of the project, ensuring the labels could be applied consistently.

Secondly, the two sets of records (distribution ledgers about review copies, and scrapbooks of reviews) were linked. It was clear from the correspondence and other business files that Angus & Robertson used these two collections alongside each other to shape and refine their promotional strategy. The publishers spoke of having to "hunt up" newspaper editors who had received a review copy but failed to return a review.[5] The publishers were also prepared to strike papers from their distribution ledgers if this inattention continued over time, explaining to one editor, "we did not receive any copy of the papers containing these reviews, and therefore did not send any further books".[6] Despite this interrelationship between the ledgers and scrapbooks, it is difficult to see or analyse correlations between the collections when just using the paper-based archive. The collections could, however, be directly linked in the *Angus & Robertson Book Reviews Database* via Heurist's record pointer function. This was a complex and time-consuming process, involving hours of manual labour, mostly relying on various search filters, but the outcome is one of the most valuable parts of the project. It makes it possible to see if an individual review copy of a specific book sent to a specific newspaper led to a review and, if it did, to immediately navigate to that review. Linking the two collections in this way also allows for quantitative analysis of return rates. That is, how many copies Angus & Robertson distributed to the press compared to how many reviews they received back. I found the publishers had an overall return rate of 24% (indicating the effectiveness of their mass-review strategy), though this was highly variable based on book genre, author reputation and newspaper/periodical.[7]

Thirdly, I added information from other archival sources to enrich the individual stories. In a letter to Angus & Robertson, author Katharine Susannah Prichard asked, about her novel, *The Wild*

---

5    F. S. Shenstone (deputy publisher at Angus & Robertson) to author George Essex Evans, 21 February 1907 (ML MSS 314, Volume 29, Item 2, p. 657). See also George Robertson (co-founder of Angus & Robertson) to manager of *Country News* (Adelaide, SA, Australia), 8 July 1929 (ML MSS 314, Volume 19, Item 3, p. 595).

6    Rebecca Wiley (head of Mail Department at Angus & Robertson) to editor of *North Otago Times* (Oamaru, New Zealand), 24 July 1930 (ML MSS 314, Volume 63, Item 1, p. 221).

7    Return rates by genre, for example, ranged significantly from 10% (educational publications related to mathematics and civics) to 45–46 % (art books and non-fiction ethnographies).

*Oats of Han* (1928), why "booksellers in Perth do not seem to know Han".[8] Publisher George Robertson responded they had distributed 145 review copies, "liberally notified" the Trade, and collected 150 reviews.[9] Similarly, the publishers were able to inform author Doreen Puckridge that they had distributed 124 copies of her children's book, *King's Castle* (1931), to the press, accounting for 10% of the total print run.[10] This book does not appear in the surviving distribution ledgers, so this letter is an important referent. Many letters in the Archive help explain the cessation of review copies to specific places, the types of support that Angus & Robertson received from booksellers and the press, and the publishers' rationale for various business decisions. For example, one page of the scrapbooks carries a quick handwritten annotation that Angus & Robertson were no longer distributing review copies to the *Murray Pioneer*, a weekly newspaper based in Renmark in South Australia, due to "some unpleasantness" between Robertson and the paper's editor, Henry Samuel Taylor.[11]

Finally, supplementary information was sourced from online catalogues and bibliographic databases such as *AustLit*, the *Australian Dictionary of Biography*, *Trove*, *GeoNames*, *Papers Past* and *World Cat*, as well as from various secondary sources.[12] Long-form, discursive details were recorded, while other information was categorised or standardised across the database. Types of information recorded at this stage included biographic details for authors and reviewers (gender, life dates, occupations and, where known, identities of pseudonymous reviewers), bibliographic information about books

---

8    Katharine Susannah Throssell [née Prichard] to George Robertson, 22 October 1928, and 6 January 1930 (ML MSS 314, Volume 83, Item 1, pp. 227, 233).

9    George Robertson to Mrs Throssell [Katharine Susannah Prichard], 30 January 1930 (ML MSS 314, Volume 82, Item 1, p. 239).

10   Walter Cousins (deputy publisher at Angus & Robertson) to Doreen Jenkin [née Puckridge], 17 March 1931 (ML MSS 314, Volume 40, Item 2, p. 455).

11   See "Why America Should Forego Her War Debt Claims," review of *Honour or Dollars?* by Frederick Peabody, *Murray Pioneer* (Renmark, SA), 4 May 1928 (ML MSS 3269, Box 501, Volume 76).

12   *AustLit* is an online database of Australian literature. *Trove* and *Papers Past* are collections of digitised newspapers for Australia and New Zealand respectively. The *Australian Dictionary of Biography* is a collection of biographical information about eminent Australians. *WorldCat* is an online catalogue of 170 international library records. *GeoNames* is an international database of places, including discrete latitudes and longitudes.

(namely genre, edition printing date/s and place of publication), and latitude/longitude of geographic locations. Details about newspapers and periodicals (such as run dates, periodicity, affiliations, circulation figures, place of publication, known editors and proprietors, title changes and amalgamations) and descriptions of bookstores were also recorded. Heurist's capacity for incremental structure creation and simple procedures for inputting data means additional information can continue to be added in the future.

## Outputs

The Heurist team—namely designer Dr Ian Johnson and the Community Technical Advisors, Dr Michael Falk and Dr Maël Le Noc—aided in the construction of a public interface for the *Angus & Robertson Book Reviews Database*, with embedded explore, rank, search and mapping capabilities to improve functionality for current and future users. In the spirit of open DH, that interface has been published under a Creative Commons Attribution International 4.0 license, which enables the use, redistribution and expansion of materials as long as the original source is appropriately credited, and all changes are acknowledged.

In the future, the functionality and usefulness of the database could further be enhanced by adding digitised copies of the reviews and subsequent application of Optical Character Recognition (OCR). This would allow researchers to study the corpus more closely, including for evidence of repetition between the reviews. The data might also be combined with or connected to existing projects to meet principles of findability, accessibility and interoperability (Hagstrom, 2014). Potential partners include 'Linked Archives', which seeks to bring together related but disparate collections including the Angus & Robertson Archive (see Bones, 2019), and *AustLit*, a digital database that aims to be "the definitive information resource and research environment for [national] literary, print, and narrative cultures" but does not yet contain much information about reviewing. Even without such additions, though, the *Angus & Robertson Book Reviews Database* is already an original, useful DH output in its own right.

Publishing the digital outputs of research in this way is an important aspect of the digital revolution and is an ethical imperative for publicly funded projects (Bode, 2019). It also ensures transparency, allows others to check, corroborate or challenge conclusions presented in written outputs, and enables future researchers to ask and answer innumerable questions related to their own work. Publishing digital projects, especially with a Digital Object Identifier, enables them to be (potentially) counted towards an individual's research output. As Kerry Kilner noted in her discussion of *AustLit* in 2009:

> Are we nearing a time when a research outcome comprised of a web-based artefact which takes a highly detailed but visual approach to the analysis of an author's oeuvre might be formally recognised as a top-level publication? Could a piece of scholarship comprising an exegesis with an interoperable dataset be understood as of high a value as a 5000-word essay... or even a single-authored monograph? It is very likely that these types of scholarship already being developed across many humanities disciplines will begin to be regarded as at least as valuable as traditional forms (2009, pp. 300–301).

In the 15 years since Kilner posed such questions, there have been some shifts towards such recognition, though there is still a long way to go in this area.

One important issue when considering the long-term value of such outputs is the risk of impermanence. Claire Brennan (2018, p. 5) points out that digital objects are "inherently less stable than the physical objects they at times completely replace" as technology is always superseded, leaving objects unreadable and hardware unusable. Unlike many other database applications, Heurist has been conceived for the sustainability of the data. Firstly, it is built on MySQL (the most widely used open-source server DBMS) and, secondly, there is internal documentation of structures. Thirdly, the associated website is integrated as data within the database itself and, lastly, there is the option to download a self-documenting archive. That archive contains an SQL dump of the entire database, a comprehensive XML rendering of the database content, file structures containing uploaded files, icons and custom formats, and documentation of the structure of these resources to allow them to be interpreted into the future. These archive files can also be automatically uploaded to a memory institution repository, depending on configuration.

A more immediate contribution to database sustainability is the ongoing software development and centralised maintenance of the platform by the Heurist project team. The team, led by Heurist creator Ian Johnson, monitors and updates public servers supporting hundreds of projects, independent of individual project funding. Legacy projects beyond their funding life are thus supported by contributions from projects with current funding, applying a "Robin Hood" strategy (Ian Johnson, personal communication).

It is also important to acknowledge other limitations of DH projects. Digital outputs are often seen as more objective than physical equivalents and are idealised as more democratic. Katherine Bode (2008) describes how DH can help "denaturalise" the canon and avoid "hierarchical, qualitative judgements and selections," while David Berry (2011, p. 8) writes about the possibility of DH projects bypassing "traditional gatekeepers of knowledge". Paul Fyfe (2016, p. 548) notes such sources "seem to erase any intermediary state between source object and digital surrogate in the cloud". Helen Bones (2019) suggests "the incomplete nature of the material being searched is less obvious in digital form".

Yet, just like physical archives, digital projects involve acts of human mediation and often reinforce, rather than challenge, canonicity and so continue to exclude alternate voices (Earhart, 2012; Wilkens, 2012). Scholars should therefore communicate, and actively reflect on, the human decisions involved in the construction processes. Jason Ensor (2009b, p. 244) talks about offering the "necessary apologetics and methodological uncertainties that contextualise analytical labour" while Paul Fyfe (2016, p. 550) endorses releasing "para data" including "procedural contexts, workflows, and intellectual capital generated by groups through a project's life cycle". In surveying global digitised newspaper collections, Tessa Hauswedell et al., (2020, p. 142) recommend the creation of explanatory texts to accompany digital archives. More broadly, a *Checklist for Digital Outputs Assessment* (2021), produced by Arianna Ciula for King's College, describes the need to provide "a description and essential information on the digital output's scope, limitations, date of public release and intended audiences" as well as "the content of the output and the decisions made in all key steps of its curation".

In response to such suggestions, each tool offered within the interface of the *Angus & Robertson Book Reviews Database* (such as the map, rank and search functions) is accompanied by clear instructions for use. This is particularly important given the 'novice DH-er' theme of my project. Furthermore, the interface includes an "Overview" and detailed "User Guide" to outline record types, define key terms and describe curation processes including decisions around inclusion, exclusion, and data cleaning. For example, the User Guide explains that the term "printing date/s" is used throughout the project because the Angus & Robertson reviewing records typically cite the date of distribution instead of the date of publication and do not differentiate clearly between impressions and editions. The database is also impacted by mediation processes previously imposed on the physical archive. From the 1890s onwards, Angus & Robertson staff removed "worthless and uninteresting letters" from their correspondence files (Tucker & Anemaat, 1990, p. 12). Other documents have been lost to time. Further alterations to the collection were made by State Library of NSW curators who made decisions about the arrangement of materials and discarded items such as "recent invoice books and computer printouts of stock holdings" because "the information contained therein was trivial or because it was recorded in some other part of the archives" (Brunton, 1980). Critically reflecting on the patchy, mediated nature of the physical collection and database alike contextualises conclusions arising from subsequent research. Communicating that information to other users of the digital outputs ensures that future research based on the database can similarly acknowledge how mediation processes have impacted findings.

## Outcomes

When first designing the *Angus & Robertson Book Reviews Database*, I envisaged a fairly simple digital index of the relevant reviewing records. I was primarily focused on retrievability: creating a DH tool that would help when writing up my thesis by allowing me to find records more quickly. If I wanted to write about reviewing practices in Ballarat, for example, I could quickly produce a list of review copies, reviews, newspapers and reviewers associated with that location (there are 1,324 records about Ballarat). Alternatively, if I was interested in a specific book—say May Gibbs' *Wattle Babies* (1918) or P. S. Cleary's *The One Big Union* (1919)—I could retrieve all review copies and reviews in a single search (a total of 762 records for *Wattle Babies* and 683 for Cleary's book). In these cases, the records are spread across multiple volumes in the physical archive, with no clear way of identifying them all without spending hours leafing through every page and, even then, no simple technique for linking them together in a meaningful way. The database resolves that issue.

Another form of retrievability was identifying statistically significant or otherwise interesting case studies worthy of closer, more qualitative research. Using the database in this way made it possible to look beyond canonical texts and contextualise all cases within broader histories to understand their relative exceptionality or conventionality. As Jason Ensor (2009, p. 200) notes in his study of Angus & Robertson, data thus acts as "starting points for greater discussion, not end points". For example, the *Angus & Robertson Book Reviews Database* made it possible to determine that the most-promoted titles in the collection were C. J. Dennis' *Doreen* (1,079 copies across multiple editions) and the *Common-Sense Hints on Plain Cookery* (919 copies). The most reviewed titles were *My Life and Work* by Henry Ford (359 reviews) and, in literature, *The Songs of a Sentimental Bloke* by Dennis (331 reviews). Banjo Paterson's debut novel, *An Outback Marriage*, fell into third position in both lists (849 copies and 294 reviews).

I could also determine that the *Sydney Morning Herald, Brisbane Telegraph, Hobart Mercury* and *Adelaide Advertiser*—all large dailies in Australian capital cities—were returning the most reviews to Angus & Robertson (with an average of 830 reviews per paper). Outside of the capital cities, regional dailies like the *Newcastle Sun* and *Bendigo Advertiser* were also returning significant numbers of reviews, and even some small country papers had impressive coverage. Having identified these cases, I could then quickly navigate to the relevant reviews to undertake more discursive analysis. In doing so, the iconic Sydney *Bulletin* emerged as an interesting case study. It became clear that the number of review copies flowing to that periodical was directly correlated to the tenures of its various editors. Angus & Robertson sent relatively few review copies to the *Bulletin* when the position of literary editor was filled by A. G. Stephens between

1896–1906, and, later, David McKee Wright from 1916–1926, as they disagreed with some opinions of those critics.[13] The publishers sent significantly more copies to the *Bulletin* when Douglas Stewart, with whom they had a more positive relationship, took up the position of editor in the 1940s.[14]

While retrievability remains an important function of the *Angus & Robertson Book Reviews Database*, other uses soon became apparent. In particular, the database makes it possible to resolve gaps in the physical records. Three illustrative cases are discussed here.

## Case 1

The *Aussie* was a Sydney-based journal that, from 1923, had a New Zealand supplement. Some clippings in the Angus & Robertson Archive do not specify which version of the paper they had appeared in. Using the database to identify all *Aussie* reviews across various scrapbooks in the physical archive revealed distinct tendencies in each version. The Sydney paper ended reviews with bibliographical details (title and author imprint, followed by an endash, then the price) while the reviews in the New Zealand supplement usually ended with the price or a statement that the book under review could be purchased from local retailers. Observing this trend meant it was possible to ascertain the likely place of publication for the unattributed *Aussie* reviews and add that information to the database.

## Case 2

In the 1920s, Angus & Robertson launched their *Platypus* series (mostly consisting of reprints). The *Platypus* books were assigned a series number upon publication. Often, Angus & Robertson would only

---

13   For complaints from Angus & Robertson staff about the *Bulletin*, see F. S. Shenstone to Dale Collins, 13 October 1924 (ML MSS 314, Volume 19, Item 1, p. 211); and George Robertson to Walter Murdoch, 21 November 1930 (ML MSS 314, Volume 62, Item 1, p. 215).

14   Angus & Robertson staff complained about how the *Bulletin* had treated their books from the 1890s onwards. See, for example, F. S. Shenstone to Dale Collins, 13 October 1924 (ML MSS 314, Volume 19, Item 1, p. 211) and George Robertson to Walter Murdoch, 21 November 1930 (ML MSS 314, Volume 62, Item 1, p. 215).

record the number in their reviewing records rather than the title or author. This meant the distribution records were not clearly associated with a specific title, making it difficult to draw any conclusions about the books or link pairs of reviews and review copies together. The Angus & Robertson catalogues that do survive reveal that numbers were assigned by genre rather than chronologically, with numbers 1–5 reserved for children's literature and the 30s relating to novels, while books numbered from 80 onwards were general non-fiction. I knew from the distribution ledgers that review copies of multiple *Platypus* books tended to be distributed at one time, so it seemed likely the same books would also be reviewed together. However, the reviews had been split into "paras" for each book and filed across several scrapbooks, so it was necessary to first conduct structured searches in the database. To take just one instance, *Platypus* books #83 and #84 were sent to the press in June 1924 alongside #34. A preserved catalogue identified #83 and #84 as the twin volumes of *Studies of Australian Crime* by John Fitzgerald. I then searched the database for reviews of novels that had been published on the same day and in the same papers as the reviews of Fitzgerald's books. Through this process, it was possible to conclude, with a reasonable degree of certainty, that *Piebald, King of Bronchos* (a novel by Clarence Hawkes) was the elusive #34. I was then able to update the database accordingly, with due acknowledgement of the residual uncertainties, and, importantly, link the review copies of #34 to the reviews of *Piebald*.

## Case 3

Multiple reviews in the Angus & Robertson Archive were signed "CL" (see Figure 8.3). These reviews appeared in nine different papers across four Australian states from 1934–1948 so were likely from more than one reviewer, but the physical records do not offer any explanation of the identity of the reviewer/s. By comparing these reviews with attributed reviews in the database, particularly looking for correlations in dates and locations, it is possible to resolve some of these cases. The Perth 'CL' was probably by C. Lemon, who was actively writing book reviews under his full name for the Western Australian press in the 1930s. Meanwhile, other 'CL' reviews were presumably written by Clem Lack, a journalist and historian who produced various types of content, including book reviews, for the Brisbane *Telegraph* in the early 1940s and then for the Melbourne *Age* in 1945–1947. It is possible that Lack also wrote some of the other 'CL' reviews through his continued connections with various Australian newspapers. Having made these identifications, it was possible link the requisite records in the database.

Through the same process, it can be assumed 'JKE' was John Ewers, an author and journalist who also wrote under the pen name 'Yorick', and that 'ARC' was critic A. R. Chisholm. Dozens of other cases can also be posited with varying degrees of certainty. Melbourne reviewer 'CT' might be journalist Clive Turnbull, 'HRR' could be Auckland Professor of Economics Harold Rione Rodwell and 'GM' might have been George Mackaness, an educationist and Angus & Robertson author in his own right. Such findings would not have been possible using the physical archival records in isolation.

| Book Title | Newspaper | Year | Identity of Reviewer |
|---|---|---|---|
| Marsden and the Missions | Daily News (Perth) | 1936 | C Lemon |
| Papuan Wonderland | Daily News (Perth) | 1936 | C Lemon |
| Only the Stars are Neutral | Unlisted | *ca*.1942 | Unconfirmed |
| The Keys of the Kingdom | Telegraph (Brisbane) | 1942 | Clem Lack |
| The Drums of Morning | Unlisted | *ca*.1943 | Unconfirmed |
| Dress Rehearsal | Telegraph (Brisbane) | 1943 | Clem Lack |
| Guadalcanal Diary | Telegraph (Brisbane) | 1943 | Clem Lack |
| I Escaped from Hong Kong | Telegraph (Brisbane) | 1943 | Clem Lack |
| Australia's Changing Constitution | Telegraph (Brisbane) | 1943 | Clem Lack |

| Such is Life | Telegraph (Brisbane) | 1944 | Clem Lack |
|---|---|---|---|
| The Incredible Year | Telegraph (Brisbane) | 1944 | Clem Lack |
| Isles of Despair | Age (Melbourne) | 1947 | Clem Lack |
| Henry Lawson | Age (Melbourne) | 1947 | Clem Lack |
| Flying Doctor Calling | Age (Melbourne) | 1947 | Clem Lack |
| Practical Homes | Country Life (Sydney) | 1947 | Unconfirmed |
| Shannon's Way | Advocate (Melbourne) | 1948 | Unconfirmed, possibly Lack |
| Gone Tomorrow | ABC Weekly (Sydney) | 1948 | Unconfirmed |
| Bradman | Advocate (Melbourne) | *ca.*1948 | Unconfirmed, possibly Lack |
| Stone of Destiny | Advocate (Melbourne) | 1949 | Unconfirmed, possibly Lack |

Fig. 8.3 All reviews signed 'CL' in the Angus & Robertson Archive (by date).

Beyond these functions of retrievability and filling in gaps in the physical materials, the database offers additional uses that are not evident within the physical Angus & Robertson Archive. For example, the addition of a higher-level decade field simplified the process of conducting chronological searches and analyses. This enabled discussion about changes in Angus & Robertson's publishing output and review strategy over time. I was able to graph the number of review copies and reviews per decade, finding a significant increase from the 1910s and, particularly, during the 1920s (see Figure 8.4). It was also possible to translate these figures to average copies/reviews per book title to take into consideration the growth in the firm's publishing schedule, finding that the peak of Angus & Robertson's distribution strategy occurred in the 1910s despite the constraints of the First World War (Figure 8.5).

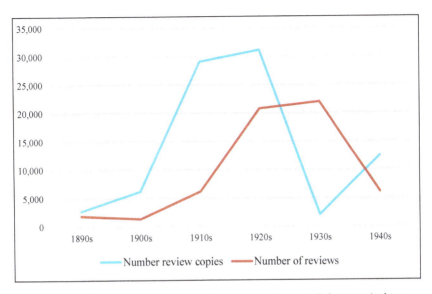

Fig. 8.4 Number of review copies and reviews in Angus & Robertson Archive (over time).

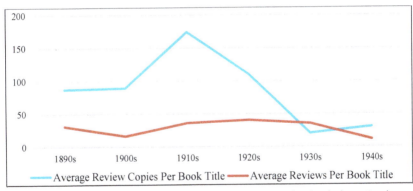

Fig. 8.5 Average number of review copies and reviews per book title (over time).

Another example of new information made visible by the database is the extent of Angus & Robertson's engagement with the booksellers. By creating a record type for the booksellers, I was able to identify 732 retailers involved in Angus & Robertson's promotional strategy across 1895–1949, including 556 in Australia (see Figure 8.6). I have also been able to enrich some of those records via secondary research, particularly using *The Early Australian Booksellers* (1980) and *The Golden Age of Booksellers* (1981). Within my doctorate, this inclusion of booksellers has shaped discussions of the highly networked nature of Angus & Robertson's promotional strategy. The publishers deliberately involved other bookish actors in their processes, seeking to create a collegial trade and strengthen their own relationships with local retailers around the country. More broadly, in place of any surviving or complete list of domestic booksellers, this aspect of the database reveals the breadth of the Australian book trade in the 20th century.

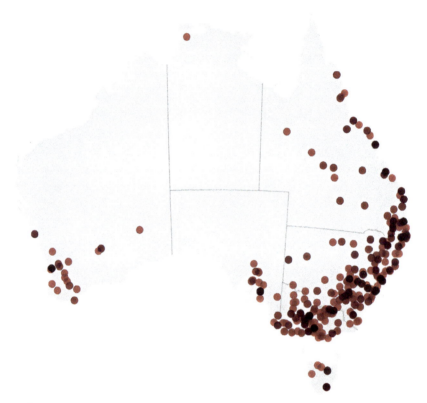

Fig. 8.6 Map of Australian retailers involved in Angus & Robertson's promotional strategy.

Beyond the specific case of Angus & Robertson, my database contributes to understanding of the nature and characteristics of reviewing. Tracking bylines revealed that 93.6% of reviews stored in the Angus & Robertson Archive were anonymous, and that even many of the attributed reviews masked reviewer identity with pseudonyms or initialisms (a further 4.3%). Categorising the length of reviews revealed the majority were brief, usually a single paragraph (38.8%) or less than a column in a standard broadsheet (42.1%). These findings—alongside general observations that most reviews tended to be enthusiastic and descriptive—led to the conclusion that the majority of the Angus & Robertson reviews were general notices rather than literary criticism. Multiple types of book reviewing were therefore occurring in the late 19th and early 20th centuries, even though most scholarship focuses to an exclusionary extent on long-form evaluative reviews. The database therefore makes it possible to tell new stories about Angus & Robertson and their reviewing strategies, as well as about book reviewing and the 20th-century print industry.

## Coda

Even as a self-proclaimed novice DH-er, I was able to conduct most of this work independently. Any coding bugs that did emerge were resolved via consultation with the Heurist team. For example, at one stage several title masks disappeared from my database for no apparent reason (see Figure 8.7), but Johnson and Le Noc were able to rapidly resolve this in the backend. This points to the advantage of a centrally managed platform with technical staff on call to assist with various projects, rather than a locally installed application where fixes are dependent on the vagaries of technical staff availability and knowledge.

Fig. 8.7 Sample of database entries, showing the disappearance of constructed titles for some records.

My project barely scratches the surface of what is possible using the *Angus & Robertson Book Reviews Database*. Countless other aspects could be taken up by others in future research projects in small or significant ways, including to address questions that have not been conceived of yet. In this way, the database—like all DH projects—is not just a tool that helped with my own thesis, it is an original and significant research output in its own right: one that even novice users can create and use effectively.

Looking outwards, this discursive account of my own lived experiences in DH demonstrates the transformative potential of low-threshold, user-friendly, readily available digital platforms like Heurist and others. By dismantling technical barriers that may otherwise hinder entry to the field, these platforms allow researchers with diverse disciplinary backgrounds to become novice, then expert, DH-ers. This influx of voices, perspectives and approaches fosters a more inclusive and innovative research environment. Established DH tools therefore afford new opportunities to people without programming backgrounds, and in turn, those people beneficially expand the field of DH.

# Works Cited

Angus & Robertson Book Reviews in Bound Volumes. (1894–1970). Collection 3, Series 4, Sub-Series 1. ML MSS 3269 Boxes 478–531. https://collection. sl.nsw.gov.au/record/1bGdoprY

Angus & Robertson Ltd Business Records. (1885–1973). Collection 3, Series 1, Sub-Series 1. ML MSS 3269 Boxes 1–25. https://collection.sl.nsw.gov.au/ record/n5lXBlg9

Angus & Robertson Publishing Files and Associated Papers. (1858–1933). Collection 1, Series 1. ML MSS 314 Volumes 1–90. https://collection.sl.nsw. gov.au/record/9gkdb8X9

*AustLit: The Australian Literature Resource.* (2002). University of Queensland. www.austlit.edu.au

Australian Booksellers Association. (1980). *The Early Australian Booksellers.* Australian Booksellers Association.

*Australian Dictionary Biography* (n.d.). Canberra: National Centre of Biography, Australian National University. https://adb.anu.edu.au/

Barker, A.W. (1982). *Dear Robertson: Letters to an Australian Publisher.* Angus & Robertson.

Berry, D. (2011). The Computational Turn: Thinking About the Digital Humanities. *Culture Machine 12.* http://sro.sussex.ac.uk/49813/

Bode, K. (2019). Large, vigorous, and thriving: Early Australian publishing and futures of publishing studies. In M. Weber & A. Mannion (Eds). *Book*

*Publishing in Australia: A Living Legacy.* (pp. 1–28). Monash University Publishing.

Bode, K. (2008). Beyond the colonial present: Quantitative analysis, 'resourceful reading' and Australian Literary Studies. *JASAL* Special Issue, 184–197. https://openjournals.library.sydney.edu.au/JASAL/article/view/10212

Bones, H. (2019). Linked digital archives and the historical publishing world: An Australian perspective. *History Compass* 17(3), https://www.doi.org/10.1111/hic3.12522

Bourdieu, P. (1996). *The Rules of Art: Genesis and Structure of the Literary Field.* Stanford University Press.

Brennan, C. (2018). Digital Humanities, digital methods, digital history, and digital outputs: History writing and the digital revolution. *History Compass* 16(10). https://www.doi.org/10.1111/hic3.12492

Brunton, P. (1980). The Angus & Robertson Archives. *Bibliographical Society of Australia and New Zealand Bulletin* 4(3), 191–201. https://search.informit.org/doi/abs/10.3316/ielapa.801027903

Ciula, A. (2021). *Checklist for Digital Outputs Assessment.* King's College London. https://zenodo.org/records/3361580

Crymble, A. (2021). *Technology and the Historian: Transformations in the Digital Age.* University of Illinois Press.

Earhart, A.E. (2012). Can information be unfettered? Race and the New Digital Humanities Canon. In M.K. Gold (Ed.). *Debates in the Digital Humanities.* (pp. 309–331). University of Minnesota Press.

Edmonds, E., & Peck, A. (2016, October). Literary giants: Revealing the Angus & Robertson Collection. Paper presented at the Australian Society of Archivists National Conference, Parramatta. https://www.sl.nsw.gov.au/sites/default/files/ literary_giants_-_revealing_the_angus_robertson_collection_presentation.pdf

Eliot, S. (2002). Very necessary but not quite sufficient: A personal view of quantitative analysis in book history. *Book History 5,* 283–293. https://www.doi.org/10.1353/bh.2002.0006

Ensor, J. (2009a). Still waters run deep: Empirical methods and the migration patterns of regional publishers: Authors and titles within Australian literature. *Antipodes* 23(2), 197–208. https://www.jstor.org/stable/41957815

Ensor, J. (2009b). Is a picture worth 10,175 Australian novels? In K. Bode & R. Dixon (Eds). *Resourceful Reading: The New Empiricism, eResearch, and Australian Literary Culture.* (pp. 240–273). Sydney University Press.

Fyfe, P. (2016). An archaeology of Victorian newspapers. *Victorian Periodicals Review* 49(4), 546–577.

*GeoNames.* (n.d.). https://www.geonames.org/

Hagstrom, S. (2014). The FAIR data principles. *The Future of Research Communications and e-Scholarship.* https://force11.org/info/the-fair-data-principles/

Hauswedell, T., Nyhan J., Beals, M.H., Terras, M., & Bell, E. (2020). Of global reach yet of situated contexts: An examination of the implicit and explicit selection criteria that shape digital archives of historical newspapers. *Archival Science 20*, 139–165. https://www.doi.org/10.1007/s10502-020-09332-1

Kilner, K. (2009). AustLit: Creating a collaborative research space for Australian literary studies. In K. Bode & R. Dixon (Eds). *Resourceful Reading: The New Empiricism, eResearch, and Australian Literary Culture.* (pp. 299–14). Sydney University Press.

Mahony, S., & Pierazzo, E. (2012). Teaching skills or teaching methodology? In B. Hirsch (Ed.). *Digital Humanities Pedagogy: Practices, Principles and Politics.* (pp. 215–25). Open Book Publishers. https://www.doi.org/10.11647/OBP.0024

McCarty, W. (2012). The PhD in Digital Humanities. In B. Hirsch (Ed.). *Digital Humanities Pedagogy: Practices, Principles and Politics.* (pp. 33–46). Open Book Publishers. https://www.doi.org/10.11647/OBP.0024

Moretti, F. (2005). *Graphs, Maps, Trees: Abstract Models for a Literary History.* Verso.

*Papers Past.* (n.d.). Auckland: National Library of New Zealand. https://paperspast.natlib.govt.nz/

Riddell, E. (Ed.). (1981). *The Golden Age of Booksellers: Fifty Years in the Trade.* Abbey Press.

Spiro, L. (2012). Opening up digital humanities education. In B. Hirsch (Ed.). *Digital Humanities Pedagogy: Practices, Principles and Politics.* (pp. 331–363). Open Book Publishers. https://www.doi.org/10.11647/OBP.0024

Times Literary Supplement. (n.d.). *Historical Archive, 1902–2019.* Gale Primary Sources. https://www.gale.com/intl/c/the-times-digital-archive

*Trove.* (n.d.). National Library of Australia. https://trove.nla.gov.au/

Tucker, S., & Anemaat, L. (1990). *Guide to the Angus & Robertson Archives in the Mitchell Library.* Library Council of NSW.

Ward, R. (2018). Publishing for Children: Angus & Robertson and the Development of Australian Children's Publishing, 1897–1933. Master's thesis, Western Sydney University. http://hdl.handle.net/1959.7/uws:51862

Ward, R. (2023). *Angus & Robertson Book Reviews Database.* https://heuristref.net/Rebekah_ARBookReviews

Wilkens, M. (2012). Canons, close reading, and the evolution of method. In M.K. Gold (Ed.). *Debates in the Digital Humanities* (pp. 249–258). University of Minnesota Press.

*WorldCat.* (n.d.). www.worldcat.org/

# 9. Are we ready to 'screw around' together? Barriers to institutionalisation of DH pedagogy in literature departments

*Ritam Dutta*

## Abstract

Founded on the philosophy of the constructivist and collaborative pursuit and production of new knowledge, pedagogy is at the very heart of Digital Humanities (DH). However, among the challenges for the institutionalisation of DH pedagogy, particularly in literature departments, is a dearth of sufficient literature on DH pedagogy—a concern echoed in "Where's the Pedagogy?" by Stephen Brier (2012) among other scholar-practitioners of DH. As Hirsch (2012a) points out, the focus of the literature is predominantly "on the theories, principles, and research practices associated with the Digital Humanities—past and present—and not on issues of pedagogy". Teaching is often "bracketed off" as an afterthought in the discussion on DH, which is a reflection of the practical realities of DH studies, particularly in literature departments. Hirsch argues that the bracketing off or complete exclusion of pedagogy in critical discussions of the Digital Humanities, as is often the case, reflects, and reinforces, the conflicting contrast between teaching and research of DH in academia.

The chapter highlights the discrepancy between traditional pedagogical approaches prevalent in literature departments, especially in India, and the collaborative, hands-on methods

https://doi.org/10.11647/OBP.0423.09

intrinsic to DH practice. Traditional approaches often focus on the delivery of content from teacher to student, whereas DH emphasises inquiry-based learning, experimentation, and collaboration among peers and instructors. In the context of DH, a "pedagogy of digital experimentation" involves students actively engaging in making and doing, mirroring the work of DH professionals. This approach encourages collaborative exploration and discovery, aligning with the core tenets of DH, such as practice, discovery, and community. However, many literature departments are not prepared to embrace this approach, which involves what Ramsay (2010/2014) terms "screwing around" or "surfing and stumbling" as part of the research methodology.

Shifting towards a pedagogy of active experimentation requires a significant paradigm shift, challenging traditional notions of teaching and learning. This shift may lead to discomfort or uncertainty for both teachers and students as they navigate unfamiliar territories. Bonds (2014) suggests that this discomfort arises from the need to co-produce knowledge in a constructivist manner, rather than passively receiving it. To bridge the gap between traditional pedagogy and DH practices, there needs to be a re-evaluation of entrenched ideas about teaching and scholarship. This re-evaluation should challenge limited perceptions of the teacher's role and the connection between teaching and scholarship. Without this re-evaluation, Digital Humanities risks being confined to superficial applications like computer-assisted text analysis, rather than realising its full potential in higher education. Bringing pedagogy to the forefront of Digital Humanities in literature programs requires a fundamental reconsideration of educational practices and the roles of teachers and students. Embracing collaborative, experimental approaches can pave the way for the integration of DH into mainstream educational frameworks, fostering innovation and deeper engagement with humanities disciplines.

# Keywords

Pedagogy; digital experimentation; collaborative venture.

# Introduction

The 21st-century pedagogical practices have been shaped immensely by the phenomenal growth of the internet and digital technologies. New modes of research and teaching have been devised, and these have claimed niches in academic departments in universities all over the world. Therefore, these new developments, including the emerging discipline of Digital Humanities (DH) studies, warrant our attention to understand what has changed and what new possibilities have emerged for pedagogical practices after the digital turn—especially in the field of humanities, which was previously considered to be the most divorced from technology.

However, research (Shanmugapriya & Menon, 2020) has found that DH programs and courses in higher education in India are few and far between, although several critical events in the recent past, such as the launch of Digital Humanities Alliance of India in 2018, governments projects like "Digitize India"[1] and "Digital India,"[2] and an increase in the number of DH courses, conferences, workshops, and seminars indicate that DH in India is steadily moving forward. Additionally, several academic institutions and individual humanities scholars have helped to create awareness about DH through focused networks in the last couple of years. These developments have resulted in the introduction of DH programs in many more universities across the country (Diwan, 2016).

However, Shanmugapriya and Menon (2020) also indicate that despite a discernible trend for employing "computer applications as an 'appendix' of various disciplines" (n.p.; para 12), including that of humanities, "to ensure employment opportunities in the digital era and to meet the global demands" (n.p.; para 12), attempts at "humanities-based critical inquiry [...] is absent in the curricula of the academic universities [...] [and] while there is an evidence of engagement with digital technologies for higher education and digital pedagogy" (n.p.; para 12), it doesn't often extend to "the critical realm of inquiry and investigation in the field of humanities" (n.p.; para 12).

This is due to multiple challenges, including some multifaceted

---

1    See https://www.digitizeindia.gov.in/
2    Ibid.

infrastructural challenges. For instance, negotiating the digital divide in higher education in India is still a big challenge. Pedagogical content development and instructional design for multi-lingual and socio-culturally diverse classrooms, integration of archival materials, training teachers and researchers in new technologies, easy access to DH labs and related digital infrastructures, challenges related to development and theorisation of digital pedagogy, and paucity of funding and institutional support for DH programs in Indian universities are also areas that require intervention. Other challenges include defining and locating the subject within discipline-specific boundaries, the absence of a theoretical framework around questions of DH pedagogy, the learning environment in traditional teacher-centric classrooms, and teachers' beliefs about how students learn or should learn (Sneha, 2016).

Due to lack of space, I shall focus only on the challenges of the learning environment in traditional teacher-centric classrooms and teachers' beliefs about how students learn or should learn in the rest of this exposition on the present realities of DH pedagogy in India.

## Making sense of DH pedagogy

Based on the philosophy of constructivism and collaborative production of new knowledge, pedagogy is at the heart of Digital Humanities. However, DH scholar Sneha notes:

> [I]nstitutional efforts at building curricula specifically around DH-related concerns have been few, with the prominent ones in India being the courses at Jadavpur University and Presidency University in Kolkata, and more recently Srishti School of Arts, Design and Technology in Bangalore (2016, p. 45).

A reason for this might be that the possibilities of DH have still not been explored adequately, and to what extent DH might contribute qualitatively to addressing or even furthering some specific disciplinary concerns in the humanities remains open to speculation, even as the field gains institutional stability in India as in the other parts of the world.

Generally understood as an exploration of the "intersection between information technology and humanities, DH has grown to become [a highly funded] interdisciplinary field of research" (Sneha, 2016, p.14) in humanities over the last couple of decades. Nevertheless, as Sneha points out, studies on DH mark the difficulties in defining and locating the subject within discipline-specific boundaries, as Digital Humanities research spans archives, to social media, and everything in between, which is a specific obstacle for the "curriculisation" of DH:

> [DH has been] called a phenomenon, field, discipline and a set of convergent practices—all of which are located at and/or try to understand the interaction between digital technologies and humanities practice and scholarship (Sneha, 2016, p. 14).

However, the field has rapidly become popular in India, with several universities now pursuing DH studies, and not just with interdisciplinary teaching and research within existing humanities or media science departments, but to explore and invent creative and inventive knowledge-making processes in functional institutional spaces of its own. However, there is a still lack of consensus on what a DH pedagogy entails and scholars and practitioners in many instances have stopped short of fully embracing it as a discipline (Sneha, 2016).

The lack of a precise definition of DH and its location within established disciplinary contexts, coupled with the near absence of a theoretical framework around questions of DH pedagogy, are also obstacles to understanding what the field entails and its many future possibilities in the Indian context (Sneha, 2016). Our limitations in comprehending the disciplinary area have, therefore, effectively limited the prospects of DH pedagogy in India to that of 'training' for increasing students' employment prospects after graduation and for channelling greater funding for the humanities (Bonds, 2014). The question that we need to ask ourselves is: can we conceptualise a role for DH pedagogy in India beyond skill-building to that of helping students to critically engage with questions of socio-political concern?

## Curriculisation of DH

The curriculisation of DH has its problems. As Sneha (2016) points out, the curriculisation of DH courses in three universities in India indicates the "specific academic concerns [for DH] in the Indian context, and the disciplinary challenges and questions that it may open up for the teaching-learning process" (p. 45).

Among these challenges, particularly in literature departments, is a dearth of literature on DH pedagogy—a concern echoed in Brier (2012), among other scholar-practitioners of DH. For instance, echoing Brier, Hirsch (2012b) points out that the focus of the literature is predominantly:

> [...] on the theories, principles, and research practices associated with the digital humanities—past and present—and not on issues of pedagogy (Hirsch, 2012b, p. 4).

Teaching, Hirsch (2012b) adds, is often "bracketed off" as an afterthought in discussion on DH, which is a reflection of the practical realities of DH studies. Hirsch (2012b) argues that the bracketing off of or complete exclusion of pedagogy in critical discussions of Digital Humanities, as is often the case, reflects and reinforces the conflicting contrast between the teaching and research of DH in academia.

One reason for the lack of sufficient literature on DH pedagogy could be that we have not been able to define DH adequately, far less fully understand the constantly evolving nature of the digital and its changing facets in the context of DH. Moreover, as Sneha (2016) points out, we are still passing through the transition "from the analogue to the digital", and the simultaneous existence of both modes makes it challenging to teach DH (p. 45). Another crucial reason is that the constructivist, collaborative nature of DH studies does not fit our traditional approaches to formal education, including instructional designs, institutional policies, and teachers' beliefs.

## Project-based learning

DH studies often follow a pedagogical approach based on constructivist and collaborative methodologies. Consequently, learning in DH is frequently 'project-based'. This makes curriculum design and course evaluation difficult, particularly in the Indian context, where project-based learning, at least in most humanities and social science departments, is still not very common. Most Indian teachers are not adept at teaching and evaluating students through project-based learning, which differs significantly from traditional coursework and requires teachers to possess a particular skillset and mindset needed for teaching collaboratively. Similarly, it requires that students possess some specific interpersonal and technical skills that "many students have not yet developed" (Bonds, 2014, p. 149).

DH scholar Alan Liu believes that the:

> ... 'co-developing' model of teaching with technology supplement[s] the usual closed discursive circuit of the instructor-talking-to-the-student (and vice versa) with an open circuit of the instructor-and-student talking to others (2009, p. 20).

Students typically learn to co-produce knowledge collaboratively with their teacher(s) and peers through 'practice' and 'discovery'—or, in other words, through "screwing around" as a methodology (Ramsey, 2014). Such a methodology, where teachers and students collaboratively produce knowledge through experimentation rather than pursue the normative methodology of direct transfer of knowledge from the teacher to the students (known as the 'banking model'), warrants a pedagogical paradigm shift that could create an unsettling learning environment for both the teacher and her students (Fyfe, 2011). However, Fyfe (2011) also believes that it "can also be a terrific opportunity" for engaging students "in shared projects of inquiry" and exploration, only if we could "imagine a pedagogy of digital experimentation" (p. 85)—one that prompted Ramsey to ask if we are ready to accept "screwing around" as research (and may I add, pedagogical?) methodology (Ramsey, 2014).

## Constructivism: A pedagogical paradigm shift

Instead of inculcating deep learning, which should be the goal of education, the current education system in India focuses on preparing students for examinations, often through rote memorisation. The traditional lecture-based teaching method in schools, colleges, and universities propels students towards rote memorisation instead of creative thinking and collaboration. Teaching in this manner often creates cognitive dissonances for the students, because learning in our lifeworld is inter-personal and inter-textual, spanning multiple contexts, multiple social worlds, and various 'funds of knowledge' that we already possess. Since learning involves meaning-making, learning in our lifeworld is also essentially dialogic and extends beyond the classroom space, both temporally and spatially. That is, it seeks to connect with the students' present, past, and possible (future) life experiences (Bruner, 1996), both inside and outside the classroom (Dutta, 2015a; 2015b).

According to Fink's (2013) taxonomy, significant learning includes several components besides "foundational knowledge", that is, understanding and recalling information and ideas taught in classrooms. Some of the other areas of Fink's taxonomy of significant learning are: "application", "integration", "human dimension", and "caring". Therefore, significant learning is not (and cannot be) limited to simply memorising information and being able to recall it when required (Ayling, 2010). Significant learning involves much more, not the least of which is being able to make connections between one's life and one's learning—that is, in acting on the knowledge, in connecting the proverbial dots. However, the goal-based, task-oriented curricula of most schools often do not allow room for such an active pursuit after connections (Dutta, 2015b).

The multiple funds of knowledge that students bring to the classroom are often not acknowledged. Students "are often implicitly asked to set aside what and how they have come to know in the world" (Moje et al., 2004., p. 5) in favour of the dominant ways of knowing valued in the classroom. Many scholars have also pointed out how schools often, in practice, fail to acknowledge and tap into students' "knowing-in-the-world" (Moje et al., 2004; Dyson, 1993; Tagore, 2009). Indeed, some have even argued that far from acknowledging students' "knowing-in-the-world", schools often actually perpetuate a sort of epistemic violence on students by cutting them off from the pulse of their cultural and social lives (Gruenewald, 2003; Tagore, 2009). This excision makes education "unreal, heavy and abstract" (Tagore, 2009) and causes disconnect (Dyson, 1993; Noddings, 2005) and ennui or boredom (Sidorkin, 2004) in students (Dutta, 2015a; 2015b). The root of the problem is the teacher-centric learning environment of conventional classrooms, where instruction is typically always unilateral. Therefore, we must embrace a different pedagogical pathway that would allow our students to develop their autonomy, augment their sense of self as young scholars, and promote interpersonal growth and dialogic learning through collaborations.

Constructivism is one such pedagogical approach that encourages students to research, reflect, collaborate, take ownership of their learning, and be both critical and creative through learning projects that are intrinsically meaningful and motivating for them. As an approach, it is best suited for learning through the 'making and doing' philosophy at the heart of DH pedagogy. Constructivism as an epistemological philosophy of knowledge acquisition prioritises knowledge construction over knowledge transmission. According to constructivist philosophy, new knowledge is socially constructed by learners, based on their prior knowledge, through collaboration on meaningful and authentic tasks (Sneha, 2016). Thus, within a constructivist pedagogy, activities supplement lectures, and students are encouraged to build upon their prior knowledge or their 'knowing-in-the-world'.

Dyson (1993) shows how this can be achieved in the classroom space through a permeable curriculum—a porous curriculum that allows for the percolation of the "outside", like the playground, the community, the church, and the *āddā*, into the classroom. It is a curriculum that allows and makes provision for connecting the various unofficial social worlds (such as the "peer sphere" and the "home sphere") of the student with the official school world ("official sphere") and encourages students to draw from their various "funds of knowledge" (Moll et al., 1992). A permeable curriculum allows us to acknowledge all the diverse lived experiences of our students and their ways of taking and meaning-making in the world—at home, in the community, in interaction with peers, and through participation in popular culture—as valid sources of knowledge, informing their learning in school. Thus, constructivism emphasises a learner-centric, and learner-directed, collaborative pedagogic style that allows students to learn by participating in authentic tasks with scaffolding from teachers.

Vygotsky (1978) argued that knowledge is inseparable from the socio-cultural context it is embedded in and that all higher-order mental functions are social in nature. Therefore, within the social constructivist approach to pedagogy, the role of the teacher is no longer that of the sole dispenser of knowledge but rather that of a motivator, mentor, guide, and resource person to the students.

Constructivism does not acknowledge the possibility of any objective knowledge that is "out there" independent of the knower. According to the constructivist philosophy, the only knowledge is that which we construct for ourselves socially through collaborative engagements within our "own world". Differentiating between the world "out there" and the students "own world" allows a teacher to choose the type of pedagogy to follow in a constructivist classroom (Bonds, 2014). An effective educator within a constructivist paradigm must primarily engage with and build upon students' "funds of knowledge" (Moll et al., 1992) or the prior knowledge and beliefs about the lived world that students already possess and bring with them into the classroom. Students' prior knowledge or knowing-in-the-world forms the base on which new knowledge is built within a constructivist paradigm. A constructivist educator must then help students realise that there are multiple ways of making meanings of any act or utterance, and we dialogically negotiate meaning from our unique ideological positions within the particular context of an act or utterance (Bakhtin, 1984). Therefore, paying attention to students' experiences in local contexts and allowing them the autonomy to take ownership of their learning lives is essential for teachers. But being moored to a "school-centric curriculum" (instead of a student-centric curriculum), most teachers fail to surmount the "Berlin Wall" that their syllabi erect between their teaching and the rich pedagogical possibilities afforded by the cultural lives of their students outside of classrooms (Dutta, 2015a).

Trying to choose between the world "out there" and the students' "own world" (Bonds. 2014) (which includes the home, the playground, the canteens, the *āddā*s, popular culture, and even the third spaces inside the classrooms) often puts the teacher in an acute dilemma. However, simply choosing the latter over the former usually does not help much, because teachers often do not have much control over the curriculum, the learning environment in an institution, the instructional design of courses, and students' learning habits—all of which require an overhaul if we are to succeed with constructivist pedagogy. We need a constructivist instructional design that does not direct students towards singular solutions to problems—academic or otherwise—but rather, through social constructivism in the classroom, helps students to develop social, emotional, and cognitive skills; in other words, life skills.

# Problems with learner-centric education reforms in India

Despite sustained endeavours to move from the teacher-centric paradigm to a more learner-centric paradigm, the Indian education system is still dominated by rote learning. Research (Brinkmann, 2015; Schweisfurth, 2011; Vavrus, 2009) suggests several prevalent cultural beliefs opposed to the tenets of learner-centric education (LCE) as the reason for such conservatism. Unfortunately, as Sneha (2016) notes, these cultural beliefs, which are one of the primary impediments to a fully-fledged national implementation of LCE, have not yet been adequately researched in India. It is, however, important to engage with cultural beliefs, particularly those to which many educators subscribe, if we hope to make our education system learner-centric and constructivist (Brinkmann, 2015; Richardson, 1996; 2003; Sanger & Osguthorpe, 2011).

Besides the beliefs of individual teachers, there is also the influence of the "folk psychology" of culture (Bruner, 1996) on teachers. Each culture, according to Bruner (1996), has a distinctive "folk psychology", or "deeply ingrained culturally inherited beliefs [...] [that] are difficult to override" (Brinkmann, 2015, p. 344). Similarly, other researchers like Robin Alexander (2001) who studied pedagogical differences across five countries (India, Russia, France, the UK, and the USA), have argued that culture has a powerful influence on teachers' thinking and practice. Clarke (2001), Rao et al. (2003), Sarangapani (2003), Gupta (2006), and Batra (2009) have also noted that a large majority of the pedagogical beliefs of Indian educators are rooted in their cultural perspectives on class, caste, gender, social inequality, etc., making it difficult for them to change these beliefs.

Besides cultural perspectives, the beliefs of teachers are often also shaped by the educational contexts they find themselves in, including how they are treated and supported (or not) by their superiors—both at the institutional level and within the larger educational system. The educational context often plays a significant role in mediating between a teacher's beliefs and her praxis: even teachers with learner-centric beliefs would struggle to ditch the chalk-talk or board-work, unless the class strength, the examination practices, the prescribed textbooks, the school administration, etc., are conducive to learner-centric pedagogy.

Without professional autonomy, foundational knowledge, or practical skills, a teacher's learner-centric beliefs on their own will not effectively create a learner-centric environment or bring about any change in the pedagogical practices in her classroom—which is one of the limitations of the scant research done on this topic in India thus far (Brinkmann, 2015). However, 'teacher beliefs' is nevertheless an important but relatively unexamined area in the literature on Indian educational reform and, therefore, warrants our focus.

Brinkmann (2015) argues that we cannot wholly comprehend the beliefs of teachers without considering the cultural contexts shaping these beliefs. Thus, it is vital to identify the shared cultural patterns in individual teacher's beliefs. However, in order to shift to a learner-centric education system from a teacher-centric one, there also needs to be institutional changes, including changes in the schools' systemic contexts and teachers' professional identity and autonomy (Brinkmann, 2015). Scholars like Batra (2005), Dyer et al., (2004), and Ramachandran et al., (2008) argue that, rather than considering teachers rightly as reflective practitioners, we presently view them "as technicians who must passively implement pre-designed ideas from outside 'experts'" (Brinkmann, 2015, p. 354)—which is another challenge for creating learner-centric, constructivist classroom environments necessary for DH pedagogy, based on a philosophy of experimentation or "screwing around" (Sneha, 2016).

## Conclusion

Learning through experimentation—that is, through "making and doing", or "through building"—is at the heart of DH pedagogy (Ramsay, 2013, p. 245). Learning in a constructivist manner like this adds to what Fink would have called students' "life file [...] where they put the lessons from everyday life" to draw from when needed (Bonds, 2014, p. 153). In India, particularly, for want of a precise theorisation of the key concerns and objectives of the discipline, practice mapping is presently the only viable option through which one may hope to realise the contents, structures, and methods of instruction in Digital Humanities pedagogy. However, research suggests that, whether because of teachers' beliefs, folk psychology, or the adverse educational context that teachers regularly find themselves in, we are still not quite ready to experiment or 'screw around' with how our students might learn in classrooms. Consequently, instead of growing into an emergent field of critical scholarship with immense possibilities, Digital Humanities—an area whose institutional success hinges on scholar-practitioners "screwing around together" (Ramsay, 2010) as research and pedagogical methodology—is presently relegated to the domain of skills-training for the better employability of students. Until the time we are equipped to consider Digital Humanities pedagogy as more than just skill training, DH studies will remain unrelated to and ill-defined in relation to higher education goals (Bonds, 2014).

# Works Cited

Alexander, R.J. (2001). *Culture and Pedagogy: International Comparisons in Primary Education*. Blackwell.

Alvarado, R.C. (2012). The Digital Humanities Situation. In M.K. Gold (Ed.). *Debates in the Digital Humanities* (Vol. 1). University of Minnesota Press. https://doi.org/10.5749/9781452963754

Aoki, T.T. (1986/1991). Teaching as Indwelling between Two Curriculum Worlds. In W. Pinar, & R. Irwin (Eds). *Curriculum in a New Key: The Collected Works of Ted T. Aoki*. (pp. 159–165). Lawrence Erlbaum Associates.

Arms, W., & Larsen, R. (2007). *Building the Infrastructure for Cyberscholarship*. National Science Foundation.

Ayling D. (2010). Designing Courses for Significant Learning. http://tlcommunityunitec.ning.com/profiles/blogs/designing-courses-for

Bakhtin, M.M. (1984). *Problems of Dostoevsky's Poetics*. University of Minnesota Press.

Batra, P. (2005). Voice and agency of teachers: A missing link in the National Curriculum Framework. *Economic and Political Weekly 40*(36), 4347–4356.

Batra, S. (2009). Inequalities in elementary education. In P. Rustogi (Ed.). *Concerns, Conflicts and Cohesions: Universalization of Elementary Education in India*. (pp. 102–124). Oxford University Press.

Bhaba, H.K. (1990). The third space: Interview with Homi Bhabha. In J. Rutherford (Ed.). *Identity: Community, Culture, Difference*. (pp. 207–221). Lawrence & Wishart.

Bonds, E.L. (2014). Listening in on the conversations: An overview of Digital Humanities pedagogy. *The CEA Critic* 76(2), 147–157. https://dx.doi.org/10.1353/cea.2014.0017

Brier, S. (2012). Where's the pedagogy? The role of teaching and learning in the Digital Humanities. In M.K. Gold (Ed.). *Debates in the Digital Humanities* (Vol. 1). University of Minnesota Press. https://doi.org/10.5749/9781452963754

Brinkmann, S. (2015). Learner-centred education reforms in India: The missing piece of teachers' beliefs. *Policy Futures in Education 13*(3), 342–359. https://doi.org/10.1177/1478210315569038

Bruner, J. (1996). *The Culture of Education.* Harvard University Press. https://doi.org/10.4159/9780674251083

Burdick, A., Drucker, J., Lunenfeld, P., Presner, T., & Schnapp, J. (2016). *Digital Humanities.* MIT Press. https://mitpress.mit.edu/books/digitalhumanities

Cantu, D.A. (2001). *An Investigation of the Relationship Between Social Studies Teachers' Beliefs and Practice.* Edwin Mellen Press.

Chakrabarti, M. (1993). *Tagore and Education for Social Change.* Gian Publishing House.

Chan, K.W., & Elliott, R.G. (2004). Epistemological beliefs across cultures: Critique and analysis of belief structure studies. *Educational Psychology 24*(2), 123–142. https://doi.org/10.1080/0144341032000160100

Clarke, P. (2001). *Teaching and Learning: The Culture of Pedagogy.* Sage.

Clarke, P. (2003). Culture and classroom reform: The case of the district primary education project, India. *Comparative Education 39*, 27–45. https://doi.org/10.1080/03050060302562

Clement, T. (2012). Multiliteracies in the undergraduate digital humanities curriculum: Skills, principles, and habits of mind. In B.D. Hirsch (Ed.). *Digital Humanities Pedagogy: Practices, Principles and Politics.* (pp. 368–388). Open Book Publishers.

Collins, K.M. (2013). *Ability Profiling and School Failure: One Child's Struggle to be seen as Competent.* Routledge. https://doi.org/10.4324/9780203802533

Dagar, V., & Yadav, A. (2016). Constructivism: A paradigm for teaching and learning. *Arts and Social Sciences Journal 7*(4), 1–4.

Diwan, R. (2016). State of Digital Humanities in India. *Hastac.* https://www.hastac.org/blogs/radhikadiwan/2016/10/12/state-digital-humanities-india

Dutta R. (2015a). The integrated curriculum and the place(s) of learning in higher education: Notes from an Indian university campus. In F. Uslu (Ed.). *Proceedings of INTCESS'15–2nd International Conference on Education and Social Sciences.* (pp. 1394–1407). OCERINT.

Dutta, R. (2015b). "Let's Talk": Promoting dialogue and answerability in critical humanities education with permeable curriculum and an āddā-based pedagogy. *Kultura-Społeczeństwo-Edukacja 7*(1), 35–59. https://www.doi.org/10.14746/kse.2015.1.3

Dyer, C., Choksi, A., Awasty, V., & et al., (2004). Knowledge for teacher development in India: The importance of 'local knowledge' for in-service education. *International Journal of Educational Development 24*, 39–52. https://doi.org/10.1016/j.ijedudev.2003.09.003

Dyson, A. H. (1993). Negotiating a permeable curriculum: On literacy, diversity, and the interplay of children's and teachers' worlds. *NCTE Concept Papers 9*, 1–40. National Council of Teachers of English.

Edmond, J. (2016). Collaboration and Infrastructure. In S. Schreibman, R. Siemens, & J. Unsworth (Eds). *A New Companion to Digital Humanities*. Wiley & Sons, Ltd. https://doi.org/10.1002/9781118680605.ch4

Eshach, H. (2007). Bridging in-school and out-of-school learning: Formal, non-formal, and informal education. *Journal of Science Education and Technology 16*(2), 171–190. https://doi.org/10.1007/s10956-006-9027-1

Fang, Z. (1996). A review of research on teacher beliefs and practices. *Educational Research 38*(1), 47–65. https://doi.org/10.1080/0013188960380104

Fink, L.D. (n.d.). A self-directed guide to designing courses for significant learning. *Teaching and Learning Community at Unitec*. http://tlcommunityunitec. ning.com/

Faull, K.M., & Jakacki, D.K. (2015). Digital learning in an undergraduate context: Promoting long-term student-faculty place-based collaboration. *Digital Scholarship in the Humanities*. https://doi.org/10.1093/llc/fqv050

Fink, L.D. (2013). *Creating Significant Learning Experiences: An Integrated Approach to Designing College Courses*. John Wiley & Sons.

Freire, P., & Ramos, M.B. (Trans.). (1970). *Pedagogy of the Oppressed*. Continuum.

Fyfe, P. (2011). How to not read a Victorian novel. *Journal of Victorian Culture 16*(1), 84–88. https://doi.org/10.1080/13555502.2011.554678

Gold, M.K. (2012a). Day of DH: Defining the Digital Humanities. In M.K. Gold (Ed.). *Debates in the Digital Humanities* (Vol. 1). University of Minnesota Press. https://doi.org/10.5749/9781452963754

Gold, M.K. (Ed.). (2012b). *Debates in the Digital Humanities* (Vol. 1). University of Minnesota Press. https://doi.org/10.5749/9781452963754

González N., Moll L., Deborah N., Amanti C. (2005). *Funds of Knowledge: Theorizing Practices in Households, Communities, and Classrooms*. New Jersey.

Gruenewald, D.A. (2003). Foundations of place: A multidisciplinary framework for place-conscious education. *American Educational Research Journal 40*(3), 619–654. https://doi.org/10.3102/00028312040003619

Gupta, A. (2006). Early childhood education, postcolonial theory, and teaching practices. In *India: Balancing Vygotsky and the Vedas*. Palgrave Macmillan. https://doi.org/10.1057/9780312376345

Hirsch, B.D. (2012a). Introduction: Digital Humanities and the place of pedagogy. In B.D. Hirsch (Ed.), *Digital Humanities Pedagogy: Practices, Principles and Politics.* (pp. 3–30). Open Book Publishers. https://www.doi.org/10.11647/OBP.0024

Hirsch, B.D. (Ed.). (2012b). *Digital Humanities Pedagogy: Practices, Principles and Politics.* Open Book Publishers. https://www.doi.org/10.11647/OBP.0024

Ives, M. (2014). Digital Humanities pedagogy: Hitting the wall and bouncing back. *CEA Critic 76* (2), 221–224. https://dx.doi.org/10.1353/cea.2014.0016

Jakacki, D., & Faull, K. (2016). Doing DH in classroom: Transforming humanities curriculum through digital engagement. In C. Crompton, R. J. Lane, & R. Siemens (Eds). *Doing Digital Humanities: Practice, Training, Research.* (pp. 358–372). Routledge.

Liu, A. (2009). Digital Humanities and academic change. *English Language Notes 47* (Spring/Summer), 17–35. https://doi.org/10.1215/00138282-47.1.17

Liu, A. (2012). Where is the cultural criticism in the Digital Humanities? In M.K. Gold (Ed.). *Debates in the Digital Humanities* (Vol. 1). University of Minnesota Press. https://doi.org/10.5749/9781452963754

Liu, A. (2013). The meaning of the Digital Humanities. *PMLA/Publications of the Modern Language Association of America 128* (2). https://doi.org/10.1632/pmla.2013.128.2.409

McClurken, J., Boggs, J., Wadewitz, A., Geller, E., & Beasley-Murray, J. (2013). Digital literacy and the undergraduate curriculum. In D.J. Cohen & T. Schienfeldt (Eds). *Hacking the Academy: New Approaches to Scholarship and Teaching from Digital Humanities.* University of Michigan Press. https://www.doi.org/10.3998/dh.12172434.0001.001

Moje, E.B., Ciechanowski, K.M., Kramer, K., Ellis, L., Carrillo, R., & Collazo, T. (2004). Working toward third space in content area literacy: An examination of everyday funds of knowledge and discourse. *Reading Research Quarterly 39*(1), 38–70. https://doi.org/10.1598/RRQ.39.1.4

Moll, L.C., Amanti, C., Neff, D., & Gonzalez, N. (1992). Funds of knowledge for teaching: using a qualitative approach to connect homes and classrooms. *Theory into Practice 31*(2), 132–141.

Munby, H. (1982). The place of teachers' belief in research on teacher thinking and decision making, and an alternative methodology. *Instructional Science 11*(3), 201–225. https://doi.org/10.1007/BF00414280

Murray, P.R., & Hand, C. (2015). Making culture: Locating the Digital Humanities in India. *Visible Language 49*(3), 140–155.

NCF. (2005). National Curriculum Framework. NCERT.

Noddings, N. (2005). Place-based education to preserve the Earth and its people. In N. Noddings (Ed.). *Educating Citizens for Global Awareness.* (pp. 57–68). Teachers College Press.

Nyhan, J., & Vanhoutte, E. (Eds). (2013). *Defining Digital Humanities. A Reader*. Ashgate Publishing.

O'Connell, K.M. (2008). Freedom, creativity, and leisure in education: Tagore in Canada, 1929. *University of Toronto Quarterly 77*(4), 980–991. https://doi.org/10.3138/UTQ.77.4.980

Pajares, F.M. (1992). Teacher's belief and educational research: Cleaning up a messy construct. *Review of Educational Research 62*(3), 307–322. https://doi.org/10.3102/00346543062003307

Ramachandran, V., Bhattarcharjea, S., & Sheshagiri, K.M. (2008). *Primary School Teachers: The Twists and Turns of Everyday Practice*. Educational Resource Unit.

Ramsay, S. (2010/2014). *The Hermeneutics of Screwing Around: Or What Do You Do with a Million Books*. (pp. 111–120). https://libraries.uh.edu/wp-content/uploads/Ramsay-The-Hermeneutics-of-Screwing-Around.pdf

Ramsay, S. (2013). On building. In *Defining Digital Humanities: A Reader* (pp. 243–245). Ashgate Publishing.

Ramsay, S., & Rockwell, G. (2012). Developing things: Notes toward an epistemology of building in the Digital Humanities. In M.K. Gold (Ed.). *Debates in the Digital Humanities* (Vol. 1). University of Minnesota Press. https://doi.org/10.5749/9781452963754

Rao, N., Cheng, K.M., & Narain, K. (2003). Schooling in China and India: Understanding how socio-contextual factors moderate the role of the State. *International Review of Education 49*(1/2), 153–176. https://doi.org/10.1023/A:1022969922200

Raths, J. (2001). Teachers' beliefs and teaching beliefs. *Early Childhood Research and Practice 3*(1), 1–10.

Rehbein, M., & Fritze, C. (2012). Hands-on teaching digital humanities: A didactic analysis of a summer school course on digital editing. In B.D. Hirsch (Ed.). *Digital Humanities Pedagogy: Practices, Principles and Politics*. (pp. 47–78). Open Book Publishers.

Richardson, V. (1996). The role of attitudes and beliefs in learning to teach. In J. Sikula (Ed.). *Handbook of Research on Teacher Education*. (pp. 102–119). Macmillan.

Richardson, V. (2003). Preservice teachers' beliefs. In J. Raths & A.C. McAninch (Eds). *Teacher Beliefs and Classroom Performance: The Impact of Teacher Education*. Information Age Publishing.

Sanger, M.N., & Osguthorpe, R.D. (2011). Teacher education, preservice teacher beliefs, and the moral work of teaching. *Teaching and Teacher Education 27*(3), 569–578. https://doi.org/10.1016/j.tate.2010.10.011

Sarangapani, P.M. (1999). The child's construction of knowledge. In T. Saraswathi (Ed.). *Culture, Socialization and Human Development: Theory, Research and Applications in India*. (pp. 85–122). Sage Publications.

Sarangapani, P.M. (2003). *Constructing School Knowledge: An Ethnography of Learning in an Indian Village*. Sage Publications.

Schweisfurth, M. (2011). Learner-centred education in developing country contexts: From solution to problem? *International Journal of Educational Development 31*(5). https://doi.org/10.1016/j.ijedudev.2011.03.005

Schweisfurth, M. (2013). *Learner-centred Education in International Perspective: Whose Pedagogy for whose Development?* Routledge. https://doi.org/10.4324/9780203817438

Shanmugapriya, T., & Menon, N. (2020). Infrastructure and social interaction: Situated research practices in Digital Humanities in India. *Digital Humanities Quarterly 14*(3). http://digitalhumanities.org:8081/dhq/vol/14/3/000471/000471.html

Sidorkin, A.M. (2004). *In the event of learning: Alienation and participative thinking in education*. (Faculty Publications Paper 12, pp. 1–11). Rhode Island College. https://doi.org/10.1111/j.0013-2004.2004.00018.x

Sneha, P.P. (2016). *Mapping Digital Humanities in India: Vol. CIS Papers 2016.02*. The Centre for Internet and Society, India. https://cis-india.org/papers/mapping-digital-humanities-in-india

Svensson, P. (2010). The landscape of Digital Humanities. *Digital Humanities Quarterly 4*(1).

Tagore, R. (2009). *The Oxford India Tagore: Selected Writings on Education and Nationalism*. U. D. Gupta (Ed.). Oxford University Press.

Tatto, M.T. (1996). Examining values and beliefs about teaching diverse students: Understanding the challenge for teacher education. *Educational Evaluation and Policy Analysis 18*(2), 155–180. https://doi.org/10.3102/01623737018002155

Taylor, S. (2013). Collaborative approaches to the Digital in English Studies. *Computers and Composition 30*, 180–182. https://doi.org/10.1016/j.compcom.2013.06.003

Vavrus, F. (2009). The cultural politics of constructivist pedagogies: Teacher education reform in the United Republic of Tanzania. *International Journal of Educational Development 29*, 303–311. https://doi.org/10.1016/j.ijedudev.2008.05.002

Vygotsky, L.S. (1978). *Mind in Society: The Development of Higher Psychological Processes*. Harvard University Press.

# 10. Literary masterpiece as a literary bank: A digital representation of intertextual references in T.S. Eliot's *The Waste Land*

*Aditya Ghosh and Ujjwal Jana*

## Abstract

This chapter attempts to model a digital representation of all the intertextual references alluded to in T.S. Eliot's *The Waste Land*. It encompasses the references Eliot incorporated into this masterpiece, from Classical and Biblical texts to his contemporary literary texts, followed by an inventory of post-*Waste Land* texts which borrowed from the text in question. This work produced by Eliot throws any reader or scholar into a labyrinth of intertextuality and literary allusions, the sheer magnitude of which can potentially confuse as the range of the references reaches far and wide. There is a scholarly dispute about the changing paradigm of critical research works under the veneer of digital technology, as many are apprehensive about losing epistemological and ontological aspects of critical research work in the field of humanities under the sustained pressure of employing a digital medium.[1] But, having the benefit of an archival digital

---

1   In the past few years  there has been a tremendous momentum shift towards adopting digital technologies in India in all spheres of life, including the education sector and governance. The Indian government has allocated funds and aggressively pushed for Digital India, Digital Economy and many other initiatives to foster digital growth. As part of this drive the Indian education system has been reformed and more focus has been given to technological innovations and digital drives such

    https://doi.org/10.11647/OBP.0423.10

repository and its capability to quickly access multiple texts from various resources corroborates the view that technology can facilitate the creation and dissemination of knowledge in the field of humanities. The main objective of this research is to create a repository where all the intertextual references of Eliot's poem *The Waste Land* could be stored. This chapter will employ three different steps to demonstrate different sources of references and allusions that were used in the production of *The Waste Land*.

## Keywords

Digital representation; Digital Humanities; digital technology; intertextuality; T.S. Eliot.

## Introduction

Discussion and research on and about Digital Humanities (DH) have rapidly increased in intensity in Indian academia in the last eight to ten years. Research in literary fields has primarily been analytical and qualitative. On the other hand, digital methods and computational works primarily focus on data-driven quantitative research. Although the marriage between these two fields seems unlikely on a surface level, there is a recent trend in which scholarly activities flourish at the intersection of digital technologies and the disciplines of humanities (Buzzetti, 2019; Edmond, 2020; Jockers & Underwood, 2016; Pokrivcak, 2021; Schwandt, 2021). Using new applications and techniques, Digital Humanities makes new kinds of teaching and research possible, while at the same time studying and critiquing how these impact cultural heritage and digital culture (Wilkens, 2012; McPherson, 2012; Fiormonte, 2012; Hankins, 2023). In its attempt to bridge the gap between traditional knowledge-based domains and modern skill-based fields, DH aims to "use information technology to illuminate the human

---

as MOOC, SWAYAM, and NPTEL courses. The private sector have an increasing influence on the Indian education system providing funds and economic backing to technology and data-driven areas. On the contrary, traditional humanities feel alienated, reeling with lack of funds and resources. There is a constant pressure to fit in the current 'digital mania', to either adapt to digital technology or perish.

record and [bring] an understanding of the human record to bear on the development and use of information technology" (Scheibman et al., 2004, p. xiii). Therefore, Digital Humanities situates itself at the centre of many divergent areas and operates as "a nexus of fields within which scholars use computing technologies to investigate the kinds of questions that are traditional to the humanities, or, [...] ask traditional kinds of humanities-oriented questions about computing technologies" (Fitzpatrick, 2012, p. 12).

The drive towards digital technologies has changed human perspectives rapidly in the 21st century. Cultural and intellectual consciousness has gone through a massive transformation. India has quickly participated in this transformation and devoted much intellectual and economic capital to this digital drive through Digital India, Bharat Net, UPI, Broadband Highways, Aadhar, DigiLocker, and Digitize India Platform. The postmillennial generation is swiftly moving away from the pen-paper-print medium to the digital mode, and this trend is influencing the traditional knowledge-based fields that have predominantly depended on physical books, pen and paper. Humanities departments are going through a crisis at this critical juncture, as students of this generation are more tech-savvy than 'bookworm'. Humanities teachers and researchers are embracing digital modes in their pedagogical styles, as well as digitisation in study materials and research endeavours. Significant emphasis has been placed upon the adoption of digital technologies in humanities studies in the past decade.

As Dash states, there has been the rise of an:

> [...] interactive interface for the new generation of scholars to enable them to extend their studies and research of humanities under a digital platform and gives them the power to apply traditional skills of the humanities (e.g., critical thinking) to understand digital culture while learning how digital technology can enable them to explore the key questions in the humanities (Dash, 2023, p. 38).

Digital Humanities have presented us with an alternate mode of study and research within the traditional domain of knowledge production. It has created an opportunity to explore the traditional knowledge system in a fresh manner, keeping it relevant to the current generation as it involves, "collaborative, transdisciplinary, and technologically engaged analysis, research, development, teaching, resource generation and making them available for the new generation of users" (Dash, 2023, p. 38).

Keeping this transformation in mind, this chapter aims to contribute to the alternative ways of studying canonical literature by adopting Digital Humanities methodology, keeping T.S. Eliot's *The Waste Land* at the centre of the chapter. Literature with the epic proportions of Eliot's *The Waste Land*, Milton's *Paradise Lost*, Joyce's *Ulysses*, Hindu epics *Ramayana* and *Mahabharata*, Greek epics *Aeneid* and *Metamorphosis*, or Dante's *Inferno* is difficult for students and teachers to lucidly elaborate in the classroom. It becomes all the more challenging for contemporary students who are estranged from studying physical materials and who are more oriented towards using technological devices.

This chapter presents a digital model, which acts as a repository of all the allusions and intertextual references in Eliot's *The Waste Land*. This approach offers access to information about all of the poem's references in one place. The chapter is a part of a bigger hypertext project, similar to the Victorian Web, which develops a digital platform that presents the allusions and referenced texts in one place, with access to these referenced texts that are either quoted in *The Waste Land* or other post-*Waste Land* texts that were inspired by Eliot's work. This chapter only presents a visual representation of the repository through graphs and diagrams of the project, to generate interest among students and to inspire further research in the Digital Humanities. The authors are part of the larger project currently building a database for the visual representation of Eliot's *The Waste Land*. This chapter introduces and models the database that is enabled by the collection of the data after a detailed study of the intertextual references. Diagrams and graphs have been prepared for this chapter with the help of digital technology. As the building of *The Waste Land* database will be through the affordances of digital technology, this chapter is likewise undoubtedly the product of Digital Humanities research.

Computational methods in the Digital Humanities have the potential to trace patterns in literary works which can inform qualitative analysis. The structuralist paradigm has demonstrated how elements in different cultural activities, for example, literature and movies, can be organised within a semiotic system. For example, most of the detective stories, irrespective of their sources, for centuries have followed a common structure.[2] Similarly, all superhero movies follow a pattern or a structured narrative. A close analysis of Victorian novels reveals that they follow an underlying pattern or structure which remains the same while individual stories differ, along with characters and plotlines (Hingston, 2019; Garrett, 1977; Valint, 2021). Russian structuralist critic Vladimir Propp made an extensive study of hundreds of Russian folktales and discovered a pattern of underlying structures for these stories (Propp, 1968). Although they were different on an individual level and consisted of different characters and settings, all of them had seven character types—hero, villain, donor, provider, princess, fake hero and dispatcher—and all these stories served similar purposes.

What is important here is that, although the primary research work in literary fields involves qualitative analysis, most scholars ignore the quantitative nature of their work. These examples suggest that research work in literary fields also is "implicitly quantitative, pattern-based, and dependent on reductive models of the texts they treat" (Wilkens, 2015, p. 11). Computational methods in Digital Humanities help in "identifying and assessing literary patterns at scales from the individual text to whole fields and systems of cultural production" (Wilkens, 2015, p. 11). Digital Humanities has bridged the gap between these two fields and offers new approaches to carrying out innovative ground-breaking research. Digital Humanities, therefore, is "an interdisciplinary area of research, practice and pedagogy that looks at the interaction of digital tools, methods and spaces with core concerns of humanistic enquiry" (Sneha, 2016, p. 10). Maintaining a holistic approach and keeping the theoretical concerns and the possibilities of further emergence in mind, *Digital Humanities Quarterly* considers that:

> Digital humanities is a diverse and still emerging field that encompasses the practice of humanities research in and through information technology, and the exploration of how the humanities may evolve through their engagement with technology, media, and computational methods (Sneha, 2016, p. 10).

---

2    A crime is committed; police fail to solve the case; a detective is called upon; the crime seems to be a perfect crime; the detective has a personal friend who is primarily a narrator of the story; the detective solves the case at the end; the criminal is caught and punished; justice prevails; truth wins.

Research work in the Digital Humanities has largely focused on literary texts. English departments, specifically, have been important to Digital Humanities research. Some of the ground-breaking research projects on Digital Humanities have given birth to The Victorian Web, the Shakespeare Electronic Archive, The Whitman Archive and many more. The Victorian Web is a repository of various Victorian digital objects. It is "a hypertext project derived from hypermedia environment, Intermedia and Storyspace" (Victorian Web, 2024). Although the repository had around 1500 documents including Victorian texts when it was created, it boasts of having nearly 128,500 items currently. Shakespeare Electronic Archive and The Whitman Archive are archival works generated by Digital Humanities projects. Shakespeare Electronic Archive was created to keep all "electronic texts of Shakespeare's plays closely linked to digital copies of primary materials" (Shakespeare Electronic Archive). This archival work includes images from the *First Folio,* collection of arts and illustrations from *Hamlet* and many digitised items from film on *Hamlet.* The Whitman Archive has documented and stored Whitman's life and works, including his letters and essays.

Apart from the hypertext model adopted by the Victorian Web and many archival repositories, Digital Humanities research has significantly focused on text modelling and encoding for critical analysis and to evaluate patterns and forms of literary works (Argamon & Olsen, 2009; Jannidis & Flanders, 2012; Kralemann & Lattmaan, 2013; McCarty, 2004; Marrus & Ciula, 2014; Sharma & Sharma, 2021). This indicates that literary works and literary figures are often the subject of significant Digital Humanities research projects. Matthew Kirschenbaum (2016) argues that "after numerical input, text is the most traceable type of data for computers to manipulate", and "there is the long association between computers and composition" (pp. 8–9). Computational methods, digital data and digital databases:

> [...] have become indisputable resources for literary study, not just for archival research but also literary interpretation, and the amount of data available in text form—think Google Books, Project Gutenberg, and UPenn's Online Books Page—continues to grow at an astonishing rate (Pressman & Swanstorm, 2013).

Like many literary stalwarts, T.S. Eliot has also been the subject of many Digital Humanities research works. Arbuckle (2014) discusses the preparation of *The Waste Land* for iPad. She points out that although it is widely successful, it is not free of issues. He further discusses the importance of robust collaboration and reconciliation between scholarly practices and computational designs in the creation of cultural content through digital means.

Kim et al., (2020) make an extensive study of many modern writers, with a particular focus on Eliot. With the use of computational methods, they try to discover some patterns of vocabulary density and the occurrence of nouns and adjectives in *The Waste Land*. Juan Antonio Suarez (2001) emphasises Eliot's dependency on technological devices through his special connection to the gramophone. Although Eliot never flaunted his affection for technological gadgets, their impact on modern society is well documented in his literary production. Suarez argues that: "Eliot's writing, like Warhol's multimedia projects, was uneasily entangled in gadgets, circuits, media networks, and technologies of textual production and reproduction" (2001, p. 747). An extensive review of these research articles reveals that, although Digital Humanities research has focused on many aspects of Eliot's *The Waste Land*, little research work has been carried out to explore the work's extended references, which range from classical literature to Eliot's contemporaries.

The objective of this chapter is to fill that gap. It aims to model a digital representation of all the intertextual references in T.S. Eliot's *The Waste Land*. It encompasses Eliot's interests that he incorporated into this masterpiece as well as other literary works. It also includes books that were published later and borrowed from *The Waste Land*. The sheer magnitude of Eliot's poem can potentially confuse both lay readers and scholars, as the range of the references reaches from Classical literature, to Biblical allusions, to the contemporaries of Eliot's time. This research creates a repository that provides the intertextual references in one place, thereby making it a kind of literary bank.

## I.

*The Waste Land* is Eliot's masterpiece in the history of literature. In this work, Eliot discusses the morally corrupt, degenerate condition of modern society. He provides hundreds of literary allusions for his representation of a horrific social situation. Despite making giant economic strides and technological advancements, Eliot views his society as one whose heart and soul have become hollow. In Eliot's outlook, society is morally corrupt; there is political instability, and social values have given way to jealousy envy, revenge, greed and betrayal. People are alienated, fragmented, mentally deranged, joyless and sexually aberrant so that lechery and debauchery thrive (Bellour, 2016; Hoover, 1978; Karim, 2019; Maheswari, 2016; Qasim, 2022).

To portray the sordid account of this degenerate society, Eliot sources intertextual references from Classical texts, Biblical texts and many literary texts as follows:

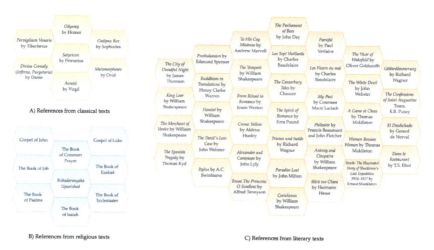

Fig. 10.1 The allusions from Classical texts, Biblical texts and literary texts in *The Waste Land*.

In the beginning of the poem, references to Classical texts like Virgil's *Aeneid*, Ovid's *Metamorphosis*, and Dante's *Inferno* are used extensively (Bhardwaj & Kumar, 2023; Donker, 1974; Rapa, 2010). With these allusions we revisit, for example, Satan, Hell, the Cumaean Sibyl, and the rape of Philomela in *Metamorphosis*. Eliot makes it clear that modern cities are like Hell, in which people suffer, are punished, and are mentally tormented. There is sexual exploitation, perversion and debauchery everywhere. There are references to Sophocles and Seneca's texts, because Eliot suggests that, like the city of Thebes in *Oedipus Rex*, the modern city of London also is going through a pandemic (Saxby, 2020). People are restless as they are fragmented morally and psychologically and lust for each other's downfall. There is anarchy everywhere. There is sterility and society is decaying.

Though the poem deals with themes of decay and degeneration, the turn towards a solution to arrest this decline is underpinned by many Biblical references (Alahdal, 2017; Kumar, 2018; Mahmud, 2020). Eliot is also searching for a resolution for the rebirth of society. His search for this holy grail draws on intertextual references to the search for the Holy Grail of Christ. "The Burial of the Dead" in *The Waste Land* provides a reference to the Anglican Book of Common Prayer which suggests that death is necessary for rebirth and revival. Throughout Eliot's poem, there are abundant references to The Book of Common Prayer, The Book of Job, the Gospel of John, the Gospel of Luke, The Book of Ezekiel and The Book of Ecclesiastes (Ananda, 2023; Lauren, 2003).

In the beginning of the poem, the reference to "broken images" (L. 22–23) provides an allusion to Ezekiel's narration of God's judgement of people worshipping idols. The reference compares the idolisation of money by modern society and God's judgement accordingly, which leaves them without souls and with many psychological traumas. In the Bible, Hebrews are seen lamenting for the lost city of Jerusalem after they are exiled to Babylon. Eliot uses this reference to the loss of a glorified past in his lamentation for a hopeless, degenerate society that is hollow, corrupt and volatile. Apart from these references to Classical and Biblical texts, there are various connections to many other literary texts, including those by Shakespeare, Chaucer, Spenser, Marvell, Webster, Middleton, Huxley, Baudelaire, Milton and Wagner.

## II.

The Canterbury Tales by Chaucer | Aeneid by Virgil | Metamorphoses by Ovid | Oedipus Rex by Sophocles | Philaster by Francis Beaumont and John Fletcher

The Book of Common Prayer | The Book of Ezekiel | The Book of Ecclesiastes | My Past by Countess Marie Larisch | Crome Yellow by Aldous Huxley | Oedipus Rex by Sophocles | Itylus by A.C. Swinburne | Purgatorio by Dante

Metamorphoses by Ovid | Satyricon by Petronius | Purgatorio by Dante | The Spirit of Romance by Ezra Pound | Tristan und Isolde by Richard Wagner | The Tempest by William Shakespeare | The Merchant of Venice by William Shakespeare

The Book of Job | Inferno by Dante | From The Princess: O Swallow by Tennyson | Blick ins Chaos by Hermann Hesse

The White Devil by John Webster | Les Fleurs du mal by Charles Baudelaire | El Desdichado by Gerard de Nerval | King Lear by William Shakespeare

**The Waste Land**

A Game at Chess by Thomas Middleton | Hamlet by William Shakespeare | Spanish Tragedy by Thomas Kyd | Dans le Restaurant by T.S. Eliot | The White Devil by John Webster

Gospel of John | Prothalamion by Edmund Spenser | Pervigilium Veneris by Tiberianus

Antony and Cleopatra by William Shakespeare | The Vicar of Wakefield by Oliver Goldsmith | Parsifal by Paul Verlaine | Götterdämmerung by Richard Wagner | The Confessions of Saint Augustine | Brihadaranyaka Upanishad | Coriolanus by William Shakespeare

Gospel of Luke | Paradise Lost by John Milton | Alexander and Campaspe by John Lyly | The Devil's Law Case by John Webster | Buddhism in Translations by Henry Clarke Warren | To His Coy Mistress by Andrew Marvell | The Parliament of Bees by John Day | Oedipus Rex by Sophocles | The Book of Psalms

From Ritual to Romance by Jessie Weston | Les Sept Vieillards by Charles Baudelaire | Women Beware Women by Thomas Middleton | South: The Story of Shackleton's Last Expedition, 1914–1917 by Sir Ernest Shackleton | The City of Dreadful Night by James Thomson

Fig. 10.2 A visual representation of allusions in *The Waste Land*: i) rectangular boxes (yellow), which are closest to the title of the poem, contain texts from which lines have been directly borrowed; ii) rectangular boxes (pink) consist of texts from which phrases and names have been borrowed; iii) the outermost rectangles (blue) contain other thematic references to various texts.

In the above image, the closest rectangle to the title of *The Waste Land* contains texts from which Eliot directly quoted lines for his work. The next set of rectangles consists of texts from which Eliot borrowed phrases and names for intertextual references, and the outermost rectangles contain texts that the poem references indirectly, but from which Eliot has borrowed no direct quotations, phrases or names. For example, the epigraph of *The Waste Land* is taken from *Satyricon*, written by Petronius, whose translation reads: "For on one occasion I myself saw, with my own eyes, the Cumaean Sibyl hanging in a cage, and when some boys said to her, 'Sibyl, what do you want?' she replied, 'I want to die'" (Rainey, 2005, p. 75). Eliot directly quotes "*Frisch weht der wind/*

*Der Heimat zu,/ Mein Irisch Kind/ Wo weilest du?*" [Fresh blows the wind / To the homeland; / My Irish child, / Where are you tarrying?] (L. 34–38) from Richard Wagner's *Tristan and Isolde*. This text tells the story of Tristan and Isolde and how they fell in love on their journey from Cornwall to Ireland. Eliot uses this allusion at the beginning of the poem to suggest that Death is the ultimate cure for all the decay, corruption, sterility and sexual debauchery that has taken hold of society. *Tristan and Isolde* begins and ends with death.

Eliot extensively quoted from Shakespeare's works. "Those are pearls that were his eyes" (L. 48) is a direct quotation borrowed from *The Tempest*. The farewell words "Good night, ladies, good night, sweet ladies, good night, good night" (L. 171–172) of the ladies in the bar in the closing lines of *A Game of Chess* resemble Ophelia's "farewell to the Queen and other ladies of the castle" (Purwarno, 2003, p. 132) in Shakespeare's *Hamlet*.

Eliot borrows the phrases "—Hypocrite lecteur,—mon semblable,—mon frère!" [Hypocrite reader!—You!—My twin!—My brother!] from Baudelaire's poem *Les Fleurs du Mal*. He also provides an allusion to Spenser's *Prothalamion* and directly borrows a quotation: "sweet Thames, run softly, till I end my song" (L. 176). Next, Eliot quotes directly "Et O ces voix d'enfants, chantant dans la coupole" [And O those voices of children singing under the cupola] (L. 202) from Paul Verlaine's poem *Parsifal*. Eliot used this line to turn the attention towards a longing for the innocence of childhood and the sanctity of the church. "When lovely woman stoops to folly" (L. 253) is from Oliver Goldsmith's *The Vicar of Wakefield*. This refers to a lamentation because of the seduction of money and physical pleasure and its negative moral effect on modern people. It refers to the envy, corruption, debauchery, and sexual perversion of the modern world.

The phrase "burning burning burning burning" (L. 308) is taken from Buddha's *Fire Sermon*. It describes the "burning of passion, attachment and suffering" (Sharma, 2020, p. 7). "Datta. Dayadhvam. Damyata" (L. 433) is taken from *The Brihadaranyaka Upanishad* in which God preached to men who have gone astray to return to the life of giving, which is to be kind and offer help, show compassion to others, and to rein in unruly behaviour and aggression. Eliot ends the poem with "Shantih Shantih Shantih" (L. 434) which is also taken from *The Brihadaranyaka*

*Upanishad.* "Shantih" means "peace", and is necessary for an ordered human existence. People in this wasteland are suffering from mental unrest, they are alienated, they are lost, they are without hope and traumatised. If they want to get back to the glorified peaceful past and have Shantih in life, they have to practice Datta. Dayadhvam. Damyata.

III.

Fig. 10.3 All the texts that have borrowed references from or been inspired by Eliot's *The Waste Land*.

*The Waste Land* not only references past works, but the poem itself has influenced many future texts. The title of Evelyn Waugh's novel, *A Handful of Dust* (1934), which satirises human values, morality, mortality and all human endeavours, is borrowed from *The Waste Land*. Much more recently, Kenzaburo Oe published *Death by Water* in 2009, a novel set against the backdrop of World War II that narrates a man's search to uncover the mysteries surrounding the death of his father. The influence upon the title of Stephen Dedman's short story *Waste Lands* is obvious, while Dedman's other short story, *The Lady of Situations*, is inspired by Madam Sosostris's tarot reading in Eliot's poem. Not only is the title of Francesca Lia Block's novel *Wasteland* (2003) influenced by Eliot's work, but the novel quotes extensively from the poem towards the end—as does Stephen King's novel *The Dark Tower III: The Waste Lands* (1991), which quotes many lines from the poem in the opening pages as well as borrowing its title.

Not all of the references are reverential. H.P. Lovecraft wrote a parody of the poem, *Waste Paper: A Poem of Profound Insignificance*. He considered *The Waste Land* a meaningless poem that accumulated quotations and references from hundreds of books throughout literary history to no purpose; a waste of materials and time that lacks significance.

## Conclusion

There exist intellectual and scholarly disputes about the changing paradigm of critical research methods that use digital technology. The advantages of an archival repository and access to multiple texts suggest that the affordances of technology can facilitate the creation and dissemination of knowledge in the field of humanities. Moreover, interpretative, generative and qualitative research enabled by the intersection of humanities and the digital medium has already demonstrated that Digital Humanities can offer access to research sources and materials. DH enables scholars to access and analyse vast corpora of materials from various sources and synthesise with close-reading method of traditional research which brings in new insights and allows for a fresh interpretation. By providing plethora of data and statistical methods, DH helps researchers to analyse and understand the patterns of literary production in any particular age, external factors which shape the literary tradition of any decade or century, literary movements and their influences on author/reader etc. Therefore, DH does not undermine or neglect the nuances of traditional research methods nor does it reject the close-reading of literary texts, instead it enhances further research possibilities with its wider reach to far away materials and providing data-driven statistical methods. In the case of this chapter, bringing the intertextual references of Eliot's masterpiece *The Waste Land* into the framework described will prove a lasting resource for scholars and educators alike.

# Works Cited

Alahdal, M., Ahmed, Y., & Mane, D.R. (2017). Sterility as a recurring theme in Eliot's *The Waste Land*. *Indian Scholar 3*(4), 78–82.

Arbuckle, A. (2014). Considering *The Waste Land* for iPad and Weird Fiction as models for the public digital edition. *Digital Studies/le Champ Numérique 5*(1). https://doi.org/http://doi.org/10.16995/dscn.50

Argamon, S., & Olsen, M. (2009). Words, patterns, and documents: Experiments in machine learning and text analysis. *Digital Humanities Quarterly, 3*(1).

Bellour, L. (2016). The religious crisis and the spiritual journey in T. S. Eliot's *The Waste Land*. *Arab World English Journal 7*(4), 422–438.

Bhardwaj, P., & Kumar, D. (2023). A deep reflection of disorder and decay in *The Waste Land*. *Humanities and Social Sciences 83*(1), 115–122.

Birsanu, R. (2010). Intertextuality as translation in T. S. Eliot's *The Waste Land, SUNDEBAR 21*, 21–35.

Buzzetti, D. (2019). The origins of humanities computing and the Digital Humanities Turn. *Humanist Studies & the Digital Age 6*(1). https://doi.org/10.5399/uo/hsda.6.1.3

Chaudhuri, S. (2021). The game's the thing: Politics and play in Middleton's *A Game at Chess. Études Épistémè. Revue de littérature et de civilisation (XVIe–XVIIIe siècles) 39*. https://doi.org/10.4000/episteme.11534

Dash, N.S. (2023). Digital Humanities: Harnessing digital technology for sustenance and growth of the Humanities. In Mandal, Pranab, Kumar, and Ghosh, Sankha (Eds). *The Incandescent Classroom: Essays in Honour of Prof. Satyaki Pal.* (pp. 38–55). RK Mission Residential College Press.

Donker, M. (1974). *The Waste Land and The Aeneid. PMLA 1*, 164–173. https://doi.org/10.2307/461679

Edmond, J. (Ed.). (2020). *Digital Technology and the Practices of Humanities Research*. Open Book Publishers. https://doi.org/10.11647/OBP.0192

Eliot, T.S. (1922). *The Waste Land*. Binker North.

Fiormonte, D. (2012). Towards a cultural critique of the digital humanities.

*Historical Social Research* 37(3), 59–76. https://doi.org/10.12759/hsr.37.2012.3.59-76

Fitzpatrick, K. (2010). Reporting from the Digital Humanities 2010 Conference. In *The Chronicle of Higher Education*. http://chronicle. com/blogs/profhacker/reporting-from-the-digital-humanities-2010-conference/25473

Garrett, P.K. (1977). Double plots and dialogical form in Victorian fiction. *Nineteenth-Century Fiction 32*(1), 1–17.

Griffith, J. (2020). Victorian structures: Architecture, society, and narrative. *Nineteenth-Century Contexts 44*(5), 543–544.

Haas, L. (2003). The revival of myth: Allusions and symbols in *The Waste Land*. *Ephemeris* 3(8). https://digitalcommons.denison.edu/ephemeris/vol3/iss1/8

Hankins, G. (2023). Reproducing disciplinary and literary prestige: The index of major literary prizes in the US. *International Journal of Digital Humanities*. https://doi.org/10.1007/s42803-023-00082-x

Hingston, K-A. (2019). *Articulating Bodies: The Narrative Form of Disability and Illness in Victorian Fiction*. Liverpool University Press. https://library.oapen.org/handle/20.500.12657/52808

Hoover, J.M. (1978). The urban nightmare: Alienation imagery in the poetry of T. S. Eliot and Octavio Paz. *Journal of Spanish Studies: Twentieth Century 6*, 13–28.

Jannidis, F. & Flanders, J. (Eds). (2012). Knowledge organization and data modelling in the humanities: An ongoing conversation. *Workshop at Brown University*.

Jockers, M.L. & Underwood, T. (2016). Text-mining the Humanities. In S. Schreibman, R. Siemens, & J. Unsworth (Eds). *New Companion to Digital Humanities*. John Wiley & Sons.

Karim, Md., Rezaul. (2019). Spiritual barrenness, war, and alienation: Reading Eliot's *The Waste Land*. *IJRHAL, 7*(6), 393-404.

Khan, A.B., Mansoor, H.S., & Khan, M.Y. (2015). Critical analysis of allusions and symbols in the poem *The Waste Land* by Thomas Stearns Eliot. *International Journal of Multidisciplinary Research and Modern Education 1*, 615–619.

Kim, S., et al., (2020). Implications of vocabulary density for poetry: Reading T. S. Eliot's poetry through computational methods. *Digital Scholarship in the Humanities*, 1–12. https://doi.org/10.1093/llc/fqaa009

Kirschenbaum, M. (2016). What is digital humanities and what's it doing in English departments? In M. Terras, J. Nyhan, & E. Vanhoutte (Eds). *Defining Digital Humanities*. (pp. 195–203). Routledge.

Kralemann, B. & Lattmann, C. (2013). Models as icons: Modelling models in the semiotic framework of Pierce's theory of signs. *Synthese 190*(16), 3397–3420. https://www.doi.org/10.1007/s11229-012-0176-x

Kumar, S. (2018). The theme of decay and destruction in Eliot's *The Waste Land*. *Parisheelan*, XIV(2).

Maheswari, C., Baby N. (2016). Modern life as a waste land in Eliot's *The Waste Land*. *IJELLH*, *IV*(*XI*).

McCarty, W. (2004). Modelling: A study of words and meanings. In S. Schreibman, R. Siemens, & J. Unsworth (Eds). *A Companion to Digital Humanities*. Blackwell.

McPherson, T. (2012). Why are the digital humanities so white? Or thinking the histories of race and computation. *Debates in the Digital Humanities 1*, 139–60.

Mahmud, R. (2020). Spiritual barrenness and physical deformities of the distressed modern people in T. S. Eliot's *The Waste Land*. *Language in India 20*(7).

Marras, C. & Ciula, A. (2014). Circling around texts and language: Towards 'pragmatic modelling' in Digital Humanities. *Digital Humanities— Book of Abstracts*, 255–257. http://www.digitalhumanities.org/dhq/vol/10/3/000258/000258.html

Patil, U. (2023). A critical study of the myths, classical references and allusions in T. S. Eliot's *The Waste Land*. *IJFMR 5*(6).

Pokrivcak, A. (2021). Digital Humanities and Literary Studies. *Trnava 5*(7).

Pressman, J., & Swanstrom L. (2013). The literary and/as the Digital Humanities. *DHQ: Digital Humanities Quarterly 7*(1). https://www.digitalhumanities.org/dhq/vol/7/1/000154/000154.html

Propp, V. (1968). *Morphology of the Folktale*. University of Texas Press.

Purwarno, P. (2003). Echoes of Shakespeare in T. S. Eliot's *The Waste Land*. *JULISA 3*(2), 128–137.

Qasim, M. (2022). The land and the waste: Meaninglessness and absurdity in T. S. Eliot's *The Waste Land*. *SJESR 5*(4), 141–146. https://doi.org/10.36902/sjesr-vol5-iss4-2022

Rainey, L. (Ed.). (2005). *The Annotated Waste Land with Eliot's Contemporary Prose*. Yale University Press.

Rapa, J. (2010). Out of this stony rubbish: Echoes of Ezekiel in T. S. Eliot's *The Waste Land*. Master's Theses. 692. https://scholarworks.gvsu.edu/theses/692

Saxby, G. (2020). *The Waste Land* by T. S. Eliot: Is it a dialectic text? *Swinburne University of Technology*, https://www.doi.org/10.13140/RG.2.2.28389.63205

Scheibman, S., Siemens R., Unsworth, J. (2004). The Digital Humanities and Humanities Computing: An Introduction. In S. Scheibman, R. Siemens, J. Unsworth (Eds). *A Companion to Digital Humanities*. Blackwell.

Schwandt, S. (Ed.). (2021). *Digital Methods in the Humanities: Challenges,*

*Ideas, Perspectives*. Bielefeld University Press. https://library.oapen.org/handle/20.500.12657/47133

Sneha, P.P. (2016). Mapping Digital Humanities in India. *The Centre for Internet & Society*. https://cis-india.org/papers/mapping-digital-humanities-in-india

Shakespeare Electronic Archive. https://shea.mit.edu/shakespeare/htdocs/main/index.htm

Shakespeare, W. (2019). *Antony and Cleopatra*. Maple Press.

Shakespeare, W. (2014). *King Lear*. Maple Press.

Sharma, K.S., & Sharma, A. (2021). Literature and Cultural Studies Through Data Mining. *ICFAI Journal of English Studies 16*(4), 119–125.

Sharma, L.R. (2020). Detecting major allusions and their significance in Eliot's poem *The Waste Land*. *Journal for Research Scholars and Professionals of English Teaching 21*(4), 1–9.

Suarez, J. (2001). T. S. Eliot's *The Waste Land*, the gramophone, and the modernist discourse network. *New Literary History 32*(3), 747–768. https://www.doi.org/10.1353/nlh.2001.0048

Valint, A. (2021). *Narrative Bonds: Multiple Narrators in the Victorian Novel*. The Ohio State University Press.

Victorian Web. (2024). In *Wikipedia*. https://en.wikipedia.org/wiki/Victorian_Web

Wilkens, M. (2012). Canons, close reading, and the evolution of method. In M. Gold (Ed.). *Debates in the Digital Humanities*. University of Minnesota Press.

Wilkens, M. (2015). Digital Humanities and its application in the study of literature and culture. *Comparative Literature 67*(1), 11–20. https://www.doi.org/10.1215/00104124-2861911

# 11. Hypertext as a 'palimpsestuous' construct: Analysing Shelley Jackson's *Patchwork Girl*

*Lopamudra Saha and Ujjwal Jana*

## Abstract

This chapter analyses how the hypertext fiction *Patchwork Girl* (1995) functions as a palimpsest in its postmodern multimodal rewriting of the myth of *Frankenstein; or, the Modern Prometheus* (1818). Since digital culture is one of the major postmodern offshoots, and the idea of the hypertext is the product of literary culture and digital innovations, new possibilities have been brought about that unsettle the traditional conceptualisation of the novel as the printed word. This chapter, therefore, proposes the study of the concept of the hypertext as 'palimpsestuous' relativity, with special reference to *Patchwork Girl*. To serve this purpose, the traditional idea of the 'palimpsest' as a parchment undergoes revision in the light of the affordances of multimedia. This enquiry also uncovers the changing dynamics of readership that the new media intervention has brought about. Finally, the discussion highlights how hypertextual rewriting induces the ideas of multivocality, fragmentariness, non-linearity and interactivity through the application of the inter-semiotic paradigm.

## Keywords

Palimpsest; hypertext; multimodal; *Patchwork Girl*; Frankenstein.

https://doi.org/10.11647/OBP.0423.11

# Introduction

The digital era has diverted the attention of the traditional book reader from turning pages to browsing web pages across digital screens. In 1997, Espen Aarseth defined this new coda of literature as 'ergodic' where "non-trivial effort is required to allow the reader to traverse the text" (Aarseth, 1997, p. 1). In other words, the reader must be engaged in the active creation of the text with a traversal dynamic previously unattained. The process of narrative co-construction was furthered by David Ciccoricco (2007) in *Reading Network Fiction*, where he posits that network fiction not only blurs the boundary between author and the reader, but by analysing formal elements and aesthetic novelty he argues that they enter into a dialectic with the cultural and technological shifts brought about by the proliferation of digital technology. With the ever-existent and all-encompassing presence of the digital in our everyday life, and the prevalence of multimedia technologies—images, videos, audio, graphics, animations—on the screens of our electronic devices such as smart phones and laptops simply through a click, the scope and possibilities of ergodic literature grew rapidly. Digital Humanities, as an area of scholarly activity that functions at the intersections of these new digital innovations and literary culture, has gained global scholarly attention in recent times.

Electronic Literature, which is a subgenre of Digital Humanities and an instance of ergodic literature, basically embodies a multimodal genre of writing that aims to associate multimedia technologies with the printed word. N. Katherine Hayles' (2008) understanding of electronic literature, in her seminal *Electronic Literature: New Horizons for the Literary*, as integrating computational processes and interactive structures, situates this genre of writing as giving birth to and interacting with issues of identity, embodiment and narrative aesthetics in the digital age. These are born-digital works of literature that are also meant to be read digitally on the various social media platforms, blogs, and YouTube videos that are the very sites of Electronic Literature production. Here, the Electronic Literature Organisation (ELO) definition of Electronic Literature aptly fits—that is, Electronic Literature refers to works that make use of the materiality of the computational culture. One of the various forms of Electronic Literature that have come to exist in the digital age is hypertext fiction.

The idea of the hypertext was introduced by Vannevar Bush in 1945[1] and was simultaneously realised and given its contemporary shape by Theodor Nelson. Nelson coined the term 'hypertext', which refers to:

> [...] non-sequential writing—text that branches and allows choices to the reader, best read at an interactive screen. As popularly conceived, this is a series of text chunks [lexias] connected by links which offer the reader different pathways (Landow, 2006).

According to Paul Delany and John Landow, hypertext can be defined as "the use of computer to transcend the linear, bounded and fixed qualities of the linear text" (Delany & Landow, 1994, p. 6). The earliest instance of literary creation that used this method was *Afternoon, a Story* by Michael Joyce in 1987. The work was written in 'Storyspace', a software program developed by Joyce himself along with Jay David Butler, for creating, editing, and reading hypertext fiction.

The hypertext fiction *Patchwork Girl* (1995) was written by the American author Shelley Jackson and published by Eastgate Systems. The myth upon which this electronic fiction is based, calls to mind the famous gothic novel published by the British author Mary Shelley in 1818, *Frankenstein; or, the Modern Prometheus*.[2] The narrative of this hypertext fiction, *Patchwork Girl*, documents the resurrection and journey of the female monster, forsaken by Dr Frankenstein in the original novel, across a span of 175 years, where, unlike her male predecessor, she successfully evolves to become an independent member of contemporary American society. This chapter aims to highlight the palimpsestuous relation between these two texts, the latter of which has often been explored as a new-media rendition of an old Promethean myth. It will also analyse how new digital art forms revolutionise traditional concepts of

---

1    Bush introduced the revolutionary idea of the 'hypertext' in his essay "As We May Think" (published in *The Atlantic*) through the hypothetical machine called Memex, which enables its users to browse through a wide range of documents stored on microfilm, connected through linkages, thereby anticipating the hyperlinked structure of the internet today. Ted Nelson, the pioneering figure in the introduction of hypertext, is indebted to Bush's vision.

2    *Frankenstein; or, the Modern Prometheus* was considered to be one of the earliest examples of gothic science fiction. It is an epistolary novel that narrates the life experiences of the scientist Victor Frankenstein after the unnatural creation of his assembled Creature.

adaptation, thereby enhancing the tech-savvy reader's understanding of the postmodern concepts of fragmentation, multivocality and multilinearity.

## The revised idea of the 'palimpsest' in the digital age

The term 'palimpsest' generally refers to a parchment or some other writing surface on which the original text has been effaced and then overwritten by another. In the Middle Ages, these parchments were recycled pieces of vellum treated by chemical agents to erase the existing text. The new text was then superimposed upon the erased surface. Thus, a palimpsest becomes a multi-layered record upon which the remnants of previous writing persist.

Sarah Dillon (2007) extended the meaning of this word beyond its paleographic status. She argues in her doctoral thesis, *The Palimpsest: Literature, Culture and Theory*, that palimpsests have "a continuing contemporary relevance" (p. 12). The imperfect retention and co-existence of the new and old texts "change the very way we interpret and know the past" (p. 12) and at the same time they intrigue the readers by simultaneously capturing "the mystery of the secret, the miracle of resurrection and the thrill of detective discovery" (pp. 12–13). Dillon uses another term, "palimpsestuous", that refers to the "simultaneous relation of intimacy and separation" whereby the distinctiveness and individuality of each text is preserved and, at the same time, "essential contamination and interdependence" (p. 3) is allowed. Therefore, a palimpsest is a composition of different writings that are interwoven in an elusive manner.

Hypertext, as a genre of writing, acts as a palimpsest and exhibits the properties of fragmentariness, association and dissociation simultaneously, through its basic configuration as an association of hyperlinks. The re-emergence of the erased texts render the structure with a unique heterogeneity. In this context, Dillon also closely develops the concept of intertextuality initially introduced by Julia Kristeva in her essay, "Word, Dialogue and Novel" (1986). Although the palimpsest does not essentially seek to explore the relation of the text with its context, a constructive relation could be drawn between the concept of palimpsest and the concept of intertextuality. Derived from the Latin term, 'intertexto', meaning to intermingle while weaving, intertextuality, according to Kristeva, perceives any text as a constructed "of a mosaic of quotations; any text is the absorption and transformation of another" (Kristeva, 1986, p. 66). The very idea of the coalescence of different textual fragments unfolds palimpsestuous properties.

## A general note on the selected text

The author of *Patchwork Girl* invites the reader to virtually 'patch together' the female monstrous counterpart of Dr Frankenstein's creation. As the reader enters the textual narrative, they encounter five routes to explore the story at the very title page, which qualifies as a sort of sequential narrative progression. The story is divided into five sections, namely "A Graveyard", "A Journal", "A Quilt", "A Story" and "Broken Accents". The graveyard section enlists the names and stories of the donors of the various patched-up body parts of the monster. The section, "A Journal" captures the relationship between the author of *Patchwork Girl* and her creation, narrated through the voice of the fictional authorial presence of Mary Shelley as the creator of the female monster. Hence it is a repository of Mary Shelley's emotions. Predominantly narrated from the creator's perspective, "Crazy Quilt" entails the process of the Patchwork Girl's construction, weaving together textual appropriations, references, and citations from various texts. The next section, "A Story" is narrated by the Patchwork Girl and offers her perspective on her life. Finally, "Broken Accents" offers reflections on the process of hypertext fiction writing.

To explore *Patchwork Girl*, the reader can either enter the text in the prescribed format given on the title page, or they can opt for a non-sequential narrative progression wherein entering and exiting each section is guided by one's own choice of nodes. The textual threads that comprise the body of *Patchwork Girl*, known as "lexias", construct a web of relations between the various units of the work either in the form of images or chunks of texts. The term "lexia" had its genesis in Roland Barthes' essay *S/Z* (1970). It is referred to there as "a series of brief contiguous fragments" (p. 13). In the present hypertextual context, the individual screens of texts or images that form the units of the multimedia novel are referred to as a lexia. Overall, this hypertext fiction consists of "323 lexias, which are joined by over 400 links" (Sarkar, 2020, p. 3).

The reader ensures their virtual presence within the body of the hypertext using the cursor icon as a navigational tool. With every click, the reader is transported via hyperlinks to the different sections. By concretising the narrative possibilities of the text with his critical engagement through a virtual presence, the reader is transformed from a passive consumer to an active participant in the meaning-making process.

## Discussion

The present study argues that *Patchwork Girl* can be said to qualify as a palimpsest at two levels in an initial analysis. The text of *Patchwork Girl* as a reworking of *Frankenstein* is united with the source text through an eternal chain of reference and significance. The source text, itself, however, has undergone a preservatory procedure and developed as a palimpsest, despite an array of corrections and editing made by Mary Shelley's husband, the famous Romantic poet, Percy Bysshe Shelley (Henthorne, 2018). Mary Shelley's authorial instinct has been 'checked' and simultaneously 'framed' by her husband, and therefore *Frankenstein*, very much like the piece of vellum, the surface of which endures rewritings and erasures post-chemical processing, has survived as a document paradoxically preserving, underneath its story, the voices of both Mary and Percy Shelley. The re-emergence of the authorial voice of Mary Shelley finds expression within the layers of the palimpsestuous construct, *Patchwork Girl*, a voice that was repressed through editorial interventions.

Secondly, the body of the monster itself functions as a palimpsest as the different constituent parts encapsulate stories of the different donors of her limbs and organs. As the reader enters into the first section, "A Graveyard", the protagonist states: "I am buried here. You can resurrect me, but only piecemeal. If you want to see the whole, you will have to sew me together yourself". This leads us to a "Headstone" lexia in which the various body parts are listed: "Here lies a Head, Trunk, Arms (right and Left), and Legs (Right and Left) as well as diverse Organs Appropriately Disposed May they Rest in Piece". The pun on the word 'piece' exhibits the very idea of the fragmentariness of the monstrous frame. It highlights how 'piece by piece' the structural whole has been woven together so that the various constitutive elements assimilate to give life to the monstrous whole and at the same time retain their individuality. The numerous voices that emerge from the gravestone detail the donors of the monster's body parts to assert the same idea of individuality and fragmentation, "intimacy and separation" (Dillon, 2007, p. 3), that captures the essence of a palimpsest. Furthermore, Jackson endowing each tale with a distinctive voice creates scope for Bakhtinian multivocality.

An exploration of the various body parts of the monster suffices to indicate the inference. For instance, on clicking on the monster's "left leg" we encounter a lexia that encapsulates the history of its donor. The left leg belonged to:

> Jane, a nanny who harbored under her durable grey dresses and sensible undergarments are membrane of a less sensible time: a tattoo of a ship [...] knew some stories that astonished her charges, and though the ship on her thigh blurred and grew faint and blue with distance, until it seemed that the currents must have long ago finished their work, undoing its planks one by one with unfailing patience, she always took the children to the wharf when word came that a ship was docking, and many a sailor greeted her by name (Jackson, 1995).

On clicking on the "right arm" lexia we witness that it has two parts: "the upper belonged to Tristessa, a woman known in the ship yards for her deadly aim with a bottle", while the lower portion encapsulates the tale of a "lady very dexterous with the accoutrements of femininity". However, this cohering of pieces to create a disjointed whole that makes the digital reader aware of the materiality of the medium also foregrounds the fragmentariness of both the medium and the product. The monster is an artificial construct—both at an anatomical and a metaphorical level. Her artificiality is foregrounded by the reader's physical presence on the screen of the text as a virtual entity, who, through his clicks, invokes life into the story.

In another lexia titled "metaphorme", the monster claims that the "metaphorical principle is my true skeleton". Here the hybrid nature of the Patchwork Girl as a mixed metaphor of borrowed organs finds further expression. Her hybridity is anatomical and textual for she has been birthed twice, "under the needle, and under the pen". A relation between the body and the text as an artificial construct has been established. In the lexia "lives", this metaphorical principle has been elaborated: "we live in the expectation of traditional narrative progression; we read the first chapters and begin already to figure out whether our lives are romantic comedy, or high tragedy, mystery or adventure". Here, the idea of linear progression undergoes palimpsestuous rendition through the medium of hypertext. The expectation of a traditional reader for an author-guided progression is subverted through the array of choices the virtual reader can exercise with the drag of the cursor.

The body is also described in the lexia "swarm" as "a multiplicity of anonymous particles" with "no absolute boundaries: I am a swarm". The idea of being constituted through a multiplicity of particles evokes the existence of discrete elements with no significant agent of association, yet bound together through a complexity of disparate connectivity. This, however, time and again, underlines the fragmentariness of the body of the monster. The materiality of the body is emphasised in the lexia "seemed adhesive", where the patched-up body "being seam'd with scars" was both a fact of 18th-century life and a metaphor for dissonant inferences ruining any finely adjusted composition. In the lexia "her", the graphical presentation of a woman's body dissected using multiple dotted lines exhibit the scars of her patched-up anatomy. Similar dotted lines intersect in the lexia "phrenology", where the image of a giant head divided into different sections is given a sidewards glance. Aesthetics of fragmentation and assemblage pervade the work.

The very idea of the dotted line has a palimpsestuous quality, for it signifies both association and dissociation between the various pieces it moves across. The association is established when the dotted line functions as a thread that joins disparate pieces. Dissociation is constituted by the non-dilution of the borders of each piece into a unified whole. However subtle and fine the sewing of the entrails might be, the idea of a patched entity ultimately persists throughout the work. This idea finds expression in the "sequence" lexia: "An electronic river washes out my scent in the intervals. I am a discontinuous trace, a dotted line".

The revival of the once-discarded bodily elements of the female monster becomes the site of palimpsestuous inquiry. Her multi-layered identity is evoked through her fragmented, hybrid constitution. While in *Frankenstein* the idea of fragmentariness is limited to the body of the Creature produced by Victor Frankenstein, in *Patchwork Girl*, fragmentariness is embodied even in the essence of the digital medium. It is an inherent quality of the hypertext format, as pages of the hypertext fiction pop up as lexias or text chunks. In this respect, even the functioning of the internet posits itself as a palimpsest. Each webpage, like a parchment of vellum, undergoes continuous refreshment and re-inscription with the click of a button. The hypertext, with its multi-linear embodiment, facilitates play across multiple screens of texts. Not only does the literal body of the Patchwork Girl exhibit fragmentariness but also its very gender encompasses the essence of convoluted identities. In the lexia "I am", Jackson's creature accepts that her confused, and electronically constructed gender identity makes her "belong nowhere". Her androgynous nature is the result of the assimilation to form a disparate whole, as can be explored in the stories of the organ donors. It is because of this reason that "women and men alike mistake my gender and both are drawn to me".

A further point of association between the two texts begins when the real-life author of *Frankenstein* is portrayed as a character in the hypertextual context. Hence the author herself becomes a site of intertextual relativity. In the section "Journal", Mary Shelley recounts her relationship with her creation. The very idea of the Creature as a "hideous progeny" (Shelley, 1831, p. 11) undergoes extensive erasure and rewriting or revision in *Patchwork Girl*. Although the female monster does consider herself "a disturbance in the flow", thereby reinforcing the idea of the grotesque or the inhuman that is usually associated with the image of a monster, the reaction of the creator upon beholding her progeny for the first time speaks the contrary. While Frankenstein's disgust is voiced in the line, "[b]ut now I went to it in cold blood, and my heart often sickened at the work of my hands" (Shelley, 1818, p. 118), the sympathetic acceptance and compassion, followed by the simultaneous erotic, incestuous, homosexual feelings that the fictional character of Mary Shelley feels towards her female creature are a palimpsestuous reworking of the terror and disgust that Frankenstein once felt at the very sight of his progeny. The lexias "my walk" and "sight" within the section "A Journal" illustrate the observation:

Yesterday I went for a walk down the lane that branches off at the holly tree from the main road [...] when I saw on the far side of the span a sight that made me stop ankle-deep in mud and stare (Jackson my walk). It was my monster, stark naked, standing still as if I had not yet breathed life in to her massive frame, and waiting for me [...] I could not help but quail before the strangeness of this figure, from which, I fancifully imagined the very blades of grass seemed to shrink, but curiosity, and a kind of fellow feeling was the stronger impulse, and I forced myself to continue.

This could be read in comparison to the experience related by Frankenstein at a similar sudden encounter:

I looked on the valley beneath; vast mists were rising from the rivers which ran through it, [...] I suddenly beheld the figure of a man, at some distance, advancing towards me with superhuman speed [...] his stature also, as he approached, seemed to exceed that of man. I was troubled: a mist came over my eye and I felt a faintness seize me, but I was quickly restored by the cold gale of the mountains. I perceived, as the shape came nearer (sight tremendous and abhorred!) that it was the wretch whom I had created. I trembled with rage and horror, resolving to wait his approach, and then close with him in mortal combat. He approached; his countenance bespoke bitter anguish, combined with disdain and malignity, while its unearthly ugliness rendered it almost too horrible for human eyes (Shelley, 1818, pp. 97–99).

Though each textual extract describes a reaction from the beholder, the stronger sympathetic impulse of the female creator overshadows the fear of the male creator.

The subversion of the terror upon beholding an anomaly functions as a reworking of the properties of gothic novel as a genre of writing that revels in the macabre, the grotesque, and the horrific. The notorious excerpt in which Frankenstein confronts his male Creature with terror in the creation scene, finds a magical fairy tale rendition in the hypertext fiction. Frankenstein's visits to charnel houses are subverted by the description of "magic lanterns, peepshow box", "materials necessary to new creation" to frame the female counterpart. The next lexia, "labor", relates to the moment of genesis of the female monster and copies extensive quotes from the source text: "My candle was nearly burnt out, when, by the glimmer of the half-extinguished light, I saw the dull yellow eye of the creature open". Furthermore, there is a reference to "a magician lean[ing] over" the monster to shake" from the bottle some grains". The various layers of palimpsest that form this lexia voice are working of the old myth through a new medium. As the traditional conceptualisation of a monster as hideous undergoes reworking in the hypertext novel, various terms usually identified with a monster, such as grotesque, deviant, abject or abnormal are given a positive connotation when the monster herself states in the lexia "why hideous?": "every part of me is human and proportional to the whole. Yet I am a monster because I am multiple, and because I am mixed".

The idea of the palimpsest is, therefore, contained within the configuration of the creature, the act of its creation, and in the very functioning of the medium as well. The intertextual association between the two texts begins with an examination of the two titles. The subtitle of *Patchwork Girl* as *A Modern Monster* can be seen as a rewriting of the subtitle of *Frankenstein*, as *the Modern Prometheus*. The erasure of the mythological status attributed to the scientist in Shelley's text has been revised to demonise the progeny at the very outset of the hypertext novel. Hence the creator as the subject is replaced by the creation as the subject in the digital adaptation. The refashioning of the title of the hypertext brings about the "simultaneous relation of intimacy and separation" (Dillon, 2007) that the concept of the palimpsest embodies. The two titles are intimately related to and, at the same time, dissociated from their individual peculiarities.

The association however extends beyond the titles and finds expression in the first part of the section "A Story", which literally incorporates quotes from Shelley's novel. Seen in the light of *Patchwork Girl*, the various allusions function as implants of alien tissues in a piece of fiction. In the section "Crazy Quilt", Jackson produces a palimpsest of direct quotations from Derrida,[3] Baum (2013), Stamford's (1991) *Body Criticism* and so on. The narrative becomes a mosaic of textual fragments synthesised through intertextuality. The virtual quilt with its dotted lines invokes the traditional arts of sewing or weaving to form a "palimpsestuous surface [wherein] otherwise unrelated

---

3    In the lexia entitled "Mementos", Derrida comes "home mumbling about a she-monster who beset him in the woods" (Jackson, 1995). Jackson intertextualises fragments of excerpts from Derrida's *Disseminations* (Derrida, 1981) into her own work.

texts are involved and entangled, intricately woven, interrupting and inhabiting each other" (Dillon, 2007, p. 4). Hence the remnants of the previous writing persist, coexisting and contending with the newer appropriations upon the body of the text to produce new meanings, as was the case with the inscriptions on the vellum. The lexia "plea", for instance, records the Creature's request to his creator Frankenstein to gift him with a female counterpart. The lexia "promise" entails the initial agreement and the lexia "treachery" captures the ultimate refusal on the part of the scientist to fulfill the Creature's wishes. The fear of the female counterpart "becom[ing] ten thousand times more malignant than her mate and delight[ing] for its own sake, in murder and wretchedness" (Shelley, 1818, p. 165) accounts for Frankenstein's refusal of the Creature's demands. It is this resurrection of the female monster from the relics that were once thrown into the sea that is secretly accomplished by the fictional Mary in Jackson's novel.

A being that was thought to be too hideous and uncanny by the scientist, transforms herself into a modern woman in the digital paradigm and ventures across the American metropolis until death or disintegration dismantles her. Unlike her male counterpart, who encountered a catastrophic fate and ultimately vanished in the northernmost extremity of the globe, the Patchwork Girl re-instantiates her identity as a global citizen despite her monstrous selfhood. In this aspect, the death of each monster is comparable:

> The dispersal and multiplying of identity is not seen as monstrous by Jackson but as an acceptable and even normalizing experience. The final message carried by the image and metaphor of the hybrid subjectivity of the cyborg is that the only chance for individual coherence is not striving towards unity and balance, but accepting one's multiplication (Glavanakova-Yaneva, 2003, p. 73).

Contrary to the romantic disposition of the male Creature, the Patchwork Girl disintegrates to underline her postmodern assemblage as she recognizes herself to be "gathered together loosely [...] in a way that was interesting". A similar interest is aroused in the audience to undertake the whole journey of constructing the plot of the story in the multimodal medium.

In the context of the palimpsest, the term 'grafting' bears special significance, as the concept from gardening can be seen as a reworking of the traditional idea of giving birth. While exploring the hypertextual relationship of hypertext with "hypotex", Gerard Genette brings in the metaphor of grafting in his famous book *Palimpsests* (1997): "any relationship uniting a text B (which I shall call the hypertext) to an earlier text A (I shall, of course, call it the 'hypotext'), upon which it is grafted in a manner that is not that of commentary" (Genette, 1997, p. 5). Jackson plays with this concept in the literal 'grafting of skins' in two consecutive lexias, namely "surgery" and "join", where a piece of skin from the body of Mary Shelley is grafted upon the body of the monster. The female monster is not born 'biologically' through a woman's womb; rather her constituent parts are grafted or implanted in the digital medium through sewing as evidenced in the presence of the dotted line. The sexual identity of the monster is simultaneously grafted, thereby giving an androgynous layer to her seemingly feminine frame. As has been stated by Hayles (2002) in her book *Writing Machines*, the relationship between different media could be a parasitic one; the grafting of a story from a printed novel into a virtual medium entails the parasitic remains of the printed word being brought into the digital ecosphere. The new art form becomes the repository of the older and therefore is like the parchment where the source text, despite undergoing revision and erasure, still exists. The transition between different mediums, however, invites questions about traditional reading habits.

Finally, the hypertextual adaptation exhibits the very properties of a palimpsest through the act of creative writing and reading. A connection is drawn between writing and sewing in the lexias "written" and "sewn" which could be read as delving into the various layers of creative writing as an artist and engaging in the traditionally feminine art of stitching. The material moment of undertaking the act of writing by the fictional authorial persona of Shelley Jackson is incorporated in "this writing" lexia. The peculiarities of the processes of hypertextual creation and consumption are stated as:

> [...] assembling these patched words in an electronic space [...] as if the entire text is within reach, but because of some myopic condition I am only familiar with from dreams, I can see that part most immediately before me, and have no sense of how that part relates to the rest (Jackson, 1995).

Jackson elaborates how the linear, page-bound construction of a printed novel is "restful" and its very act of reading is "spatial and volumetric". On the contrary, the multifarious digital configuration of the hypertextual novel evokes a sense of getting lost among the multitude of reading options: "But where am I now?" This is followed by the lexia "reading", where the confusing and often exhaustive process of exploration in hypertext fiction is given emphasis.

## Conclusion

In *Patchwork Girl*, the discarded idea of the female companion to the "hideous progeny" created by Dr Frankenstein in Shelley's text is seen to be resurrected by Shelley herself through the hypertextual medium. That the male predecessor was the outcome of extensive technological invention has been virtually realised by Jackson's multimodal text. The medium facilitates a real-time encounter with the very process of the scientist's sewing together of the various parts, thereby reinforcing an act of witness to the anatomical process of resurrection, which was limited simply to the imaginary in the reading of the printed novel. The hypertextual medium can function as a palimpsest only through the implementation of multifarious digital tools. The new media platform is facilitated by multimedia technologies that were once unthinkable in print. Jackson's text adapts the myth of the Romantic era to the postmodern environment. *Patchwork Girl* reinforces the idea of fragmentariness and hybridity when analysed under the lens of palimpsest. The reader, at once, is turned into a scientist and a creative artist in the process of weaving together the textual fragments of the text. The resurrection of the digital monstrous entity is superimposed upon her predecessor.

Exploiting the interactivity of hypermedia, hypertext fiction caters for its audience with a mosaic of hyperlinks. This, in turn, initiates interactivity on two levels—to begin with, the audience enters a play with the screen of the electronic device using the cursor. Secondly, the various hyperlinks initiate a sort of play within the body of the text. Hence, multiple dimensions of interactivity can be understood in *Patchwork Girl*; firstly, the navigational intent initiates an interactive relationship between the medium, the work and the reader. Interaction occurs when the reader uses computer interfaces such as the mouse to click, drag, and scroll across the body of the text. Secondly, the various hyperlinks create a web of interconnected relationships wherein clicking on one, effortlessly transports the reader to a gallery of simultaneous links. It is perhaps in this context that Landow suggests "all writing becomes collaborative writing" with hypertext (Landow, 1992, p. 88).

# Works Cited

Aarseth, E.J. (1997). *Cybertext: Perspectives on ergodic literature.* Johns Hopkins University Press. https://williamwolff.org/wp-content/uploads/2013/01/aarseth-ergodic-ch1-1997.pdf

Barthes, R. (1977). The death of the author (S. Heath, Trans.). *Fontana*, 142–8.

Barthes, R. (1980). *S/Z: An Essay.* Siglo XXI.

Bell, A. (2010). *The Possible Worlds of Hypertext Fiction.* Palgrave Macmillan.

Baum, F. (1990). *The Patchwork Girl of Oz.* Caliber Press. https://theodoresinger.wordpress.com/wp-content/uploads/2015/09/the_patchwork_girl_of_oz.pdf

Bush, V. (1945, July). As we may think. *The Atlantic Monthly.*

Carazo, C.S.P., & Jiménez, M.A. (2006). Gathering the Limbs of the text in Shelley Jackson's *Patchwork Girl. Atlantis*, 115–129.

Ciccoricco, D. (2007). *Reading Network Fiction.* University of Alabama Press. http://www.movingimages.info/class/wp-content/uploads/2010/06/CiccRead.pdf

Delaney, P., & Landow J. (1994). *Hypermedia and Literary Studies.* MIT Press.

Dillon, S. (2007). *The Palimpsest: Literature, Criticism, Theory.* Bloomsbury Publishing. https://doi.org/10.1093/res/hgn156

Doležel, L. (1998). Possible worlds of history and fiction. *New Literary History*, 785–809.

Genette, G. (1997). *Palimpsests: Literature in the Second Degree* (Vol. 8). University of Nebraska Press.

Glavanakova-Yaneva, A. (2003). Body Webs: Re/constructing boundaries in Shelley Jackson's *Patchwork Girl. Journal of American Studies of Turkey 18*, 65–79.

Hayles, N.K. (2000). Flickering connectivities in Shelley Jackson's *Patchwork Girl*: The importance of media-specific analysis. *Postmodern Culture 10*(2). https://dx.doi.org/10.1353/pmc.2000.0011

Hackman, P. (2011). 'I am a double agent': Shelley Jackson's *Patchwork Girl* and the persistence of print in the age of hypertext. *Contemporary Literature 52*(1), 84–107. https://doi.org/10.1353/cli.2011.0013

Hayles, N.K., & Burdick, A. (2002). *Writing Machines* (Vol. 10). MIT Press. https://doi.org/10.7312/aloi19666-031

Hayles, N.K. (2008). *Electronic Literature: New Horizons for the Literary*. University of Notre Dame. https://dl.acm.org/doi/abs/10.5555/1795941

Henthorne, T. (2018). Shelley Distributed: Material Assemblages of Frankenstein, Mary, and Percy [Thesis, Georgetown University]. In *Georgetown University-Graduate School of Arts & Sciences*. https://repository.library.georgetown.edu/handle/10822/1050771

Jackson, S. (1995). *Patchwork Girl*. Eastgate Systems.

Kilgore, C.D. (2013). Rhetoric of the network: Toward a new metaphor. *Mosaic: A Journal for the Interdisciplinary Study of Literature*, 37–58.

Kristeva, J. (1986). *Word, Dialogue and Novel: The Kristeva Reader*. T. Moi (Ed.). Basil Blackwell.

Landow, G.P. (1991). *HyperText: The Convergence of Contemporary Critical Theory and Technology*. Johns Hopkins University Press.

Landow, G.P. (2006). *Hypertext 3.0: Critical Theory and New Media in an Era of Globalization*. Johns Hopkins University Press.

Modir, L., Guan, L.C., & Aziz, S.B.A. (2014). Text, hypertext, and hyperfiction: A convergence between poststructuralism and narrative theories. *Sage Open 4*(1). https://doi.org/10.1177/2158244014528915

Rajakannan, R., & Rukmini, S. (2021). Reading paradigms of digital narratives: Reception of hypertext fictions and its implications. *Journal of Narrative and Language Studies 9*(18), 357–380. http://nalans.com/index.php/nalans/article/view/450

Sarkar, J. (2020). Reading hypertext as cyborg: The case of *Patchwork Girl*. *Rupkatha Journal on Interdisciplinary Studies in Humanities 12*(5), 1–7. https://dx.doi.org/10.21659/rupkatha.v12n5.rioc1s2n2

Sánchez-Palencia Carazo, C., & Jiménez, M.A. (2006). Gathering the limbs of the text in Shelley Jackson's *Patchwork Girl*. *Atlantis 28*(1), 15–29.

Shelley, M. (1818). *Frankenstein*. Lackington, Hughes, Harding, Mavor, & Jones.

Stafford, B.M. (1991). *Body Criticism*. The MIT Press.

# 12. Narratives of the self: Comments and confessions on Facebook

*Rimi Nandy*

## Abstract

Narratives are structured around events, which are used to tell a story. The self is perpetually being constructed through narratives of experience. This chapter focuses on the phenomenon of Facebook confession pages and how they contribute to the construction of digital identity. Drawing on insights from my project on the role of Facebook College Confession pages, the chapter examines how these platforms have transformed the way users express and shape their identities. The anonymity provided by these pages allows users to post confessions without revealing their identities, encouraging a form of virtual self-exploration. These confessions, often written by nameless authors, generate a complex and ongoing narrative of identity, shaped by the interaction of multiple voices and viewpoints. The chapter also explores the motivations behind sharing personal confessions, even when the responses may be negative, and how this contributes to the perpetual construction of the digital self. By examining the intersection of public and private spheres in these online spaces, this chapter highlights how the breaking of the public-private divide enables users to create and negotiate their identities in a digital, networked world. The narrative constructed is endless, and the post is not an end in itself. It paves the way for the generation of an endless narrative by multiple authors with

https://doi.org/10.11647/OBP.0423.12

multiple viewpoints. This chapter explores the reasons behind sharing such posts on Facebook, even if the comments are negative in tone. It will refer to Anthony Giddens' concept of time-space "distanciation" (Keefer et al., 2019) to show how multiple tellers through their narratives help to build the complex networked identity of a user. The study will also analyse the role played by the breaking of the public-private divide in creating such spaces for the construction of a private self through public voices.

## Keywords

Facebook; anonymous; messages; private; public; time-space; identity.

## Introduction

We are creating a world where anyone, anywhere may express his or her beliefs, no matter how singular, without fear of being coerced into silence or conformity (Barlow, 2016).

Cyberspace has changed the very structure of society. Within the binary expanse of cyberspace, identity has become enormously fluid. The notion of 'identity' refers to the basic characteristics and features that help to identify a person and distinguish them from others. When a real-life identity enters cyberspace, it transforms into a digital identity. In cyberspace, one can create a new identity that might not reflect even the tiniest feature of the 'actual' identity. The introduction of a culture provided by the Internet and social media platforms transformed how we interpret and interact with time and space which, have become fluid and unstructured. The lure of cyberspace lies in this enormous power of creating an identity that need not be the true reflection of the actual person. The digital identity helps to self-select the desired characteristics to remake one's visible identity to be performed before the digital audience. Cyberspace also provides the option of choosing the audience before whom one can act as digitally disguised.

# Methodology

This chapter is an outcome of a minor research project titled "Confessions in the Digital Age". This was a part of a larger project, "Mapping Digital Humanities in India", sponsored by the Centre for Studies in Culture and Society in Bangalore. The data collected during this project functions as a primary source. The methodology utilised in this chapter incorporates a qualitative approach focused on the exploration of Facebook College Confession Pages in India. This qualitative method is pivotal for understanding the nuanced ways in which digital platforms, specifically Facebook, mediate and transform the traditional concept of confession into a public, interactive, and anonymous format. The methodological framework involves the collection of data through the analysis of various Facebook Confession Pages, supplemented by online questionnaires and interviews with users of these pages. This approach allows for an in-depth examination of the changing attitudes towards confession, the role of anonymity, and the social dynamics within these digital spaces

In the context of Digital Humanities, qualitative methods used in tandem with quantitative data are essential to capture the complex interactions between technology and human behaviour. This often involves the interpretation of digital texts, online communities, and the use of digital platforms, requiring researchers to engage deeply with both the content and the context of digital interactions. Such methodologies are significant for our understanding of digital cultures that have become all-pervasive in the contemporary age. This approach is crucial in the context of this project, where the aim is to understand not just the content of digital confessions but also the broader social and cultural implications of these practices. It emphasises the importance of qualitative research in uncovering the ways digital technologies shape social practices, identities, and communities (O'Sullivan, 2023). By employing a qualitative methodology, this project aligns with contemporary Digital Humanities research that seeks to map the cultural and social impacts of digital media on traditional practices like confession.

The following confession pages from Facebook Confession Pages in India were critically studied. Data collection was difficult as Facebook policies do not allow scraping data. The other major issue faced while writing this chapter was the unavailability of data collected during 2013.

A few of the confession pages from this year have been removed from the Facebook platform. As a result, the data collected from these pages could not be used as they could not be cited. The dynamic nature of social media platforms also makes it difficult to study a particular trend over a long period.

| Srl No. | Name | URLs |
|---|---|---|
| 1. | IIT KGP Confessions | https://www.facebook.com/iitkgpconfession1 |
| 2. | Unofficial IIT K Confessions | https://www.facebook.com/iitkconfessions |
| 3. | IIT Delhi Confessions V2.0 | https://www.facebook.com/profile.php?id=100063743602772 |
| 4. | IIT B Confessions | https://www.facebook.com/iitbConfessions |
| 5. | IIT Confessions | https://www.facebook.com/IITConfess |
| 6. | IIT Crush Confessions | https://www.facebook.com/iit.crush |
| 7. | Presidency College Confessions | https://www.facebook.com/profile.php?id=100068683026177 |
| 8. | IIMA Confessions | https://www.facebook.com/profile.php?id=100067731219912 |
| 9. | JU Confessions | https://www.facebook.com/Jadavpur.32 |
| 10. | BESU Confessions | https://www.facebook.com/BesuConfessions |
| 11. | UOH Confessions | https://www.facebook.com/HcuConfessions |
| 12. | Hindu College Confessions | https://www.facebook.com/profile.php?id=100069835615326 |
| 13. | JNU Confessions | https://www.facebook.com/JnuConfessions |
| 14. | Jammu Confessions | https://www.facebook.com/profile.php?id=100064825685367 |
| 15. | Indian Armed Forces Confessions | https://www.facebook.com/IndianArmedForcesConfessions |

| 16. | Delhi Metro Confessions/ Compliments | https://www.facebook.com/ DelhiMetroConfesssion |

Fig. 12.1 List of Facebook confessions pages used in this study.

## Digital confessions in the Information Age

The digital citizens of today's world socialise on virtual platforms using various social networking sites like Facebook, Instagram, and LinkedIn. Among these social networking sites, Facebook is the leading platform. Across the world, Facebook has touched the lives of millions of people. India has the second largest number of Facebook users in the world. Facebook is a place that does not have any boundaries, be it gender, age, race or country, and the advancement in networking technology has reduced the time and space gap. Physical boundaries no longer determine social interaction and friendship is no longer restricted by geographical boundaries. The very idea of sharing posts and pictures is a way of acknowledging existence. Existence of the self, of ideas, dreams, desires and fears, everything is recognised once it enters cyberspace. Facebook helps in community building, and the criteria for building a community can be varied and not restricted by the usual codes of conduct. The communities on Facebook are created around shared interests, ideologies, likes and dislikes. One such community formation is aided by the numerous confession pages flooding Facebook.

The idea of 'confession' originated among the Greeks (Hymer, 1995). According to the great Greek philosophers such as Seneca, confession was a medium for self-improvement. This act consisted of revisiting one's actions at the end of the day, to give a better understanding of a person's character. This could involve an analysis of one's behaviour and actions on one's own, or writing about it for the perusal of another person who can provide an unbiased opinion and judgement. The method and meaning of confession have undergone various degrees of change from its point of origin when confession was mainly a process of purging one's soul of any impurities. The Christian notion of confession is a mix of the Celtic rituals of penance, and the Hindu beliefs followed by the ascetics. The religious practice of confession is a tool for purifying the soul and getting rid of the stains of the various sins performed by a confessor. But the role of 'confession' was not restricted to relieving the confessor of the burden of guilt; instead, it was also used as an agent to instil fear and enforce power mechanisms. In the words of Michel Foucault:

> The confession is a ritual of discourse in which the speaking subject is also the subject of the statement; It is also a ritual that unfolds within a power relationship, for one does not confess without the presence (or virtual presence) of a partner who is not simply the interlocutor but the authority who requires the confession, prescribes and appreciates it, and intervenes in order to judge, punish, forgive, console, and reconcile; a ritual in which the truth is corroborated by the obstacles and resistances it has had to surmount in order to be formulated; and finally, a ritual in which the expression alone, independently of its external consequences, produces intrinsic modifications in the person who articulates it: it exonerates, redeems, and purifies him; it unburdens him of his wrongs, liberates him, and promises him salvation (Foucault, 1978, pp. 61–62).

In the 19th century, confession took a different form. It was no longer a religious act; instead it became a scientific discourse in the hands of psychoanalysts (Taylor, 2009). In this form of confession, the process could only be completed after the interpretation of the confession given by the psychoanalyst. This was based on very different power dynamics; the entire control was in the hands of the psychoanalyst and the confessor was just an instrument.

The power dynamics reflected in the use of confession as a tool against perceived repression are furthered in the context of confession under police interrogation. In earlier ages, methods of physical torture were used to get false confessions from the accused. In the present day and age, physical torture has been substituted by psychological tactics. At times, certain people make false confessions even without any coercion. This may be due to the innate need to gain fame, acceptance and acknowledgement (Taylor, 2009).

Closely related to the coerced confessions of criminals is the culture of confession practised in China during the Cultural Revolution. In China, a form of confession called *suku* (speaking bitterness) was performed before the public. The government reached out to people from different walks of life, to narrate the hardships they faced in bygone days before they were rescued by the Communist Party. According to Ann Anangnost, this kind of public confession was used to drive into the minds of the people the importance of a "disciplinary state" (Yu, 2009, p. 69).

The desire to confess on Facebook Confession Pages can be analysed through the lens of Michel Foucault's ideas about the desire to confess, as outlined in his seminal work, *The History of Sexuality, Volume I*. Foucault argues that the act of confession has transformed over centuries from a religious ritual into a pivotal mechanism of power within society (Foucault, 1978). This transformation is particularly evident in the context of Facebook Confession Pages, where individuals voluntarily share personal, often intimate, details about their lives in a public or semi-public digital space.

Foucault posits that confession is a technique of power that compels individuals to articulate their innermost thoughts and desires. In the digital age, this compulsion finds a new outlet on platforms like Facebook, where the act of confessing is not mediated by a priest or therapist but is broadcast to an anonymous or semi-anonymous audience. The desire to confess, in this context, is intertwined with the construction of identity and the negotiation of social relationships in digital spaces. The practice of confession in the present day and age has evolved to suit the changing times. The confession pages on Facebook typically cater to educational institutes, companies, or various other organisations with shared beliefs and ideas. Each of the confession pages on Facebook has an administrator who selects which confessions to post and which to reject. Anybody can become a member of any number of confession pages by sending a request that is either approved or denied by the administrator. The confessions are usually made using Google Forms, and then scrutinised and published for the readers' perusal. The meaning of confession associated with Facebook has undergone an enormous change from the religious ideas that used to be related to it. Though it is still used to unburden one's soul, it has become much more than that. On the virtual platform, the present-day confession has become the mode of creation of the self. The note of regret and repentance in confession has been replaced with a boastful and challenging tone. The digital confessors, in most cases, use the instrument of anonymity to defy and deny the rules set by the society at large.

The trend of Facebook confession pages started in Western countries and slowly found its way into the Indian subcontinent. In the modern age, according to Anthony Giddens (1995), social relations are stretched across time and space with the availability of modern technologies such as the internet . In traditional societies, interactions happened only in direct proximity. However the Internet enables interactions which transcend temporal boundaries and spaces. Social practices are no longer restricted to local society alone. With the introduction of the internet and mobile technologies, vast spaces are being brought closer together, while also being connected to the expanse of time; the distance between time and space has increased to a greater extent than in pre-modern society. Social practices are no longer restricted to local society alone. With the introduction of the internet and mobile technologies, vast spaces are being brought closer together, while also being connected to the expanse of time. The effect of this transformation can be seen in the establishment of the trend of Facebook confession pages, later followed by other anonymous messaging services. The first confession page is believed to have been started by Stanford University (Kadvany, 2020). This idea then spread like wildfire across the various schools and colleges in the United States of America. In India, the first Facebook confession page was reportedly started by Bombay IIT (Indian Institute of Technology), followed by other Institute of Information Technologies, and various colleges and universities across India. Now it is no longer restricted to educational institutions. It has taken root in various IT companies like TCS and Infosys. There are also confession pages for the Delhi Metro and Mumbai local trains, Indian Armed Forces Confessions, Jammu Confessions, 18+ Confessions and countless other such pages catering to young people.

The confession page has become an instrument to bring together like-minded people. According to one of the users, it "[b]uilds a sense of community for the students, lets us know that we aren't alone in certain things" (see Appendix 1). In support of this idea, Dr B. R. Madhukar, a leading Bangalore psychiatrist, says:

> Initially, people would write letters or make phone calls, but social media allows you to reach a much larger audience, and a lot of these young people need to tell the world that 'they are there'. While the tendency to sensationalize is inevitable, there is also the hope that someone, somewhere, can understand, can empathise (Krishnaswami, 2013).

The topics discussed on these pages include various issues beginning from love problems, teenage problems, life problems to politics and social issues. The reasons behind the popularity of these pages is based on its ability to provide entertainment. Most users of the confession pages read it to enjoy the 'funny' content and to feel a sense of community and belonging. In the words of one of the frequent readers of the confession, he reads them,

> To think deeper on certain matters, and enhance my views. To get a laugh, to learn more about the people in my community, to help them out with their problems if I can. I'm a frequent commenter and my responses range from humorous and sarcastic to longer, thoughtful responses. I also use the opportunity to spread wisdom, positivity, and empathy, whenever I can.
>
> A bit of the notoriety I've gained IRL from being a prominent commenter never hurt either." (See Appendix 1).

The role of the administrator of the confession pages is that of a guardian as well as a keeper of this virtual social space. It is the task of the administrator to read through all the confessions submitted using Google Forms and then select the ones that go up on the page. The role of the administrator, according to the administrator of the Delhi Metro Confessions/Compliments page is: "Well as an admin. We have to make sure that we post entertaining stuff! People liked this page for some fun and here we are to provide them with entertainment." The criteria for selection, as per the administrator, are: "It should be humorous, realistic, and should touch the reader's heart!" (Anonymous, 2015b).

Many of these pages, were pulled down at different times only to resurface again. In general, administrators of the institutions played an important role in putting a stop to the confession pages. The image created in the digital space is boundless and uncontrollable. One's identity is no longer in one's hands. It is extremely fragile and can easily be broken. It is essential to "[...] project the right image, at the right time to the right audience" (Cerra & James, 2012, p. 11). In such a scenario, the fear of an institution's administration is understandable, as they do not want the name of their institution to be associated with the kind of confessions made on the confession pages. In my opinion, the institutions are worried about tarnishing their image in front of potential students. This hypothesis is supported by the experience of an alumni of IIT Kharagpur:

Yesterday I received a forwarded email from Dean, SA, cc-ed to the Director, harshly discarding the content of this page, and asking me to take immediate actions for bringing this page down. Attached to the email was a letter sent by a media person [from outside the institution] expressing her shock as how could "students malign their esteemed college's reputation on public portals.

Considering the gravity of the issue right now, I seriously request you to take this page down immediately, to avoid any kind of disciplinary issues. Please do the needful, and let me know" (Sethi, 2017).

A few alumni of IIT Kharagpur also felt that the confession page was destroying the image of the institution:

Disappointing to say the least. I was disappointed by the admin who started such a ridiculous page knowing nothing good can come of it. Hasn't he seen the state that the other pages—IITK Confessions, IITK Proposals—reached, the people who provided their so-called "rage" and the people who merrily liked the page and the statuses in which their fellow students were being ridiculed.

I believe that the posts were never about rage. I don't think people had so much anger stored in them, as it showed in the posts. It was always about ridiculing the person they don't like in a public forum. "The other person may not have affected my life, but I simply don't like him and he/she should suffer." This kind of attitude was not expected from IITK students and I was disappointed. But what hurt me most was that even 5th-yearites and female residents of our campus were not excluded from this madness.

I was also apprehensive about this event getting media attention. The IITK Confessions incident got published in the *Times of India* and we all know what all confessions featured in that article. And this incident would have provided just the right "masala news" to them.

And finally I was happy that the campus community reacted in a very strong way to such a lowly and derogatory act which ultimately led to the closure of the page. FAITH IN HUMANITY RESTORED"[1] (Anonymous, 2013a).

A few people were of the opinion that the power provided to the students by their anonymity was excessive:

---

1    The quotations have been transcribed exactly as they were posted in the Facebook Confession Pages. The idiosyncratic spellings and grammar appears in the original posts and therefore have not been changed or edited in any manner.

The page was downright Freudian and in the beginning, it was an amusing microcosmic social experiment, but then it just showed what happens when a mob goes Beserk

    as in it was an aggressively pushed for initiative which if done under a proper social mannerism could be healthy, but quite obviously when you have a bunch of Lemur like admin/admins, playing to the gallery was more important than supporting an initiative

    i am totally fine with the idea as long as it has some level of etiquette, but the fact that finally the posts were downright nauseous goes to say maybe we weren't prepared for so much freedom (Anonymous, 2013a).

The popularity of the confession pages rose very suddenly in 2013, and quite suddenly they went out of fashion. According to the administrator of Jai Hind College Confessions:

"The age is old... the trend is over... so I receive less confessions". He further comments, "Everything has its time... it's like product life cycle... it had a great craze... reached a maturity level and now the craze is gone" (Anonymous, 2015a).

The end of this trend is further evidenced by the fact that, on most of the confession pages, there has been no activity since December 2013 or January 2014.

    There are a few confession pages that are still active. Some of them have even become a tool for citizen journalism. The phenomenon of ordinary citizens reporting about events or sharing their views on particular issues has become a trend on the social media platform. Facebook being the largest social media platform offers greater potential and reach to citizen journalism.

    Various social and political issues are discussed across the confession pages. For example, the Delhi Metro Confessions/Compliments page has taken up the issue of net neutrality in India. Similarly, issues related to women's emancipation has also been discussed in a few pages. For example, the following post from UoH Confession Page comments on the generally held view that women are raped due to improper clothing:

I wanted to say just a few things, first of all no women wants to expose her body wantedly and if it is the reason for rape attempts, then you can find many women at railway stations, roads, and slums exposing their body due to lack of proper clothing, why doesn't any 1 attempt a rape on them,, dear brother it's not what women expose that matters its what a men's mind is exposed to,that matters. Instead of suggesting them to properly dress up, why don't u ask ur brothers to stay in home, instead ... Even this will solve the problem. ... By Raghav Singh ..."(Singh, 2013)

The following post from Jammu Confessions page talks about another prevalent issue faced by society at large:

#7272
F
Jammu

.

plz don't mention my name
female
hlo frnds ...mene abi tk k almost sbi post read kiye hai ..comments bi kiye hai..
aap sab se ek request hai .aaj hamare neighbor me ek or young boy ki death ho gyi due to overdose of heroine...mujhe injection smack in sab ki bahut zayda knowledge hai ..bahut tension hoti hai ...my real brother also doing this ...jb bi Ghar se late night call aati hai bas darr lg jata hai ki kahi kuch ho na gya ho...mene bahut socha ki kuch aisa kru jis se youth ko in sab cheezo se durr kru...kya kru kuch samaj ni aata mene apni life me bahut se logo ko overdose se marte dekha Hai...aap sab aisi koi ngo ya kuch bi open krne ka socho jisme hum sab involve ho ...jis se kuch to sudaar ho apni society me..plzz

Facebook translates this as:

#7272
F
Jammu

.

plz don't mention my name
female
Hello friends ... I have read almost all the posts till now. Commented as well.
I have a request to all of you. Today one more young boy died in our neighbor due to overdose of heroine... I have a lot of knowledge about injection smack. There is a lot of tension ... my real brother also doing this ... Whenever I get a late night call from home, I am afraid that something might have happened. I thought a lot to do something which can keep youth away from these things... I don't understand what to do. I have seen many people die of overdose in my life. You all think of opening a NGO or something in which we are all involved ... The one who improves our society. Please

In another comment from Delhi Metro Confessions/Compliments, a user shares their complicated relationship situation, akin to a taboo which has to be hidden or confessed anonymously:

> F 18
> DELHI..
> its for the first time...I'm confessing something
> so here it actually goes...
> I'm in a relationship with a guy from past 3 years...I'm in a quiet serious relationship...so do he....but he is very much egoistic n even he is at times have a very much non caring... I dun care kind of attitude...if we aren't talking he will also wont take a charge to text or call...his stupid ego comes in between...
> but he still says he loves me a lot.. and if I ever left him it will be the last one...he wont love anyone else again...I seriously don't just get this he do love me..or its just like he thinks he do but in reality its nowhere...
> and even from past some months his paternal uncle (mamu) who's unmarried and not too elder to me...we started having some conversations n they increased with the time! we even talk late nights for hrs n hrs.
> now I even think I'm falling for him (Anonymous, 2013c).

Foucault's exploration of confession as an interplay of power and knowledge and the inherent desire in the human psyche to confess can be traced in the above post. By articulating her feelings publicly, the confessor navigates her sense of identity and truth, engaging in a self-reflective process influenced by the anticipation of public acknowledgement or response. The act of confession, according to Foucault, also functions as a form of self-surveillance, where the individual judges herself against societal constructs. The confession highlights internal conflicts and societal expectations about loyalty, relationships, and emotional fidelity, showcasing the confessor's negotiation of personal desires against perceived norms. The Facebook Confession Page, in this case, acts as a contemporary confessional booth, where digital technologies facilitate new forms of self-expression and communal engagement with personal truths.

The following post from IITK Confessions page depicts how confession is used as a means of subverting and challenging acceptable behaviour regarding self-care and health issues. The mocking tone used in juxtaposing a global phenomenon like COVID-19 with a seemingly irresponsible act that could be damaging to one's health reiterates Foucault's concept of normalising and deviance (Taylor, 2009).

#744
Just got my first vaccine dose today. Apart from the normal symptoms of headache, fever, and body ache, I am experiencing a little tripiness. IDK if it is due to the vaccine, the paracetamol tablet or the Blenders Pride I used to swallow down MDMA.

In this post, the closing plea is most striking. It is an indirect acknowledgement of the fact that, very often, most of the confessions are made fun of and the confessor ridiculed. In a slightly humorous tone, the following post talks about the complexity arising on social media platforms due to 'friending' family members (i.e., connecting your profiles so that you can see what each other posts online), which becomes a form of surveillance.

Relationship status "Single" doesn't always mean that you are alone. Sometimes it means "family members are there in the friends list.... (Anonymous, 2014)

The Indian Armed Forces Confessions page is quite different from any other. It is informative and helps to spread respect for the army. The confessions on this page revolve around love for the army and aspirations to join the army.

#638
Hello Everyone,
More than a confession, consider this a testimonial to my love. He is going to join Air Force Academy in January first week in Flying. And trust me, its not easy picturing him like that. We have been together for 4 years now and he has become a part of me. But because THIS life is what he has chosen for himself, I'll be a part of it happily. I'll spend my days, my weeks or even months waiting for that one call of his well being. I'll wish for these five months to get over as early as possible and those 1 month vacation to actually never end. Silly me, forcing him to take transport and stay away from combat as much as possible, now i want to see him as a fighter pilot, my fighter pilot. And no matter how much these things will weaken me, i'll be a strong would be Army wife, now and forever.
To you baby- come back soon, with those wings you had always wanted. I don't understand military things much, but i understand these wings will be above everything else on this earth for you. I was, i am and i will be always proud of you. And yes, i'll miss you badly but never let you fall apart.
Lastly, i am badly waiting to be a part of this military life, so come soon and marry me please 😘 😛 😛

(To Admin: Please post this, this is for him and i want him to stay strong)
🙂

(admin: we have posted though late. )😃
(Anonymous, 2013b).

The criteria for the confessions, according to the manager of the page, are that the posts should not be boring, false, or hateful and no racism or comment against religion is allowed. The page posts photographs of deceased army personnel, and female army personnel who have achieved a lot. It gives the readers a picture of the life, dreams and aspirations of the army personnel. This presentation of the idea of patriotism has the potential to attract Indian youth to join the Indian Armed Forces.

Most people believe that these confessions are true; some believe that they are not true, yet read them for the sake of entertainment; and a few do not care whether they are true or not. In certain cases, it becomes a matter of cyberbullying. The confessor is mostly anonymous, but the people about whom the confessions are made are unable to hide their identity and protect their image.

The confessions are mostly gendered, as the number of confessions made by males about females is much more than that of women making confessions about men.

The confession pages were extremely popular between 2013 and 2014. At the time of writing they are slowly falling into disuse. Most of the confession pages have been inactive since early 2015.[2] This craze for confessing online anonymously seems to have run its course. An analysis of the confession pages shows that a few pages are still active or have been restarted as different versions of the existing pages. By observing the posting patterns it can be deduced that the COVID-19 period saw a resurgence of the Facebook confession pages.

Although the trend of the Facebook confession pages has slowly dissipated, it has been reframed on anonymous messaging platforms such as Stulish and Sarahah, to name a few. Sarahah was initially formed to provide positive feedback for posters. However, very often, insulting comments or body shaming appear on such messaging platforms. This platform became popular during 2017–18 when many Facebook users

---

2    Refer to Appendix 1.

followed the trend of sharing the Sarahah link to collect comments, both positive and negative. The right to share the comments rests in the hands of the users alone.

This trend can be explained with the help of Judith Butler's (2009) *On Performativity*. The actions of Facebook users are directly connected to their sense of themselves. Their identity is founded to a significant extent on social acceptance. The act of following the trend of sharing posts received via platforms like Sarahah is intended to gain acceptance and confirmation. Butler posits that identity is not an inherent or static quality but a product of repeated social acts. In the digital context, especially on anonymous Facebook confession pages, users construct and negotiate their identities through confessional posts.

These online spaces allow individuals to perform aspects of their identity in front of an audience, where the anonymity of the platform encourages users to confess thoughts, desires, and actions that they might not express in real life. This echoes Butler's idea that identity is continuously shaped by repeated acts performed in a social space. The confessions on Facebook, therefore, serve as performative acts where users try out different versions of the self to see how they are received and to participate in collective narratives.

For example, a user confessing their feelings about taboo topics (such as relationships or personal failures) may be performing an identity that defies societal norms. This performance aligns with Butler's argument that such acts are not purely expressive of a pre-existing self but rather, they constitute the self through the act of performance. The feedback loop on social media—likes, comments, and shares—reinforces or reshapes this digital self, much like how social norms in the physical world shape identity through recognition or rejection .

Thus, Facebook confession pages, with their anonymous and performative nature, can be seen as digital stages where identity is constantly constructed and reconstructed, embodying Butler's notion that identity is not a stable essence but something created through ongoing social interaction.

# Conclusion

Whether the confession pages will be revived is still to be seen. What the pages have left behind gives a picture of the attitude and expectations of young people to and from society. Anonymity will always be useful as it helps a person to dissociate from a nasty comment being made. With their true identity hidden from the public eye, no one can be held responsible for the words they use and their consequences. Confessions have been an integral part of human life in every age, and with Facebook confessions losing their importance, this practice might take a different form. Only time can tell how it might be revived. Further research should be conducted on the subject matter and meaning of the posts using textual analysis tools and sentiment analysis tools.

# Works Cited

Anonymous. (2013a). IITK Rage - IIT K: What do you feel about the IITK Rage page which went viral recently and was closed down? *Quora*. https://www.quora.com/IITK-Rage-IIT-K-what-do-you-feel-about-the-IITK-Rage-page-which-went-viral-recently-and-was-closed-down

Anonymous. (2013b). *Indian Armed Forces Confessions | Facebook*. https://www.facebook.com/IndianArmedForcesConfessions/posts/pfbid08veaxEBYVzyunRN9K9G2QnS2w1n6eTspEbL3Gi1MdsWvuY5Gtvzvbp7oAty6KjZsl

Anonymous. (2013c). *Delhi Metro Confessions/Compliments | Facebook*. Facebook. https://www.facebook.com/DelhiMetroConfesssion/posts/pfbid02y3x22ECB75CxbnnMQDXyomvojXzqzyw4sjBuzrqCWuYnwXLKA2VnSfxXJZUC76Wrl.

Anonymous. (2014). *JAMMU Confessions | Facebook*. Facebook. https://www.facebook.com/jammuconfess/posts/pfbid02QFBWrP5wxg1fGWTKE1fWBbxSsKFNRn6NvBqn1VAbQdVMFjGbGdB9GqgCrSfqZ1UAl.

Anonymous. (2015a). *Jaihind College Confessions*. https://www.facebook.com/messages/jaihindconfessions

Anonymous. (2015b). *Delhi Metro Confessions*. https://www.facebook.com/messages/delhimetroconfessions

Barlow, J. P. (2016). *A Declaration of the Independence of Cyberspace*. Electronic Frontier Foundation. https://www.eff.org/cyberspace-independence

Butler, J. (1999). *Gender Trouble: Feminism and Subversion of Identity*. Routledge.

Cerra, A., & James, C. (2012). *Identity Shift: Where Identity Meets Technology in the Networked-Community Age*. John Wiley & Sons, Ltd.

Foucault, M. (1978). *The History of Sexuality* (Vol. 1). Penguin Books.

Hymer, S. (1995). Therapeutic and Redemptive Aspects of Religious Confession. *Journal of Religion and Health* 34(1), 41–54.

Kadvany, E. (2020, March 6th). Anonymous Confessions pages are surging in popularity on high school and college campuses. Why? *Palo Alto Online*. https://paloaltoonline.com/news/2020/03/06/anonymous-confessions-pages-are-surging-in-popularity-on-high-school-and-college-campuses-why

Keefer, L.A., Stewart, S.A., Palitsky, R., & Sullivan, D. (2019). Time-space distanciation: An empirically supported integrative framework for the cultural psychology of time and space. *Time & Society* 28(1), 297–332. https://doi.org/10.1177/0961463X17716736

Krishnaswami, N. (2013, March 10th). Letting it all out, anon. *Times of India*.          https://timesofindia.indiatimes.com/home/sunday-times/deep-focus/letting-it-all-out-anon/articleshow/18887520.cms

Sethi, A. (2017). Who started the confessions rage on Facebook? *Quora*. https://www.quora.com/Who-started-the-confessions-rage-on-Facebook

Singh, R. (2013). *UoH Confessions—#326: @320 I wanted to say just a few things,... | Facebook*. https://www.facebook.com/HcuConfessions/posts/pfbid02H5kDnxo4mDGSjiS2c7BnyWeoELgCawQV8jKrTWUV1kxnYcTQMFvQEWTw7u88LTtwl

Taylor, C. (2009). *The Culture of Confession from Augustine to Foucault A Genealogy of the 'Confessing Animal'*. Routledge.

Yu, H. (2009). *Media and Cultural Transformation in China*. Routledge.

# Appendix 1

Appendix 1 is available online at https://hdl.handle.net/20.500.12434/c6e9e696

# PART 3
# DIGITAL HUMANITIES AND TECHNOLOGY: METHODS AND METHODOLOGY

# 13. Code against code: Creative coding as research methodology

## Cameron Edmond and Tomasz Bednarz

### Abstract

Machine writing—where computing methods are used to create texts—has risen in popularity recently, diversifying and expanding. Machine writing itself could be seen as a subset of the creative coding discipline. Emblematic of the contemporary turn in machine writing is Darby Larson's *Irritant*. Impenetrable by traditional reading standards, the text is governed by code. The reader of *Irritant* faces similar challenges to the Digital Humanities scholar attempting to analyse large textual corpora. As such, *Irritant* becomes a useful case study for experimenting with reading methodologies.

We approach *Irritant* from a computational criticism perspective, informed by the same creative coding methods that spawned it. Our objective is to reverse engineer *Irritant*, scraping its repetitions and variables using Python within a live coding environment. We position creative coding as a research methodology itself, especially suited for analysing machine-written texts.

This chapter details our process of back-and-forth iteration between the researcher and the text. The 'hacking' of the text becomes critical practice itself: an engagement with the coded artefact that meets it on even ground. What our analysis finds, however, is more questions. Our exploration of *Irritant* fails to unravel the novel's code in the way we planned, but instead reveals more thematic depth. Far from the post-mortem of a failed experiment, this chapter presents creative coding as a research methodology and interrogates its benefits and challenges via the *Irritant* case study.

## Keywords

Machine-writing; distant reading; graph theory; algorithmic literature; creative coding.

## Introduction

In something of red lived an irritant. Safe from the blue from the irr. And this truck went in it. Safe. Something of red in it back to the blue to the red. This truck and something extra (Larson, 2013, p. 1).

So begins Darby Larson's monolithic text *Irritant* (2013). And so it continues, winding through surreal, asemantic statements that challenge reader comprehension. *Irritant* represents the creative coding practice of machine writing, where computing methods are used to create texts (Edmond, 2016, p. 4–5). As a textual practice, machine writing has experienced renewed interest within both popular (Heflin, 2020) and academic discourse (Orekhob, 2020). A lingering question of these interrogations is what methodologies are best suited for analysing machine-written texts, especially those generated from large textual corpora (Fullwood, 2014) or that are interactive (Walton, 2019). In this context, Larson's *Irritant* is an interesting beast. *Irritant's* construction is far more simplistic, using simple generative and cut-up methods akin to William S. Burroughs and the Dadaist movement (Robinson, 2011, p. 1–20). However, the abrasive prose of *Irritant* defies traditional reading standards. Rather than a traditional, temporal narrative, *Irritant* treats the text of the novel more like a texture. A single, monolithic paragraph is repeated, with each repetition featuring slightly altered sentences with objects, characters and actions changed. These actions are incremental, causing a slow rise and fall of these entities and actions throughout.

Despite its form, one could take a linear approach to reading *Irritant*. However, the veracity of such a reading is questionable. While the theme of relentless, linguistic oppression will be apparent, making sense of anything else requires a more systemic approach, one that can find the mutations within the sea of sameness. This observation leads us to inquire as to whether the computational criticism of the Digital Humanities (DH) can help us make sense of machine-written texts.

Analysis of machine-written texts has existed within fringe groups of literary scholarship for some time. Attempts to unravel texts produced via automation date back to at least the early 1980s, when computing and tech journalism began to show interest in computational texts (Edmond 2019, p. 37). However, recent years have seen an uptick in the relevance of machine-written texts. Writing in 2023, the most recent of these developments is the proliferation of Large Language Models (LLMs) such as OpenAI's ChatGPT, which some users have used to generate novels (Coetzee, 2023). At present, it seems that this form of Artificial Intelligence (AI) tool—one that produces text that bears extreme similarity to that of the human—is only likely to become more pervasive throughout our society.

Any grievances or jubilations about the world of Generative Pre-trained Transformer (GPT) texts aside, as the textual possibilities of AI continue to extend into new directions, it is important for us to understand how we may 'read' a text that is truly machinic. The productions of these LLMs are vastly different from Larson's *Irritant*. A foundational understanding of how one might speak to 'code through code' is important for the DH researcher of the future, and we believe doing so on the level of the machine—rather than when it is trying its hardest to appear human—may be the best way to get there.

While many DH techniques and tools are developed for the programmatic interrogation of texts at large, we are instead proposing a close reading. Our approach is not without precedent, as evident in the *Z-Axis Tool* that transposes literary works into 3D maps (Christie and Tanigawa, 2016). However, the *Z-Axis Tool* is only useful to a reader who knows what they are looking for—that is, the relevance of particular locations. Arguably, the reader of *Irritant* is starting from a somewhat less secure position, knowing only that the text they are stepping into is literally (and literarily) inhuman. Consequently, our attention turns to Jan-Hendrik Bakels et al.'s (2020) tool for computational visualisation/ annotation of films, which they refer to as a "systemic approach to human experience" (par. 12). One of the solutions the team demonstrates involves the creation of a timeline of the media in question, complete with the audio visualised as a waveform. The resulting view is akin to what a post-production professional would view when working on a film, mimicking the process of creation and allowing the user to peer 'behind the curtain' of the artefact.

Following Bakels et al.'s (2020) lead, we approach *Irritant* with a similar deconstructive approach in mind. As Larson's text was constructed through methods of creative coding, we will attempt to use similar techniques to analyse the text. In doing so, we offer a case study into the effectiveness of creative coding as a research methodology. Our initial analysis set out to unravel the code of *Irritant* itself. However, as we plunged deeper into the text, we were left with more questions. Our analysis revealed to us new thematic avenues and possibilities, thereby shedding light on both *Irritant* and how researchers may wield creative coding to conduct research.

Our work is also aligned with several other DH practitioners currently active in this field. John Mulligan's 'middle-distant' form of reading has recently examined the tensions that exist between numerical analysis and literary theory and attempts to reconcile the two.

Furthermore, the twisting and deforming of text to divine further meaning is a practice we are certainly not pioneering. Lisa Samuels and Jerome McGann (1999) discussed the reading of a text "against the work's original grain" (Samuels & McGann, 1999, p. 28). While discussing poetry, the pair suggest a new mode of critique: do not ask what the poem means, but instead investigate how you can release and expose this meaning.

Attempting to further pinpoint all the methods influencing this practice would be a chapter in and of itself. Instead, we point towards James E. Dobson's (2019) overview of the landscape of DH reading methods. Here, Dobson discusses the concept of "surface reading", and its relationship to approaching a text without a lens of "superstition" that accompanies close reading. Indeed, many of the practices we utilise emerge within such surface-reading approaches, down to the use of Python and Jupyter Notebooks. However, we approach our study with a far different intention. While a surface-reading approach may suggest meaning sits within the text, awaiting discovery, we instead recognise our programmatic reading as a sort of close reading itself, but simply one through a different method. We have, to put it crudely, replaced our pens and margin notes with loops and arrays. Our approach is deliberately inhuman, for what we are reading is as well.

Finally, we must address that while our methodology encourages the writing of code by the critic, our enquiries and practices may also apply to other existing tools for those apprehensive about starting programming themselves. Tools such as *Voyant Tools* and *Omeka* allow the visualisation of formalist textual elements, as well as marking up and annotating them. For those unsure where to begin, we suggest these tools as a starting point along their journey.

# Creative coding

Traditionally trained artists are increasingly interested in coding, as is evident in the proliferation of tools designed to facilitate the field of creative coding directly, such as *Stamper* (Burgess et al., 2020), and texts written to introduce arts practitioners to coding (Montfort, 2016). However, there is an erroneous narrative that computational art came about post-1980s. Artut (2017) states that it was only "a limited group of engineers and scientists who became experts in computer programming" (p. 2). While Artut's (2017) statement that computing was less accessible during the 1980s is true, it oversimplifies the use of computation in artistic practice, which dates back to at least Christopher Strachey's *Love Letter Generator* (Wardrip-Fruin, 2005), and glosses over the demoscene (Hansen et al., 2014), arguably a precursor to contemporary creative coding.

Creative coding has been referred to as decidedly iterative and reflective, likened to the painter who makes some expressions on the canvas and then decides what to do next (Bergstrom and Lotto, 2015, p. 26). Essentially, planning is reduced if not eliminated. Bergstrom and Lotto (2015) extend this metaphor by describing "live coding" in which individuals write code in front of an audience (pp. 26–27). The pair also associate creative coding with hacking. Nikitina (2012) describes hackers as the tricksters of the digital age, performing inventive, barrier-crossing tasks that leverage systems in the search for creativity (pp. 133–135). Much like the trickster of mythology, the hacker manipulates the systems around them to alter their environment. Their subversion becomes their artistry. In keeping with these sentiments, our definition of creative coding encompasses the need for the act to be an iterative 'hacking' away at the subject.

Without planning too far ahead, we do need to consider what we wish to uncover from *Irritant*. Given its algorithmic form, the patterns themselves are a good starting point. This leads us back to the techniques that bore *Irritant* initially: textual manipulation. Our starting point, then, is to try and unravel the repetitions and variables of *Irritant*. As we wish to do so iteratively and reflectively, we will use a Jupyter Notebook. A Jupyter Notebook is a live programming environment, that allows users to write blocks of code and execute them as they go, creating a space for exploratory and iterative programming (Project Jupyter). Notebooks can be shared, so ours is available from http://hci.epicentreunsw.info/ creativecode.html. While we cannot upload our source material, by making our code available, we hope to encourage readers to experiment with the code in their analysis of other texts.

A note on the syntax and style of code used in this chapter. While completed code is often re-factored to appear more beautiful, function better and achieve more reliable results, our purpose here was to show the live 'hacking' experience of attempting an enquiry, learning from the result (or error message) and trying again. As such, while we stand by the methodology presented here, we make no such claims about the styling and formatting of the code. Please view the actual code presented here as scribbles in the margins, rather than completed analysis.

## Prep time

Machine writing texts such as *Irritant* are, in many ways, 'hacks' of language and literary tradition. As illustrated in the yearly submissions to NaNoGenMo (Kazemi, 2013), to practice machine writing is to play with language. Although some scholars have studied *Irritant* (Sierra-Paredes, 2017; Murphet, 2016) the question remains: how do we unravel this enigma? What is the key to opening the monolith and discovering the meaning within? We view it as a puzzle: a dense tome that challenges the reader. We must follow the clues and construct the jigsaw piece by piece, forming the picture as we go.

Larson is not the first to craft a puzzle for their reader in the form of unconventional discourse. *Life: A User's Manual* (1987) by Georges Perec refers to itself as a jigsaw puzzle in its opening pages. Similarly, as the brain in *Plus* (2014) by Joseph McElroy relearns consciousness, the reader is invited to piece together the story. However, McElroy and Perec both give the reader more clues as they go. By sheer dint of perseverance, the reader will find answers by the time they reach the final page. For the reader of *Irritant*, there is no such certainty. *Irritant* ends much as it began: the monolithic paragraph iterates a few more times and ends—almost mockingly—with the statement "this is a showboat" (Larson, 2013, p. 623).

However, Larson has left clues for those trying to solve *Irritant*. In an interview, Larson presented the code used to generate the short story "Pigs", in which a series of sentences slowly evolve, their original words being replaced with a litany of other nouns, creating a textual unravelling (Larson, "Pigs"). Larson then suggests that "similar" constraints were used to create *Irritant*, stating the original idea as "a 70-word initial set that slowly changes to a completely different 70-word final set with a one-word change occurring every 4000 words. So, 4000 x 70 is 280,000 words total" (Butler & Larson, 2013). Larson cryptically continues:

> *Irritant* ended up being quite less than 280k [...] I wrote the first 4000 words on my own, just stream of consciousness while referring to the word set. Then I randomized that and concatenated it to the original (so now 8000 words) and did one-word substitution on the new 4000, and so on and so on until all 70 words had been substituted (Butler & Larson, 2013).

From Larson's statement, we can begin to unravel *Irritant* armed with the following clues:

- The first 4000 words are completely humanly written.

- The second 4000 are randomised.

- There are 70 words that become substituted.

These points are useful, but also establish the difficulty of our task. The core of *Irritant* being written by a human rather than a machine throws it into a nether realm of study. A human-penned puzzle has its pieces placed deliberately, ready to be solved. Further, a completely machinic text would require only one cracking of the pattern to uncover its workings. *Irritant* sits between the two worlds, guarded by both humanity and machinery.

The first step, then, is to check the veracity of Larson's claim. According to the copy of the text we have, *Irritant*'s word count is 272,267. If an iteration occurs every 4000 words, and accounting for the novel's first 4000 words being 'outside' the equation and the next 4000 being iteration zero, we are left with 264,267 words (272,267 – 8,000). Dividing this by 4000, we are left with 66.1, three (and change) words shy of Larson's claimed 70 iterations. We then must ask: did Larson begin counting his iterations earlier? Did he use some sort of post-processing to remove sections that weren't interesting? And how do we account for the stray 267 words, which based on initial sums do not fit nicely into our calculations? Larson has likely both made a few tweaks in the editing room and, perhaps, forgotten the exact number of iterations contained in the book. Taking these two points as our preliminary hypothesis and armed with a digestible version of the text ready to 'hack', we begin our spelunk into the literary depths of *Irritant*.

## Hacking *Irritant*

The text of this chapter is written to present our methodology in a way that it can be reproduced. As such, we assume very little of our reader's knowledge of the Python language. However, if for no other reason than chapter length, we will not be delving into how to install Python or Jupyter Notebook. Thus, our process begins at the step of having digested *Irritant*'s text into a .txt file and opened up a Python 3 Jupyter Notebook to begin our excavation. We first import all necessary libraries and then turn our .txt file into a single string.

```
import pandas as pd
import nltk
from nltk.stem.wordnet import WordNetLemmatizer as WL
from statistics import median
import matplotlib.pyplot as plt

with open ("irritantraw.txt", "r") as irr:
    irritant = irr.read()
```

We now have our subject in a raw, textual form for processing. There are many starting points here. Given Larson's discussion of word permeation, we will first uncover exactly what words appear throughout the text by creating a list of every unique word within it. We create a version of *Irritant* that removes punctuation and capitalisation to make it easier to split into words and avoid false positives. We then transform this string into a list of all words in *Irritant*.

```
punctuation = [".",",","?","!"]
irritant_np = irritant
for p in punctuation:
  irritant_np = irritant_np.replace(p,"")
irritant_np = irritant_np.lower()
irritantlist = irritant_np.split(" ")
```

This list will certainly include duplicates, so from here we generate our new list of 'prime' words, which includes each word only once.

```
irritantwords = []
for word in irritantlist:
  if word not in irritantwords:
    irritantwords.append(word)
    print(word)
```

This gives us our list of every word within *Irritant*—a total of 478 unique words. If we still believe Larson's original claims, this leaves us with (478-70*2=) 338 'generic' words that do not evolve over the course of the system. We can assume these words are most likely articles and conjunctions, although we cannot prove this yet. Another step is to see just how many times each word appears. Because we kept both lists, we can compare them and retrieve the count of each unique word.

```
for word in irritantwords:
  count = irritant_np.count(word)
  print ("There are " + str(count) + " instances of '" +
word + "' in total.")
```

Although this method allows us to produce a plain, textual list of each word and its frequency, a list of 478 words is only marginally more readable than *Irritant* itself, and, on its own, it will not reveal much. It would be better to visualise this data. First, we will need to place unique words and their counts into a tabular dataset/dataframe. As we will be doing this a few times, we will write a function to create our graph. After a run, it became clear that visualising all 478 words was unwieldy, and it might be better to begin with the top 50 and bottom 50 words, amalgamated in Figure 13.1.

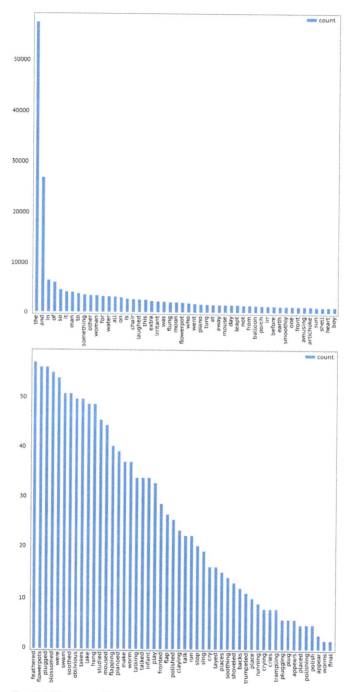

Fig. 13.1 The top and bottom 50 words in *Irritant*, sorted by frequency.

```
def visualise(uniquewords,fullcorpus):
  wordcount = []
  for word in uniquewords:
    count = fullcorpus.count(word)
    wordcount.append(count)
  df = pd.DataFrame({'word': uniquewords,'count':wordcount})
  dfsorted = df.sort_values(by='count', ascending = False).
head(50)
  dfsorted.plot.barh(x='word',y='count', figsize=(30,30),
fontsize=20)
  dfsorted = df.sort_values(by='count', ascending = False).
tail(50)
  dfsorted.plot.barh(x='word',y='count', figsize=(30,30),
fontsize=20)

visualise(irritantwords,irritantlist)
```

Looking at our top 50 words, it becomes abundantly clear that the inclusion of our generic terms—especially "the" and "and"—is obfuscating any insights. Our next step, then, is to shrink our list down so we can examine only the evolving words. There are a handful of ways we could do this. We could guess which words are generic, but we will likely miss some, making this a time consuming and error-prone method. We could comb through the text itself and find words, but this would defeat the purpose of our hack-based reading methodology. Most other solutions involve bringing in some sort of NLP library, in this case, NLTK, that offers some intelligence as to how words hang together.

First, we will try using NLTK to analyse the text and find what words are similar to one another. This should give us a good idea as to how the patterns of the text hang together. We begin by tokenising our text to make it readable to NLTK.

```
text = nltk.word_tokenize(irritant)
irritanttagged = nltk.pos_tag(text)
context = nltk.Text(word.lower() for word in text)
```

Through this method, we should receive a list of every word used in similar settings to the eponymous "irritant", one of the words we propose is evolving throughout the text. We run the code "context.similar('irritant')", which returns "woman porch water morning moon turq chair other evening man sun balloon corner door kitchen artichoke weather flowerpot infant blue".

This isn't particularly insightful. While it does indicate we are on the right track (nouns appear to be replaced by nouns), it is hardly a conclusive list. Moreover, running the query on "the" ("context.similar('the')"), yields a few of the same words, such as "moon".

While these results are discouraging, they do create some inroads into Larson's linguistic puzzle box. If "the" and "irritant" share similarities, this implies that Larson's pattern does not follow a traditional syntactical pattern. So, we will now see if we can retrieve all nouns and verbs from the text to map what structure does exist. NLTK can help us do this, as it tokenises and tags words based on their lexical role. For instance, conjunctions are tagged with "CC", common nouns with "NN", proper nouns with "NNP", etcetera. Following the creative coding mantra of "leap before you look" (Greenberg et al., 2013, p. xxiii), we will begin by creating a new list of all nouns, pronouns, adverbs and verbs. To start, we first want to get a lead on what tags are present in the text, so we don't waste time having our code look for tags that don't appear.

```
alltags = []
for word, tag in irritanttagged:
  if tag not in alltags:
    alltags.append(tag)
    print (tag)
```

An interesting observation is that when our script returns the list, it includes "FW", which NLTK assigns to non-English words.[1] By probing what this word is:

```
for word, tag in irritanttagged:
  if tag == "FW":
   print (word)
```

It is revealed that the word is "masked", rather than the far more likely invented words of *Irritant*, such as "turq" (a contraction of turquoise, perhaps?) and "elbowthumbs" (an impossible body part?). This exercise reminds us of the limitations of our method. The delegation of "masked" as "foreign" aside, we can use this information to generate a

---

1    The relegation of all non-English words to the category of "foreign" is somewhat problematic.

much shorter list of words and get closer to understanding how *Irritant's* patterns manifest. Firstly, we define a function for simplifying words to avoid repetition. At the moment, all this function will do is change a word to lower case and add it to our working 'evolving words' list.

```
def simplify(word, targetlist):
  word = word.lower()
  if word not in targetlist:
    targetlist.append(word)
```

We then identify all tags we wish to keep and simplify the associated words.

```
goodtags = ['NN,','JJ','VBD','PRP','NNP','RB','NNS','VBN','V
B','PDT','VBG',
 'PRP$','VBP','VBZ','RBR','JJR','UH','JJS','FW']
evolvingwords = []
for word,tag in irritanttagged:
  for gt in goodtags:
    if tag == gt:
      simplify(word,evolvingwords)
print (evolvingwords)
print (len(evolvingwords))
```

The resulting list is not perfect, coming in at 332 words and featuring several duplicates in the form of plurals and different tenses. We test its use by first running it through our word count function from earlier ("visualise (evolvingwords,irritantlist)"). Our resulting graphs were better, but a few words have slipped through the categorical cracks, such as "is" and "as". We can quickly remove them and run our code again: the results are depicted in Figure 13.2. Interestingly enough, this level of manual editing moves us closer to Larson's practice, as he made a few changes to his output. However, we are still maintaining a computational slant by not directly deleting data points and instead using scripting to do so.

```
badwords = ['is','as','so','it']
for bw in badwords:
  evolvingwords.remove(bw)
visualise(evolvingwords,irritantlist)
```

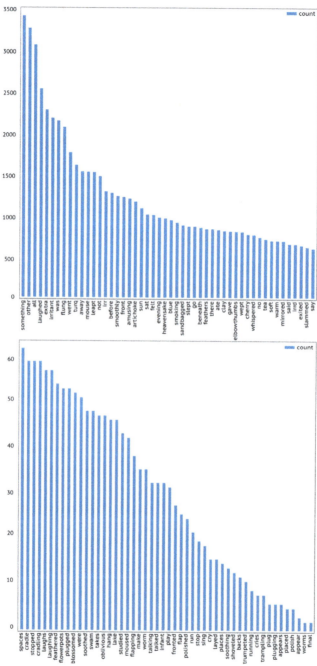

Fig. 13.2 The top 50 and bottom 50 of our "evolving words" in *Irritant*, sorted by frequency.

Our resulting visualisations show a lot more promise. The most common word in the text appears to be "something", indicating that it either never evolves, or is the final piece to do so. "Irritant", "irr" and "irrd" all make the top 50, which is unsurprising. The absence of "red" is interesting. The novel's opening would make it seem that "red" will feature prominently. Instead, "blue" steals the show.

It is here we start to question what constitutes a unique 'word' in Larson's pattern. Are "cough" and "coughed" unique permeations, or the same permeation but with the tense skewed either by code or by Larson's hand? If the former, then the permeations are greater than Larson stated. If the latter, then having a list to access the permeations directly would go a long way towards unravelling *Irritant*. We could achieve this by reducing each instance to its base form. NLTK can achieve this via the "lemmatize()" function. Adding this to our simplify function has unintended consequences, as it converts "went" to "go", "ground" to "grind" and a few other transformations that make our list too divorced from the original text to be useful. Perhaps we need to flip the script and search for the words around the permeations. We fall again to our creative coding mantra of experimentation and attempt to retrieve some sort of 'boilerplate' of *Irritant*. We first create a new list of every sentence.

```python
badpunctuation = ["?","!"]
irritantcleaned = irritant
for bd in badpunctuation:
    irritantcleaned = irritant.replace(bd,".")
    irritantsentencelist = irritantcleaned.split(". ")
for sentence in irritantsentencelist:
    print (sentence)
    print (len(irritantsentencelist))
```

We then filter this down to just the unique sentences.

```python
irrusentences = []
for sentence in irritantsentencelist:
    if sentence not in irrusentences:
        irrusentences.append(sentence)
        print (sentence)
print (len(irrusentences))
```

While the novel contains 20,724 sentences, only 1612 of these are unique. This leaves us with 19,112 repetitions throughout the novel. This is

interesting, as a cursory look over *Irritant* gives the appearance that
sentences change constantly, if only slightly. We will return to this number
soon, but first we want to finish what we started and try to find the
boilerplates of the text, replacing each evolving word with "<BLANK>".

```
boilerplates = []
irritantcleanlist = irritantcleaned.split(" ")
irritantnewlist = []
evolvingwords_punctuated = []

missedwords = ["flowerpot", "chair", "porch", "truck",
"carpenter", "door", "shell", "piano", "kitchen",
"showboat", "hearth", "balloon", "woman", "moon", "man"]

for mw in missedwords:
  evolvingwords.append(mw)

for word in evolvingwords:
  evolvingwords_punctuated.append(word + ".")

for word in irritantcleanlist:
  if word in evolvingwords or word in evolvingwords_
punctuated:
    irritantnewlist.append("<BLANK>")
  else:
    irritantnewlist.append(word)

irritant_boilerplated = " ".join(irritantnewlist)
boilerplates = irritant_boilerplated.split(". ")

boilerplates_unique = []
for sentence in boilerplates:
  if sentence not in boilerplates_unique:
    print (sentence)
    boilerplates_unique.append(sentence)

print (len(boilerplates_unique))
```

As we peruse our results, it becomes clear that certain obviously evolving
words such as "flowerpot" have evaded NLTK's categorising. The
results are noisy, and don't seem to show any patterns. Our hypothesis
of some 'generic' words and some 'non-generic' words may have been
inaccurate. Perhaps all words are permeating. If so, what method is
keeping these sentences 'in check'? Perhaps reducing each sentence to
its semantic NLTK tags will help shed our text of any noise.

```
justtags = []
for word, tag in irritanttagged:
  justtags.append(tag)

irritanttags = " ".join(justtags)

irritanttagsents = irritanttags.split(". ")

for sent in irritanttagsents:
  print (sent + " ---------> " + str(len(sent.split(" "))))
```

Still no discernible patterns seem to emerge. Word type and sentence length are arbitrary, with no overarching patterns. While this might be discouraging, it is par for the course: our philosophy of hacking away at this novel has already dramatically changed our understanding of how it works. Larson's claims seem to be completely false, or else made obsolete by his human-level tampering. Instead, the abstracted, hacked artefact of *Irritant* is forming into something far different. But we aren't done yet.

While we are unable to find patterns on this macro level, due to the difference in size between our complete sentence list and our unique sentence list, we know there is repetition. So, how often does a new sentence manifest? We can better understand this by visualising it, charting each period of repetitions and how many sentences repeat between them.

```
repeatcount = 0
repeats = []
periods = []
periodcount = 0
newsentences = []
irritantsentencelist = irritantcleaned.split(". ")
for sentence in irritantsentencelist:
  if sentence not in newsentences:
    if repeatcount != 0:
      periodcount += 1
      periods.append(periodcount)
      repeats.append(repeatcount)
      repeatcount = 0
      newsentences.append(sentence)
    else:
      repeatcount += 1

df = pd.DataFrame({'period': periods, 'length':repeats})
ax = df.plot.barh(x='period',y='length', figsize=(20,500),
fontsize=20)
```

Fig. 13.3 All intervals between new sentences in *Irritant* and their lengths. Each column represents 300 intervals.

The result is depicted in Figure 13.3, which we have cropped and edited for readability. The resulting graph shows us that the intervals fluctuate in length, but overall become longer as the text continues. Many short intervals are slowly littered with longer ones, peaking at the 585th mark and slowly shrinking again, with the final few intervals shorter than the first bout. What does this tell us about *Irritant*? Sierra-Paredes (2017) refers to the "slow rhythm" (p. 31) of *Irritant* created by its repetitions. However, this rhythm is hard to discern. Via our visualisation, it becomes manifest.

The themes represented by the irritant itself are becoming clear. There are over sixteen intervals in *Irritant* where the gap between new sentences is over 100, with the largest gulf between repetition and permeation being 157. The maelstrom of repetition and monotony, disturbed by the spectre of allegory, that the reader must endure between each glimmer of newness is quantified. Due to such a high degree of repetition, we are left to wonder if most readers would even be aware of when repetitions were occurring. In effect, the clarity of our visualisation makes *Irritant's* obscurity more evident.

There is one last process we wish to perform. It is likely that all words permutate, and that Larson's clues were red herrings. However, we are still interested in *when* some of the more prominent words appear. Perusing our earlier lists and counts, we notice that the "infant"—a symbol for the future and a linguistic warping of "irritant"—erupts into the text towards its end. Perhaps more meaning lies in mapping some of the other terms, plucking them from the maelstrom of conjunctions and articles to better understand the presence of flowerpots, women, blue and even the irritant itself.

We initially experimented with visualising the occurrence of each evolving word per sentence, but with over 20,000 sentences (retrieved via "print (len(irritantsentencelist))"), it would be difficult to meaningfully visualise within the Jupyter notebook environment. Additionally, each word is only going to appear in a sentence once or twice, meaning any visualisation is going to be one of many ups and downs, without a clear view of how words rise and fall on a meaningful scale. We return to Laron's clues and divide *Irritant* into "chunks" of 4000 words, yielding 69 chunks in total.

```
span = 4000
irritantchunks = []

for i in range(0, len(irritant_np.split(" ")), span):
  irritantchunks.append(irritant_np.split(" ")[i:i + span])
print(len(irritantchunks))
```

This code creates 36 graphs, which together act as a sort of summary of the novel. Unsurprisingly, some of these "scenes" are more interesting than others. In our first plot (Figure 4), "extras" has many mentions early on, but then drops off dramatically before we hit 10 chunks. "Safe" meets a similar fate, although it never had much power to begin with. "Red" has a few in the early chunks and then disappears before we get to chunk 20.

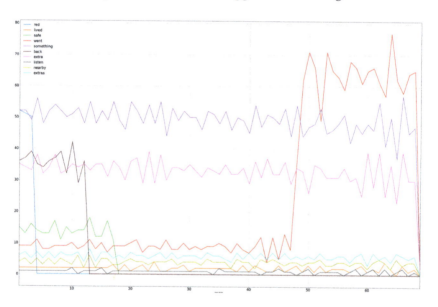

Fig. 13.4 Our first-word progression plot, depicting the words "red", "lived", "safe", "went", "something", "back", "extra", "listen", "nearby" and "extras".

Of course, the novel's namesake is worth interrogating. As shown in Figure 13.5, the irritant entity makes it through almost the entire novel. Far from the most popular entity, the irritant lurks within the permutations, popping up here and there, occasionally announcing itself before slinking back into the darkness. Much like the reader's search for resolution, the "irritant" itself is just out of reach, skulking between linguistic twists and turns. In our graph, however, we do see some resolution: the irritant disappears towards the end of the novel completely, dropping to zero appearances before all is said and done.

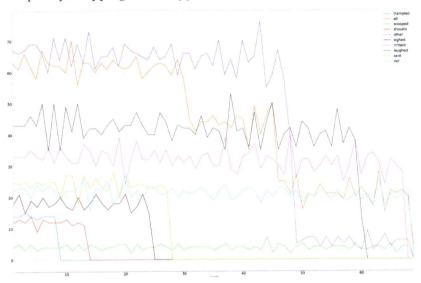

Fig. 13.5 A plot that shows the frequency of "irritant" throughout the novel.

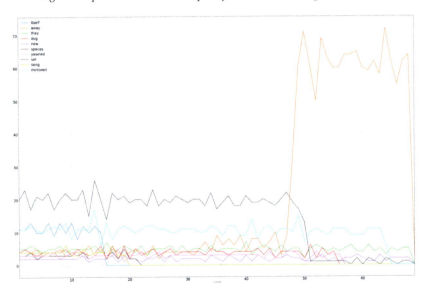

Fig. 13.6 A plot showing the frequency of "away", illustrating how it dwarfs the terms it was featured with.

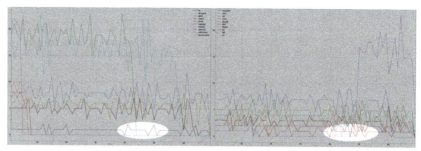

Fig. 13.7 Two plots showing the similar patterns of "have" and "seemed", which have been spotlighted for clarity.

Some patterns emerge that may simply be red herrings. "Away" dwarfs the words it is visualised with (Figure 13.6) but may not seem so mighty if grouped with others. As Figure 13.7 shows, "seemed" and "have" feature similar patterns between chunks 40 and 50, but is this at all noteworthy? While some instances show large intervals between our word lines, others bunch together, creating interesting patterns, as seen in Figure 13.8.

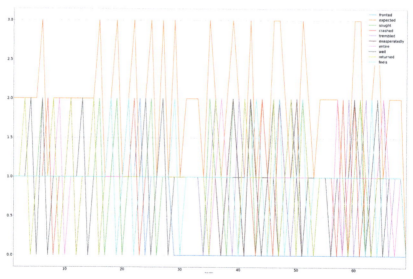

Fig. 13.8 A plot showing the interesting pattern that emerges when the frequencies of "fronted", "expected", "sought", "crashed", "trembled", "exasperatedly", "entire", "well", "returned" and "feels" are featured together.

These visualisations illustrate the importance of filtering our data. As a final visualisation, we take 10 words that we believe—together—will tell us more about *Irritant*. The words chosen are "irritant", "infant", "finally", "weeping", "digest", "clay", "whispered", "slammed", "cried" and "showboat", as displayed in Figure 13.9. Comparing these words tells the story of *Irritant*: we see the irritant persist throughout, suffering a dip about a fifth of the way into the text, but then rising again multiple times. Ultimately, however, the irritant falls, eclipsed by the infant. In the background, the nature of the world is changing: the world of clay is replaced by one of whispering and slamming, emotions running high before the outburst of crying that usher in the infant's arrival. A dangerous and primordial (clay) world is replaced with one of new beginnings and emotional relief. Meanwhile, a Greek choir of weeping and showboats bubbles beneath the surface, almost unnoticed throughout. Of course, this is the showboats' plan, appearing as the final word of the text, and thereby one of its most memorable.

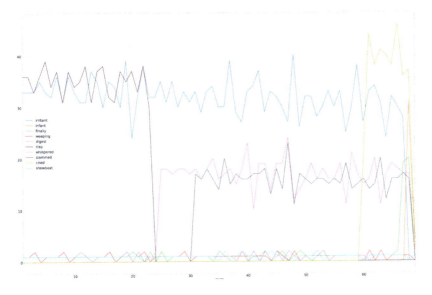

Fig. 13.9 Our final visualisation of *Irritant*, comparing the frequencies of "irritant", "infant", "finally", "weeping", "digest", "clay", "whispered", "slammed", "cried" and "showboat".

# Conclusions

Our final plot, while interesting, is simply one interpretation. Were we to select a different set of 10 words, we would be presented with a far different story. Our visualisation of the irritant yielding to the infant, along with our other visualisations, word counts and missteps along the way, provide us insight into how creative coding may function as a method of close computational criticism. We conclude our experiment yielded a form of analysis that was both interpretive and performative.

As an interpretation, our methodology provides an additional layer. We become divorced from the text proper, with our visualisations becoming the actual texts that we 'read' and interpret. However, this act of interpretation is preceded by many more interpretations. Every time we choose a method of representation or retrieve data, we are making a judgement as to what elements are relevant. If our analysis had begun with a shorter or longer list of 'evolving words', we may have ended up with far different conclusions. This extra layer is useful but has its flaws. As the reader explores the text through abstraction and selection, elements may be lost or forgotten. Of course, we can always return to the initial text, but it certainly suggests one can become 'lost' within their quantified text. We should consider the ramifications of representation when conducting these changes. Could a reader inadvertently erase the stories of marginalised groups within a text through these methods, with their resulting plots distorting the messages of the original text? The problem is not indomitable, but we must be wary not to let abstraction obfuscate the original text.

As a performance, the breakdown of the text and its abstraction is a sort of live sculpting. The original text, as data, is honed and reformed multiple times, revealing its different textures and contours with each iteration. We align ourselves here with the philosophy behind *LitVis*, a data visualisation tool created to allow data communicators to iterate on their visualisations, reflecting as they go (Wood et al., 2018). This chapter is a testament to that, acting as a sort of memoir of analysis, containing observations and reflections alongside findings. Returning to our hacker concept, the creative coding critic becomes the trickster of mythology, the text itself their sphynx, labyrinth, or gorgon. In truth, a creative coding methodology needn't be performative, but simply presenting the resulting visualisations does little to advance knowledge of the text. Indeed, we hope this chapter has contributed knowledge on *Irritant*, as well as the use of computational mechanisms to deconstruct a text itself.

Creative coding is itself, a creative practice. As our analysis has shown, this is not a methodology steeped in calculated pre-theorising and planning. Instead, our approach suggests a sort of *performance* of criticism. Harkening to DH's older ethos of performativity and aesthetics (Svensson, 2010), we present a method that places the digital humanist in a dance with the textual object: offering, receiving, analysing, repeating. We do not seek to replace these more carefully planned forms of analysis, but instead offer another approach that asks the digital humanist to embrace playful analysis.

Our method of creative coding as research methodology is presented as an additional tool in the arsenal of the literature/media analyst. Far from the distant reading techniques typical of DH, our approach places us closer to the text, forced to enter into, pull apart and remould the text itself. The algorithmic structure behind *Irritant* was not 'cracked' as we first set out to do. It appears there is no consistent morphing of each word, nor does there seem to be consistency of sentence structure/length. However, in our process of trying to unravel *Irritant's* mysteries, we have found new themes and patterns. Given this chapter is a relatively brief exploration of what is a thick tome, it is likely that far more lies beneath *Irritant's* surface, and that some of it can perhaps only be revealed by further trying to beat the book at its own game. In this way, our work aligns with Saum-Pascual's (2020) view of "critical creativity", which he describes as something "wildly transformative that disrupts and changes the way we say, make, and do things. Creativity becomes a ballast to rationality" (par. 36). Far from the end of this story, our plunge into the depths of *Irritant* offers a few introductory steps into a method of close reading that conceives of the writer as puzzle maker, reader as hacker, and pits code against code.

# Works Cited

Artut, S. (2017). Incorporation of computational creativity in Arts Education: Creative coding as an Art Course. *SHS Web of Conferences 37*. https://www.doi.org/10.1051/shsconf/20173701028.

Bakels, J-H., et al., (2020). Matching computational analysis and human experience: Performative arts and the Digital Humanities. *Digital Humanities Quarterly 14*(4). www.digitalhumanities.org/dhq/vol/14/4/000496/000496.html

Bergstrom, I., & Lotto, R.B. (2015). Code bending: A new creative coding practice. *Leonardo 48*(1), 25–31. https://www.doi.org/10.1162/LEON_a_00934

Burgess, C., et al., (2020). Stamper: An artboard-oriented creative coding environment. *CHI EA '20L Extended Abstracts of the 2020 CHI Conference on Human Factors in Computing Systems*, 1–9. https://www.doi.org/10.1145/3334480.3382994

Butler, B., & Larson, D. (2013, September 11). If you build the code, your computer will write the novel. *Vice*. www.vice.com/en/article/nnqwvd/if-you-build-the-code-your-computer-will-write-the-novel

Christie, A. & Tanigawa, K. (2016). Mapping Modernism's Z-axis: A Model for Spatial Analysis in Modernist Studies. In S. Ross & J. O'Sullivan (Eds). *Reading Modernism with Machines*. (pp. 79–107). Palgrave Macmillan. https://doi.org/10.1057/978-1-137-59569-0_4

Coetzee, C. (2023, March 24). Generating a full-length work of fiction with GPT-4. *Medium*. https://medium.com/@chiaracoetzee/generating-a-full-length-work-of-fiction-with-gpt-4-4052cfeddef3

Digital Scholar. (2024). *Omeka*. https://omeka.org/

Dobson, J.E. (2019). *Critical Digital Humanities: The Search for a Methodology*. University of Illinois Press.

Edmond, C. (2016). The poet's other self: Studying machine writing through the Humanities. *Humanity 7*, 1–29. novaojs.newcastle.edu.au/hass/index.php/humanity/article/view/46

Edmond, C. (2019). *Poetics of the Machine: Machine Writing and The AI Literature Frontier*. Macquarie University. Thesis. https://doi.org/10.25949/19436060.v1

Fullwood, M. (2014). Twide and Twejudice at NaNoGenMo 2014. *Michelle Fullwood*. michelleful.github.io/code-blog/2014/12/07/nanogenmo-2014/

Greenberg, I., et al., (2013). *Processing: Creative Coding and Generative Art in Processing 2*. Springer.

Hansen, N., et al., (2014). Crafting Code at the Demo-scene. *DIS '14: Proceedings of the 2014 Conference on Designing Interactive Systems*, 35–8. https://www.doi.org/10.1145/2598510.2598526.

Heflin, J. (2020, March 3). How Do You Map an AI Art World? *Immerse*, immerse.news/how-do-you-map-an-ai-art-world-8beb3e77a52b

Larson, D. (2011). Pigs. *Sleeping Fish*. web.archive.org/web/20180118034035/http://www.sleepingfish.net/X/070911_Larson/

Larson, D. (2013). *Irritant*. Dznac Books.

McElroy, J. (2014). *Plus*. Dznac Books.

Montfort, N. (2016). *Exploratory Programming for the Arts and Humanities*. MIT Press.

Murphet, J. (2016). Short Story Futures. In D. Head (Ed.). *The Cambridge History of the English Short Story*. (pp. 598–614). Cambridge University Press.

Mulligan, J. (2021). Computation and Interpretation in Literary Studies. *Critical Inquiry 48* (1), 126–143. https://doi.org/10.1086/715982

Nikitina, S. (2012). Hackers as tricksters of the digital age: Creativity in hacker culture. *The Journal of Popular Culture 45*(1), 133—52.

Orekhob, B., & Fischer, F. (2020). Neural reading: Insights from the analysis of poetry generated by artificial neural networks. *ORBIS Litterarum*, 230–46. https://www.doi.org/10.1111/oli.12274.

Perec, G. (1987). *Life: A User's Manual* (D. Bellos, Trans.). Godine.

Project Jupyter. *Jupyter Notebook*. jupyter.org/

Robinson, E.S. (2011). *Shift Linguals: Cut-Up Narratives from William S. Burroughs to the Present*. Rodopi.

Samuels, L., & McGann, J. (1999). Deformance and interpretation. *New Literary History 30*(1), 25–56. https://dx.doi.org/10.1353/nlh.1999.0010

Saum-Pascual, A. (2020). Digital creativity as critical material thinking: The disruptive potential of electronic literature. *Electronic Book Review*. https://www.doi.org/10.7273/grd1-e122

Svensson, P. (2010). The Landscape of Digital Humanities. *Digital Humanities Quarterly 4* (1).

Sierra-Paredes, G. (2017). Postdigital synchronicity and syntopy: The manipulation. *Neohelicon* 44, 27–39. https://www.doi.org/10.1007/s11059-017-0379-8

Sinclair, S. & Rockwell, G. (2024). *Voyant Tools*. https://voyant-tools.org

Kazemi, D. (2013). *NaNoGenMo*. nanogenmo.github.io/

Walton, N. (2019). *AI Dungeon 2*. www.aidungeon.io/

Wardrip-Fruin, N. (2005). Christopher Stratchey: The First Digital Artist? *Grand Text Auto.* grandtextauto.soe.ucsc.edu/2005/08/01/christopher-strachey-first-digital-artist/

Wood, J., et al., (2018). Design exposition with literate visualization and computer graphics. *IEEE Transactions on Visualization 25*(1), 759–68. https://www.doi.org/10.1109/TVCG.2018.2864836.

# 14. Digital Humanities for a different purpose

*Julian Walker, Miyuki Hughes, Madeleine Leehy and Peter Mauch*

## Abstract

This chapter explores the recent application of Digital Humanities (DH) methods to a database for Australia-Japan Research and Industrial Collaboration (DAJRIC) and assesses their potential utility to a project outside of traditional scholarly purposes. The primary objective of this chapter is twofold: (i) to evaluate the effectiveness of this approach in serving our purposes, and (ii) to consider the scalability of the pilot database to accommodate numerous yet unfunded Japanese-Australian research projects. By developing a Heurist database, the project can harness the intuitive design principles that make DH methods so effective and appealing for scholarly purposes to users unfamiliar with these research fields. Throughout this process, the project team has discovered the challenges of raw data, ontology development, and bilingual functionality that face a project of this scale, whilst also realising the potential of Digital Humanities' techniques in providing improved user interactivity and search functionality through record types and their connections with each other, and through data visualisation. These techniques, when applied with knowledge organisation techniques, enable a scalable database that can organically grow with the hundreds of projects to be entered in the future. As such, this project provides a valid example of how scholarly techniques within the Digital Humanities can

https://doi.org/10.11647/OBP.0423.14

be applied successfully to projects that act as a gateway between academia and other sectors.

## Keywords

Digital Humanities; Heurist databases; databases; ontology development; translation; data visualization; knowledge organisation.

## Introduction

This chapter introduces readers to a recent attempt at applying Digital Humanities techniques for reasons other than the scholarly: we are developing a database that will showcase a large range of Japanese-Australian collaborative technological-industrial-scientific-academic ventures. Funded by the Australia-Japan Foundation, the database aims to provide a gateway for investors and to facilitate corporate funding for Japanese-Australian translational research.

The project seeks to serve an emerging community between collaborative researchers and industry funding in the bilateral Australia-Japan relationship. Functioning as a repository for this information, a significant amount can be learned from digital libraries and their definitions of sustainable preservation of digital metadata. That said, there are varied definitions of what sustainability entails, especially when dealing with a database that seeks to connect academia and industry in such a way. Therefore, sustainability in this case is best defined as the ongoing maintenance of the platform to ensure continued access for both researchers and funders (Edmond & Morselli, 2020, p. 1022).

Digital Humanities techniques are applicable because the search functions of the database must necessarily be intuitive and all users, regardless of their level of familiarity with the Japanese-Australian research landscape, need to be able to find projects of interest with ease. This includes the ability to simplify technical jargon across various research fields. The discussion in this chapter centres on a pilot project, which involved the construction of a database based on ten research projects funded by the Foundation for Australia-Japan Studies. The success (or otherwise) of the pilot database would determine whether

(i) the DH techniques under discussion in this chapter would serve our purposes, and (ii) the pilot database could be scaled up so that it included several hundred as yet unfunded Japanese-Australian research projects.

This process has uncovered various challenges and obstacles that stem from dealing with dense raw data specifically tailored for specialist audiences in their original form, and the objective of bilingual functionality. Furthermore, the significant desire to create a database that develops organically in a self-sustaining manner raises concerns about scalability in both key terms and search functionality. Yet for each challenge, the nature of DH methodologies provided alternative solutions to our problems, such as creative search functionality through Heurist record types and their connections with one another; data visualisation through a map to demonstrate the transnational research collaboration simply; and the usage of Heurist's database structures to ensure scalability for such projects.

## Raw data

The raw data for the pilot project were the research proposals that research teams submitted to the Foundation for Australia-Japan Studies. These proposals fell into one of the following priority areas: (i) medical science and technology; (ii) materials and energy technologies and systems; (iii) computing, digital and AI applications and developments; (iv) food, marine and agriculture science and technologies; and (v) social and physical infrastructure.

Each proposal included (i) project title, (ii) project summary, (iii) project salience, (iv) innovation, (v) project team members' track record, (vi) networks, (vii) sustainability, (viii) diversity, and (ix) financial contributions from sources other than the Foundation for Australia-Japan Studies.

The raw data is dense, full of discipline-specific phrasing and terms, and not necessarily easy for the layperson to digest. The principal issue for the database involved making this data digestible for a wider audience, so that, for example, an employee at a capital-rich corporation looking for projects to support financially can quickly and easily locate projects of potential interest.

# Database construction

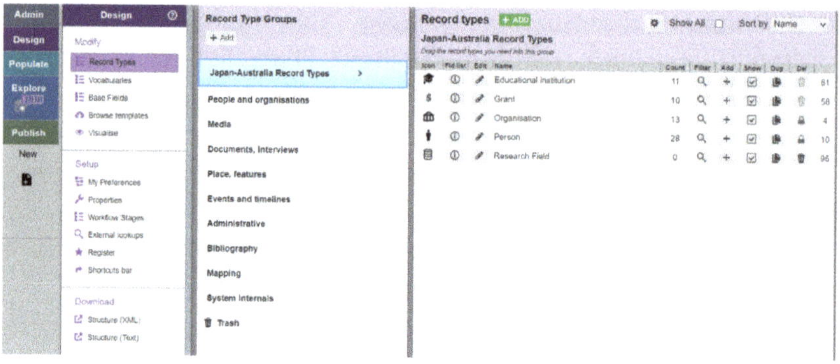

Fig. 14.1 Database interface.

The project team used Heurist, which is an open-source online database builder and CMS publisher designed for Humanities research data and collections. In Heurist, we created our own "record types," creating records for "educational institutions" and "organisations", "persons" (meaning researchers), and the "research field" of a project (see Figure 14.1). By creating these categories, database users can search projects by research field, keywords, institution, organisation, keywords, etc.

While our initial steps looked simple, we later realised these "record types" actually affect the database's user-friendliness. For example, we initially grouped universities and companies in one category called "organisations." But if a third party is looking in this database for a project to fund, they will probably be interested in, e.g., industrial partners on any project. The database therefore needs to filter companies from universities. We had to differentiate and separate these record types so that the database now includes separate entries for "educational institutions" and "organisations".

Heurist includes DH functionality that is beneficial to the database. We have been able to make connections between items so that, e.g., the database connects "researchers" to "educational institutions", "organisations" to "projects", or "projects" to "researchers". This allows users to also search by a researcher's name to see what project they are working on, or to search by the university to see what other projects are based there. This functionality contributes directly to the user-friendliness of the database.

# Ontology building

As part of producing content for the database regarding the project proposals, we were tasked with building an ontology. This involved identifying keywords and phrases while considering the specific users of the database, such as academics and individuals from the corporate world (Noy & McGuiness, 2001, p. 6). We concerned ourselves with likely search items that would enable database users to find proposals and key information (Jones et al., 1998). Ultimately, we were concerning ourselves with how users would interact with the database.

The process of ontology building began with reading through each proposal a couple of times to understand both the intent of the author and the material being presented. While reading through the proposal, speciality terms such as 'fluorescence in situ hybridisation' were researched, defined and noted within their context.

When building the list of keywords, the aim was not to duplicate the terms within the proposal document as these were to be uploaded into the database to enable a free search of terms. For example, if you search 'fluorescence', even though this was not included within the list of keywords, the proposal would still emerge as it was included in the raw data.

There were a range of things to consider in building an ontology as a distinct entity from the data present in the proposal document. For example, we had to consider pluralisation; various terms within the proposal document were treated as singular, but what happens if the database user, e.g., attempts to search for "blood cancers" rather than "blood cancer"?

We also had to consider multiple expressions for the same term. The use of synonyms proved the most expansive element of the list. There are so many different terms used for the phrase "blood cancer research", what happens if a database user searches for "blood cancer interventions", or "blood cancer imaging", or "blood cancer monitoring", or "blood cancer study", or "blood cancer diagnostics"? The list just keeps going and continues to grow if we move beyond the more generalised terms to include higher-order concepts. For example, instead of "blood cancer research" database users may search for more abstract terms such as "haematology", "biomedical research" and "phenotype research".

As mentioned, the material is dense and not easily digested by the layperson, and so keywords and phrases had to be simplified and redefined to increase accessibility for database users. For example, users interested in interventions within blood cancer research may not be searching for the specific term "in situ hybridisation" but may use layperson terms such as blood cancer treatments and blood disorder initiatives.

The last thing we considered was spelling localisation, for example using an 's' or 'z' in 'hybridisation' as per British English or American English. This localisation was especially important as generally American English is used within Japan. However, British English is used in Australia, leading to differences in search terms as well as the free search of the proposal depending on what type of English the author used.

The ten projects in our pilot database gave rise to a total of 1353 keywords. This is a mean number of keywords of 140.5 per project. As mentioned, by using Excel, data was produced on a line-by-line basis, thus it could be easily transposed to the database after checking the lists for clarity and spell-checking. Thus, keywords can be easily updated, which is essential as the number of keywords is always growing. There will always be new terms to add and consider and more terms will develop over time. This is an essential aspect of ensuring that the database is organic and growing constantly as it incorporates new data and new projects.

## Bilingual issues

Target users of the database will mostly be based in Australia and Japan. If the database is to be user-friendly, it needs to be a Japanese-English bilingual database. This has created various issues. For reasons of brevity, we have restricted our discussion to several illuminative examples (Figure 14.2).

| | | Taro Tanaka |
|---|---|---|
| Kanji | Chinese characters | 田中太郎 |
| Hiragana | The basic Japanese phonetic alphabet. (It is primarily used for function words and inflexions.) | たなか　たろう |
| Katakana | The basic Japanese phonetic alphabet. It is often used for the transcription of loan words from foreign languages. | タナカ　タロウ |

Fig. 14.2 Japanese has three spelling systems.

As this table demonstrates, the Japanese language has three types of characters. Should we enter every Japanese word in all three characters? In the context of personal names, as a rule, personal names are written in kanji (Chinese characters). But if a database user wants to search by researcher name, even though they don't know the exact kanji that the researcher uses for their name, the database user is likely to use either hiragana or katakana—they are essentially searching by phonetics. In short, a search for a particular researcher in the database might take one of the following three forms: "田中太郎"; "たなかたろう"; "タナカ タロウ".

One problem is that the raw data includes no Japanese text (the proposals were written only in English), so the team constructing the database cannot always be certain of the kanji that a researcher uses to write their name. At the very least, it involves a lot of cross-checking, by consulting, for example, at the university where the researcher is based, to see whether the raw data includes the researcher's name written in kanji.

| Circumstances | Issues | Examples |
| --- | --- | --- |
| When we know how to pronounce the name. | It would have some variations depending on how you hear it. | Madeleine [ˈmadəlɪn, -lèɪn]<br>マデライン；マドレイン；<br>マドリーン；マドレーン；<br>マドレーヌ |
| When we do not know how to pronounce the name. | We may transcribe it completely wrong. | Peter Mauch<br>(How do you pronounce it?)<br>ピーター・マウチ (Mauch?)<br>ピーター・マーク (Mark?)<br>ピーター・モーク (Mork?) |

Fig. 14.3 Non-Japanese names.

The second question was, if we enter Japanese researchers' names in both English and Japanese (Fig. 14.3), should we do the same for non-Japanese researchers? Would it affect the search results if only Japanese researchers had entries in. both languages? To answer this, I thought about how we could add non-Japanese researchers' names in Japanese. Two problems arose.

The first problem arises when we know how to pronounce the name. We can write a non-Japanese person's name in Japanese according to the phonetic sounds. However, we are just sorting the sounds that do not exist in Japanese into the closest Japanese sounds. The result would have some variations depending on how you hear it. This may cause problems later. For example, Figure 14.3 indicates the possible spellings of Madeleine in Japanese, and they all sound similar but are spelled slightly differently.

The second problem is when we do not know how to pronounce the name. In this case, we could record it completely incorrectly. Let us use the surname 'Mauch' as an example. If we don't know how to pronounce this name, the way we write it phonetically in Japanese becomes nothing more than guesswork. Possible renderings in Japanese are マウチ, マーク, and モーク. They are quite different.

| Cancer |
| --- |
| 癌<br><br>Cancer in epithelial tissue<br><br>e.g., Skin cancer, stomach cancer |
| がん<br><br>All types of cancer<br><br>e.g., Insurance for cancer, cancer research centre<br><br>The visual impression is softer than Katakana |
| ガン<br><br>All types of cancer |

Fig. 14.4 Keywords.

Similarly, a database user might conduct a keyword search for 'cancer' in one of three different ways: 癌、がん、or ガン. These variables become more difficult and more complex when we consider variations in English-language terms. Sometimes each English-language variation offers multiple possible Japanese-language translations, so that the process of database construction becomes almost endless. Figure 14.5 below includes a few examples.

| Possible variations | Examples |
| --- | --- |
| Use of hyphen | shelf-life / shelf life |
| Singular/ plural | tumour / tumours |
| Multiple expression | medical implant / biological implant / biomedical implant<br><br>chromosomal abnormalities / abnormal chromosomes |
| Acronyms | Fluorescence in situ hybridisation / FISH<br><br>Magnesium / Mg |
| Spelling (US/UK/AUS) | haemato- (US) / haemato- (UK)<br><br>Tumor (US) / Tumour (UK) |
| Technical term / layman's term | Multiple myeloma / Bone marrow cancer |

Fig. 14.5 English variations and multiple translations.

## Visualising data

We have also considered how users might choose to visualise the data. A map seemed like a logical choice as it demonstrates not only the transnational Japanese-Australian connections between the proposals, but it also increases user interactivity by making searching through the database functional, rather than just relying on the free search/ categorical search function. Geotagging was used on both the proposals and educational institutions, which can be searched and identified on the map, ultimately linking to the proposal as the final function. The map widget also has a built-in timeline function that demonstrates when the proposed research began and finished, in other words, the lifespan of the proposal.

The use of a map tool to present data within our database gives rise to additional issues. As mentioned, one of the initial goals of the database was for it to be bilingual. As the map is primarily visual, it allows people with limited language capability to access information, which is highly important in its current state as a largely English-language-dominant site (while the more difficult elements of producing a bilingual database are resolved). Using the map also allows the layperson to engage with it, as it requires a minimal level of skill—just clicking around and exploring a map, rather than having to click through various menus or attempt to freely search if a user has no idea what they are trying to look for or is attempting to engage with the database for various purposes.

As mentioned previously, using the map as a visual representation of data demonstrates the global connections between proposals. As one of the major goals of this database was to produce international collaborations between both Japan and Australia, and to allow engagement with various stakeholders external to close-knit academic circles, the map draws various connections and reinforces the close links between Australia and Japan, especially regarding research. Further, mapping international data points draws attention to foreign facilities that may not be recognised by someone overseas but are generally well known in the country of origin, as demonstrated by the mass connections to this data point.

In another vein, it may also draw attention to smaller facilities that have great potential to produce future work and demonstrate unexpected connections. For example, one of the proposals regarding autonomous robots generated contributions from researchers in Jamaica, outside of the realm of an exclusive Australian and Japanese relationship. This demonstrates unexpected connections that would not have been picked up on the initial reading of the proposal or the database entry. In contrast, you can also examine which proposals involve prestigious organisations—for example, the National Institute for Quantum Science and Technology in Japan was involved in various proposals. Users may be interested in what these large organisations are focusing on, as well as the connections between pieces of work, which is demonstrated clearly through the visual map function.

We have begun to explore how filters, such as searching for organisations, countries, and whether the data points are linked to an industry partner impact the effectiveness of establishing connections and increase the discoverability of proposals. For example, the field "industry partner" enables users to examine organisations outside of close-knit academic circles for possible collaboration. The timeline function supports the aim for the database to be a living thing, and also helps to build the reputation the grant proposal program as a whole, as it demonstrates the history of providing funding and the length of the body of work.

Although a map appears to be a clear benefit to the database and a valuable tool for representing the data, we also attempted other forms of modelling, such as network maps to demonstrate connections between different identifiers including the grants, organisations, researchers, institutions, etcetera. But it became eclectic very quickly as there are too many variables to consider at this early stage and we have not yet identified a key area of focus for connections and how to filter these. This might be something to discuss as we move into presenting the database to focus groups—what are the most important factors that individuals who use the database want to search for, and do visualisations such as network maps aid in the discoverability of proposals and in people's understanding of the database as a whole?

# Scalability and usability

One of the challenges with large-scale projects such as this database is scalability and usability for end users. This requires good knowledge organisation (i.e., the organisation of the data itself), and streamlined ontologies that are easily understood by the end user. Such a requirement often emerges in Digital Humanities (DH) tools where the intuitive design makes substantial projects possible for broad audiences (Golub & Liu, 2022, p. 2). The Heurist platform enables humanities scholars to enter data and create front-end websites, just as easily as an end user can search and use that database for their purposes. But this hurdle can result in overwhelming ontologies both in size and in complex jargon. While terminology is beneficial for those familiar with the applicable fields, it is fundamentally confusing to lay users. Therefore, this project in its second year has devoted time to streamlining the vast ontology to become more direct for point A to point B searches, whilst also laying the foundations for large-scale knowledge organisation that further acts as a filter for the expansive categorisation of projects.

## Knowledge organisation and databases

How a database organises its data is an important task, and thus it is the focus of much scholarly inquiry, especially in the Digital Humanities. DH researchers commonly face the realities of ad hoc solutions for data collection management and find themselves suffering from scalability issues (Golub & Liu, 2022, p. 1). Part of this stems from the sheer scale of digitalised material Digital Humanities researchers collect, annotate, and analyse (Robinson, 2014, p. 247).

For this database, however, we focus on the closely related field of information retrieval. While the database, and how data is organised, is crucial, the objective of the database is to be quickly and easily searchable for the layperson outside of science, technology, engineering, and medical (STEM) fields. This requires data to be organised for the fundamental purpose of retrieval rather than analysis. It is critical to note that, while users may be competent in searching during their day-to-day lives, they will not necessarily be experts nor familiar with these cutting-edge projects (Hjørland, 2015, p. 1570).

# Nested vocabularies

Yet searchability is vital for the success of the database's objective, which is to connect funding to collaborative research projects. All projects within this database are located within priority areas as defined by the Foundation of Australia and Japanese Studies, and as such, these categories become the foundation of the nested vocabularies. This top-down approach takes broad conceptions, the priority areas, and narrows them down into specialisations or specific areas of interest (Noy & McGuiness, 2001, p. 6). For example, the generalised priority area of "Food, Marine, and Agriculture" has split into areas of specific interest such as "food", "marine", or "agriculture". In a similar sense, it also required us to further define the meaning of the priority area of "Social and Physical Infrastructure" into categories of "renewable energy", and "resource security" to enable users to immediately understand what the priority area holds.

Further examples include "Medical Science and Technology" being broken down into smaller categories familiar to broader audiences, such as "cancer", "genetics", and "surgeries". This also applies to the priority area of "Materials, Energy Technologies, and Systems", where sensor and measurement devices are bundled together with "systems" and "energy". This approach allows the database, for those managing it, and for the end users, to take broad categories and begin to narrow them down for their respective purposes. This is a core principle for nested vocabularies, whose emphasis on filtering down vast categories into smaller sections is one solution to the scalability problem faced by a database that seeks to be as organic as possible.

# Streamlined ontologies

The key to knowledge organisation within large-scale projects aimed at non-specialist users lies in an easily understood, usable, and streamlined ontology. This can be achieved in multiple ways, involving a "standard and systematic procedure to use, and categorise information" that can be searched and obtained from a database (Ezhilarasi & Kalavathy, 2023, p. 54). This project has approached this standard and systematic process through the construction of an ontology during the pilot year. This ontology was applied to both searchable tags and simple searches. The streamlined ontology, however, uses the currently existing ontology as a foundation to create a set of tags that improves the user's ability to find information easily (Hepp, 2007, p. 90). This new ontology is designed to improve scalability by being specific yet not overly technical or redundant. Tags used in the search fields aim to be clear, precise, and concise in their usage. For example, the various ways of searching for implants have been reduced to a single keyword. Specific terms, such as types of cancers, have remained for scalability purposes. This enables the user to traverse the projects in the database in a fast and direct manner in three ways. They can either: 1) use the nested vocabularies of priority areas to find a certain selection of projects; 2) use these streamlined tags to find a certain project; or 3) search the database more broadly using the vast ontology previously developed.

Another vital aspect of streamlined ontologies is its maintenance and application. A dedicated ontology can be additionally purposed for user self-entry into the database and would require little maintenance, whereas an overly expansive one can quickly run rampant as more users enter data into the database. This allows the database to become more of a repository that other sectors such as agriculture, information and technology, or scientific fields already utilise significantly. The database would evolve from one that primarily stores data for the sole purpose of connecting funder to researcher, into a self-sustaining repository for these projects that grows over time.

## Future enhancements

The scalability changes have been successfully implemented in the pilot database. Furthermore, these enhancements for knowledge organisation and optimised ontology have been extended to the Japanese sister site, aligning with the database's ultimate goal of bilingual functionality. Looking ahead, the most significant challenge the database will encounter is archiving completed projects from the Search Projects page.

Currently, this issue is addressed through a filtering process in search fields. However, as the database grows, a maintenance process will be necessary to ensure that completed projects are appropriately archived in a separate location. This measure is crucial to prevent finished projects from overshadowing unfunded projects and maintaining the integrity and relevance of the database's content.

# Discussion

In this section, we discuss how the evolution of the database over the pilot process has many implications for the use of Digital Humanities technologies and techniques in connecting academic approaches to external opportunities. Does it justify the use of Digital Humanities techniques in non-academic spaces, and is this approach scalable to accommodate large-scale and continuous data entry?

The primary obstacle to applying DH approaches to databases like this is the acquisition of raw data. However, our research has shown that not only can this obstacle be overcome, but it can also be implemented without necessitating knowledge from the end user. DH functionalities provided by platforms like Heurist, such as establishing "relationships" between different types of records (e.g., "researchers" and "organisations"), enhance user-friendliness by enabling users to search for specific researchers, universities, or industries of interest directly.

Furthermore, our study has highlighted how DH approaches can address the challenges of bilingual databases in Australian-Japanese collaborations. For instance, we explored complexities related to the Japanese writing system, which complicates English-to-Japanese translations for keywords developed in the ontology, as well as translating English names into Japanese. Additionally, managing English variations and multiple translations poses ongoing challenges as the database progresses beyond the pilot stage. However, DH techniques offer innovative solutions to overcome these challenges.

One such solution provided by Heurist is the ability to leverage data visualisation tools such as maps, which not only showcase transnational collaborations between researchers, organisations, and industries but also enhance usability by allowing users to interact with the database intuitively, without needing to know specific search terms. This demonstrates the versatility and effectiveness of DH techniques in improving accessibility and usability for diverse audiences. Yet, the exploration has also revealed that this process requires strict streamlined ontologies and knowledge organisation to ensure that projects remain scalable and useable for the end user. This challenge is unique to non-scholarly applications of DH techniques, as the database's primary purpose is to become a self-sustaining repository for research projects, as opposed to its traditional purpose as a tool to analyse vast quantities of data. By using Heurist's intuitive vocabulary functions, we can streamline the ontology that can grow alongside the vast number of projects in the future.

The limitations of this chapter are primarily attributable to the project being in its pilot phase. However, this limitation also serves as an opportunity for future research and a re-evaluation of how DH techniques can be further applied to the database once it becomes self-sustaining. Despite being in the early stages, these findings hold significance as they demonstrate the feasibility and success of DH approaches for non-academic purposes. With careful refinement, these techniques can be scaled to accommodate large and ongoing data entry.

The insights gleaned from this study should encourage others in similar or related fields to explore the potential of DH techniques beyond academic research. By showcasing the adaptability and effectiveness of DH methodologies on a broader non-scholarly scale, this chapter provides a compelling case for the wider adoption of such approaches in various contexts.

# Conclusion

This chapter presents a novel application of Digital Humanities techniques aimed at lay audiences in the creation of a database highlighting a diverse array of Japanese-Australian collaborative research endeavours spanning technological, industrial, scientific, and academic domains. The primary objective is to establish connections between corporate or industry funding and these collaborative projects in a manner that is transparent and easily accessible by all stakeholders.

The database contains a vast amount of complex raw data, posing a significant challenge in simplifying specialised terminology for lay audiences. However, the Heurist platform offers innovative and user-friendly solutions to address this issue by facilitating simple and filtered searches, thus enhancing accessibility.

Furthermore, the database's aim to support Japanese-Australian research projects necessitates bilingual capabilities, which pose distinct challenges. Translating English keywords into Japanese and selecting the appropriate Japanese spelling system present initial hurdles. Moreover, the intricate task of translating Japanese text back into English adds another layer of complexity.

For a project of this magnitude, managing hundreds of projects awaiting data entry, and anticipating future expansions necessitates a scalable ontology and search functionalities. To tackle these challenges, nested vocabularies have been employed to enhance knowledge organisation and establish a flexible structure capable of accommodating the organic growth of the database. This approach significantly enhances the ability of the database to achieve bilingual functionality.

This project's application of Digital Humanities methods is not only justified, but it also serves as a model for collaborations between academia and industry within the DH space. By leveraging techniques commonly employed in traditional DH projects dealing with large datasets, this project demonstrates the potential to effectively overcome knowledge and language barriers. Consequently, it showcases a viable and efficient pathway for future projects using DH approaches outside the realm of academia.

# Works Cited

Department of Foreign Affairs and Trade. (2024). Australia-Japan Foundation. https://www.dfat.gov.au/people-to-people/foundations-councils-institutes/australia-japan-foundation

Ezhilarasi, K., & Kalavathy, G. (2023). Development of Contextual Crop Ontology for Effective Information. In *Proceedings of 3rd International Conference on Recent Trends in Machine Learning, IoT, Smart Cities and Applications: ICMISC 2022* (pp. 53–65). Springer Nature Singapore. https://doi.org/10.1007/978-981-19-6088-8_6

Foundation for Australia-Japan Studies (n.d.). https://www.fajs.org/

Golub, K., & Liu, Y.H. (Eds). (2021). *Information and Knowledge Organisation in Digital Humanities: Global Perspectives*. Taylor & Francis. https://www.doi.org/10.4324/9781003131816

Gunjan, V.K., & Zurada, J.M. (2023). Development of contextual crop ontology or effective information retrieval. In *Proceedings of 3rd International Conference on Recent Trends in Machine Learning, IoT, Smart Cities and Applications* (Vol. 540, pp. 53–65). Springer. https://doi.org/10.1007/978-981-19-6088-8_6

Hepp, M. (2007). Possible ontologies: How reality constrains the development of relevant ontologies. *IEEE Internet Computing 11*(1), 90–96. https://doi. org/10.1109/MIC.2007.20

Hjørland, B. (2015). Classical databases and knowledge organization: A case for Boolean retrieval and human decision-making during searches: Classical databases and knowledge organization. *Journal of the Association for Information Science and Technology 66*(8), 1559–1575. https://doi.org/10.1002/ asi.23250

Jones, D., Bench-Capon, T., & Visser, P. (1998). *Methodologies for Ontology Development.* University of Liverpool. https://cgi.csc.liv.ac.uk/~tbc/ publications/itknows.pdf

Noy, N.F., & McGuinness, D.L. (2001). *Ontology development 101: A guide to creating your first ontology.* https://corais.org/sites/default/files/ontology_ development_101_aguide_to_creating_your_first_ontology.pdf

Robinson, P. (2014). Digital Humanities: Is bigger, better? In P.L. Arthur & K. Bode (Eds). *Advancing Digital Humanities.* (pp. 243–257). Palgrave Macmillan UK. https://doi.org/10.1057/9781137337016_16

# 15. Online dating: Transformations of marriage arrangements through digital media technologies in Australia's Indian community

*Asha Chand*

## Abstract

Marriage and migration are twin global forces that have reshaped Australia's identity from a white nation to a multicultural melting pot. India has become the largest contributor to immigration in Australia, with 710,380 permanent migrants. Indians are Australia's second largest migrant community (after England), equivalent to 9.5% of Australia's overseas-born population (Australian Bureau of Statistics, 2021). This study, built within the context of a postmodern society that is networked, mobile and global, examines the use of new media technologies in finding a marriage match, known to the Indian diaspora as a way of life. The research seeks to understand the sociological impacts of hyper-communication, especially the use of dating sites and social media platforms such as Facebook, in forming intimate relationships online. This chapter evaluates the aspirations among the Indian diaspora to maintain cultural identities through marriage (which also feeds migration) by seeking life partners with similar background via online dating websites. Globalisation, while opening a world of possibilities, simultaneously helps to lock the Indian community into its own cultural cluster through online dating and marriage. Using Information and Communication

https://doi.org/10.11647/OBP.0423.15

Technologies (ICT), the community is basking in this newfound freedom to pick and choose, reinforcing the centuries old tradition of ensuring compatibility when forming relationships. Levels of education, professional status and family values stand out as key attributes being sought by men and women who engage on the dating sites in this study. This study builds on earlier research (Chand, 2012) that presents the fabric of family as vital to the Indian social structure. This study is important as it attempts to understand the cultural negotiations specific to the Indian diaspora, which is vibrant and growing in the Australian landscape. The influence of Bollywood, which has enraptured Western societies, coupled with India's resurgence as a superpower, adds value and significance to this research which provides an understanding of the importance of marriage to Indians. This research is timely and relevant to the public, including Western societies, which not too long ago saw 'matchmaking' as backward.

## Keywords

Marriage; matchmaking; new media technologies; online dating; Indian diaspora; weddings; Bollywood

## Introduction

The landscape of modern romance has undergone a significant transformation with the advent of digital technologies. In an era when education and career pursuits often dominate our lifestyles, millions turn to the digital highways in search of love and marriage. Scholars like Schmitz and Schmitz (2017) have explored this phenomenon, framing online dating as a digitally unified marketplace where symbolic goods are exchanged as individuals engage in a process of digital partner choice. This perspective underscores the role of technology in facilitating connections and shaping romantic narratives within contemporary society.

Reinforcing this notion, Sautter, Tippet, and Morgan (2010) argue that online dating has transitioned into a mainstream tool for meeting potential partners. Their research highlights that the primary predictors

ngaging in online dating are one's single status and internet usage
its. This indicates a widespread acceptance and integration of
ne dating platforms into the fabric of modern relationship-seeking
aviours. Cacioppo et al., (2013) introduce the access hypothesis,
ch offers insight into the demographic factors driving the adoption
online dating. According to this hypothesis, individuals who face
llenges in meeting potential partners face-to-face due to constraints
h as limited time, demanding careers, or other commitments are
e likely to turn to online dating platforms.

The role of convenience and accessibility in shaping the preferences
behaviours of digital daters has thus become important, and hence
convergence of technology, societal shifts, and individual preferences
led to the proliferation of online dating as a prominent avenue for
king and forging romantic connections, redefining the landscape of
temporary romance. Conceptualising online dating as "relationship
pping", Heino, Ellison, and Gibbs (2010) argue that daters see
platform as a virtual market where numerous potential mates are
ilable and desired ones can be found by simply entering partner
cifications. It has also been speculated that the shopping mentality
atively affects commitment and satisfaction with dates.

The 21st century is a blessing and a curse, where a robust environment
online dating sites has attracted people from all walks of life and
m all over the world. Several niche sites specifically target ethnic or
gious groups. Among Indians, for whom arranged marriage has
n a part of their social, cultural, and religious fabric for centuries,
ine dating sites provide a high-tech means of matchmaking. India is
world's second-largest market for dating apps behind the US Sites
h as Shaddi.com, IndianDating.com, IndianCupid.com, iMilap, and
trimony.com are popular among Indian users of dating sites. Some of
se were established before many of the current users were born. Each
has enhanced user capabilities, such as introducing video technology,
ert matchmaking services and different dialects common among
diaspora, to remain competitive in the market. Many of the sites
w initial free access with personality and algorithm-based matching
izzes. To go to the next step of 'meeting' prospective partners, clients
required to pay fees. Online dating was a US $40 million business in
)1 and by 2008 it had grown into a $600 million industry, involving

more than 800 businesses (Epstein, 2007).

Using the theoretical framework of selective self-presentation, Walther (1996) argues that online communicators have at their disposal an arsenal of technological affordances that enable them to exercise more control over their statements than in face-to-face communication. The asynchronicity of the internet enables daters to take time to construct their profiles, editing and refining statements to strategically present themselves, but these opportunities also afford an optimal amount of deception in portraying the self. Researchers such as Ellison, et al., (2006) say that impression management (in presenting personal profiles), is appealing because it can help daters stand out and gain attention from potential mates. Daters also manage tensions by presenting elements of their ideal self, an enhanced, yet attainable version of self.

## Research objective

The central aim of this research is to understand why and how the digital media environment is the new platform for finding partners for Indians who have been accustomed to traditional arranged marriage through matchmaking. Historically, this was done by the village matchmaker and more recently by parents, families, and acquaintances. The other objective is to understand why online dating is replacing and extending the traditional methods of introducing couples. The significance of marriage from traditional and modern perspectives is presented to evaluate how online dating impacts the institution of marriage in a modern, western society where affluence also dictates the elaborate wedding ceremonies, which are mostly influenced by Bollywood celebrity weddings, and weddings of the rich and famous, such as the 2024 wedding of Anant Ambani and Radhika Merchant which Australian media report as having cost $600 million, an eyewatering sum that accounts for only 0.5% of the Ambani fortune (Ellis-Petersen, 2024). The public display of the glitter and glamour from such weddings (Bollywood) on the silver screen and private ones on the multitude of social media sites feed the ideals of marriage and wedding.

Photos and videos taken by professional photographers at engagements and weddings are regularly posted on social media by both women and men. These photos enhance the look of the couple and comments via the "like" columns include positive and flattering remarks. Online exposure through video and photo sharing enables even those who may not know the couple to copy fashions from such photos, which in turn, at a psychological level feeds the imagination of idealistic trends in Bollywood and silver-screen celebrity marriages, as well as other fashion trends.

This research brings out the level of matchmaking and compatibility by detailing what people seeking partners post on their profiles, for example, the presence of columns with the kinds of attributes being 'sought' and 'presented' by participants. This research thus aims to provide an understanding of the role of online dating sites in the modern era of sharing private information in public spheres to find a partner for marriage.

## Methodology

This investigation focuses on the use of new media technologies in finding matches for marriage through five online dating sites as well as Facebook, which facilitates the 'posting' of personal profiles and the first secret meeting online. The sites evaluated for this study include Shaadi. com, IndianDating.com, IndianCupid.com, iMilap.com and Matrimony. com.

The study explores the types of profiles being posted to understand the common criteria, values and attributes presented and sought by marriage partners. This exploration helps to frame an understanding of values and priorities that are important in relationships to modern-day Australian Indians. A comparative study, through literature reviews, seeks to present what the common ideals are when marriage partners are being sought. This work records the influence of new media technologies in dictating descriptors about private and personal aspirations in public media spaces.

The dating sites were accessed online and evaluated for the services they offer, statements they make about their business, and their target markets (people from various language backgrounds within the Indian diaspora). The study involved examining key personal descriptors by those seeking partners, focusing on how women described themselves and what they sought in their ideal partners. Similarly, the research considered how men described themselves and their preferences in their partners. This focus is an extension of the author's PhD research (Chand, 2012) which evaluated matchmaking within the Fijian Indian community in Sydney (2008–2012) when newspaper advertisements seeking partners were popular in the ethnic media. The research found the use of similar descriptors, although skin colour, which was one of the most common descriptors in advertisements, was missing in the online profiles.

Studies by Gibbs, Ellison and Heino (2006) found that 80% of online daters registered concerns that others misrepresented themselves, and research by Brym and Lenton (2001) note that fear of deception is the biggest perceived disadvantage of online dating. To this end, this research has focused on the personal descriptors and attributes being sought in prospective partners. The aim was to see if there is a common aspiration among the Indian diaspora when choosing partners. Goffman (1959) defines self-presentation as a process of packaging and editing the self to create certain impressions upon the audience. Ellison, Heino, and Gibbs (2006), Schlenker (2003), Toma et al., (2008), argue that online daters make choices regarding the information they present to attract desirable potential mates. The latter argue that the daters' choices are guided by two underlying tensions. The first is self-enhancement, or the desire to appear as attractive as possible to be noticed. The second is to be authentic, with the need to appear honest in their descriptions of themselves.

The theoretical framework of selective "self-presentation" (Walther, 1996) has also been explored in this research. This theory posits that online communicators have at their disposal an arsenal of technological affordance that enables more control over their statements than face-to-face communication. The asynchronicity involved in online interactions affords them time to construct, edit, revise and refine claims until they are optimal, and develop a strategic self-presentation that draws upon their actual and ideal selves.

This study has not considered the use of profile photos, which is a central component of online self-presentation, especially on social networking sites such as Facebook and Instagram. Research by Humphreys (2004) found that profiles containing photographs were contacted approximately seven times more than those without a photo. The focus of this research is to understand the characteristics being sought in a partner.

A comparison with the popular Australian dating site RSVP.com.au adds new perspectives to this work. The comparison helps to provide an understanding of the Indian-specific attributes being sought in dating or prospective marriage partners, further helping to understand the cultural continuity of seeking a 'match' in Indian marriages in the digital age.

## Indian diaspora and weddings

The Indian diaspora is destined to continue its upward trajectory of migration to Australia, given the increased political connections Australia has developed with India in the last few years. This is noted in the Parkinson review of Australia's migration system (Parkinson, Howe & Azarias, 2023) that offers a blueprint for increasing migration which is much needed with the post-COVID-19 skills shortage, Australia's aging population and the need to attract international students to study and work in Australia to fill the gaps. Indian migrants therefore play an important part in this strategy.

The Indian diaspora celebrates major cultural events, including weddings, in bold and unique ways. Indian weddings in Australia breathe fun, pomp, and ceremony with many replicating wedding scenes from Bollywood movies. Affluence in Australia, and the trend of sharing wedding photos online via Instagram or Facebook, also mean that many brides and grooms copy what Bollywood stars wear during their weddings. The mass circulation of Bollywood celebrity wedding videos, clips, and photos, as well as on-screen weddings from movies, add to Indians' desire and anxiety for marriage.

The diaspora of mostly Hindu Indians legitimises its social structure through marriage as a sacrament. New generations of Indians copy Bollywood stars and weddings to add 'masala' (spice) to wedding rituals. Weddings in Australia are choreographed events featuring the expert work of wedding planners and DJs. Each wedding ritual, such as the henna night, is captured on video and loaded onto Instagram and Facebook, personal websites, and other Social Networking Sites (SNS) instantaneously and shared/reshared across all media and personal online sites. Easy access to Bollywood, television soaps, and other forms of media including Zee TV, Netflix, YouTube, home wedding videos circulated among families and friends around the globe via mobile phones, and multiple other forms of digital media, has spawned newer and high-tech additions to wedding ceremonies. Professional wedding planners combine old, new, borrowed and invented ideas to make each wedding unique and special.

The yearnings of a community sharing a common culture, identity and values are thus maintained through the institution of marriage and marrying within its cultural cluster. Indian weddings represent a new epoch, characterised by flux, change, modernity, affluence, globalisation, and the use of information technology to transform the once humble home event into an occasion to be viewed across the globe through multimedia platforms. Presenting a range of discussions with viewers, Pfleiderer (1985) sees Hindi films as stabilising the social system by repressing new needs and, at the same time, mythologising tradition. Dwyer (2004) also sees weddings as grand events, arguing that:

> The wedding is a major spectacle, Indians being known for the grandeur and splendour of their weddings even within families of modest means. These views [of the Indian community] are further reinforced through the Indian movies where weddings are also presented as a grand spectacle. It is rare for a Bollywood film not to have a wedding scene for the hero and heroine or for another couple. Cinema is interpretative art and expands our sense of the possible (Dwyer, 2004, p. 66).

Songs give an 'intravenous shot of adrenaline' to those watching Bollywood movies. These are then replayed in real-life weddings. Songs like "chote bhaiyon ke bade bhaiya aaj bane kisi ki saiya chote—the oldest brother of small brothers is today becoming a husband" from *Hum Saath Saath Hai* (1994) is replayed as the groom arrives for the wedding ceremony in real life (personal observation since 1998 in Sydney). Like the fanfare the families and friends enjoy at weddings on screen, such forms of entertainment have become an integral element of social and cultural continuity for those 'on the ground'.

Raheja and Kothari (2004) say that the language and lyrics of Bollywood are not abstract critical theories, but a living, breathing reality providing depth and unexpected synthesis, enriching the consumers' day-to-day lives. The community's fascination with Bollywood-style weddings in Australia is fulfilled largely by the commercial activities of wedding planners, caterers, invitation card manufacturers, fashion houses, DJs, photographers, and videographers. While those involved in establishing such businesses capitalise on the available opportunities, members of the community mostly feed their fascination and desire for grand weddings by copying Bollywood, how Bollywood stars and the rich and famous from the diaspora, get married. Many choose 'destination weddings' and share photos online, adding to the cycle of copying from others. Distributing wedding video links among families and friends and posting engagement and wedding photos online via Facebook, Instagram and other sites, enables the couples and their families to 'show and tell'. All these are linked to the aspirations and dreams of the Indian diaspora when finding a marriage partner.

## Matchmaking online

According to a BBC poll of 11,000 internet users in 19 countries, 59% of Indians and 60% of Pakistanis use the internet to search for a potential partner (Asian News International, 2010). As a society, Australian Indians rely heavily on social media platforms to receive and deliver social happenings. The extremely fast rate of delivering information and communicating means that social networking sites (SNSs) such as Facebook, Instagram, and WhatsApp create a virtual world that is seen by many as replicating their 'real world' existence. The explosion of SNSs in the early 2000s ushered in the internet as a 'social space' for users, who use technology to create content such as videos, text, and pictures to share. Nentwich and König (2012) see such technology as the "catalyst" for social engagement on the internet. They argue that Web 2.0 developers tried to take advantage of the interactive functions of their tools (2012, p. 6), giving context to "user-generated content". For Indians in Australia, and indeed individuals around the globe, social media and social networking have become an integral part of their social lives and personal expression.

# Research findings

The online dating sites that were evaluated for this study present insights into the ways technologies have enabled the choice and selection of partners for marriage in the Indian diaspora. The process used for the evaluation included accessing the site, reading company statements, taking note of the services provided and the steps involved in uploading profiles and checking for matches. All the sites evaluated for this study claimed to be the 'go-to place' to find a match. Two of the sites have branched into several other lucrative wedding businesses. One site launched an Elite Matrimony site in 2008, an invitation-only, fee-paying section for rich people who are time-poor but are seeking matrimonial alliances via a matchmaking service (matrimony.com).

## Shaadi.com

Shaadi.com is owned by People Interactive (I) Pvt Ltd, which is an internet-based company that provides a range of internet-based services to the Indian diaspora all over the world. The services range from Shaadicentre (matchmaking and wedding planning), to Shaadilive, which is an official blog for shaadi.com. It features an "Ask an Expert" section which is a relationship counselling service. Shaadi. com was founded in 2006 by Anupam Mittal, who says in a message online that his objective was to provide "superior matchmaking by expanding opportunities to meet potential life partners." The website claims to have helped millions of people across the world find marriage partners. It is the "world's largest online matrimonial site" and has won several awards. The site allows each member to search for partners in their country or according to the language spoken (Bengali, Gujarati, Hindi, Kannada, Malayalam, Marathi, Marwari, Punjabi, Sindhi, Tamil, Telugu, and Urdu). Members are asked to state their gender, DOB, religion, mother tongue, the country they live in, their mobile number, if they are creating this profile for themselves or someone else (son, daughter, brother, sister, relative or friend), marital status, height, diet, if they smoke and drink alcohol, personal values (traditional, moderate, liberal), complexion, body type, medical conditions, country/ies they grew up in, the state/city in which they are living, residency status, education level, education field (tourism, engineering, architecture etc.), type of company they work for, industry they work in, annual income, a description/ mini-biography, and to upload a photo, which is mandatory. On average, the mini biographies were only several sentences long and often used abbreviations and text message spelling.

The phrases that women used to describe themselves were much more detailed than those used by men. Also, more profiles were created by family members for females than for males. When searching for a partner, members are asked to specify the following criteria: looking for bride or groom, age bracket (ranging from 18 to 71), mother tongue (52 options, mostly for languages spoken in or around India; also the choices of "doesn't matter" or "other" is an option). The list of attributes being sought and presented shows the top mother tongues searched for, caste/sect, country, height range for partner, education, diet, partner's marital status, *manglik* (birth sign) complexion, industry, type of company they work for (private company, defence, government, civil service, self-employed, non-working), residency status, whether they smoke or drink alcohol, any special cases (people with disability), HIV status. In 2023 the site claims to facilitate 10 meetings in an hour with prospective partners.

Clicking on the site takes one to a happy photo of a couple. The home page has a set of questions: I am looking for, age range, religion, and country living in. After these questions are answered, one must answer who the profile is for; options include me, son, daughter, brother, sister, relative, followed by information on the person seeking a partner, such as name and date of birth, religion. One must sign up (register for free and load a profile) and connect with the matches. However, to interact, one must become a premium member.

Three couples share their testimony of how they met on the site, fell in love, got married or are marrying in 2023. A digital wedding album of a beautiful bride and groom is used as a backdrop.

## IndianDating.com

IndianDating.com is operated by Cupid plc. It is not exclusively a matrimony website and states that it helps Indians find "love, friendship and romance" (IndianDating.com, 2012). It also states that it helps members find "local" matches and asks for their postcodes. Members are asked to state personal details. Age, gender and date of birth are mandatory. Non-mandatory information includes drinking/smoking status, religion, interest in children, education, and occupation.

Users are also asked to upload a photo, fill in an "about me" section (mini biography), write a short section about "what I am looking for" and score themselves on a Likert Scale about how loving, confident, successful, faithful, flirty, compassionate, extroverted, caring, patient, adventurous, and healthy they are. There is a lifestyle setting where they are asked to state three activities for the following categories: entertainment, hobbies, favourite music genres, favourite food, sports watched, sports played, and favourite TV genres. Users can also record a video greeting.

The mini biography sections were more likely to be left blank than those of the Shaadi.com site. As with Shaadi.com, there was a tendency towards 'text message' spelling, and almost 100% of the profiles in the random sample had no regard for grammar. When searching for a partner, members are asked to specify the following criteria: gender of partner, what they are looking for (friends, email, nothing serious, marriage), partner's orientation, smokes or drinks, relationship status, ethnicity, height, eye colour, build, hair colour, and/or their location in Australia.

## IndianCupid.com

IndianCupid.com is owned and operated by Cupid Media Pty Ltd, a company that "specialises in 'database-driven dating sites'" (indiancupid.com). It offers a site tour and testimonials from happy customers. Members are asked to provide the following information about themselves: gender, date of birth, the country they are living in, ethnicity (non-Asian ethnicities are also listed), complexion, occupation, income, residency status, parents' occupation, siblings and if they are married, *nakshatra, manglik* (birth sign). Users are asked if they are creating this profile for someone else, to provide a mini-biography and to write a little about what they are looking for in a partner.

Most profiles for males and females did not have photos. The female members of this site are the most likely to list specific criteria when describing themselves and their ideal match. Members are asked to specify the following: gender and age they are interested in, the country their partner should be living in, state, city, what radius of the city they are in, the option of only showing matches who have pictures on their profile, and the last time the member was active in searching for a partner.

The website says the company is based in Southport, Queensland and has a revenue of $11.8m.

The following dialogue from the movie "Bride and Prejudice" (Chadra, 2004) captures the feelings of Indian mothers, aunts and grandmothers who have a similar off screen 'talk' with their daughters and female relatives.

> "Hurry up, you silly girls! We must make sure Jaya meets this Mr Balraj from London before anyone else".
>
> Lalita: All mothers think that any single guy with big bucks must be shopping for a wife.
>
> Jaya: I am embarrassed to say, but I hope he is.
>
> Lalita: What, shopping or loaded?
>
> Jaya: Well, both.
>
> In response to her younger daughter wanting to wear a low cut blouse, Mrs Bakshi says: "But we want Balraj to look into Jaya's eyes, not your mames. She is our only hope ... if we do not get the eldest married first; we'll never be able to marry the rest of you for the shame."
>
> When the scenes switch to the wedding hall, the bride's friends run onto the dance floor in their Indian finery and dance to pulsating bhangra (Punjabi music), teasing the men from the groom's party. The two groups tease and dance. The lyrics are:
>
> "Oh these pretty girls ... fluttering temptingly like kites without string. These girls are like naked live wires. If you get too close, you'll get an electric shock of love."

## iMilap.com

iMilap is operated by BroadLink LLC and seeks to connect millions of Indian men and women all around the world (imilap.com, 2012). It stresses that matrimonial/dating relationships are its prime focus, and that its service allows its members to get in touch with their "soul mates" (imilap.com, 2012).

When creating a profile, members are asked to provide the following information about themselves: gender, country, state, city, date of birth, if they are creating this profile for themselves, marital status, number of children, height, complexion, hair colour, eye colour, if they have a disability, country of birth, looking for dating or marriage, country of birth, religion, caste, mother tongue, *manglik*, cultural values, education, profession, employer, diet, smoking habits, drinking habits, living situation, type of housing, phone number (optional if displayed publicly), immigration status, citizenship, do you believe in horoscopes, time of birth, place of birth. Then members are asked to fill in "about me" and "partner expectation" sections.

When searching for a partner, members are asked to specify the following: Searching for a male or female, what kind of relationship they are looking for, age and height range, country of birth, residency, citizenship, marital status, religion, caste, cultural values, education, profession, diet, smoking and drinking status.

This site does not have an "about us" section and does not provide any information about its history or objectives.

## Matrimony.com

Matrimony.com says its flagship brand is BharatMatrimony—a network of matchmaking services employing 4000 people across 20 offices in India, US, Dubai, and Bangladesh. It claims to provide personalised matchmaking services for busy professionals. It launched its premium service, Elite Matrimony, in 2008, which caters to wealthy individuals or their families seeking matrimonial alliances. Services are available to invited members who must pay a matchmaking service fee ranging from 60,000 to 2,220,000 rupees ($1,117 to $41,364 Australian). In 2012 the company started a matrimony directory with a wedding-vendors-classified portal featuring over 50,000 wedding-related services such as creating designer wedding invitation cards, outfits for bride, groom and family, venue hire and catering services. In 2021, Matrimony.com launched a *jodii* (match) app—a vernacular app in Tamil for lower-income and blue-collar workers. It claims to provide services to 7.5 million people monthly.

The home page says, "Take first steps to your happy marriage" and offers an online registration form. The form asks "Matrimony profile for" with options to choose myself, son, daughter, relative, friend, brother, sister. Other questions are name, gender, date of birth, religion, mother tongue, caste/division, country living in, mobile and email. The next step is to create a password and register.

The site claims to be India's first Consumer Internet Company to be listed on the Bombay Stock Exchange. It says that its "flagship brand BharatMatrimony is India's largest and the Most Trusted Matrimony Brand (as per the Brand Trust Report 2014). Over 3000+ associates serve millions of active members. The company has a market capitalisation of over Rs. 2,300 crores".

The company provides both matchmaking and marriage-related services through websites, mobile sites and mobile apps and is also complemented by 110+ company-owned retail outlets. Its flagship matchmaking services are BharatMatrimony, EliteMatrimony and CommunityMatrimony. Besides this, *Jodii*, a matchmaking service for non-graduates, is available in 10 Indian languages. Their home page describes them as follows:

> With strong leadership in online matrimony, the company has been expanding into the highly unorganised $55 billion marriage services industry. The goal is to build a billion-dollar revenue company and a long-lasting institution with a legacy for generations to come (Bharat Matrimony.com).

Their offerings in the marriage services business are WeddingBazaar and Mandap.com.

## RSVP.com and comparison with US data

RSVP.com.au is a partially free dating website that operates in Australia. Members can create their own profiles and browse other members' profiles as well as contact them via "kisses" for free. Beyond this, members can pay to have their profile appear at the top of all searches and control whose searches their profile shows up in. It is the only site evaluated in this research that allows the user to search for bisexual partners.

When creating a profile, members are asked to specify the following: if they are seeking a male or female, their current relationship status (including if they are currently married), a "headline" (a sentence-long summary of themselves), height, body type, smoking status, upload a photo of themselves, relationship status (including whether they are currently in a relationship), if they have children, if they want children, personality, eye colour, hair colour, nationality, ethnic/cultural background, religion, political persuasion, zodiac sign (automatically shows according to one's birthday), drinking habits, diets, if they have pets, education, industry, job, type of music they listen to, type of books they read, favourite TV shows and movies, sports they are interested in and other interests.

In the aggregate, all the websites had more male than female users. 80% of the aggregate profiles were for males. The group most likely to have a profile on one of these websites is men aged 21–40. Men aged 21–30 make up 47% of the aggregate profiles, and men aged 31–40 make up 22% of the aggregate profiles. 51% of the Indian website users are in the 21–30 age categories.

The median age of the Australian population is 37, while the median age for new arrivals (immigrants who came to Australia after 2007) is 27 (Australian Bureau of Statistics, 2012). This is partially due to the criteria set for skilled migrants, stating that a migrant should not be older than 50 (Australian Bureau of Statistics, 2012).

Under each website's heading, tables show how members describe themselves and their ideal partners. Figures 15.1 and 15.2 below show the results of all these tables. Some people did not fill this section of their profile, and some phrases were used only once so they were not included in this graph. This data was not included for RSVP.com as it is not an Indian-specific site.

These results show the most used phrases and expressions in a random sample of 50 men from the websites.

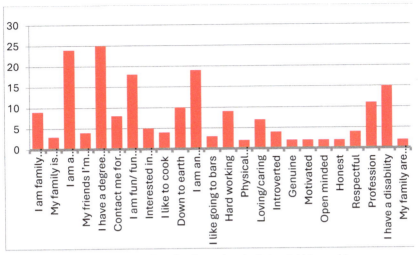

Fig. 15.1 How men describe themselves in their mini biographies.

These are the aggregate results from a random sample of 50 female profiles from the five Indian dating and matrimony websites. Some people did not fill in this section of their profile, and some used unique phrases that have been omitted from this graph.

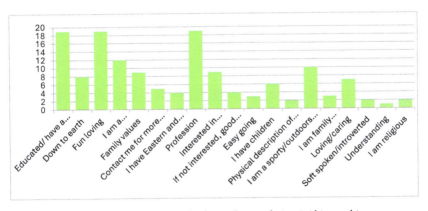

Fig. 15.2 How women describe themselves in their mini biographies.

## Education, profession, and fun-loving top features of dating sites

As shown in the tables above, having a degree, education, and being in a profession as well as being fun-loving are characteristics women value and use to describe themselves. The new digital environment where they easily express such attributes has given them a new status and sense of purpose, where they have the power to make choices from a wide range of available men. Busy lifestyles filled with work and study mean that women, like men, have limited or little time to socialise. As most Indians living in Australia work outside the home, finding a match for marriage in social settings is less common than for their Australian counterparts, mainly because Indians (generally) tend not to participate in the evening socialising culture in pubs or clubs, something that is common among younger Australians. Engaging with new media and social networking sites (SNS) provides other opportunities and fills any gaps.

The research indicates that men have resorted to online dating in much larger numbers than women. Their profiles show that they too prioritise education and work, as indicated by their tertiary and higher qualifications and skilled positions. The other common descriptor used by men is "simple, average, normal guy, fun-loving, outdoors/sporty person". For women, profession and education are top of the list while they also describe themselves as fun-loving and average, normal people. It is important to also note that, although these women are educated and working outside the home, many still rely on parents and families to find them a match. This view is confirmed by Nancy Netting (2010) whose study of arranged marriage in India demonstrates the duty to marry daughters remain the responsibility of the father. Appadurai (1996, p. 44) describes marriage as "the meeting points of historical patterns of socialization and new ideas of proper behaviour."

The above descriptions are based on the aggregate data from the websites evaluated for this study. These research findings demonstrate that dating, especially online dating, has become a new steppingstone to marriage among Indians in Australia. The new high-tech communication environment ushered in by globalisation has allowed individuals more control when seeking a partner, while demoting the role of the village headman who traditionally enjoyed the status of key matchmaker for people reaching puberty.

Like all people around the globe, Indians have become discerning in taste and seek out the maximum personal advantages in dating relationships and marriage. Indian women are now more empowered and no longer confined to the role of homemaker. Joshi and Kumar (2012. p. 58) argue that the online matrimony market is "a popular and efficient way for busy singles to find love interests". They say that the amount of "valuable" information that can be uploaded onto the site about a prospective partner could potentially reduce divorce rates and "other types of unsuccessful relationships" (p. 58).

The age at which community members marry is increasingly delayed: women are waiting until their late 20s–early 30s while men are delaying until their early to mid-30s. Although this is consistent with the Australian statistics on marriage (30.8 for men and 29.4 for women) (ABS, 2021) delaying marriage also means that many people end up seeking partners online, in many instances as a last resort. Also specific to online dating is the easy method of viewing photos as a first option before reading profiles. Many use Facebook to search for other photos and information about the person posting a profile on the online dating site. Previous unsuccessful attempts at meeting a potential partner face-to-face may cause a person to feel lonely, and therefore seek a partner online. Lawson and Leck (2006) found that using the internet to contact potential partners increased the self-confidence of those who were self-conscious about their appearance. This would be in line with Lawson and Leck's (2006) finding that all the research participants felt lonely.

One nationally representative sample of US adults shows that 22% of heterosexual couples who met between 2007 and 2009 did so online (Rosenfield & Thomas, 2010), making the internet the second most likely way to meet a partner, after meeting through a friend. Another study shows that more than one-third of Americans who married between 2005 and 2012 had met online (Cacioppo, Gonzaga, Ogburn, & VanderWeele, 2013).

## Importance of marriage

Jones and Ramdas (2004) argue that alongside the physical intimacy of marriage, the deeper intimacy of daily sharing and living together in marriage makes it a most profound way of ever knowing another person as well as oneself. As a result of this knowledge, Singer (2009) presents marital love in a different category from romantic love. Cavell (1981) argues that marital love, presented through film, demonstrates a way to happiness.

> Since this happiness is expressed as marriage, we understand it as simultaneously an individual and social achievement. Or rather, we understand it as the final condition for individual and for social happiness, namely the achieving of one's adult self and the creation of the social. The achievement of human happiness requires not the perennial and fuller satisfaction of our needs as they stand but the examination and transformation of those needs (Cavell, 1981, pp. 4-5).

Hindu traditions and the community's social structures create important sites for the ideological transformation of the Indian culture, values, and morals of marriage into the modern world; in the face of popular culture which gives the Indian diaspora a new reality on its identity. Conservatively constructed, the family values presented in this research are indeed a reflection of the ambivalence and anxieties of the community, juxtaposed in a complex multicultural setting, having to choose between love and arranged marriage, western cultural markers, and their own value system, all challenging their everyday existence in Australia's physical spaces. Marriage also feeds migration as the online daters also aspire to migrate (from India and other parts of the world to Australia and vice versa). This research has not explored the aspects of migration.

## Seeking cultural similarity in matchmaking

A significant finding of this research is that the those participating in the online dating sites prefer a same race partner with similar status(homogamy). The sites also facilitate an efficient selection by the cultural, language and other descriptors that are important for the diaspora, in keeping its identity. Kilminjin (1998) says that expectations for cultural similarity and the advantage of being matched to someone with similar values such a lifestyle and interests present an individual's predilections for the members of their own group, making cultural capital highly dependent on racial background.

Chiswick and Houseworth (2011) posit that selecting a culturally competent partner enables an 'effortless' attainment and transfer of cultural practices to the next generation. Much earlier works of Bogardus (1947) presents an argument that a strong sense of community and identity within one's racial group produces feelings of separation from other groups, and a hesitancy to engage with them.

Based on the stated preference on the sites under study for this chapter, racial preferences seem to prevail when seeking partners. However, further detailed research in this area is needed to gauge a deeper understanding on online dating scene in relation to race identity in multicultural Australia where there are opportunities to meet people from other races and cultures.

In providing an understanding on this situation, Chand (2012) argues that young adults from the Indian diaspora are caught in between stages of change where they do not hold clearly defined positions within their social system or network. They therefore feel marginalised, excluded and without identity and influence. For them assimilation into a new environment poses many challenges.

While outsiders can be located outside a social structure and may not have the intention or ability to re-enter the space, marginals, according to Turner (1969) are "simultaneously members of two or more social groups whose social definitions and cultural norms are distinct from, and often even opposed to, one another" (p. 233). Stonequist (1965; 1937) describes a marginal as an individual who through migration, education, marriage, or some other influence, leaves one social group or culture without making a satisfactory adjustment to another and who finds himself or herself on the margin of each but a member of neither.

Pundit Narayan Bhatt, a marriage celebrant in Sydney, said he is "constantly inundated" with requests from Indians to match kundalis (birth/zodiac sign) with prospects of marriage. "I get an average of about 50 requests per month" (Bhatt, 2013). Birth date compatibility is also checked online discreetly, with priests practising in Australia and internationally. This method of matchmaking is common among the Indian diaspora. Bhatt says that Indians see marriage as an important milestone in the lifecycle of a family and the community. In the context of the extended family as well as the community, the young married couple is expected to maintain family unity as well as fulfil filial obligations.

This chapter reiterates the general view in the community that women are past their 'use-by date' if they are not married by age 25 or 28. Men are expected to be married by age 28 to 32. This is also in keeping, although moderated in view of the dynamics of modernisation, with the traditional Hindu beliefs and cultural norms about the stages of life.

Social scientists have for a long time recognised the importance of networks, especially among migrant communities. Such networks are sets of interpersonal relationships; sometimes deep ties based on friendship, kinship and shared history or nationality which provide a connection among migrants and members of other communities in host countries and former homelands (Massey et al., 1993). As a result of creating this network such migrants contribute significantly towards an important source of social capital (Portes, 1995). In the case of the Indian diaspora living in Sydney, this level of social capital (Bourdieu, 1990) is developed and maintained in a closely networked environment in the online spaces as well as their cluster-style living in physical spaces.

## Downsides of online dating

With the internet giving access to anyone, there is always the possibility of people creating fake identities, enhancing photos, and losing money through scams. The lack of monitoring of such sites also presents the possibility that the owners of the site itself might generate "hits" to demonstrate traffic flow. This is similar to sites offering free searches whereas paid subscribers may end up paying large amounts for a service that might not lead to a satisfactory outcome or result in a mismatch, although the latter is possible irrespective of the means engaged. Most websites visited for this research included warnings and advice for staying safe when online and when arranging to meet someone for the first time. The advice sections caution users to be wary of those asking for money.

Dating website executives agree that online platforms make it quicker and easier for members to connect with a larger pool of potential partners than they'd encounter offline (Slater, 2013). This abundance of options can make people less inclined to commit to a life partner, as they are always exploring other possibilities. Moreover, Paumgarten (2011) notes that in environments with plenty of choices, like online dating, people are more likely to engage in "trading up"—i.e., switching partners once they find someone who they think is better. The problem is that this cycle is potentially endless. With more people joining dating sites, there is a constant pool of new potential partners, which could contribute to higher divorce rates and ultimately challenge traditional views of marriage (Slater, 2013).

## Conclusion

This study delves into a worldwide phenomenon where busy lifestyles are prolonging the period of singledom for individuals. Social media platforms have adapted to offer diverse choices when individuals are ready to explore romantic options. However, within the Indian community, marriage remains deeply ingrained as the societal norm. In the past, Indians heavily relied on familial networks to arrange matches, but with the diaspora dispersed across the globe, technology has replaced the traditional village marriage broker, with online dating emerging as the predominant method. This shift has given rise to numerous business opportunities, turning marriage into a multi-billion-dollar industry on a global scale.

For the Indian diaspora, globalisation has broadened the scope of potential marriage partners who share similar cultural, religious, and physical backgrounds. The parental role in matchmaking has evolved, with parents utilising online platforms to search for suitable matches for their children. Those unable to navigate these sites seek assistance from businesses specialising in online matchmaking services. Interestingly, the stigma associated with being single or without a partner is diminishing, partly due to the tailored profiles crafted by date coaching specialists.

Marriage dynamics among Australian Indians are significantly shaped by the influences of globalisation, new media platforms, and the glamorised portrayals of celebrity weddings in Bollywood films. The Indian-specific dating sites analysed in this study showcase individuals' expressed preferences and life priorities. Drawing from the notion of racial homogamy in dating, which suggests strong preferences for partners of the same racial background within racial groups, this research also underscores assimilation theory. This theory suggests that shared racial identity strongly influences in-group marital preferences.

The affluence of, and myriad opportunities available to the Indian diaspora in Australia afford them a broader spectrum of choices in terms of who to date, when, how, and where within their community.

Despite the evolution of online dating platforms, the attributes being sought when matchmaking remains largely unchanged, albeit with a major shift in setting due to the advent of online dating. Marriage continues to be a cornerstone of the Indian social fabric, with young adults, their families, and the broader community holding it in high regard. New media has injected fresh energy into this cultural cornerstone, presenting innovative and captivating platforms that facilitate dating as a precursor and pathway to marriage. Platforms like Facebook exemplify this new community-driven approach to matchmaking, enabling members to involve friends and family in the process by browsing profiles, evaluating potential matches, and providing feedback. This modern twist on matchmaking reflects a reinterpretation of traditional practices within the context of contemporary digital culture.

## Works cited

Anonymous. (2010, December 29). Love at first Byte. *The Economist*, 51–54.

Asian News International. (2010). Indians, Pakistanis biggest fans of online dating. New Dehli, India

Appadurai, A. (1996, 1949). *Modernity at Large: Cultural Dimensions of Globalization*. University of Minnesota Press.

Atkins, K. (2001). Online dating new twist to ancient Indian tradition. *The Gazette*, p. B2.

Australian Bureau of Statistics. (2012). Australian Demographic Statistics. Canberra, Australia

Australian Bureau of Statistics. (2021). Australia's Population by Country of Birth. ABS. https//www.abs.gov.au/statistics/people/population/australias-population-country-birth/latest-release

Australian Bureau of Statistics. (2012). Cultural Diversity in Australia. Canberra, Australia. https://archive.org/details/2071.0-cultural-diversity-in-australia

Azhar, A. (2007). RSVP to end online dating stigma. Sydney, NSW, Australia.

Barjatya, S.R. (Director). (1999). *Hum Saath Saath Hai* [*We Stand United*]. Rajshri Productions.

Bhatt, N. (2013, 2009). *Pundit*: Hindu priest in Liverpool. [personal interview].

Blackwell, D.L., & Lichter D.T. (2004). Homogamy among dating, cohabiting, and married couples. *Sociological Quarterly 45*(4), 19–37. https://doi.org/10.1111/j.1533-8525.2004.tb02311.x

Bogardus, E.S. (1947). Measurement of personal-group relations. *Sociometry 10*(4), 306–311. https://doi.org/10.2307/2785570

Bourdieu, P. (1990). *The Logic of Practice*. Stanford University Press.

Brym, R.J., & Lenton, R.L. (2001). Love online: A report on digital dating in Canada. *MSN. ca, February, 6*.

Chadha, G. (2002). *Bride and Prejudice* Bride Productions. [Film]

Cacioppo, J.T., Cacioppo, S., Gonzaga, G.C., Ogburn, E.L., & VanderWeele, T.J. (2013). Marital satisfaction and break-ups differ across on-line and off-line meeting venues. *Proceedings of the National Academy of Sciences 110*, 10135–10140. https://doi.org/10.1073/pnas.1222447110

Cavell, S. (1997). *Pursuits of Happiness: The Hollywood Comedy of Remarriage. 1981.* Harvard University Press.

Chand, A. (2011). *The Chutney Generation: Fiji Indian Migration, Matchmaking and Media in Sydney* (Doctoral dissertation). University of Western Sydney. https://researchdirect.westernsydney.edu.au/islandora/object/uws:20650/datastream/PDF/view

Chiswick, B.R., & Houseworth, C. (2011). Ethnic intermarriage among immigrants: Human capital and assortative mating. *Review of Economics of the Household 9*, 149–180. https://doi.org/10.1007/s11150-010-9099-9

Clark, S. (1998). Dating on the Net: Teens and the rise of "pure" relationships. In *Cybersociety 2.0: Revisiting computer-mediated communication and community*. (pp. 159–181). Sage.

Cocks, H.G. (2009). *Classified: The Secret History of the Personal Column*. Random House.

Dwyer, R. (2004). A suitable boy: Marriage market issues in India: Yeh shaadi nahin ho sakti!. In G.W. Jones & K. Ramdas (Eds). (*Un*) *Tying the Knot: Ideal and Reality in Asian Marriage*. (pp. 59–90). Singapore University Press.

Ellison, N., Heino, R., & Gibbs, J. (2006). Managing impressions online: Self presentation processes in the online dating environment. *Journal of Computer Mediated Communication 11*, 415–441. https://doi.org/10.1111/j.1083-6101.2006.00020.x

Ellis-Petersen, H. (2024, July 13). Ambani wedding: After months of celebrations, the 'Windsors of India' finally set to marry. *The Guardian*. https://www.theguardian.com/world/article/2024/jul/12/ambani-wedding-india-anant-radhika-merchant-mumbai-guests

Epstein, R. (2007). The truth about online dating. *Scientific American Mind 18*(1), 28–35.

Gibbs, J.I., Ellison, N.B., & Heino, R.D. (2006) Self-presentation in online personals: The role of anticipated future interaction, self-disclosure, and perceived success in Internet dating. *Communication Research 33*, 1–26. https://doi.org/10.1177/0093650205285368

Goffman, E. (1959). *The Presentation of Self in Everyday Life*. Doubleday.

Gordon, M.M. (1964). *Assimilation in American Life: The Role of Race, Religion, and National Origins*. Oxford University Press.

Heino, R.D., Ellison, N.B., & Gibbs, J.L. (2010). Relationshopping: Investigating the market metaphor in online dating. *Journal of Social and Personal Relationships 27*, 427–447. https://doi.org/10.1177/0265407510361614

Humphreys, L. (2004). Photographs and the Presentation of Self through Online Dating Services. Paper presented at the *National Communication Association, Chicago, II.*

imilap.com. (2012). *About iMilap.* http://www.imilap.com: http://www.imilap.com/matrimonialSitesaustralia.asp

indiancupid.com. (n.d.). *About Us.* www.indiancupid.com: http://www.indiancupid.com/About.cfm

IndianDating.com. (2012). *Home.* http://www.indiandating.com/

Jones, G.W., & Ramdas, K. (Eds). (2004). (*Un*)*tying the knot: Ideal and reality in Asian marriage* (No. 2). NUS Press.

Jones, G.W. (2004). When to marry but whether to marry. In G.W. Jones & K. Ramdas (Eds). (*Un*) *Tying the Knot: Ideal and Reality in Asian Marriage.* (pp. 3–58). Singapore University Press.

Joshi, K., & Kumar, S. (2012). Matchmaking using fuzzy analytical hierarchy process, compatibility measure and stable matching for online matrimony in India. *Journal of Multi-Criteria Decision Analysis 19*(1–2), 57–66. https://doi.org/10.1002/mcda.487

Joyner, K., & Kao, G. (2005). Interracial relationships and the transition to adulthood. *American Sociological Review 70*(4), 563-8, https://doi.org/10.1177/000312240507000402

Kadar J., & Kumar, S. (2012). Matchmaking using fuzzy analytical hierarchy process: Compatability measure and stable matchmaking for online matrimony in India. *Journal of Multi-Critera Decision Analysis*, 57–66. https://doi.org/10.1002/mcda.487

Kalmijn, M. (1998) Intermarriage and homogamy: Cases, patterns, trends. *Annual Review of Sociology 24*, 395–421. https://doi.org/10.1146/annurev.soc.24.1.395

Karandashev, V. (2024). Within-cultural and inter-cultural interpersonal attraction. In *The Varieties of Love as Interpersonal Attraction*. Springer. https://doi.org/10.1007/978-3-031-63577-9_6

Kelly, T. (2011, April 15). Woman sues match.com after alleged sexual assault. *Time.* http://newsfeed.time.com/2011/04/15/woman-sues-match-com-after-alleged-sexual-assault/

Kennedy, H. (2005, November 18). Call 'em Match.con. *Daily News.* http://web. archive.org/web/20070222150633/http://www.nydailynews.com/front/story/367167p-312443c.html

Kothari, J., Raheja, D., & Merchant, I. (2004). *Indian Cinema: The Bollywood Saga.* Aurum Press.

Lal, B. (2006). *The Encyclopedia of the Indian Diaspora.* University of Hawai'i Press.

Lawson, H.M., & Leck, K. (2006). Dynamics of internet dating. *Social Science Computer Review* 24(2), 189–208. https://doi.org/10.1177/0894439305283402

Massey, D. (1993). Politics and space/time. In K.M. Keith & S. Pile (Eds). *Place and Politics of Identity.* (pp. 141–61). Routledge.

Miller, C.T. (2011). The Cultural Adaptation of Internet Dating: Attitudes towards Online Relationship Formation. *University of New Orleans Theses and Dissertations.* Paper 1332. https://scholarworks.uno.edu/td/1332

Matrimony.com. (2023). About Matrimony.com—India's Most Trusted Matrimonial Service.

National Institute of Science Technology and Development Studies. (2009). *Migration of Indians Abroad.* http://www.nistads.res.in/indiasnt2008/t1humanresources/t1hr8.htm

Nentwich, M., & Konig, R. (2012). *Cyberscience 2.0: Research in the Age of Digital Social Networks.* Campus Verlag.

Netting, N.S. (2010). Marital ideoscapes in 21st-century India: Creative combinations of love and responsibility. *Journal of Family Issues* 31(6), 707–726.

Parkinson, M., Howe, J., & Azarias, J. (2023). *A Migration System for Australia's Future: A Review of the Migration System.* Department of Home Affairs. https://www.homeaffairs.gov.au/reports-and-publications/reviews-and-inquiries/departmental-reviews/migration-system-for-australias-future

Paumgarten N. (2011, June 27). Looking for someone. *The New Yorker.* https://www.newyorker.com/magazine/2011/07/04/looking-for-someone-online-dating

Pfleiderer, B., & Lothar, L. (1985). *The Hindi Film: Agent and Re-agent of Cultural Change.* Manohar.

Portes, A. (Ed.). (1995). *The Economic Sociology of Immigration: Essays on Networks, Ethnicity, and Entrepreneurship.* Russell Sage Foundation.

RSVP.com. (n.d.). RSVP — Australia's most trusted dating site.

Rosenfeld, M.J., & Thomas, R.J. (2010). How couples meet and stay together. Wave 2 version 2.04. *Machine Readable Data File.* Stanford University Libraries.

Sautter, J., Tippett, R.M., & Morgan, S.P. (2010). The social demography of Internet dating in the United States. *Social Science Quarterly 91*, 554–575. https://doi.org/10.1111/j.1540-6237.2010.00707.x

Schmitz, A., & Schmitz, A. (2017). Online Dating: A Meeting Point for the Modern Individual and Traditional Individualism. *The Structure of Digital Partner Choice: A Bourdieusian perspective*, 13–28. https://doi.org/10.1007/978-3-319-43530-5 2

Schlenker, B.R. (2003). Self-presentation. *Handbook of self and identity 2*, 542–570.

Shaadi.com. (2012). *About Us.* http://ww2.shaadi.com/introduction/index/about-us

Singer, I. (2009). *The Nature of Love: Courtly and Romantic* (Vol. 2). MIT Press.

Slatter, D. (2013, January/February). A million first dates: How online dating is threatening monogamy. *The Atlantic Monthly 311*, 41–43. https://www.theatlantic.com/magazine/archive/2013/01/a-million-first-dates/309195/

Stonequist, E.V. (1965, 1937). *The Marginal Man: A Study of Personality and Culture Conflict.* Russell & Russell.

The Indian Express. (2011, October 24). More people prefer to date online than in bars and clubs. https://indianexpress.com/article/news-archive/print/more-people-prefer-to-date-online-than-in-clubs-and-bars/

Toma, C.L., Hancock, J.T., & Ellison, N.B. (2008). Separating fact from fiction: An examination of deceptive self-presentation in online dating profiles. *Personality and Social Psychology Bulletin 34*(8), 1023–1036.

Turner, V. (1969). *The Ritual Process: Structure and Anti-Structure.* Aldine Publishing Company.

Walther, J.B. (1996). Computer-mediated communication: Impersonal, interpersonal, and hyper personal interaction. *Communication Research 23*, 3–44. https://doi.org/ 0.1177/009365096023001001

Wibowo, A.A. (2011). Online dating services: Chronology and key feastures in comparison with traditional dating. *Competition Forum*, 481–488.

Zee News. (2012, January 29). Lonely hearts in Britain spend £3 billion looking for love. https://zeenews.india.com/entertainment/sex-and-relationships/lonely-hearts-in-britain-spend-3-billion-looking-for-love_104836.html

# 16. The digital mediation of film archives from the Strehlow Research Centre

## Hart Cohen

### Abstract

This chapter is concerned with the history of the Strehlow Research Centre (SRC) with a special emphasis on the how the film collection has been handled at various points in the institution's history. As an archive and research centre, the SRC has evolved from an earlier series of controversies around cultural ownership to become a leading innovator of the digitisation of parts of its collection. The digitisation of the films of T.G.H. Strehlow have led the collecting institutions sector, not only in technological innovation but also in outreach and engagement with its Aboriginal constituency. The example of the Strehlow Film Collection, and its evolution as a database and focus for community engagement, resonate with the issues that have recently emerged around archive/counter archive projects and participatory archives (Huvila) which have re-capitulated the role of archives in recovering the space of cultural memory and cultural practice. The chapter will test the proposition that "[...] the archive as a site for creative intervention, is one that enables new possibilities for preserving and representing individual memory within a larger historical consciousness" (Kashmere, 2021).

https://doi.org/10.11647/OBP.0423.16

## Keywords

Archive; digital; Strehlow; Arrernte; database.

## Introduction

The Strehlow Collection is an archive composed mainly of works collected and created by the Australian anthropologist and linguist T.G.H. Strehlow in relation to Aboriginal people of Central Australia. While the archive includes multiple media and artefacts, my research has focused on 16mm ceremonial footage Strehlow filmed during the period from 1935–1970. My encounter with this film archive, which was orphaned for many years, was respectfully to catalogue these film works and to re-mediate footage fit for public viewing to tell multiple stories in an episodic mode as a biographic landscape. The result of this work culminated in the broadcast film, *Mr Strehlow's Films* (2001), for the Australian-based Special Broadcasting Service (SBS).

This archival film collection relocates cultural memory and, as ceremonial footage, still contains within it the traces of what Dick Kimber describes as:

> [...] images [...] which were themselves imbued with the spirit of the actors and the ancestors and therefore took on the secret-sacred element about them that goes above and beyond our conventional concepts of film [...]" (Kimber in Cohen, 2001).

This relates to the idea of the "anarchival materiality" of the archive (Hennessy & Smith, 2022) where the archive points to unusual and unpredictable challenges to re-mediation, especially where the work differs substantially from the context in which the archival material was first filmed.

Strehlow's ceremonial film archive is held at the Strehlow Research Centre, Alice Springs, Northern Territory and is closed to public viewing. Over time, its digital re-inscription and re-curation has made it available to those Aboriginal people who have legitimate cultural connections to its spiritual significance. This chapter is concerned with connecting this film collection with the issues that have recently emerged around archive/counter archive projects and participatory archives (see I. Huvila (2011) What are Participatory Archives? For Real?) which have re-capitulated the role of archives in recovering the space of cultural memory. The chapter will test the proposition that "[...] the archive as a site for creative intervention, is one that enables new possibilities for preserving and representing individual memory within a larger historical consciousness" (Kashmere, 2021).

## The Strehlow Research Centre, Alice Springs 1991–2023

The Strehlow Research Centre (SRC) has seen several transformations in the period of its own history as an institution. I use a decadal approach to offer a review of these transformations in relation to how parts of the collection intersected with its programmatic interest in the relationship between digital technologies and the collection as a public resource. The periods I propose are: 1991 (founding) to 2001; 2001–2011 and 2011 to the present.

As an archive or 'keeping place' it was, from its inception, confronted with questions of its validity as an archive. As Brett Galt Smith, the SRC's second Managing Director later wrote:

> The Strehlow Research Centre was not a popular institution in which to work from its opening in 1991. It had many local critics including Central Australian Aboriginal people and land councils (Galt Smith, 2015).

While the materials under its care range from documents to media, the most important and concerning materials are the several hundred objects or Tjurunga (Chirunga) collected by Ted Strehlow during his period of working in Central Australia. These objects have been the most contentious of what has been collected and then sequestered at the archive. The protests from the Central Land Council at the opening of the SRC were highly motivated by the presence of these objects in a place, the Strehlow Research Centre, that was considered in 1991 as inappropriate, as they belonged to Aboriginal people.

An ABC news program covered the intervention at the opening of the SRC in 1991. An on-camera speech was made by the then-Chair of the Central Land Council, Rupert (Maxie) Stuart, in which he invoked the desire to see and touch objects that he was connected to as part of his Aboriginal spiritual identity and protested against its sequestration in the SRC archive (see Cohen, 2001). The dispute around this disconnect, in which the archive removes access for its most important constituents, was somewhat softened 10 years later when the same person—Stuart—agreed that perhaps the SRC was the place for where these objects could be best protected (Cohen, 2001). There has been an illegal trade in these sacred objects and, understanding this, perhaps, for Stuart, the SRC became the lesser of two evils. There is a continuing persistence in the potential problems that these objects can cause, because they remain powerful things that can by their very presence cause havoc and even death if not treated with care.

In moving beyond the first decade of the SRC's existence as an archive, some important changes occurred in both the nature of how the collection was managed and how it presented itself to the public. As Galt Smith wrote:

> By 2002 the SRC had become well and truly open for business with requests from Aboriginal men to store their sacred objects for safe keeping; regular visits by Aboriginal people to view objects, films and photographs and to listen to sound recordings... Dr Mike Smith of the National Museum of Australia described as its transformation (in museum terms) from 'a kind of North Korea to a Switzerland' (Galt Smith, 2015).

This attribution does capture the challenges posed to the SRC in its early days and its subsequent emergence as a focus for outreach to its Aboriginal constituents. In its second decade, the SRC introduced repatriation in a policy revision of earlier legislation, re-invigorated the Board of the SRC by adding Aboriginal members, and hired Aboriginal people in research assistant positions. The latter showed immediate results, with renewed efforts to digitise more of the collection's media resources, expanding the database for a catalogue to these resources across a greater range of media (including sound) and links to documentation, much of it Ted and Carl Strehlow's work on genealogies and word lists.

The eventual appointment of a woman (Felicity Greene) to act as Director of the SRC addressed the issue of gender bias, given that the collection was mostly (but not exclusively) an archive of cultural ceremony (films, photographs and objects) to do with men or to what is sometimes referred to as 'men's business'. The appointment showed that with flexibility and careful planning, the gender restrictions could be respected with a female chief administrator. However, it was through a greater Aboriginal presence in research that the outreach to Aboriginal elders and traditional custodians increased contact and engagement with this important group. In its third decade, the SRC moved to employing Aboriginal people in both research and administrative roles in relation to the collection.

## Digitising the collection

Cutting across the SRC's emergence as an archive and research centre is the history of its collection as an archive. When I first visited the SRC in 1995, the work on transforming the collection into an archive was only in its early phases. The priority was given to ensuring the objects were safely and securely stored; a number of Strehlow's written materials including diaries and letters were also worked on. The film collection had gone through a form of preservation through the copying of films onto 1-inch video and ½-inch video tape. There was no catalogue to the film at this point, though the original 16 mm film itself was held in vaults at the National Film and Sound Archive (NFSA) in Canberra.

The late 1990s saw the emergence of a number of collecting institutions turn to what was then new media technology—specifically digitisation—as a means of preserving the materials, offering greater access as computing expanded to personalised computers. It was in this period that the SRC first opted to digitise the film collection with the assistance of the NFSA. At the same time, an Australian Research Council funded a project developed by the then University of Western Sydney (now Western Sydney University) in partnership with the SRC to catalogue the film material. This first catalogue was published in 2003 as "The Filmworks of TGH Stehlow 1935–1962" and notes:

> The listing is based largely on Strehlow's annotations that he maintained as part of his field diaries in relation to the films. The document lists the year in which the films were shot, a time-coded index and a brief description of the film's content. The time code follow the format given to it by Screensound (now the NFSA) when it copied the material from the original 16mm to 1-inch video. This listing is now searchable to a new Digital Video copy of the films with the assistance of Screensound for the Strehlow Research Centre (Cohen, 2003).

By way of an example of the catalogue's approach to listing the video the following is excerpted:

| Timecode | Designation | Year | Initials | Number |
|---|---|---|---|---|
| 0:1:10 | Video Reel 1 | 1935 | TGHS | NO 1A |
| | | | | |
| Strehlow Collection 1935 Reel 1 of 2 ID NO 55966 | | | | |
| 0:01:10 | Video Reel 1 | 1935 | TGHS | No 1A |
| 0:01:23 | Todd in Flood. Aboriginal girls playing in and near the flowing water. | | | |

Fig. 16.1 Excerpt from catalogue

This catalogue resulted from the first digitisation of this film collection, albeit one that was 'orphaned' in that no access had been granted to view these films for decades. Further, it was one of the first times a collecting institution in Australia digitised a part of its collection, and represents an early example of Humanities Computing or what we now refer to as the Digital Humanities.

In this early period of digitisation, collecting institutions were quickly developing the means to not only re-record the materials in digital formats but to also develop databases through which media resources collected could be accessed online. Some of the most prolific of these initiatives included Paradisec (https://www.paradisec.org.au/) which focused on Indigenous archives, Ara Irtitja (https://irititja.com/), and Our Stories (https://lant.nt.gov.au/) which focused on the media and other sources first at Ernabella, SA, then at Darwin's Northern Territory Library Service.

## 2001–2011

In the decade (2001–2011) following the publication of the catalogue, more access was given to traditional custodians to the films at the SRC but, in most instances, access to view the films could only be arranged as on-site viewings as few people had the technical and material means to access these films online. Further, there was some anxiety around the insecurity of online presentations of Aboriginal cultural material especially in the context of restricted or culturally sensitive information.

The emergent technical capacity to protect these sites was a work in progress in conjunction with those interested in testing the boundaries of security for sometimes nefarious reasons. These concerns and the responses to them pre-empted our contemporary digital landscape where insecure data storage has shown to be vulnerable with devastating consequences.

In this decade, mainly under the direction of Brett Galt Smith, the SRC was more active in outreach activities to its Aboriginal constituents and especially open to researchers seeking to work with the collection. It was this decade that saw the emergence of Barry Hill's biography (2002), my own documentaries (*Mr Strehlow's Films*, 2001; *Cantata Journey*, 2006) and database extending the book, *Journey to Horseshoe Bend* to a digital scholarly edition. Gordon Williams and Andrew Schultz' *Cantata, Journey to Horseshoe Bend* (2003) and Diane Austin-Broos's monograph, *Arrernte Present, Arrernte Past* (2009). By 2011, several research collaborations and these creative and academic works presented the life and work of the Strehlows (Carl and T.G.H.) and Arrernte cultural history to both Australian and international publics. This decade also saw the exponential growth of digital technologies, especially in how information circulated on the Internet and via social media on mobile phones.

## 2011–present

In the decade from 2011–2023, some important shifts occurred in the SRC's sense of how Aboriginal people would participate in the archives— both as users of the archive and for those employed in support of the archive.

The next phase of digitisation brought the film and other media parts of the collection into a mature Digital-Humanities-style database. Shaun Angeles, a Norther Arrernte man from Yambe, was working as a research assistant as this third decade at the SRC got underway. As part of the film project, *Ntaria Heroes*, Shaun was one of the cinematographers and more importantly was a strong voice as an interviewee throughout the film. *Ntaria Heroes* was conceived as a participatory archives project in the manner defined by Histo Ivula as:

> [...] decentralising curation, radical orientation towards users and

contextualisation of records and the entire archival process [...] (Ivula, 2021).

A summary of the film as indicated by the title is provided by the anthropologist at the SRC, Adam Macfie:

> In many ways what we are calling [...] Heroes in the title of this film are those people who worked with the Strehlows in order to have their culture documented with the intention of to have it preserved and looked after [...] that is why we have called them 'heroes' [...] (Macfie in Cohen, 2018, p. 128).

Shaun Angeles in an interview also offered a sense of the impact the project had on the youth who were invited to access the SRC archives, especially the genealogies and still photographs through which they were able to identify relatives and become familiar with skin names and skin groups, including their own skin names (new to this group of young people).

> The last few weeks we've had school students from Ntaria School come in to have a look [at] the material—some of the material—the appropriate material from the Strehlow Research Centre. They have been coming in looking at genealogies and looking at old photographs and it has been powerful for them and even for us [...] (Angeles in Cohen, 2016, p. 128).

The film documents how the project fostered a relationship with the Ntaria School through mentoring and engaging students in filmmaking. Here the use of mobile phones and iPads were already ubiquitous among young people, and their use facilitated the various creative inputs made by the students. In a sense, this project and its extension to a film was intent on marrying the SRC's archival materials—especially its world-class collection of genealogical information and photographs—with the cultural knowledge objectives of the School and Aboriginal community. As cultural research of this kind often privileges the past and cultural traditions, for young people the new media technologies allowed the connections to these traditions to appear new and engaging. For this reason, this project far exceeded the conventional relationships in the context of a collections institution and moved to a more intense level of participation in the SRC archive than had hitherto been the case.

As Shaun Angeles put it:

The work that we do here and the power of the material here [and how it] can change young people's lives for the better [...] We need to be urgent with this. We need to do as much as we can with young people now while their elders are still around [...] there is still lots of knowledge out there with our old people; knowledges, sacred site, songlines, songs, ceremonies are still going today [...] (Angeles in Cohen, 2016, p. 129).

Here, Shaun is explicit about how he felt the cultural knowledge so essential for a young person's Aboriginal identity and well-being was being lost. As he noted early in our interactions with these young people, most of them did not know their skin names, which moved Shaun to ask rhetorically, "Is this the first generation of Aboriginal people who will not know who they are?" He goes on:

We still feel it now, when we go to a ceremony or when we sit down with old people and they start singing a song; it hits you, it fills you up, it gives you goosebumps, it makes you cry. And this is the power of this stuff (Angeles in Cohen, 2016. p. 129).

This is Shaun's most emphatic plea for the continuation of this process of engagement with the Aboriginal constituents—especially the traditional custodians of the SRC archive. It is not surprising then that Shaun is at the forefront of an expansion of the SRC's media archive database.

Working with the source materials of film, but expanding to still images, Shaun built a much more expansive database to serve the demands of the Strehlow Collection. Moreover, Shaun developed this work in close consultation with elders, some of whom visited the SRC, but others were contacted on field trips. Visiting the country and meeting the elders was something Shaun always spoke of as "a great privilege" and, using laptops, he was able to glean a surfeit of information about the media resources he was attempting to document.

In an email sent to me in 2021, Shaun summarises his approach:

The editing process involved cross referencing the catalogue you produced, Strehlow's ceremonial film scripts and the field diaries. From this I developed a searchable spreadsheet that collates a broad cross section of data associated with these performances such as:

Celebrated totemic ancestor.

Animal or plant species and/or element (Fire, water, wind Associated site(s).

Performers.

Owners of acts.

People who revealed acts.

Associated SRC secret sacred objects, ceremonial songs and photographs (Angeles, 2021, personal communication).

He goes on to describe the impact of this new stage of database development:

> This work not only made sense of the ceremonial film but began to consolidate large sections of the collection by linking the different cultural assets within it. We are effectively re-piecing the collection together how it was originally recorded by using the film as a reference point.

The point here is that what was considered a marginal feature of the collection, the films shot by Strehlow over 35 years, have become the resource upon which a comprehensive database of the whole collection with its multiple connections is made. In an account of one of the key performers who worked closely and frequently with Strehlow, Shaun provides an in-depth description of how this person is seen today. It is this attention to the elders who worked with Strehlow, whom we named "Ntaria Heroes" that Shaun sees as the key to the survival of Aboriginal cultural knowledge and cultural practices and, by extension, the next generation of Aboriginal people.

> Quantifying this data has taught us many things about the visionary men who co-created this collection, particularly their profound contribution and dedication to this unique record. For example, we see that Sidi Ross was the primary actor in over sixty acts which span six language groups across Central Australia over a fifteen-year period from 1950–1965. Or Lockey Tjituma, the primary actor in over seventy acts spanning eight language groups over a thirty-year period working with Strehlow. Lockey first enters the record in 1933 at Horseshoe Bend and the last moving imagery of him is in 1965 on the Goyder River where he is still performing ceremonies as an elderly man (Angeles, 2021, personal communication).

This is valuable information that has never been available and is now brought to light in the context of this recent phase of database development. It suggests that the further development of an archive's resources in relation to the affordances of new media technologies opens up important information and knowledge about the archive's historical foundations, including, in this instance, the extensive participation of Aboriginal informants for T.G.H. Strehlow's ceremonial films. It is to Shaun Angeles that credit should flow for underpinning his technological achievements in the archive with the participation of traditional custodians to both assist with the task and offer cultural legitimacy to this important heritage-preserving work.

Even as the work expanded the known ceremonies and song cycles, Shaun pointed out how the process also identified missing materials which were eventually found. From this, we can see how the process added to the collection because of the work that had proceeded to take place:

> Through this process we were able to identify missing acts which were subsequently found while conducting research at the NFSA. This ceremonial footage was from 1949/50 at the Iltirapota Festival and for some unknown reason wasn't in the SRC collection. This particular footage taught us more about the different ceremonial classifications within the films. At Iltirapota we see a number of performances where women and children are present which is contrary to the common narrative around the collection being strictly a men's only ceremonial collection. This find opens other opportunities in the way we work with the archive.

With Shaun's work, the edited films are becoming a wonderful resource for traditional owners. Senior elders are using them as a teaching tool that is nurturing intergenerational transmission of cultural knowledge by allowing the younger generation of men to view these films. Some men are able to see their fathers and grandfathers performing in the films, which often provokes emotions, memories and thought. The films inspire men to revitalise ceremonies that have not been performed for generations. Shaun has also indicated that consolidating the film catalogue has now led us to work with the ceremonial sound recordings. This component of the collection has been completely absent from any earlier catalogue work or digitisation as it was simply too difficult, however, the work on sound is now yielding results. The holy grail of synchronising the film with the correct songs is now within reach.

## Recent developments in the SRC's digitisation program

The Museum and Gallery of the Northern Territory (MAGNT) and the SRC have collaborated with the NFSA to re-digitise the entire AV collection. The NFSA have begun with the film catalogue and copies of this important footage are now available in 4K. To further the achievements of the last few years, an on-country digital studio has been built in Alice Springs to allow traditional owners to access the files. This facility is intended to encourage the intergenerational transfer of knowledge. One of the potential consequences of this focus on the films is the re-awakening of Aboriginal languages long repressed by the colonialisation of Aboriginal people, assimilation policies, and official government policy prohibiting the use of Aboriginal language in public institutions.

The re-digitisation involved the National Film and Sound Archive's resources, once again with protocols that carefully laid out who could work on the digitisation process accompanied by consultations with senior men from the community assisting with this process. As indicated by Gil Moody:

> Those men were given the authority by the senior men from up here to be able to view or touch any of the items and hear any of the material (in Allison, 2023).

These senior men had travelled to Canberra to advise on the development of a set of protocols to ensure the materials were handled and stored in a culturally safe manner. Two restricted preservation areas were also established, limiting access to staff who had been approved by senior community men to view and handle the content (Allison, 2023).

The process is thought to be world-leading in developing protocols and processes for digitising culturally sensitive films. Out of this process has also arisen training opportunities and a concerted approach to having men local to where the SRC is located trained in audio-visual conservation, preservation, digitisation and archiving.

The proposition that "[...] the archive as a site for creative intervention, is one that enables new possibilities for preserving and representing individual memory within a larger historical consciousness" (Kashmere, 2021) is redolent of the SRC's contemporary moves in digitising its archive, in promoting Aboriginal participation in this digital renewal of its core films and doing so in a manner that respects cultural authority and traditional custodianship of culture and country.

# Works Cited

Allison, C. (2023, April 28). On-country studio to give Alice Springs traditional owners access to Strehlow Collection. *ABC News*. https://www.abc.net.au/news/2023-04-28/strehlow-collection-returned-to-central-australia/102271640

Austin-Broos, D. (2009). *Arrernte Present, Arrernte Past: Invasion, Violence and Imagination in Indigenous Central Australia*. University of Chicago Press. https://www.doi.org/10.1017/S0010417510000538

Cohen, H. (2018). *The Strehlow Archive: Explorations in old and new media*. Routledge. https://doi.org/10.4324/9781315145464

Cohen, H. (2003). *The Filmworks of TGH Strehlow 1935–1962*. Northern Territory Government.

Galt Smith, B. (2015, October 30). Journey as vehicle–Journey to Horseshoe Bend: The Trojan horse in Strehlovian politics. Paper delivered at Symposium, *Journey to Horseshoe Bend: The Repulication of an Australian Classic*. State Library of NSW, Sydney.

Hennessy, K. & Smith, T.L. (2022, April 27). Anarchival Materiality in Film Archives. Description of online presentation hosted by the *Royal Anthropological Institute (RAI)* included in *RAI* email of events.

Hill, B. (2002). *Broken song: T.G.H. Strehlow and Aboriginal possession*. Random House.

Huvila, I. (2011). What is participatory archives? For real? https://www.istohuvila.se/what-participatory-archive-real

Kashmere, B. (n.d.). Cache rules everything around me: Introduction to Issue #2: Counter-Archive. *Incite!* http://www.incite-online.net/intro2.html

Mundine, D. (2021). Remembering and forgetting: Forgiveness and not forgetting. Counter-monuments Symposium Session 3. Australian Centre for Contemporary Art. https://acca.melbourne/program/counter-monuments-session-three/

Thorsen, S. (2020). Counter-archiving: Combating data colonialism. Medium. https://medium.com/copenhagen-institute-for-futures-studies/counter-archiving-combating-data-colonialism-be17ffead4

Williams, G., & Schultz, A. (2003). *Journey to Horseshoe Bend Cantata*. ABC Classics.

# Films [All films available through VIMEO]

Cohen, H. (2001). Mr Strehlow's Films, Journocam Productions. SBSI. https://vimeo.com/177383620

Cohen, H. (2006). Cantata Journey, Research Decisions, Australian Broadcasting Corporation. https://vimeo.com/177298769

Cohen, H., Morley, R., & Salazar, J.F. (2016). Ntaria Heroes, ARC/SRC. https://vimeo.com/206014019

# Afterword

## *Michael Falk*

Why the "Indian Rim"? When we began Digital Humanities in the Indian Rim, we had the utopian desire to construct a new research network in the Global South, to rival the Atlantic network that continues to dominate scholarly life. What could digital humanists in South Asia, Australasia, East Africa and the Persian Gulf teach one another about digital scholarship? How does Digital Humanities (DH) look from the Indian Ocean?

The Indian Ocean does present challenges as a shared space to work. There are few existing institutional links, and what links there are, are typically mediated by Atlantic institutions. This was readily apparent at our first conference, "digital + humanities", held online in 2019. At that conference, we successfully attracted speakers from South Africa, Nigeria, Abu Dhabi, Mauritius, Australia and India. But our participant from Abu Dhabi worked at a satellite campus of New York University, our Mauritian colleague worked in an academic program certified by a French university, and many of our collaborators from India were either educated or held faculty positions in Britain or America. I convened the conference from my home office in England.

Is it possible—or even desirable—to try and escape the Atlantic? What have we been able to achieve, working within and across the Indian Ocean? Does it even make sense to think of the Indian Ocean as a distinct intellectual milieu, when so many scholars from the Ocean have taken up degrees or faculty positions in countries beyond its shores?

Today, India and Australia are well-established players in global DH. It is no surprise that this book, though it began with wider aspirations, has resolved into a collaboration between scholars from these two nations. As these contributions indicate, scholars in India and Australia

 https://doi.org/10.11647/OBP.0423.17

are flourishing in the mainstream of DH: they build databases, remediate archives, process cultural data, critique technology, and wonder how to convert DH from a field of research into a viable teaching program under local conditions. In these respects, neither Indian nor Australian DH need to make excuses for themselves.

This is all very well, but it is not enough to justify DH in the Indian Rim. If scholars around the Indian Ocean Rim wish to form a distinctive group, then their group must have some distinctive qualities. What are they?

As Cohen and Jana suggest in their introduction, the greatest commonality among Indian Rim countries is our shared history of colonisation. To be sure, the history of colonisation is never anywhere the same. Australia is a settler-colonial state with a white majority, hundreds of Indigenous nations and a growing plurality of global migrants—including some 600,000 from India (Chand, this volume). India is a large federation of post-colonial states, with an enormous global diaspora, and its own history of domination by caste, religion, language and region. Despite these differences, the legacy of colonisation has inflected DH in both countries and suggests that continued regional collaboration could be productive.

In what follows, I discuss three main strands of post-colonial DH, indicating how Indian and Australian digital humanists have made unique and complementary contributions to them. The strands are counter-archiving, multilingual DH, and *jugaad*, or minimal computing. Like all strands, these three are intertwined, but I hope to separate them adequately for discussion. I conclude with a reflection on possible futures for DH in the Indian Rim. Indigenous scholars are entering the Australian academy in greater numbers. Indian scholars are reviving Sanskrit learning and using it to critique dominant Western methodologies with ever greater success. These developments raise the possibility of a fundamentally new kind of DH, with new origin stories and new directions, liberated from the inspiring but also stifling myths that have hitherto given "DH-ers" their sense of academic identity (see Jones, 2016).

# Counter-archiving

Cohen presents a splendid example of counter-archiving in his chapter on the Strehlow Research Centre (SRC). In this case, the project 'counters' traditional archives by respecting the cultural authority of its subjects. Although much of the research Cohen describes is technologically at the cutting-edge, he asserts quite rightly that the project's real innovation lies "in developing protocols and processes for digitising culturally sensitive films" (this volume). The SRC is a closed, rather than an open archive. It gives Arrernte people control over their cultural heritage. As Cohen's impressive bibliography demonstrates, this closedness of the archive has not prevented research. Articles and monographs continue to flow. It is quite possible that closing the archive may have opened Arrernte people to research, by giving them confidence that they can set the terms. Of course, the most important aspect of the project is its usefulness to traditional owners, who are drawing on the archive to "revitalise ceremonies that haven't been performed for generations."

The preeminent DH theorist of counter-archiving is Indian American scholar Roopika Risam. In *New Digital Worlds* (2019), she propounds a theory of post-colonial "world-making", which can usefully be applied to Cohen's project. As Risam sees it, post-colonial DH is both critical and practical. On the critical side, post-colonial DH:

> ...addresses underexplored questions of power, globalization, and colonial and neocolonial ideologies that are shaping the digital cultural record in its mediated, material form[.]

On the practical side, post-colonial DH scholars:

> ...[design] new tools, methods, and workflows that are based in local practices [...] to create space for underrepresented communities to populate the digital cultural record with their own stories. (p. 9).

Both these sides of post-colonial DH are exemplified in Cohen's project. It began with a critique of the Strehlow Research Centre's settler-colonial heritage and morphed into a practical project to digitise the archive according to Arrernte cultural protocols.

India's history of colonisation is different to Australia's, and accordingly the critical side of counter-archiving is different. The practical side, however, is often similar. Consider the reflections of C.S.

Lakshmi, long-time curator of the SPARROW archive in Mumbai. She set up the archive to combat dominant narratives about the "Third World," which is:

> ...supposed to worry about slums, environment, legal aid for women, health care, rural development and so on (quoted in Kalra & Nene, 2020, p. 142).

Her archive allows women to tell the stories they wish to tell about themselves, rather than fit into a global developmental narrative. On the critical side, therefore, this project is quite distinct from Cohen's: Cohen critiques a settler-colonial archive in the possession of a white ruling class, and helps to return the archive to its traditional owners. Lakshmi sets up a new archive to tell stories that are missing from existing archives about the "Third World". On the practical side, however, Lakshmi's project converges with Cohen's:

> What happens is the demand for fully open archiving comes from the West. I'm not for fully-open archiving. I'll tell you why. For example, let me say I have interviewed an Indian woman worker who tells me all about her life: her personal life, her sexual life, everything. It's available with the archives. We have also digitized it in a way that people can read it on their computer; it's possible. I can give excerpts of it, for example, but we can't make the whole thing available online because I feel that when you put it on the web, millions of people can read it for no purpose (quoted in Kalra & Nene, 2020, p. 143).

Like Cohen, Lakshmi has developed protocols that rub against the dominant digital ideology of "openness" or the "free flow of information (see Tkacz, 2015, chapter 1). In this case, Lakshmi has developed protocols informally over many decades with her informants, devising a locally appropriate division between revelation and concealment.[1] Lakshmi is typical. According to Nishant Shah (2020), Indian DH has entered a "post-access" phase. Merely opening the world's digital cultural record is no longer the primary aim.

In Australia, counter-archiving is increasingly well organised, overseen by Indigenous scholars and archivists. Tahu Kukutai and John Taylor (2016) have edited a seminal collection on *Indigenous Data*

---

1    She rejects the public/private distinction: Kalra & Nene, "Ethics and Feminist Archiving in the Digital Age," p. 150.

*Sovereignty*, with contributors from Australia, Aoteoroa/New Zealand and North America. Organisations such as the Indigenous Data Network and the Indigenous Archives Collective provide platforms for Indigenous scholars and archivists to critique existing archives and organise to build new ones. They have subsequently adopted the 2022 CARE principles as core guidelines, alongside the more familiar FAIR principles.[2] Major DH archives such as People Australia, Austlit/Blackwords, and Trove have, with varying degrees of success, either brought in Indigenous managers or adopted more culturally sensitive practices.[3] Indigenous scholars are increasingly prominent in public debates about knowledge institutions. In the last two years, Kirsten Thorpe, Nathan Sentance, and Lauren Booker (2023) and Bronwyn Carlson and Lotus Rana (2024) have released highly publicised reports which starkly but constructively criticise Wikipedia, the world's preeminent knowledge institution. Although many Australian researchers (the author included) continue to work in traditional digital fields such as text analysis and cultural databasing, where openness and sharing are prized, it seems that Australia is entering its own "post-access" phase of DH.

## Multilingual DH

India and Australia are profoundly multilingual, as are most countries in the Indian Rim. More than 400 languages are spoken in India.[4] In Australia, there are more than 200 Indigenous languages,[5] and more than 20% of Australians speak a language other than English at home.[6] In this respect, DH in the Indian Rim again contrasts with its Atlantic

---

2 CARE (Collective benefit, Authority to control, Responsibility, and Ethics) emphasises the rights of groups to control data about them, as opposed to FAIR (Findable, Accessible, Interoperable, Reusable), which emphasises the importance of sharing data to guarantee the integrity of research.

3 See, for example, Trove's documentation on cultural safety for first Australians ("Cultural Safety for First Australians Trove," 2020, https://webarchive.nla.gov.au/awa/20200921070933/https://trove.nla.gov.au/help/using-trove/cultural-safety-first-australians).

4 "GlottoScope–India," *Glottolog* 5.0, https://glottolog.org/langdoc/status/browser?focus=ed&country=IN#3/24.63/70.10

5 "Glottoscope–Australia," *Glottolog* 5.0, https://glottolog.org/langdoc/status/browser?focus=ed&country=AU#4/-22.11/133.68

6 "Cultural Diversity of Australia," *Australian Bureau of Statistics*, September 2022, https://www.abs.gov.au/articles/cultural-diversity-australia#language

counterpart. Although of course there are many Indigenous languages in North America, and several European nations with more than one official language, DH in the Atlantic has seldom had to grapple with the same degree of multilingualism as DH in the Indian Rim.

In India, multilingualism is essentially compulsory. It is not possible to research digital artefacts or platforms without encountering multiple languages. This is illustrated beautifully in Chand's chapter. Chand is doubly diasporic: a member of Fiji's Indian minority, who subsequently migrated to Australia. Her research into dating apps reveals a network of languages linking members of the Indian diaspora across cities and oceans. Some languages are supported on some platforms, and some on others. She must rely on her own multilingual proficiency in order to examine and understand the platforms. Compulsory multilingualism is also a feature of Nayak and Rana's research. Even though they use an English translation of the text, they must be constantly mindful of the underlying Sanskrit. Sometimes a Sanskrit word surfaces in the English translation (e.g., *stridhana*). At other times, the translation requires careful interpretation (e.g., when the word "class" is used in the meaning of "caste"). English has not been in contact with Sanskrit as long as it has been in contact with Latin or Greek. The Indian scholar writing in English must always be aware of a gap between the text under study and the academic text they are writing. Thus, in this case, too, multilingualism is *compulsory*, where in the Atlantic world it is often avoidable.

Indian DH projects are almost inevitably multilingual. The bibliography of *Modern and Contemporary Art Writing of South Asia* records more than 12,000 pieces of art writing in 12 languages (Ragavan, 2020). The 1947 Partition Archive contains more than 10,000 oral histories in 37 languages. Bichitra, an online variorum of Rabindranath Tagore, contains a mixture of manuscripts in two languages—English and Bengali—which use different scripts. This multilingualism has shaped the project at every level, from the data model of the bibliography, the encoding scheme of the texts, and the algorithm of the collation system (Bhowmik, 2022). Even Indian projects that begin monolingual have a tendency to become multilingual. Rekhta.org began as an archive of Urdu poetry but extended in 2020 to include Hindi texts (Zaidi & Aqib, 2022).

Despite the hegemony of English, DH in Australia has been unusually multilingual for a long time. This is probably due to the relative prominence of field linguists, archaeologists and anthropologists in Australian DH. The flagship project for multilingual DH in Australia is PARADISEC, a large digital archive that conserves the cultural and linguistic heritage of the Australia-Pacific. It is a venerable project, more than 20 years old, but still expanding and improving. It contains recordings, videos and written materials in 1370 languages from across Australia and the Pacific. As I discuss in the next section, PARADISEC has taken special measures to make its materials available to the communities it represents, and has control measures in place to allow them to protect their cultural data. Other Australian projects in a similar vein include: Austlang, which provides metadata about Indigenous Australian Languages; the Living Languages Platform, which provides free dictionary apps of Indigenous Australian languages; and the AUSLAN Signbank, an innovative video dictionary of Australian Sign Language. Digital resources for Australia's many community languages, such as Arabic, Chinese or Bengali, are not so well developed.

These classic Australian examples of multilingual DH have mostly been aimed at specialist researchers and the communities they study. More recently, innovative DH researchers have found ways to reach a wider audience. As part of the *Waves of Words* project (mentioned in Burrows, this volume), Rachel Hendery and Andrew Burrell (2020) developed *Glossopticon*, a virtual reality experience in which users could explore the linguistic diversity of the Pacific with all their senses. Users could fly across the Pacific, following known canoe routes, and hear recorded speech from PARADISEC on the islands. In a different strand of the project, Antoinette Schaepper and I experimented with machine learning, concept mapping and string matching to hunt for shared vocabulary in Australian, Papuan and Polynesian languages. It has hitherto been difficult to incorporate multiple languages in the traditional DH fields of text analysis and cultural analytics. But Indian and Australian DH-ers are steadily making the effort.

## *Jugaad*; or minimal computing

One of the most important aspects of post-colonial DH is *jugaad*, or minimal computing. As the Hindi name for the practice suggests, minimal computing has been a key theme in Indian DH, where internet and computer penetration is far lower than in the Atlantic strongholds of traditional DH. *Jugaad* is an untranslatable word that intersects with the English 'makeshift' or 'hacking'. As Padmini Ray Murray and Chris Hand (2015, p. 144) observe in their canonical treatment of the topic, *jugaad* resembles other practices of "technological disobedience" in the Global South, including "*Gambiarra* in Brazil, *Rebusque* in Colombia, and *Jua Kali* in Kenya." The concept is tricky, as Souvik Mukherjee (2020) points out. If *jugaad* is an inherently disobedient practice, how can it be incorporated into the disciplined structures of an academic degree? Padmini Ray Murray (2020) herself is more sanguine, observing an interesting fact about DH pedegogy in India: India's first graduate DH degree was not founded in an English or History department, as is usually the case, but was founded in a school of Design. In India, it seems, DH lays a stronger emphasis on making things work rather than analysing the cultural record.

The same cannot be said for Australia. To my knowledge, only four Australian universities have offered teaching programs in DH: Monash University, the Australian National University, Western Sydney University and the University of Melbourne. In no case was the program offered as part of a degree in Design. Literature, Linguistics, History and Information Science have been the dominant disciplines, as far as DH pedagogy is concerned.

But there has been a role for minimal computing and critical making in Australian DH. The most poetic example again comes from PARADISEC. PARADISEC itself, like many decades-old Humanities databases, is optimised for use on a desktop connected to broadband internet. Desktops with broadband connections are relatively rare in the steamy villages of Vanuatu or the highlands of Papua New Guinea. Desktops are likewise less common than they ought to be in remote Aboriginal communities in Australia. Accordingly, the project has developed technology to enable local communities to access their data offline. Linguistic and cultural data are loaded onto a Raspberry Pi in a static format such as html. The Raspberry Pi then generates a local WiFi network, and community members can access the data using their phones (Thieberger, 2023).

In my own work, co-ordinating the Digital Studies program at the University of Melbourne, I have taken inspiration from *jugaad*. To teach my first-year students how to make computers do things, I have them play *Turing Tumble*, an AUD$100 mechanical computer. I have them create games using bitsy, a web-based '8-bit' game development program. I have them submit their assignments in the *PechaKucha* format, a highly constrained kind of slideshow. Of course, at the University of Melbourne, such constraints are artificial. We are a wealthy institution where—despite the usual grumbles—resources are plentiful, and our (mostly) privileged students are (mostly) able to obtain what they need. But the inspiring examples of my Indian colleagues—and other practitioners in the Global South—have demonstrated the value of constraint, if we want our students to make things critically.

## Futures past

DH in the Indian Rim is an incipient community. Ambassadors of Indian DH, such as Rahul Gairola and Asha Chand, have brought their knowledge to Australia. Others, such as Ujjwal Jana, Maya Dodd, Dibyaduti Roy and Nirmala Menon, have invited Australian collaborators into their circles. Building the rest of the network, across the rest of the Ocean, will take time and effort, but I am convinced that both are worthwhile.

## Works Cited

Australian Bureau of Statistics. (2022, September). Cultural Diversity of Australia. https://www.abs.gov.au/articles/cultural-diversity-australia#language

Bhowmik, S. (2022). Bichitra: The Online Tagore Variorum Project. In *Literary Cultures and Digital Humanities in India*. Routledge India. https://doi.org/10.4324/9781003354246

CARE Principles for Indigenous Data Governance ARDC. (2022, October). *Australian Research Data Commons*. https://ardc.edu.au/resource/the-care-principles/

Carlson, B., & Rana, L. (2024). *"I really like Wikipedia, but I don't trust it": Understanding First Nations Peoples' Experiences Using Wikipedia as Readers and/or Editors*. Macquarie University. https://www.doi.org/10.25949/76YK-G627

Cultural Safety for First Australians Trove. (2020). https://webarchive.nla.gov.au/awa/20200921070933. https://trove.nla.gov.au/help/using-trove/cultural-safety-first-australians

"Glottoscope – Australia." *Glottolog 5.0.* https://glottolog.org/langdoc/status/browser?focus=ed&country=AU#4/-22.11/133.68

"GlottoScope – India." *Glottolog 5.0.* https://glottolog.org/langdoc/status/browser?focus=ed&country=IN#3/24.63/70.10

Hendery, R., & Burrell, A. (2020). Playful interfaces to the archive and the embodied experience of data. *Journal of Documentation 76*(2), 484–501. https://www.doi.org/10.1108/JD-05-2019-0078

Jones, S.E. (2016). *Roberto Busa, S. J. and the Emergence of Humanities Computing: The Priest and the Punched Cards.* Taylor & Francis Group. https://doi.org/10.4324/9781315643618

Kalra, N., & Nene, M. (2020). Ethics and feminist archiving in the digital age: An interview with C. S. Lakshmi. In *Exploring Digital Humanities in India.* (pp. 141–154). Routledge India.

Kukutai, T., & Taylor, J. (2016). *Indigenous Data Sovereignty: Toward an Agenda.* ANU Press. https://www.doi.org/10.22459/CAEPR38.11.2016

Mukherjee, S. (2020). Digital humanities, or what you will: Bringing DH to Indian classrooms. In *Exploring Digital Humanities in India.* (pp. 105–123). Routledge India. https://doi.org/10.4324/9781003052302

Murray, P.R. (2020). Decolonising design: Making critically in India. In *Exploring Digital Humanities in India.* (pp. 124–137). Routledge India. https://doi.org/10.4324/9781003052302

Murray, P. R., & Hand, C. (2015). Making culture: Locating the digital humanities in India. *Visible Language 49*(3). http://radar.gsa.ac.uk/4701/1/Visible-Language-CM-2015-RayMurray-Hand-140-155.pdf

Ragavan, S. (2020). Processes of pluralisation: Digital databases and art writing in India. In *Exploring Digital Humanities in India.* (pp. 78–90). Routledge India. https://doi.org/10.4324/9781003052302

Risam, R. (2018). *New Digital Worlds: Postcolonial Digital Humanities in Theory, Praxis, and Pedagogy.* Northwestern University Press. https://www.doi.org/10.2307/j.ctv7tq4hg

Shah, N. (2020). Digital humanities on the ground: Post-access politics and the second wave of digital humanities. In *South Asian Digital Humanities.* (pp. 15–33). Routledge. https://doi.org/10.1080/02759527.2019.1599551

Thieberger, N. (2023). Doing it for ourselves: The new archive built by and responsive to the researcher. *DHQ: Digital Humanities Quarterly 17*(1). https://www.digitalhumanities.org/dhq/vol/17/1/000667/000667.html

Thieberger, N. (2020). Technology in support of languages of the Pacific: Neo-colonial or post-colonial. *Asian-European Music Research Journal 5*(3), 17–24. https://doi.org/ 10.30819/aemr.5-3

Thorpe, K., Sentance, N., & Booker, L. (2023). Wikimedia Australia and First Nations metadata: ATSILIRN protocols for description and access. https://doi.org/10.57956/B05F-CF08

Tkacz, N. (2015). *Wikipedia and the Politics of Openness*. University of Chicago Press. https://doi.org/10.7208/9780226192444

Zaidi, N., & Aqib, M. (2022). From Rekhta to rekhta.org: Digital remappings of Urdu literary culture and public sphere. In *Literary Cultures and Digital Humanities in India*. (pp. 128–152). Routledge India.

# Index

# About the Team

Alessandra Tosi was the managing editor for this book.

Proof-reading and indexing by Lucy Barnes.

Jeevanjot Kaur Nagpal designed the cover. The cover was produced in InDesign using the Fontin font.

Jeremy Bowman typeset the book in InDesign and produced the EPUB edition. The text font is Tex Gyre Pagella and the heading font is Californian FB.

Cameron Craig produced the PDF, HTML, and XML editions. The conversion is performed with open source software freely available on our GitHub page (https://github.com/OpenBookPublishers).

This book was peer-reviewed by two anonymous referees. Experts in their field, these readers give their time freely to help ensure the academic rigour of our books. We are grateful for their generous and invaluable contributions.

# This book need not end here...

## Share

All our books — including the one you have just read — are free to access online so that students, researchers and members of the public who can't afford a printed edition will have access to the same ideas. This title will be accessed online by hundreds of readers each month across the globe: why not share the link so that someone you know is one of them?

This book and additional content is available at
https://doi.org/10.11647/OBP.0423

## Donate

Open Book Publishers is an award-winning, scholar-led, not-for-profit press making knowledge freely available one book at a time. We don't charge authors to publish with us: instead, our work is supported by our library members and by donations from people who believe that research shouldn't be locked behind paywalls.

Join the effort to free knowledge by supporting us at
https://www.openbookpublishers.com/support-us

## We invite you to connect with us on our socials!

BLUESKY
@openbookpublish
.bsky.social

MASTODON
@OpenBookPublish
@hcommons.social

LINKEDIN
open-book-publishers

## Read more at the Open Book Publishers Blog
https://blogs.openbookpublishers.com

# You may also be interested in:

## Modelling Between Digital and Humanities
### Thinking in Practice
*Arianna Ciula, Øyvind Eide, Cristina Marras & Patrick Sahle*

https://doi.org/10.11647/OBP.0369

## Digital Technology and the Practices of Humanities Research
*Jennifer Edmond (editor)*

https://doi.org/10.11647/OBP.0192

## Oral Literature in the Digital Age
### Archiving Orality and Connecting with Communities
*Mark Turin, Claire Wheeler, Eleanor Wilkinson (editors)*

https://doi.org/10.11647/OBP.0032

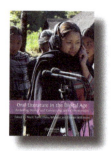

## Text and Genre in Reconstruction
### Effects of Digitalization on Ideas, Behaviours, Products and Institutions
*Willard McCarty (editor)*

https://doi.org/10.11647/OBP.0008

www.ingramcontent.com/pod-product-compliance
Lightning Source LLC
Chambersburg PA
CBHW041638050326
40690CB00027B/5269